Judicial Review and American Conservatism

The Christian Right of the 1980s forged its political identity largely in response to what it perceived as liberal "judicial activism." Robert Daniel Rubin tells this story as it played out in Mobile, Alabama. There, a community conflict pitted a group of conservative evangelicals, a sympathetic federal judge, and a handful of conservative intellectuals against a religious agnostic opposed to prayer in schools, and a school system accused of promoting a religion called "secular humanism." The twists in the Mobile conflict speak to the changes and continuities that marked the relationship of 1980s' religious conservatism to democracy, the courts, and the Constitution.

By alternately focusing its gaze on the local conflict and related events in Washington, DC, this book weaves a captivating narrative. Historians, political scientists, and constitutional lawyers will find, in Rubin's study, a challenging new perspective on the history of the Christian Right in the United States.

ROBERT DANIEL RUBIN is an independent scholar.

Cambridge Historical Studies in American Law and Society

Recognizing legal history's growing importance and influence, the goal of this series is to chart legal history's continuing development by publishing innovative scholarship across the discipline's broadening range of perspectives and subjects. It encourages empirically creative works that take legal history into unexplored subject areas, or that fundamentally revise our thinking about familiar topics; it also encourages methodologically innovative works that bring new disciplinary perspectives and techniques to the historical analysis of legal subjects.

Series Editor

Christopher Tomlins, *University of California, Berkeley*

Previously Published in the Series:

Matthew Crow, *Thomas Jefferson, Legal History, and the Art of Recollection*
Oren Bracha, *Owning Ideas: The Intellectual Origins of American Intellectual Property, 1790–1909*
Anne Twitty, *Before Dred Scott: Slavery and Legal Culture in the American Confluence, 1787–1857*
Castañeda Anastacio, Anna Leah Fidelis T., *The Foundations of the Modern Philippine State: Imperial Rule and the American Constitutional Tradition in the Philippine Islands, 1898–1935*
Robert Deal, *The Law of the Whale Hunt: Dispute Resolution, Property Law, and American Whalers, 1780–1880*
Sandra F. Vanburkleo, *Gender Remade: Citizenship, Suffrage, and Public Power in the New Northwest, 1879–1912*
Reuel Schiller, *Forging Rivals: Race, Class, Law, and the Collapse of Postwar Liberalism*
Ely Aaronson, *From Slave Abuse to Hate Crime: The Criminalization of Racial Violence in American History*
Stuart Chinn, *Recalibrating Reform: The Limits of Political Change*
Ajay K. Mehrotra, *Making the Modern American Fiscal State*
Yvonne Pitts, *Family, Law, and Inheritance in America: A Social and Legal History of Nineteenth-Century Kentucky*
David M. Rabban, *Law's History*
Kunal M. Parker, *Common Law, History, and Democracy in America, 1790–1900*
Steven Wilf, *Law's Imagined Republic*
James D. Schmidt, *Industrial Violence and the Legal Origins of Child Labor*
Rebecca M. McLennan, *The Crisis of Imprisonment: Protest, Politics, and the Making of the American Penal State, 1776–1941*
Tony A. Freyer, *Antitrust and Global Capitalism, 1930–2004*
Davison Douglas, *Jim Crow Moves North*
Andrew Wender Cohen, *The Racketeer's Progress*
Michael Willrich, *City of Courts, Socializing Justice in Progressive Era Chicago*
Barbara Young Welke, *Recasting American Liberty: Gender, Law and the Railroad Revolution, 1865–1920*
Michael Vorenberg, *Final Freedom: The Civil War, the Abolition of Slavery, and the Thirteenth Amendment*
Robert J. Steinfeld, *Coercion, Contract, and Free Labor in Nineteenth Century America*
David M. Rabban, *Free Speech in Its Forgotten Years*
Jenny Wahl, *The Bondsman's Burden: An Economic Analysis of the Common Law of Southern Slavery*
Michael Grossberg, *A Judgment for Solomon: The d'Hauteville Case and Legal Experience in the Antebellum South*

Judicial Review and American Conservatism

Christianity, Public Education, and the Federal Courts in the Reagan Era

ROBERT DANIEL RUBIN

CAMBRIDGE
UNIVERSITY PRESS

CAMBRIDGE
UNIVERSITY PRESS

University Printing House, Cambridge CB2 8BS, United Kingdom

One Liberty Plaza, 20th Floor, New York, NY 10006, USA

477 Williamstown Road, Port Melbourne, VIC 3207, Australia

4843/24, 2nd Floor, Ansari Road, Daryaganj, Delhi – 110002, India

79 Anson Road, #06–04/06, Singapore 079906

Cambridge University Press is part of the University of Cambridge.

It furthers the University's mission by disseminating knowledge in the pursuit of education, learning, and research at the highest international levels of excellence.

www.cambridge.org
Information on this title: www.cambridge.org/9781107060555
10.1017/9781107447202

First published 2017

Printed in the United States of America by Sheridan Books, Inc.

A catalogue record for this publication is available from the British Library.

Library of Congress Cataloging-in-Publication Data
NAMES: Rubin, Robert Daniel, author.
TITLE: Judicial review and American conservatism : Christianity, public education, and the federal courts in the Reagan era / Robert Daniel Rubin.
DESCRIPTION: New York : Cambridge University Press, 2016. | Series: Cambridge historical studies in American law and society | Discussing cases: Wallace v. Jaffree, 472 U.S. 38 (1985) and Smith v. Board of School Commissioners of Mobile County, 827 F.2d 684 (11th Cir. 1987) | Includes bibliographical references and index.
IDENTIFIERS: LCCN 2016041115 | ISBN 9781107060555 (hardback : alk. paper)
SUBJECTS: LCSH: Jaffree, Ishmael–Trials, litigation, etc. | Religion in the public schools–Law and legislation–Alabama–History–20th century. | Religion in the public schools–Law and legislation–United States–History–20th century. | Smith, Douglas T.–Trials, litigation, etc. | Mobile County (Ala.). Board of School Commissioners–Trials, litigation, etc. | Hand, W. Brevard.
CLASSIFICATION: LCC KF228.J34 R83 2016 | DDC 344.73/0796–dc23 LC record available at https://lccn.loc.gov/2016041115

ISBN 978-1-107-06055-5 Hardback

This book is dedicated to my wife, Sarah, and my son, Jonathan. They are the lights of my life.

Contents

Acknowledgments

I wish to thank my colleagues Michael Grossberg, Daniel Conkle, and Steven Stowe, as well as my editors, Christopher Tomlins and Deborah Gershenowitz. Thanks to Kirsti Sandy, Mark Long, and Katherine Hermes. Thanks also to Joseph Butwin and Joseph Newman for helping me carry out this project. I thank Susan Armeny, the finest critic of writing I have ever known. I am especially grateful to Julia Eulenberg and Michael Eulenberg for their boundless support, and to Barbara, Marvin, and Evan Rubin for their enduring love.

This book could never have been written without the generosity of Brevard Hand. Graciously, Judge Hand created space for us to disagree amicably. I will always appreciate his kindness.

Introduction

Conservatism and the Constitution

A tall, dignified-looking man stood at a podium one morning in May 1986, in Anniston, Alabama. The occasion was Calhoun County Law Day, and a prayer breakfast was being held inside a local Christian church. W. Brevard Hand, a federal judge and Alabama native, was there to speak of weighty and troubling matters dear to his heart. "Immorality is spreading throughout our society," Hand warned his audience. A moral epidemic had, he told, been set loose by "a weakening of the traditional religious foundation of our society"– the firm Christian foundation on which men and women acquired self-discipline. This posed a problem for lawyers and judges, who had "the obligation to know and understand the basic laws of life and our government" and needed to "stand forthrightly and insist that these be properly taught and understood in all their glory by our fellow man, so that these laws may be followed as a way of life."[1]

While traditional, Bible-based morality was being displaced from society, government, and law, Hand told the group of lawyers, so was it "fast becoming substituted by reliance on a man centered philosophy." On the basis of this man-centered, humanistic worldview, Americans were increasingly giving themselves license to rely on their own moral compasses, detached from the religious sensibilities that come from the word of God. This worldview was insidiously causing people to believe "that man is his own law giver and judge who can, by summary individual judgment, . . . determine what is moral and what is immoral, and if he so wishes change evil to good or good to evil."[2]

More than people's private thoughts and behaviors were being affected, Hand warned. Nothing less than our system for making and enforcing law – the very system that his audience was gathered that day to honor – was falling victim to the human-centered worldview. Hand was explicit. This worldview had taken hold of American culture, teaching that moral judgments ought to rest on merely subjective premises. Deluded by this worldview, legislators were less frequently grounding laws in biblical morality and more frequently treating the process of distinguishing right from wrong as a "situational and personal" matter best relegated to the private sphere. Courts had likewise been harmed. Nowadays, federal judges, under the cover of the U.S. Constitution, created personal rights that accommodated all kinds of immoral behavior. Hand concluded that the humanistic worldview was gutting the people's capacity to act in their collective best interests under law. Instead, "the lowest moral principle [had] prevail[ed]," causing society and government to become "virtually amoral."[3]

Hand had recently been mulling over legal briefs he had received, in anticipation of an upcoming trial, *Smith* v. *Board of School Commissioners of Mobile County*, over which he would preside. Hand's opinions in *Smith* v. *Board* and its earlier sister case, *Jaffree* v. *Board*, were the opinions for which he would become best known. There he was on Law Day giving a public address, prior to the *Smith* trial's commencement, revealing his affinity with a cornerstone of the plaintiffs' argument. Hand was no disinterested party to either *Jaffree* or *Smith*. Those cases provided him with a broad audience, within Alabama and among constitutional lawyers throughout America. They were the signature moments of his auspicious – or notorious – judicial activism.[4]

This book explores events in Mobile, Alabama, from 1981 to 1987. Centermost were the *Jaffree* and *Smith* cases. Most of the roles in the two cases were played by conservatives disgusted by liberal morality and liberal government. Many of them argued inside Hand's courtroom that the Supreme Court's rulings on church-state separation had run roughshod over the interests of ordinary citizens and so deserved somehow to be reversed. Over the course of the conflict, the position of some of the central characters evolved. Their actions, along with Hand's Law Day speech, reveal a conservative movement whose legal strategy confronted obstacles and underwent change at the same time as the movement was attaining unprecedented political success.

The Mobile conflict began in 1981. Ishmael Jaffree – an agnostic, African American, and parent of three students in Mobile public schools – brought suit against the Mobile County school board and the governor of Alabama. Jaffree issued what he believed to be the simple and irrefutable demands that Mobile schoolteachers cease to lead their classes in daily recitations of prayer and that a state law allowing classroom prayer be struck down. Jaffree knew that he had case law on his side, particularly the Supreme Court's 1962 *Engel* decision, which had been issued in response to a situation very similar to the one now confronting his children. Jaffree considered his case airtight.[5]

Jaffree was wrong. From the outset, his demands evoked nearly universal approbation and resistance among local residents and state officials. Jaffree ran headlong into a city whose power structure and culture were dominated by the Christian Right that had recently become more politically active and influential than at any previous time in the twentieth century. Even though African Americans played no role in the organized political resistance to Jaffree, local opposition to his suit did not vary by race or by class, with black traditional religiosity co-opted by Mobile's conservative establishment. With near uniformity, Mobilians responded not as whites and blacks but as Christians offended and outraged at this strange man who seemed to them to hate God and not care about children's souls. They understood themselves to be normal, decent people defending themselves against a foreign invasion of sorts.[6]

Jaffree's conservative opponents were informed by a worldview that cherished self-discipline, personal responsibility, private enterprise, Bible-based morality, and government by free citizens. Theirs was the worldview of the post–World War II right. Most of the characters during the story's early phase – Judge Hand, state lawmakers, evangelical attorneys, a prominent white Baptist preacher from Mobile, and his white congregants – were united especially by one element in this worldview, a mistrust of threats against Christianity. Their efforts were bolstered by a handful of local black schoolteachers and principals, whose own intense faith made them valuable allies. Jaffree's opponents were unwilling to countenance one man's brazen challenge to their right to raise children who respected God's absolute authority. As Mobile resident Hand told a local church congregation, obedience to God was something that children "have to be taught – carefully taught. And there is nothing wrong with that."[7]

When Jaffree challenged Hand's widely held assumption, he did more than contest a classroom practice and state law. Jaffree publicly defied the foundational rituals of a culture and community built on conformity with conservative Christian ideals. Jaffree's neighbors were asserting themselves in the throes of the 1960s, a period considered by many Christians to be marked by a widespread disregard for God and country. These Alabamians, along with conservatives all over the United States, took a political stand against what they saw as a culture of self-indulgence and permissiveness, a culture of decadence and immorality. For them, Jaffree signified this decadence and immorality. He threatened an educational process meant to equip children with the self-discipline needed to thrive in a free polity based on republican government.[8]

At trial, Jaffree ran head on into none other than Hand, a judge ill disposed to entertain his complaint. Jaffree also encountered an unexpected party – a group of local evangelicals whom Hand allowed to intervene in the case. Despite its status as defendant, the group did not support the teachers, local school board, and state legislature named in Jaffree's suit. Rather, the intervenors' goal was to demonstrate that they, and not Jaffree, were the true victims of practices of the Mobile public schools. The intervenors' lawyers seized on an argument, circulating in recent years, that public schools were nowadays permeated by an antitheistic religion named "secular humanism." So prevalent was this antitheistic religion, the lawyers claimed, that it assumed the power of a state establishment of religion, in violation of the First Amendment's Establishment Clause. The intervenors made this argument clearly and persuasively. In so doing they provided an odd symmetry to the *Jaffree* trial. The Mobile schoolteachers and school board sat center stage, defending themselves along two fronts. Attacking on one front was Ishmael Jaffree, attempting to eliminate all traces of traditional religion from the Mobile public schools. From the other flank came the intervenors, trying to purge Mobile classrooms of secular humanism. The plaintiff officially charged the schools with transgressing the Establishment Clause; the intervenors essentially did the same. Both challengers looked to Hand to make the schools more hospitable to people such as them.[9]

Neither challenge became the basis for Hand's ruling, even though the plaintiffs had gained Hand's notice and would stick in his mind. Hand's opinion in *Jaffree* concurred with the arguments raised by the defendants, in whose favor he found. His primary concern in the case was with the role of the federal courts over state and local policy. He and the entire federal judiciary, he ruled, had no proper jurisdiction over Alabama schools. Hand's *Jaffree* opinion was imbued with the antijudicialism that had animated conservatism since its calls for massive resistance in the wake of *Brown* v. *Board of Education*.[10]

The triumphant defendants based their case primarily on the republican majoritarianism prominent in the postwar conservative worldview – the same worldview that informed Hand. They contended that it was no business of the U.S. government, and particularly its courts, to tell state governments or local schools how to manage their church-state affairs.

Most instrumental in advancing this argument was the school board's expert witness, James McClellan. A former aid to senators Jesse Helms, Orrin Hatch, and John East, McClellan was among the most influential constitutionalists in the insurgent conservative movement of the 1970s and 1980s known as the New Right. He was highly placed in a cadre of lawyers dubbed by Sidney Blumenthal as the "counter-establishment," an influential group seeking to diminish the courts' power of judicial review, reassign power from the federal government down to the individual states, and weaken the Justice Department's commitment to rectifying violations of civil rights. McClellan was a leader among this group of constitutional lawyers with close ties to the Reagan administration. His views on the Constitution were well known in the legal establishment. McClellan brought to the *Jaffree* defendants an air of serious thinking about the issues under consideration in the case.[11]

To say that Hand was swayed by McClellan's testimony would be an understatement. Hand typically had few compunctions in crafting opinions out of arguments he encountered at trial. In finding for the *Jaffree* defendants, Hand made McClellan's position his own. Hand's opinion made copious use of not only McClellan's trial testimony but also a recent McClellan essay that spoke to these very matters. In his testimony, McClellan urged the judge to challenge Supreme Court precedent. The judge obliged. *Jaffree* was a disquieting opinion, focused entirely on reversing decades of Establishment Clause jurisprudence. The Court had interpreted "establishment" of religion too broadly, Hand contended; the Constitution's framers had intended that the government refrain from favoring only a single Christian denomination over another, not religion in general. The twentieth-century Court's erection of a "wall of separation" between church and state, according to Hand, represented an arrogant disregard for and disruption from the framers' intentions. There was thus no sound constitutional basis for finding Alabama in violation of the Establishment Clause. More startling yet was Hand's assertion that the First Amendment could not rightly constrain the individual states. Because the First Amendment did not mention the states, and because the Fourteenth Amendment did not explicitly incorporate the First Amendment, the Establishment Clause was not binding on state governments. Indeed, Hand declared – again borrowing from McClellan – that Alabama, or any other state, was free to establish a religion if it so chose. The Establishment Clause properly served to protect the states from federal interference. Even if he were to interpret the Establishment Clause broadly, as the Court had done since 1947, he still would not apply it to a state government.[12]

This book examines Hand's judicial opinions, speeches, articles, and interviews in context of a conservative worldview that took shape after World War II, and especially during the 1960s. It was, I argue, a cohesive worldview consisting of two intertwined strands. *Jaffree* combined those strands in perfect harmony. One strand was political, a stance toward government. As other conservatives had done for decades, Hand asserted the primacy of republican majoritarianism within the lawmaking process. Hand understood himself to be in complete consonance with the authors of the Constitution, who, he believed, had intended to provide for self-rule by popular majorities as executed by the people's elected representatives. The United States, through most of its history, had been a republic, Hand maintained. Judges acted at the consternation of the republic when they inserted themselves into the political process – which they did when they interpreted the Constitution so loosely as, in effect, to overrule the popular will. For him and others on the right, federal judges – Hand's colleagues – were the bêtes noires of government. The "judicial activism" perpetrated by liberal judges in particular, Hand charged, was destroying the American political system. He would do what he could to preserve democratic republicanism against their ravages.[13]

Another tenet of Hand's political conservatism was the federalism complementing his republicanism. Hand belonged to a generation of right-wing lawyers and judges who believed that a great share of sovereignty needed to be transferred from the national down to the state governments. One characteristic of republicanism on the state level, as James Madison recognized long ago, was its relative homogeneity, which gave rise to popular majorities forming more readily. This was a virtue within Hand's worldview. Popular majorities expressed the will of a discernable "people," he believed, and it was with popular will where morality and decency resided. Hand's favor toward state governments manifested in his disgust for his fellow U.S. judges who, it seemed to him, too readily struck down state laws and local policies. When they did so, those federal judges – unelected and unaccountable – frustrated popular will at the level where it operated with the greatest efficacy. One casualty of overzealous federal judicial review, Hand believed, was public policy informed by Christian values. The ubiquity of prayer in Alabama schools rested on supportive state law and local custom. When federal judges trod over the practice, Hand contended, they robbed the people of their right to build schools dedicated, as the people saw it, to the well-being of community, society, and government. Hand's colleagues eviscerated both popular sovereignty and moral education.[14]

The political majoritarianism in Hand's worldview was interconnected with a second strand, this one moral in nature. Post-Sixties American conservatives looked to the culture of "ordinary" citizens, rather than that of so-called cultural elites, to provide sustenance for popular self-government. Such ordinary citizens were more likely than others, it was said, to bequeath to their children a morality based in self-reliance, which had its roots in the work ethic historically associated with Protestantism. Such ordinary citizens were the people identified by Richard Nixon's handlers as the "silent majority." These Americans purportedly worried that the Court was doing more than violating their right to self-government. So too, they feared, was the Court, along with other institutions dominated by liberals, propagating a culture of self-indulgence and permissiveness. As much as any other institution, the Court, it was said, operated on the basis of a cultural-elite worldview that sanctioned obscenity, criminality, wanton sexuality, atheism, and socialism. Conservatives looked to the private-enterprising, God-fearing popular majority, through elected representatives, to reassert their political sovereignty and take back their government from the "robed masters" on the Supreme Court. It was especially important, for conservatives, that so-called ordinary Americans regain control over public schools from the secularists and socialists who now dominated them. Instilling Bible-based morality into children bred self-discipline and self-reliance. Informed by self-discipline and self-reliance, young citizens developed readiness for the liberty and democracy on which effective self-government was based. Self-government, in turn, reinforced the personal responsibility and initiative needed by members of a healthy, morally sound culture and society. Conservatism's moral strand sustained the political; the political strand reinforced the moral.[15]

Hand esteemed the ethic of self-reliance that, he believed, could still be found in his own local culture. To be sure, he admitted, his fellow Alabamians could and did pass bad laws. To do so was the people's right. But Hand had enough faith in ordinary Alabamians to trust that they would make laws consonant with Christian morality and the self-reliance to which it gave rise. One of the worst effects of judicial overreach, Hand believed, was to limit private morality's political capacity to strengthen states and local communities. Federal judges who enforced church-state separation within public education stifled moral instruction and thereby diminished children's opportunities to learn the self-discipline that allowed for self-government. Socialized to seek self-indulgence, many young adults of the present day preferred protection by the state over responsibility for self-rule. For Hand, federal judges were, by and large, not to be trusted because their overreach would obstruct moral reproduction and enfeeble republican rule.

Like many on the right, Hand accused the liberal establishment of weakening the character of the American people by offering to take care of them and solve all their problems. Conservatives such as Hand scorned the New Deal and Great Society largely on moral grounds. Hand believed human beings to be weak and given to temptation. All too easily, they manifested a childish dependence on government. Hand and like-minded others charged the welfare state with tempting Americans into sloth and decadence and thereby destroying their capacity to act freely and responsibly. Hand called on liberalism's opponents to instill freedom and responsibility in young citizens with care and resolve. Conservatives such as Hand saw it as crucial, now more than ever, to inculcate faith in God, reliance on self, and respect for the democratic-republican process. These would shield Americans from the liberal temptation; they would preserve individual freedom and governmental accountability.[16]

Reckoning with Hand deepens our understanding of postwar conservatism's symbiotic political and moral components. Hand's opinions exemplify conservative constitutionalism and clarify its complex relationship with conservative morality. His opinions were political writings. From the bench, as well as in speeches and articles, Hand aimed, however possible, to limit the liberal contagion. Christian habits of mind and a republican system of government were, for him, halves of a singular whole. Only a self-ruling people could reproduce self-reliance; only a self-reliant people could assert self-rule. Hand looked on the Court as the progenitor of political and cultural decline, the rapist of the Constitution. Americans seemed either not to know or not to care about the Court's destructive impact, and so he resolved to inform as many of them as he could. His rulings did not attract notice as widespread as those of William Rehnquist; his speeches were heard by fewer people than were the congressional declarations of Strom Thurmond or Barry Goldwater; his writings did not reach a public as broad as the readerships of journalists William Buckley and James Kilpatrick. But many people did take notice of Hand, albeit sometimes with disdain. His judicial opinions embodied the primary conservative conviction that a free citizenry responsible to itself needed somehow to impede its nation's descent into judicial oligarchy.[17]

The Eleventh Circuit would rebuff Hand's *Jaffree* ruling. In 1985, the appellate court's decision was upheld by the Supreme Court, even as the

Court's ruling in *Wallace* v. *Jaffree* spawned three dissenting opinions. One, by Justice Rehnquist, expounded on Hand's themes in a blistering attack on the Court's Establishment Clause jurisprudence. Notwithstanding Rehnquist's dissent, the Court remanded the case back to Hand and instructed him to ensure that Alabama schools established no religion. So ordered, Hand resolved to fulfill the mandate in an unconventional manner. He would show the justices the untenability of fully and equitably sanitizing the classroom of all religious influences. To make his point, he refocused his attention on the *Jaffree* intervenors. Although he had not based his 1983 ruling on their arguments, he had noted them favorably. Indeed, his opinion had promised that he would readdress their arguments should circumstances warrant. Hand had left open a door through which he would reenter the case if and when he was ordered to apply the restrictions of the Establishment Clause to Alabama schools. Having been directed to do just that, he returned to the intervenors' complaint and indicated that it demanded redress. Hand realigned the *Jaffree* parties, offering the intervenors, if they wished, the chance to become plaintiffs in a new case. They so wished. *Smith* v. *Board* was launched.[18]

Smith signaled a portentous moment in American jurisprudence and politics. From the 1950s onward, many on the right had bemoaned what they considered the federal courts' unconstitutional intrusion into the affairs of state legislatures. In response, conservatives attempted, over nearly three decades, to curb the federal courts' jurisdiction over state legislatures regarding a number of key issues. Among them was the right of local communities to conduct organized, aloud religious exercises in the classroom. Congress entertained numerous attempts to restore local, majoritarian control over school prayer, as well as over desegregation, busing, abortion, and other matters. Speaking as "the people," conservative activists and officials aimed to take back their government. Their goal was to restore biblical morality, self-reliance, and republican control to a government that had strayed from American values.[19]

By the time that the parties in *Smith* v. *Board* submitted their initial memoranda in 1985, it seemed as though these attempts had come to naught. For conservatives of the mid-1980s, the rights revolution overseen by the Supreme Court was proving hard to assail. Criminals were still being granted *Miranda* rights; schoolchildren continued – at least in theory – to receive Bible-free public education. It appeared that, for the foreseeable future, the constitutional rights of minorities and others marginalized by the majoritarian political process would enjoy protection by the federal courts. Some conservative intellectuals concluded that the judiciary had so usurped the people's power to rule themselves that the people might not soon regain their rightful sovereignty.[20]

Dire circumstances required bold thinking. Around the time of *Smith*, astute lawyers involved with Christian conservative causes were recognizing that not all was lost. It dawned on some that they could perhaps leverage the rights revolution to their advantage. In legislative proposals, amicus briefs, and litigation strategies, a handful of religious conservatives began calling for an expansive application of the First Amendment. Increasingly, they downplayed their longtime self-identification as "the people" besieged by the federal courts, and instead re-presented themselves as a minority within the American polity. For the first time in recent history, evangelicals solicited intervention by the federal courts on their own behalf. They asked the judiciary not to refrain from judicial activism, but to insert itself in church-state affairs. Indeed, they asked the judiciary to treat them as one of the "discrete and insular minorities" whose rights demanded special protection. Insightful Christian conservatives reimagined the judiciary as a potential friend able to help restore their lost influence in the public sphere.[21]

The lawyers for the *Jaffree* intervenors were among the growing number of Christian conservative cause lawyers writing briefs and trying cases throughout the United States. In representing the *Jaffree* intervenors, they had advanced the sort of civil-rights claims then gaining traction on the right. Their arguments had registered with Hand and would now guide him, from realignment of the *Jaffree* parties through delivery of his *Smith* opinion. Forced to recognize the federal courts' authority over the states on church-state matters, he now asserted that authority toward unusual ends. Hand applied the Establishment Clause in an expansive, unprecedented manner. Alabama, he ruled, was in violation of the First Amendment by having established the "religion" of secular humanism through its use of textbooks advancing a human-centered morality that, by its nature, denigrated God-centered religions.[22]

The rights revolution became, for Hand, a tool for protecting Christianity's place in the schools. He knew that his *Smith* ruling could not realistically be implemented; he knew that it would gain little support. That was his point. *Smith* was made tongue-in-cheek. With his admittedly outrageous ruling, he suggested to the legal establishment that, if Christian conservatives could be burdened with checking their most deeply held values at the classroom door, then liberals and secularists could be equally burdened. Liberals insisting that public education be nonreligious would be forced to apply that principle evenhandedly and remove their own worldview from the curriculum. Such a resolution, of course, was not possible. Backed against a wall, liberals would relent and permit theistic religion at least a role in the education process.[23]

Whereas McClellan had guided Hand during the *Jaffree* phase of the Mobile conflict, a different sort of conservative assisted him in *Smith*. The philosopher and critic Russell Kirk was a conservative luminary. He was one of the leading intellectuals, in the decades following World War II, to speak of a consistent, integrated conservative worldview. Throughout his career, Kirk had maintained that human freedom could thrive only in a God-based, traditional society. In the 1970s and 1980s, Kirk affirmed religion's proper place within the schools. Hand, now in search of an impartial expert witness, turned to Kirk, whose ideas about morality, freedom, and government in general were known to the judge. During the *Smith* trial, and in the opinion that resulted, Kirk played the role that McClellan had played during *Jaffree*. Hand was able to give his opinion clarity and sophistication by grounding it in the writings and trial testimony of an expert witness with a well-developed conservative worldview. Hand's civil-libertarian turn in *Smith* in no way signaled an abandonment of core conservative principles. He and the plaintiffs continued to laud Christian values and prescribe for them a role in public institutions. Civil-libertarianism served him as a strategy, but it never weakened his or the plaintiffs' commitment to the right of so-called ordinary citizens to shape law and public institutions.[24]

This book aims to demonstrate the centrality of constitutional politics to post–World War II U.S. history. Most of the rich and valuable historical literature on postwar conservatism downplays or ignores its constitutional dimension. Seeing the United States through conservative eyes requires that we take seriously conservatives' pronouncements on government, even if they sometimes seem subterfuge for malicious designs. To be sure, many conservatives resented the Court's minority rights decisions because those rulings threatened to dissolve Jim Crow social relations and Christian hegemony. But conservative resentment rested also on principled constitutional grounds. Some came to see federal judicial review as itself constitutionally suspect, a usurpation of popular majorities' political authority. Conservative intellectuals and public officials who wished to stem the Court's jurisdiction voiced genuine convictions about what the Constitution required, allowed, and forbade. Whether or not they were rationalizing does not affect their sincerity. Those evangelicals who strategically reimagined themselves as a rights-seeking bloc likewise held convictions about the Constitution. To downplay their theories about government and law as mere smokescreens for religious or racial aggrandizement is to flatten our historical knowledge.[25]

Relatedly, this book looks to demonstrate that "the Constitution" and "democracy" are evolving, contentious concepts. Although historians have paid great attention to various generations' attempts to widen or narrow democracy's scope, few studies have considered how the Supreme Court's rulings on church and state prompted different groups of citizens to define democracy and the Constitution in varying ways.[26] This book does just that. It traces the persisting influence of Alexander Bickel's 1962 claim that the Supreme Court represented a "countermajoritarian difficulty" in our essentially majoritarian system of government, that "judicial review is a deviant institution in the American democracy." Bickel's concern spurred a conservative critique of federal judicial review. Hand based his *Jaffree* ruling on that critique. For him, as for expert witness McClellan, the Constitution guarded the right of Mobile residents to allow or disallow classroom prayer, just as Alabama voters retained the right, through their chosen representatives, to encode their religious preferences into law. And nothing the courts did, they believed, could rightfully change that. Jaffree took his rather different view of democracy and the Constitution from liberals such as Justice William Brennan, who considered the protection of minorities central to democratic governance. Jaffree stood alongside constitutional theorist Ronald Dworkin, who posited that democracy required a "moral reading" of the Constitution requiring government to "treat all those subject to its dominion as having equal moral and political status" regardless of their numbers and political power.[27]

This book is a work of political history. It places federal judges and their detractors at the center of the nation's fractious and contentious battles over who ought to make laws and what kinds of laws they ought to make. Like John Jeffries and James Ryan, I assume that "the entire body of Establishment Clause jurisprudence can profitably be viewed from a political perspective." Judicial decisions and their surrounding machinations are treated here "*as if they were* products of political contests among various interest groups, both religious and secular, with competing positions on the proper relation of church and state." Debate over the Court's church-state rulings is part of a broader conflict pitting powerful segments of society – whites, anticommunists, Christians, heterosexuals, native English speakers, apparently law-abiding citizens – against advocates for society's weakest and most despised members. During the postwar years, the latter increasingly found its interests defended by federal courts committed to protecting discrete and insular minorities from the effects of legislation that disadvantaged them. To its detractors, the judiciary symbolized a federal government that had turned its back on ordinary citizens and their right to democratic governance. What critics of the courts lamented, liberal constitutionalist Laurence Tribe celebrated: that "the whole *point* of an independent judiciary is to be 'antidemocratic,' to preserve from transient majorities those human rights and other principles to which our legal and political system is committed." The federal judiciary came to signify, in the conservative imagination, the capture of government by blacks, atheists, communists, pornographers, and criminals. Those who saw themselves as on the losing end of the rights revolution adopted antijudicialism as a core tenet of their politics.[28]

Even among the enraged southern whites who pledged "massive resistance" to the Court's desegregation rulings, animosity toward the Court embodied more than hatred or resentment. As William Hustwit shows, white racism was at times subsumed within a political theory that condemned the federal government, and especially its courts, for trampling over the will of statewide majorities. Southern members of Congress signed a "Declaration of Constitutional Principles" decrying the Court's "clear abuse of judicial power" and sponsored legislation to restrict the Court's jurisdiction over the states. James J. Kilpatrick, editor of the *Richmond News Leader*, gained the support of newspaper readers and conservative intellectuals alike with his calls for local and state officials to resist the hostile and tyrannical U.S. Supreme Court. Kilpatrick's sentiments registered among whites throughout much of the nation, as witnessed by the early opposition to the civil rights movement on the part of William F. Buckley and the editors of *National Review*. Like his friend Kilpatrick, Buckley conceived his position in constitutional terms. As David Farber writes, Buckley defended "the right of local peoples to stay true to the traditions that sustained their communities" and maintained that "the federal government had no right to meddle in the affairs of individuals who wished to segregate and discriminate on racial grounds nor in the affairs of state governments who had the right to oversee local affairs." Racialist ideology became married to an anti-Court, democratic-republican philosophy of government, generating a nationwide right-wing populist movement.[29]

Had anti-Court populism targeted only the justices' desegregation rulings, its appeal would have remained somewhat limited. Instead, majoritarian critics took issue with the Court's full range of minority-rights case law. In their diatribes against judicial activism, specific issues such as race, religion, crime, and indecency blurred together. These complaints converged in a political theory that justified and explained them. Consistent with that theory, Alabama representative George Andrews responded to the Court's 1962 school prayer ruling, *Engel* v. *Vitale*, by grumbling that the justices had already "put the Negroes into the schools and now they have driven God out of them." Presidential candidates such as Barry Goldwater and George Wallace found it useful to denounce the Court as an antidemocratic monster contemptuous of small-town communities and their conventional, Christian mores. By the late 1960s, antijudicialism took root throughout American political culture. Maurice Isserman and Michael Kazin show that "a liberal government that seemed more interested in protecting esoteric and expansive notions of 'rights' for marginal groups than in protecting the lives and property of the vast majority was rapidly losing legitimacy." Increasing numbers of middle- and lower-middle-class Christian whites offended by the liberal Sixties denounced an alleged Court-sponsored ethos of moral laxity and contempt for social tradition.[30]

Widespread resentment toward the Court encouraged intellectuals who, since the 1950s, had hoped to generate a conservatism rooted in the conventional morality of ordinary people. Best known was William F. Buckley; others included philosophers Russell Kirk – expert witness for the court at the *Smith* trial – and Eric Voegelin, who argued that a free society required a firm moral order rooted in Christian devotion. Political scientist Willmoore Kendall most clearly articulated the view that American democracy ultimately rested not with personal moral autonomy but with the prescribed morality and thick wisdom found in small-town communities, and with representative government that encoded that morality and wisdom into law. More explicitly than any other conservative thinker, Kendall tied together majoritarian republicanism, religious traditionalism, and mistrust of an expansive federal government, especially its courts. Kendall's prescriptions for democracy would ultimately take root in a burgeoning conservative movement. By the mid-1960s, his majoritarian philosophy would become right-wing common sense.[31]

The moral majoritarianism championed by Kendall – government by virtuous ordinary citizens acting through their elected representatives – became a major theme of Nixon's successful presidential campaigns of 1968 and 1972. Nixon became convinced that a growing number of Americans were becoming dissatisfied with the politics of minority rights and the supposed culture of licentiousness. Two pieces of political analysis helped firm his suspicions: a series of 1968 articles by Kevin Phillips, later published as *The Emerging Republican Majority*, and Richard Scammon and Ben Wattenberg's *The Real Majority*. These works underscored what Nixon suspected: that numbers of middle- and lower-income voters were ready to leave the party of Roosevelt if it failed to repudiate the ethos of permissiveness that, in these voters' estimation, was rising to an epidemic level. A key part of Nixon's "silent majority" campaign strategy was his promise to select "strict constructionist" judges who, he believed, would be less than solicitous toward minority rights not explicitly identified in the text of the Constitution. He found political capital in denouncing liberal activist judges whose rulings infringed on decent, law-abiding citizens.[32]

From the 1970s into the 1980s, Supreme Court justices were characterized by some conservatives as members of a "new class" bent on creating public policy reflecting its own culturally elitist values. The justices, it was charged, posed as unmatched experts in matters of justice. Allegedly, like academics and liberal administrators, the justices thought they knew better than ordinary people the kinds of laws required of a good society. Proponents of the living Constitution such as William O. Douglas and William Brennan, it was said, asserted themselves as prophets who dismissed ordinary citizens as too benighted to base laws on fairness and inclusivity. These justices were accused of transgressing the parochial values on which lawmaking ought to be based. What most rankled right-wing critics of the so-called new class was its supposed disregard for the unfashionable, Bible-based mores that informed the judgment of middle America.[33]

By the early 1980s, some conservatives doubted whether majoritarian methods might ever again be a viable method for preserving conventional morality under law. Fortunately for them, elasticity in the meanings of democracy and rights enabled them to co-opt the language and legal strategies long used by liberal civil-libertarians. As the Mobile conflict evolved, the religious conservatives at its center looked to adopt and transcend Jaffree's trial position, to define democracy as solicitous toward the rights of the Christian "minority." Like Jaffree, they sought accommodation as yet another party within an inclusive classroom environment – even as they continued their quest to restore Christianity's long-lost hegemony over the public sphere. Such flexibility informed the rulings of Judge Hand. A Nixon appointee who had spent his career opposing liberal judicial activism, Hand showed great imagination in circumnavigating the roadblocks laid out by his superiors. Indeed, Hand revealed what Thomas Keck has called "a distinctive new style of conservative judicial activism" in which right-wing judges issue rulings meant to achieve their preferred political ends. The conservative activists in the Mobile conflict, including Hand, exemplified American conservatism in all its startling contradiction.[34]

Herein lies a story about the unsettled relationship between Christian conservatism and democratic republicanism. Frustrations over the failure of majoritarian politics to yield victories on school prayer prompted the subjects of this story to close some doors and open others. Seizing upon a living Constitution, they discovered uncharted legal avenues and untapped possibilities. The civil-libertarian strategy that they crafted derived, in large part, from the writings of far-right evangelicals such as Rousas John Rushdoony and Francis Schaeffer who looked askance on majoritarian sentiment. This gave rise to an ambivalence toward democracy on the part of citizens such as the *Smith* plaintiffs. If true Christians had indeed become a marginalized social group, then what did that say about the majority of Americans? Could electoral politics reliably lead to laws compatible with Christian morality? Despite these uncertainties, republican majoritarianism would continue strongly to influence Christian conservatives' understanding of their political status and identity, especially in the "red states." As with conservatives in general, Christian conservatives would persist in presenting themselves as the truest of Americans – as "the people" – even as they fretted about their own marginalization. Through state lawmaking and citizen activism, they looked to defy the so-called judicial oligarchy and its inveterate secularism. And, of course, they went to court to defend their constitutional rights.[35]

This study proceeds from the assumption that sociopolitical identities derive largely from systems of belief. My work comports with the work of cognitive linguist George Lakoff, who identifies mental "frames," or structures of thought, as the engines of conservative and liberal political behavior. Mental framework, or "worldview," provides a highly useful concept for analyzing history. My research reveals, at the heart of postwar American conservatism, a reasonably coherent worldview whose moral and political components function symbiotically. That worldview, based on Christian self-discipline and republican self-government, propelled the main characters in the Mobile story, much as it moved countless other activists, lawyers, and public officials throughout this period.[36]

Seen through the lens of worldview, postwar American conservatism does not appear as a marriage of convenience between religiously and economically motivated subgroups. My story is one about conservatives whose fears about licentiousness were inseparable from their fears of socialism. In the textbooks they targeted, the *Smith* plaintiffs detected disrespect for God, country, and capitalism. That disrespect, *in toto*, signified in their minds a monolithic secular-humanist worldview pervading American society and government. They wished, as much as possible, to supplant this progressive worldview with their own orthodox one. On the basis of their Christianity, they took aim at a supposed anti-American, socialistic atheism imposed by unelected federal judges.[37]

For many, many conservatives, commitment to private enterprise has little to do with rational self-interest. Relatively few individuals become wealthy from the operation of free markets. The vast majority of conservatives understand capitalism in moral terms, as a system that rewards self-reliance and punishes indolence and irresponsibility. Personal and social well-being can best be preserved, they believe, by a system based on private enterprise. As Lakoff puts it, "people do not necessarily vote in their self-interest. They vote their identity. They vote their values. They vote who they identify with." Conservatives identify with people for whom authority-based morality has led to self-discipline and self-discipline has opened possibilities for financial success. Self-discipline, in economics as well as religion, drives the postwar conservative worldview. David Farber rightly sees conservatives as informed by the belief that individuals need to be disciplined, and that discipline requires the risks – the rewards and punishments – that a free-market economy imposes on individuals. Without those risks, individuals behave irresponsibly. When Thomas Frank famously asked, "What's wrong with Kansas?" he failed to see that middle-American rejection of the welfare state rests on moral and political conviction rather than false consciousness.[38]

The Christians at the center of my story are conservatives oriented by a conservative worldview. Amid their shifts in legal strategy, they continued to assert their right to fashion public policy in accord with their Bible-based morality. They denounced existing religion clause doctrine as a means of depriving ordinary citizens of the right to rule themselves as they believed proper and good. They attacked secular humanism as a threat to their liberty – their liberty to fashion, for themselves and for their children, institutions that strengthened rather than diminished personal character and republican governance. They fought to save their schools and their country from an inherently un-American force, secular humanism, that was destroying citizens from within and without.

The political movement informing the subjects of this book is identified alternately as the "New Right" and "Christian Right." This inextricability between moral conservatism and conservatism in general is consonant with how many in the movement defined themselves. From the late 1970s through early 1980s, "family values" conservatives resisted supposed atheistic cultural elites who used the federal government to impose an all-powerful welfare state on a captive citizenry. The main characters of my story – Hand, McClellan, Alabama governor Fob James, presidential advisor Edwin Meese, U.S. senators Jeremiah Denton and Jesse Helms, and Supreme Court justice William Rehnquist – pursued a constitutional counterrevolution that included the right of Christians to express themselves fully within the public sphere. Even the *Jaffree* intervenors, who were motivated predominantly by religious concerns, defended a Christianity that incorporated allegiance to free-market economics and American exceptionalism. They described the secular humanism against which they rallied as an atheistic, socialistic, anti-American worldview. This broad conservatism is evident in today's far-right Tea Party, which counts, among the constitutional liberties it vigorously defends, the unfettered liberty of Christians. Hand, McClellan, and the others were informed by that constitutionalism. Seen through the lens of constitutional politics, the New Right appears as a reasonably coherent movement comprised of intertwined religious and economic strands.[39]

The intense religiosity of African Americans did not generally place them within the New Right. Theirs were not the impulses that overall drove the movement. While the New Right featured conservative Christianity as a crucial component, it did not include, among its adherents, those morally traditional Christians who favored liberal economic policies or judicial activism on behalf of minority civil rights. At the heart of New Right religiosity lay valuation of an economic individualism believed to be threatened by the welfare state. Such individualism was often irrelevant, or even anathema, to the faith of those who benefited from government assistance. The moral and cultural conservatism of many black Mobilians may have provoked in them hostility toward Jaffree, but it did not cause them to participate in the legal and political effort to protect school prayer or remove secular humanism from the curriculum. Despite their religiosity, most black Mobilians saw that effort as a distraction from the issues that mattered to them. African American schoolteachers and principals launched the initial resistance to Jaffree but soon faded into the background of the conflict. The ensuing legal and political attack was carried out entirely by whites. They personified the New Right; their black Christian neighbors did not.

The concept of majoritarianism put forward in this book should not be confused with alternative understandings of the term. First, majoritarianism here refers to a republican process in which popular sentiment is filtered through elected legislators who represent the people. I do not speak about direct democracy or plebiscitarianism; I speak about citizen majorities making their will known to and through their representatives. Second, this book identifies majorities as blocs claiming to possess, or believed by their opponents to possess, a discrete worldview or ideology. This book does not consider popular majorities as comprised of individuals belonging to a particular economic class. In the United States, socialism would likely never become a majoritarian affiliation understood in this way, no matter how many Americans might benefit economically from a government based on its principles, because collectivism violates the majority's moral sensibilities. Third, I am concerned with majorities of citizens within individual states, not with majority and minority blocs of states. The Calhounian majoritarianism about which Sam Tanenhaus writes is irrelevant to my conception. While the states of the former Confederacy might comprise a minority among all the states and therefore encounter difficulty advancing their interests at the national level, the preponderance of Christians *within* those states has fewer problems securing passage of favorable state laws. Finally, the majoritarianism discussed here is symbolic at least as much as strategic. The subjects in this study present themselves as "the people" even when their demographic standing is unclear. This symbolic dimension becomes apparent in the "real Americans" trope used by opponents of Barack Obama's successful 2008 presidential candidacy. These Obama critics, like conservatives generally, paint themselves as the heart of America – a mythical core that would purportedly reclaim its rightful sovereignty if and when the un-American political class and the cultural elites supporting it were finally brought down.[40]

The first two chapters of this book focus on the unplaying of events in Mobile. Chapter 1 charts Ishmael Jaffree's complaint about school prayer, the wall of opposition he encountered locally and statewide, and Hand's injunction against Alabama's recent school prayer law passed in response to Jaffree's complaint. In Chapter 2, several of the key conservative players, including Hand, are examined in the light of their antijudicialism. The chapter ends with the *Jaffree* trial, at which McClellan announces his vision for counterrevolution against the minority rights regime.

The next three chapters widen our gaze beyond Alabama and trace *Jaffree*'s relevance to and impact on national politics. Chapter 3 begins with Hand's ruling and ends with the Eleventh Circuit's reversal. In between, we look at the different parties' attempts to elicit sympathetic court orders, the rise of the counter-establishment surrounding the Reagan Justice Department, and the counter-establishment's bid to persuade the solicitor general to submit an amicus brief during the appellate phase of *Jaffree*. Chapter 4 continues the examination of the struggle in and around the Justice Department as *Jaffree* enters its Supreme Court phase. We look then at a parallel struggle within the Senate, where McClellan's influence among conservative lawmakers appeared to rise and wane, supplanted by the influence of advocates for equal treatment between religion and non-religion. Chapter 5 considers the Court's ongoing church-state debate, which pitted majoritarians against minority rights advocates. The chapter's spotlight falls on the Court's foremost majoritarian, William Rehnquist, whose blistering *Jaffree* dissent could not prevent the Court from upholding the Eleventh Circuit's reversal of Hand.

Chapters 6 and 7 return our attention to Mobile. Chapter 6 looks at Hand's realignment of the original parties and instigation of a new trial, *Smith* v. *Board*. The chapter examines the evolving position of the *Jaffree*-intervenors-turned-*Smith*-plaintiffs, the far-right political theology on which they drew, and the legal battle against secular humanism sparked by that political theology. The plaintiffs' stance is more fully explored in Chapter 7. Center stage is the *Smith* trial, where a parade of expert witnesses insisted that the public schools were advancing a secular religion, in contravention of the Establishment Clause. The chapter considers the influence wielded on Hand by his handpicked expert witness, Russell Kirk. Chapter 7 ends with Hand's landmark ruling – the first federal ruling ever to find a state and local government guilty of establishing the religion of secular humanism.

In the conclusion, we find that *Smith* died an ignominious death – reversed by the appellate court and abandoned by the plaintiffs. The Court would never uphold teacher-led recited prayer or the promotion of Christian ideas in the public-school classroom. Nonetheless, the logic underlying Hand's *Jaffree* and *Smith* opinions would endure. Rulings based on equal treatment between religion and secularism, it turned out, evinced unmistakable traces of religious majoritarianism. Justices Rehnquist, Scalia, and Thomas would issue opinions that more explicitly advanced that philosophy. Commitment to it would drive Attorney General Edwin Meese to instigate a public debate between himself and justices Brennan and Stevens, and other lawyers and writers as well would carry on the battle against liberal judicial activism. Intertwined throughout their declarations were the moral and political strains of post–World War II conservatism. Hand's assertions would echo among critics who blamed the Court for perpetuating a culture of permissiveness and dependency. The antijudicialism of *Jaffree* and the civil-libertarianism of *Smith* would make common cause in the continuing effort to embed Christian conservative interests in American government and law.

Notes

1 W. Brevard Hand, speech delivered at the prayer breakfast for the Calhoun County Law Day ceremony, Anniston, Alabama, May 1986, pp. 3–4, Speech file 2, W. Brevard Hand Papers (United States District Courthouse, Southern District of Alabama, Mobile, Ala.), pp. 3–4, 7.

2 Hand, Calhoun County speech, 3–4.

3 Hand, Calhoun County speech, 3–4.

4 *Smith* v. *Board of School Commissioners of Mobile County*, 655 F.Supp 939 (1987); *Jaffree* v. *Board of School Commissioners of Mobile County*, 554 F.Supp. 1104 (1983). Prior to his speech, Hand had received documents including Plaintiff's memorandum of law, *Douglas T. Smith et al.* v. *Board of School Commissioners of Mobile County et al.*, consolidated with *Douglas T. Smith et al.* v. *George Wallace*, 1983–1987: Wallace File, SG 5012, Legal Case Files, Alabama Department of Archives and History (624 Washington Ave., Montgomery, Ala.), October 10, 1985; and George Wallace, stipulation for consent decree, *Smith* v. *Board*, November 7, 1985, Wallace File.

5 [Initial] verified complaint, *Ishmael Jaffree et al.* v. *Board of School Commissioners of Mobile County et al.*, 1983–1987: Wallace File, SG 5012, Legal Case Files, ADAH, May 28, 1982; Second amended complaint, *Ishmael Jaffree et al.* v. *Board of School Commissioners of Mobile County et al.*, Wallace File, June 30, 1982. *Dare We Defend Our Rights?* (1992: L. Wade Black and the Alabama Center for Law and Civic Education), narrated by Wayne Flynt. *Engel* v. *Vitale*, 370 U.S. 421 (1962).

6 Literature on the Christian Right's rise to influence in the early 1980s is voluminous. Noteworthy works published over the past decade include Andrew Hartman, *A War for the Soul of America: A History of the Culture Wars* (Chicago: University of Chicago Press, 2015); Kevin M. Kruse, *One Nation under God: How Corporate America Invented Christian America* (New York: Basic Books, 2015); Robert Daniel Rubin, "The Righteousness of Difference: Orthodox Jews and the Establishment Clause, 1965–71," in *The Right Side of the Sixties: Reexamining Conservatism' Decade of Transformation*, ed. by Laura Jane Gifford and Daniel K. Williams (New York: Palgrave Macmillan), 121–40; Daniel K. Williams, "Richard Nixon's Religious Right: Catholics, Evangelicals, and the Creation of an Antisecular Alliance," in *Right Side of the Sixties*, ed. by Gifford and Williams, 141–60; Robert O. Self, *All in the Family: The Realignment of American Democracy since the 1960s* (New York:

Hill and Wang, 2012); Michelle M. Nickerson, *Mothers of Conservatism: Women and the Postwar Right* (Princeton: Princeton University Press, 2012); Joseph Crespino, *Strom Thurmond's America* (New York: Hill and Wang, 2012); Darren Dochuk, *From Bible Belt to Sun Belt: Plain-Folk Religion, Grassroots Politics, and the Rise of Conservative Evangelicalism* (New York: Norton, 2011); D. G. Hart, *From Sarah Palin to Billy Graham: Evangelicals and the Betrayal of American Conservatism* (Grand Rapids, Mich.: Eerdmans, 2011); Daniel K. Williams, *God's Own Party: The Making of the Christian Right* (New York: Oxford University Press, 2010); Kevin M. Kruse, "Beyond the Southern Cross: The National Origins of the Religious Right," in *The Myth of Southern Exceptionalism*, ed. by Matthew D. Lassiter and Joseph Crespino (New York: Oxford University Press, 2010), 286–307; Sarah Barringer Gordon, *The Spirit of the Law* (Cambridge, Mass.: Belknap, 2010); Max Blumenthal, *Republican Gomorrah: Inside the Movement That Shattered the Party* (New York: Nation Books, 2009); Bethany Moreton, *To Serve God and Wal-Mart: Tea Making of Christian Free Enterprise* (Cambridge, Mass.: Harvard University Press, 2009); Steven P. Miller, *Billy Graham and the Rise of the Republican South* (Philadelphia: University of Pennsylvania Press, 2009); Kim Phillips-Fein, *Invisible Hands: The Making of the Conservative Movement from the New Deal to Reagan* (New York: Norton, 2009); John G. Turner, *Bill Bright and the Campus Crusade for Christ* (Chapel Hill: University of North Carolina Press, 2008); Matthew D. Lassiter, "Inventing Family Values," in *Rightward Bound: Making America Conservative in the 1970s*, ed. by Bruce J. Schulman and Julian E. Zelizer (Cambridge, Mass.: Harvard University Press, 2008), 13–28; Paul Boyer, "The Evangelical Resurgence in 1970s American Protestantism," in *Rightward Bound*, ed. by Schulman and Zelizer, 29–51; Joseph Crespino, "Civil Rights and the Religious Right," in *Rightward Bound*, ed. by Schulman and Zelizer, 90–105; Allan J. Lichtman, *White Protestant Nation: The Rise of the American Conservative Movement* (New York: Atlantic Monthly, 2008), 330–78; and Donald Critchlow, *Phyllis Schlafly and Grassroots Conservatism: A Woman's Crusade* (Princeton: Princeton University Press, 2005), 243–95.

7 *Mobile Register*, October 6, 1986, p. 3B.

8 Self, *All in the Family*; Jonathan Zimmerman, *Whose America? Culture Wars in the Public Schools* (Cambridge, Mass.: Harvard University Press, 2002); Lichtman, *White Protestant Nation*, 2–5; George Lakoff, *Moral Politics: How Liberals and Conservatives Think* (Chicago: University of Chicago Press, 2001), ix–x, 3, 12–18, 33–36; James Davison Hunter, *Culture Wars: The Struggle to Define America* (New York: BasicBooks, 1991).

Although most of the events in this book took place in a southern city, they are not presented here as events in "southern history" as such. This is because they could have taken place in any conservative stronghold throughout the United States. As I show throughout, the actors with whom the book is concerned evince a conservatism ascendant throughout U.S. politics at the time rather than one that was regionally distinct.

9 Intervenors' Post-Trial Brief, *Ishmael Jaffree et al.* v. *Board of School Commissioners of Mobile County et al.*, 1983–1987: Wallace File, SG

5012, Legal Case Files, Alabama Department of Archives and History (624 Washington Ave., Montgomery, Ala.), January 1983. Transcript, *Ishmael Jaffree et al.* v. *Board of School Commissioners of Mobile County et al.*, Civil case no. 82–0554–H, box no. 1, accession no. 021–93–0423, location no. C0681974 SAN (Federal Records Center, East Point, Ga.), November 15–18 1982.

10 *Jaffree* v. *Board*, 554 F.Supp. 1104 (1983); *Brown* v. *Board of Education*, 347 U.S. 483 (1954); *New York Times*, March 12, 1956, pp. 1, 19.

11 Transcript, *Jaffree* v. *Board*, 519–605; James McClellan interview by Robert Daniel Rubin, October 14, 2004 (interview was conducted by telephone); Richard B. Bernstein, "R. I. P. James McClellan, 1937–2005," H-Net, June 16, 2005, http://h-net.msu.edu/cgi-bin/logbrowse.pl?trx=vx&list=HLaw&month=0506&week. Sidney Blumenthal, *The Rise of the Counter-Establishment: From Conservative Ideology to Political Power* (New York: Times, 1986); Lincoln Caplan, *The Tenth Justice: The Solicitor General and the Rule of Law* (New York: Knopf, 1987), 97–107.

12 Lincoln Caplan, "A Good Ol' Boy Sitting on the Federal Bench," *Los Angeles Times*, March 29, 1987, sec. 5, p. 3. *Jaffree* v. *Board*, 1113–15; James McClellan, "The Making and Unmaking of the Establishment Clause," in *A Blueprint for Judicial Reform*, ed. by Patrick B. McGuigan and Randall R. Rader (Washington, D.C.: Free Congress Research and Education Foundation, 1981), 295–325. Transcript, *Jaffree* v. *Board*, 556, 603. *Engel* v. *Vitale; School District of Abington, Pa.* v. *Schempp*, 374 U.S. 203 (1963); *Everson* v. *Board of Education*, 330 U.S. 1 (1947).

13 On conservatism's majoritarian dimension, see David Sehat, *The Myth of American Religious Freedom* (New York: Oxford University Press, 2011), 276–78 and *passim*.

14 Amanda Hollis-Brusky, *Ideas with Consequences: The Federalist Society and the Conservative Counterrevolution* (New York: Oxford University Press, 2015); Michael Avery and Danielle McLaughlin, *The Federalist Society: How Conservatives Took the Law Back from Liberals* (Nashville: Vanderbilt University Press, 2013). [James Madison,] "The Federalist No. 10 (1787)," in *The Federalist: The Eighty-Five Essays Written by Alexander Hamilton, John Jay, and James Madison* (New York: Random House, 1937), 60–61.

15 Kevin P. Phillips, *The Emerging Republican Majority* (New York: Anchor, 1970); Richard M. Scammon and Ben J. Wattenberg, *The Real Majority* (New York: Primus, 1970). Michael W. Flamm, *Law and Order: Street Crime, Civil Unrest, and the Crisis of Liberalism in the 1960s* (New York: Columbia University Press, 2005), 10, 159–81. On Nixon's role in the conservative imagination, see Self, *All in the Family*, 5–6, 255–60, 279; and Robert Mason, *Richard Nixon and the Quest for a New Majority* (Chapel Hill: University of North Carolina Press, 2004). My understanding of conservatism's moral strand has important similarities to the idea of "normative America" put forward in Hartman, *War for the Soul of America*, 5 and *passim*; and "moral establishment" advanced in Sehat, *Myth of American Religious Freedom*, 222–26, 235–45. The culture of right-wing populism is explored in Christopher Lasch, *The True and Only Heaven: Progress and Its Critics* (New York: Norton,

1991), 476–532. The political values of that culture are articulated most eloquently in Robert Bork, *The Tempting of America: The Political Seduction of the Law* (New York: Free Press, 1990). Criticism of the Court as purveyor of elitist liberal morality is put forward in Lino A. Graglia, "The Legacy of Justice Brennan: Constitutionalization of the Left-Liberal Political Agenda," *Washington University Law Review*, 77 (Spring 1999), 183–92; Lino A. Graglia, "Constitutional Law: A Ruse for Government by an Intellectual Elite," *Georgia State University Law Review*, 14 (July 1998), 767–79; Thomas Sowell, "How the Cultural Elite Undermine Traditional Values" *Indianapolis Star*, October 4, 1992, p. F2; and the essays collected in Mitchell S. Muncy, ed., *The End of Democracy? The Judicial Usurpation of Politics* (Dallas: Spence, 1997).

16 Bork, *Tempting of America*. See David Farber's discussion of William F. Buckley. David Farber, *The Rise and Fall of American Conservatism: A Short History* (Princeton: Princeton University Press, 2010), 47, 52–58.

17 Hand's relevance is asserted in Daniel T. Rodgers, *Age of Fracture* (Cambridge, Mass.: Belknap, 2001), 236–37. John A. Jenkins, *The Partisan: The Life of William Rehnquist* (New York: PublicAffairs, 2012). Joseph Crespino, *Strom Thurmond's America* (New York: Hill and Wang, 2012). Rick Perlstein, *Before the Storm: Barry Goldwater and the Unmaking of the American Consensus* (New York: Hill and Wang, 2001); Peter Iverson, *Barry Goldwater: Native Arizonan* (Norman: University of Oklahoma Press, 1997); Robert Alan Goldberg, *Barry Goldwater* (New Haven: Yale University Press, 1995). Kevin M. Schultz, *Buckley and Mailer: The Difficult Friendship That Shaped the Sixties* (New York: Norton, 2015); Carl T. Bogus, *Buckley: William F. Buckley Jr. and the Rise of American Conservatism* (New York: Bloomsbury, 2011); Linda Bridges and John R. Coyne, *Strictly Right: William F. Buckley Jr. and the American Conservative Movement* (Hoboken, N. J.: John Wiley, 2007); John B. Judis, *William F. Buckley, Jr.: Patron Saint of the Conservatives* (New York: Simon and Schuster, 1988).3 William P. Hustwit, *James J. Kilpatrick: Salesman for Segregation* (Chapel Hill: University of North Carolina Press, 2013).

18 *Jaffree* v. *Wallace*, 705 F.2d 1526 (1983). *Wallace* v. *Jaffree*, 472 U.S. 38 (1985); *ibid*, 91–114 (Rehnquist, J., dissenting). *Jaffree* v. *Board*, 1129–30 n41; *Smith* v. *Board of School Commissioners of Mobile County*, 827 F.2d 684 (1987), at 687–88; Memorandum on position of plaintiffs Smith, *Jaffree* v. *Board*, Sept. 16, 1985, Wallace File.

19 Barry Goldwater, Speech to the American Political Science Association, *Washington Post*, Sept. 12, 1964, p. A6; Willmoore Kendall, "The Bill of Rights and American Freedom," in *What Is Conservatism*, ed. by Frank S. Meyer (New York: Holt, Rinehart, Winston, 1964), 41–64; William F. Buckley, "Why the South Must Prevail," *National Review*, August 24, 1957, pp. 148–49; James J. Kilpatrick, *The Sovereign States: Notes of a Citizen of Virginia* (Chicago: Henry Regnery, 1957). Rehnquist critiques the Court on federalist grounds in *Fry* v. *United States*, 421 U.S. 542 (1975), (Rehnquist, J., dissenting), 557; *National League of Cities* v. *Usery*, 426 U.S. 833 (1976), (Rehnquist, J., dissenting), 845, and *Nevada* v. *Hall*, 440 U.S. 410 (1979) (Rehnquist, J. dissenting), 432–43. William M. Beaney and Edward N. Beiser, "Prayer

and Politics: The Impact of *Engel* and *Schempp* on the Political Process," *Journal of Public Law*, 13 (1964), 475–503; Bruce J. Dierenfield, "'Somebody Is Tampering with America's Soul': Congress and the School Prayer Debate," *Congress and the Presidency*, 24 (Autumn 1997), 167–204. Edward Keynes with Randall K. Miller, *The Court vs. Congress: Prayer, Busing, and Abortion* (Durham: Duke University Press, 1989).

20 *Miranda* v. *Arizona*, 384 U.S. 436 (1966); *Abington* v. *Schempp*; *Epperson* v. *Arkansas*, 393 U.S. 97 (1968). Patrick B. McGuigan and Randall R. Rader, "Judicial Oligarchy: Have the People Ceased to Be Their Own Rulers?," in *A Blueprint for Judicial Reform*, ed. by Patrick B. McGuigan and Randall R. Rader (Washington, D.C.: Free Congress Research and Education Foundation, 1981), 353–68; Lino A. Graglia, "Judicial Imperialism: The Supreme Court's Abuse of Power," *National Review*, July 21, 1978, pp. 892–96; Raoul Berger, *Government by Judiciary: The Transformation of the Fourteenth Amendment* (Cambridge, Mass.: Harvard University Press, 1977); Nathan Glazer, "Towards an Imperial Judiciary?," *Public Interest*, 41 (Fall 1975), 104–23.

21 Kevin R. den Dulk, "In Legal Culture, but Not of It: The Role of Cause Lawyers in Evangelical Legal Mobilization," paper delivered at conference on cause lawyers and social movements, University of California, Los Angeles, March 2005 (in Robert Daniel Rubin's possession); Aaron Louis Haberman, "Civil Rights on the Right: The Modern Christian Right and the Crusade for School Prayer, 1962–1996" (Ph.D. diss., University of South Carolina, 2006), 6–7, 140–76; Steven P. Brown, *Trumping Religion: The New Christian Right, the Free Speech Clause, and the Courts* (Tuscaloosa: University of Alabama Press, 2002); Stuart A. Scheingold and Austin Sarat, *Something to Believe In: Politics, Professionalism, and Cause Lawyering* (Stanford: Stanford University Press, 2004), 113–17. The "discrete and insular minorities" doctrine was first advanced by Harlan Fiske Stone in *U.S.* v. *Carolene Products*, 304 U.S. 144 (1938), 152n4. Two years later, Stone elaborated on the doctrine, declaring that the Court must not countenance "the surrender of the constitutional protection of the liberty of small minorities to the popular will." *Minersville School District* v. *Gobitis*, 310 U.S. 586 (1940), (Stone, J., dissenting), 606.

22 Plaintiff's memorandum of law, *Douglas T. Smith et al.* v. *Board of School Commissioners of Mobile County et al.*, consolidated with *Douglas T. Smith et al.* v. *George Wallace*, 1983–1987: Wallace File, SG 5012, Legal Case Files, Alabama Department of Archives and History (624 Washington Ave., Montgomery, Ala.), October 10, 1985. *Smith* v. *Board*, 655 F.Supp 939 (1987). For examples of rulings where judges had rejected such arguments, see the discussion in Chapter 6.

23 Robert Daniel Rubin, "Establish No Religion: Brevard Hand's Civil Libertarian Turn," *Journal of Church and State*, 58 (Winter 2016), 98–116. W. Brevard Hand interview by Robert Daniel Rubin, April 12, 2000, transcript, pp. 14–15 (in Robert Daniel Rubin's possession); W. Brevard Hand interview by Robert Daniel Rubin, December 5, 2000, transcript, pp. 16–17 (in Robert Daniel Rubin's possession).

24 Kirk's most comprehensive description of the conservative worldview appears in Russell Kirk, *The Conservative Mind: From Burke to Eliot* (1953; Washington, D.C.: Regnery, 1995). Russell Kirk, "Shelton College and State Licensing of Religious Schools: An Educator's View of the Interface between the Establishment and Free Exercise Clauses," *Law and Contemporary Problems*, 44 (Winter 1981), 169–84. In an essay published a few months prior to *Smith*, Kirk rehearsed his *Smith* testimony. Russell Kirk, "Traditions of Thought and the Core Curriculum," in *Content, Character, and Choice in Schooling: Public Policy and Research Implications*, ed. by Onalee McGraw (Washington, D.C.: National Council on Educational Research, 1986), 13–27. The months prior to *Smith* also saw the publication of papers from a 1984 symposium organized by McClellan's Center for Judicial Studies. Kirk edited the collection, wrote the introduction, and dedicated it to Hand. Russell Kirk, "Introduction," in *The Assault on Religion: Commentaries on the Decline of Religious Liberty*, ed. by Russell Kirk (Lanham, Md.: University Press of America, 1986), 4–7.

25 Several works provided me with instructive examples of connecting conservative worldview to constitutional theory. These included Hustwit, *James J. Kilpatrick*; Sehat, *Myth of American Religious Freedom*; R. Jonathan Moore, *Suing for America's Soul: John Whitehead, the Rutherford Institute, and Conservative Christians in the Courts* (Grand Rapids, Mich.: Eerdmans, 2007); and Laura Kalman, *Yale Law School and the Sixties: Revolt and Reverberations* (Chapel Hill: University of North Carolina Press, 2005), 1–10, 273–318. Especially helpful was Sehat's *Myth of American Religious Freedom*, which explores religious conservatives' continued legal efforts, on and off the bench, to enforce their own moral preferences and to marginalize religious dissent. Other works that examine conservatism and the law include Amanda Hollis-Brusky, *Ideas with Consequences: The Federalist Society and the Conservative Counterrevolution* (New York: Oxford University Press, 2015); Michael Avery and Danielle McLaughlin, *The Federalist Society: How Conservatives Took the Law Back from Liberals* (Nashville: Vanderbilt University Press, 2013); Steven M. Teles, *The Rise of the Conservative Legal Movement* (Princeton: Princeton University Press, 2008); and Ann Southworth, *Lawyers of the Right: Professionalizing the Conservative Coalition* (Chicago: University of Chicago Press, 2008).

26 The impact of church-state case law on democracy's definition is briefly considered in Bruce J. Dierenfield, *The Battle over School Prayer: How Engel v. Vitale Changed America* (Lawrence: University Press of Kansas, 2007); and Stephen Bates, *Battleground: One Mother's Crusade, the Religious Right, and the Struggle for Our Schools* (New York: Holt, 1993). Democracy's relationship to constitutional issues in general is given close scrutiny in Mark V. Tushnet, *The NAACP's Legal Strategy against Segregated Education, 1925–1950* (Chapel Hill: University of North Carolina Press, 1987).

27 Alexander M. Bickel, *The Least Dangerous Branch: The Supreme Court at the Bar of Politics* (1962; New Haven: Yale University Press, 1986), 16–19. Walter Berns, "The Constitution as a Bill of Rights," in *How Does the Constitution Secure Rights*, ed. by Robert Goldwin and William A. Schambra (Washington, D.C.: American Enterprise Institute, 1985), 50–73; Bork,

Tradition and Morality in Constitutional Law; Berger, *Government by Judiciary;* Philip B. Kurland, *Politics, the Constitution, and the Warren Court* (Chicago: University of Chicago Press, 1970). By the end of his life, Bickel became a critic of judicial review as it had developed. Alexander Bickel, *The Morality of Consent* (New Haven: Yale University Press, 1970). Bickel's evolution as a thinker is thoughtfully considered in Kalman, *Yale Law School and the Sixties*. A critique of rights-centered jurisprudence as potentially corrosive of democracy can be found in Mary Ann Glendon, *Rights Talk: The Impoverishment of Political Discourse* (New York: Free Press, 1991). Brennan's solicitude toward religious minorities can be seen in *Sherbert* v. *Verner*, 374 U.S. 398 (1963); *Abington* v. *Schempp* (Brennan, J., concurring), 234–41; *Marsh* v. *Chambers*, 463 U.S. 783 (1983), (Brennan, J., dissenting), 795–822; and William J. Brennan, "The Constitution of the United States: Contemporary Ratification," *South Texas Law Review*, 27 (Fall 1986), 433–45. Ronald Dworkin, *Freedom's Law: The Moral Reading of the American Constitution* (Cambridge, Mass.: Harvard University Press, 1996), 7–8.

28 John C. Jeffries Jr. and James E. Ryan, "A Political History of the Establishment Clause," *Michigan Law Review*, 100 (November 2001), 280, emphasis in original; Justin Driver, "The Consensus Constitution," *Texas Law Review*, 89 (2011), 777, 787, 801. Lucas Powe similarly declares his commitment to "reviv[ing] a valuable tradition of discussing the Supreme Court in the context of American politics." Lucas A. Powe, *The Warren Court and American Politics* (Cambridge, Mass.: Belknap, 2000), xi. Tribe quoted in John Morton Blum, *Years of Discord: American Politics and Society, 1961–1974* (New York: Norton, 1991), 217. Conservative critiques of the Court as antidemocratic are explored fully in Mark Kozlowski, *The Myth of the Imperial Judiciary: Why the Right is Wrong about the Courts* (New York: New York University Press, 2003), 1–50.

29 Numan V. Bartley, *The Rise of Massive Resistance: Race and Politics in the South during the 1950s* (Baton Rouge: Louisiana State University Press, 1969); Dewey Grantham, *The South in Modern America* (New York: Harper Collins, 1994), 208–9. Hustwit, *James J. Kilpatrick*, 41–57. Farber, *Rise and Fall of American Conservatism*, 73. George H. Nash, *The Conservative Intellectual Movement in America since 1945* (Wilmington: ISI, 1996), 185–87; Powe, *Warren Court and American Politics*, 59–62. Blum, *Years of Discord*, 190–98; Jim Newton, *Justice for All: Earl Warren and the Nation He Made* (New York: Riverhead, 2006), 385–87; Michael Kammen, *A Machine That Would Go of Itself: The Constitution in American Culture* (New York: Knopf, 1987), 324–31.

30 On the increased centrality of majoritarian theory to the thinking of conservative intellectuals, see Nash, *Conservative Intellectual Movement in America*, 199–203, 234. Andrews is quoted in Beaney and Beiser, "Prayer and Politics," 478. Dan Carter, "A World Turned Upside Down: Southern Politics at the End of the Twentieth Century," in *The Southern State of Mind*, ed. by Jan Nordby Gretlund (Columbia: University of South Carolina Press, 1999), 57; Powe, *Warren Court and American Politics*, 187–89, 361–63; David Goldfield, *Southern Histories: Public, Personal, and Sacred* (Athens: University of

Georgia Press, 2003), 55–58. Goldberg, *Barry Goldwater* (New Haven: Yale University Press, 1995), 153–55, 229–30; Rick Perlstein, *Before the Storm: Barry Goldwater and the Unmaking of the American Consensus* (New York: Hill and Wang, 2001), 425, 430. On Wallace's public criticism of the Court, see Beaney and Beiser, "Prayer and Politics," 486–87; Dan T. Carter, *The Politics of Rage: George Wallace, the Origins of the New Conservatism, and the Transformation of American Politics* (New York: Simon and Schuster, 1995), 162, 313–14, 339; and Lichtman, *White Protestant Nation*, 278–80. Maurice Isserman and Michael Kazin, *America Divided: The Civil War of the 1960s* (New York: Oxford University Press, 2000), 203.

31 Nash, *Conservative Intellectual Movement in America*, 64–68, 151–55, 160–71, 235. William F. Buckley, *God and Man at Yale: The Superstitions of Academic Freedom* (Chicago: Regnery, 1951); Kirk, *Conservative Mind;* Willmoore Kendall, *The Conservative Affirmation* (Chicago: Regnery, 1963); Willmoore Kendall, "Bill of Rights and American Freedom," 41–64.

32 Kevin Phillips, *The Emerging Republican Majority* (New Rochelle, N.Y.: Arlington House, 1969); Richard M. Scammon and Ben J. Wattenberg, *The Real Majority* (New York: Coward-McCann, 1970). Mason, *Richard Nixon and the Quest for a New Majority*, 82–86, 142–46; Lichtman, *White Protestant Nation*, 277–80, 288–91. John W. Dean, *The Rehnquist Choice* (New York: Free Press, 2001); Thomas M. Keck, *The Most Activist Supreme Court in History: The Road to Modern Judicial Conservatism* (Chicago: University of Chicago Press, 2004), 113–15; Richard M. Nixon, *RN: The Memoirs of Richard Nixon* (New York: Grosset and Dunlap, 1978), 418–24.

33 On the conservative critique of the new class, see Hartman, *War for the Soul of America*, 50–52; Rodgers, *Age of Fracture*, 83–92; and Lasch, *True and Only Heaven*, 509–22. The critique was applied to the justices in Robert Bork, "The Struggle over the Role of the Court," *National Review*, November 17, 1982, pp. 1137–39; Glazer, "Towards an Imperial Judiciary?"; and Graglia, "Judicial Imperialism." A recent articulation of the New Class critique is found in Fred Siegel, *The Revolt against the Masses: How Liberalism Has Undermined the Middle Class* (New York: Encounter, 2014), 129–30, 146–47.

34 Justin Watson, *The Christian Coalition: Dreams of Restoration, Demands for Recognition* (New York: St. Martin's, 1997), 1–27; Lichtman, *White Protestant Nation*, 1–2. Keck, *Most Activist Supreme Court in History*, 2. On Hand's impact on conservatives, see Rodgers, *Age of Fracture*, 236–37; Hartman, *War for the Soul of America*, 207; and Warren A. Nord, *Religion and American Education: Rethinking a National Dilemma* (Chapel Hill: University of North Carolina Press, 1995), 169–71, 179, 186, 190.

35 Historian Lisa McGirr emphasizes "the dual nature of modern American conservatism: its strange mixture of traditionalism and modernity, a combination that suggests the adaptability, resilience, and, thus perhaps, intractability of the Right in American life." Lisa McGirr, *Suburban Warriors: The Origins of the New American Right* (Princeton: Princeton University Press, 2001), 8. Brown, *Trumping Religion*. Political dissent and staunch Christian morality are intertwined in Rousas John Rushdoony, "The Meaning of Theocracy,"

Chalcedon position paper no. 15 (August 1979), *The Roots of Reconstruction* (Vallecito, Calif.: Ross House, 1991), 63–68; Rousas John Rushdoony, *Christianity and the State* (Vallecito, Calif.: Ross House, 1986); and Francis A. Schaeffer, *A Christian Manifesto* (Wheaton, Ill: Crossway, 1981), 46–47, 78–82.

36 George Lakoff, *Moral Politics: How Liberals and Conservatives Think* (Chicago: University of Chicago Press, 2001), ix–x, 3, 12–18, 33–36; Nord, *Religion and American Education*, 10–14. Conservatives and liberals are distinguished by their differing "moral foundations" in Jonathan Haidt, *Why Good People Are Divided by Politics and Religion* (New York: Pantheon, 2012). They are distinguished by the respective narratives they tell in Drew Westen, *The Political Brain: The Role of Emotion in Deciding the Fate of the Nation* (New York: PublicAffairs, 2007). Self confirms that "what most sharply divided Americans in these years were distinct worldviews." Self, *All in the Family*, 279. The term "orthodox" comes from James Davison Hunter, *Culture Wars: The Struggle to Define America* (New York: BasicBooks, 1991), 31–51.

37 Hunter, *Culture Wars*, 43–48.

38 George Lakoff, *Don't Think of an Elephant! Know Your Values and Frame the Debate* (White River Junction, Vt.: Chelsea Green, 2014), 17; Farber, *Rise and Fall of American Conservatism*, 2–3. Thomas Frank, *What's the Matter with Kansas?: How Conservatives Won the Heart of America* (New York: Books, 2004), 1–10. Frank's analysis is refuted in Hartman, *War for the Soul of America*, 2.

39 Theda Skocpol and Vanessa Williamson, *The Tea Party and the Remaking of Republican Conservatism* (New York: Oxford University Press, 2012), 48–51.

40 Sam Tanenhaus, "Original Sin: Why the GOP Is and Will Continue to Be the Party of White People," *New Republic*, February 10, 2013, www.newrepublic.com/article/112365/why-republicans-are-party-white-people. The "real Americans" trope is voiced in "Joe the Plumber endorses John McCain," October 30, 2008, www.youtube.com/watch?v=rL97vWgSp7U; Josh Lanier, "Hayes Explains Comments at McCain Rally," *(North Carolina) Independent Tribune*, October 21, 2008, www.independenttribune.com/news/hayes-explains-comments-at-mccain-rally/article_e96f5da0-f9c5-5eb6-9de5-51f7c9cbc50c.html; Michele Bachmann interviewed by Chris Matthews, October 17, 2008, www.youtube.com/watch?v=eJIQm_7YAUI&feature=related; "Scarborough: 'Americans Want Their President to Be a Real Man'," March 31, 2008, http://mediamatters.org/research/2008/03/31/scarborough-on-obamas-dainty-bowling-performanc/143050.

1

Massive Resistance

HERETIC

Ishmael Jaffree was perplexed. When his five-year-old son Chioke reported that his kindergarten teacher led him and his classmates in singing grace every day before lunch, Jaffree couldn't believe what he was hearing. The class said grace? Chioke's class prayed together, out loud? This perturbed the stridently agnostic Jaffree. Was this teacher not aware that nowadays, in September 1981, it was illegal for public-school teachers, in their classrooms, even in Mobile, Alabama, to conduct religious activities of any sort? The whole thing made no sense. It was troubling that his son's teacher would even consider indoctrinating her students.[1]

Jaffree felt as though his family's way of life was being threatened. He and his wife Mozelle placed great stock in raising their children as free thinkers, regularly engaging them in philosophical discourse. Five-year-old Chioke, whom he considered unusually sophisticated for his age, showed a special enthusiasm for their discussions. When Jaffree asked the boy one September evening about his day in school, as he often did, the last thing he expected to hear was that Chioke's teacher, Miss Boyd, had been directing the students to thank God for their food. Yet that was exactly what Chioke now told him. Before going on to lunch, Chioke and his classmates would stand in line behind the teacher and bow their heads. The teacher would then invite the class to join her in singing, "God is great, God is good, let us thank Him for our food," as she had done daily since the beginning of the school year.[2]

The kindergarten teacher threatening Jaffree's parental rights could not have seen the world more differently from him. Mobile native Charlene

Boyd never questioned the propriety of leading her students in grace. She never imagined that anyone would ever so object. Her own days as a student in Mobile public schools included prayer and devotional reading, and she was now continuing that tradition by praising God each day before lunch. Boyd believed that her students cherished the routine every bit as much as she did. When they asked her if they could openly thank God for their food, she turned the singing of grace into a daily practice. Most of the children would enthusiastically sing along with the "'God is good' jingle" objected to by Jaffree. And most would continue singing it voluntarily the following spring, after Boyd announced that they could remain silent if they chose. For the remainder of the 1981–1982 school year, Chioke's class, with Boyd in the lead, would continue to offer thanks to God every day before lunch.[3]

Perhaps Jaffree should have expected to encounter teachers such as Boyd in the Mobile public schools, given the city's profoundly religious character. Still, he claimed that the prayer routine shocked him. Until that moment, Jaffree maintained, he had remained "naïve" regarding prayer's continued presence in the schools. He denied any eagerness to challenge such practices, claiming that he became concerned only when Chioke informed him of the daily grace he and his classmates recited. Jaffree did recall that his own public-school experience, in Cleveland, Ohio, during the 1950s, was filled with Bible reading, religious dramatic performances, and pictures of Jesus on classroom walls. But Jaffree assumed that such practices everywhere had long since ceased. He was certain that, following the 1962 and 1963 Supreme Court decisions banning prayer and Bible reading in public schools, all religious content had been expunged from the Cleveland public schools. And he expressed great surprise that the Alabama public schools had not done likewise.[4]

When Chioke reported about the lunchtime recitation of grace, an incredulous Jaffree told his son to remind the teacher that organized prayer in the classroom violated the law. Chioke did just that, letting Boyd know that he would not be able to participate in the singing. Her reaction, he later recalled, "wasn't anything too pleasant." Chioke's protest shook and confused Boyd, who held that it was the first and only such objection she had ever encountered as a schoolteacher. Boyd had no intention of discontinuing the exercise. Wanting to spare herself further aggravation, she announced to the children that anyone who wished to remain silent could do so. But she also made clear that the rest were free to participate, and that throughout the singing of grace the others must not misbehave.[5]

Boyd could not understand why Chioke would object to saying grace. She didn't know whether praying in the classroom was in fact against the law, but she assumed that she could not be doing anything too terribly wrong, since she herself had grown up with classroom prayer. The particular grace in which she led her students was one that she had learned as a schoolgirl. For Boyd, teaching children to thank God for their food was more than a tradition – it was an obligation. Children needed to thank God, she insisted, "because ... that's who I thank." Boyd had been raised a Southern Baptist, belonged to a Southern Baptist church in Mobile, and knew nothing about any religion other than her own. She had no frame of reference in which to place Chioke's stunning request, which, to her ears, sounded utterly alien and warranted little accommodation.[6]

Jaffree's anger increased after Chioke informed him that Boyd had spurned his request to stop. "Apparently, it had no effect," Jaffree concluded. He learned from his son that Boyd continued right on "having the class line up and bow their heads and say this grace." Once again, Jaffree instructed Chioke to remind his teacher that it was against the law to lead her class in prayer; once again, she disregarded his request, instructing the boy to remain in line quietly while his classmates sang their thanks to God. In turn, Jaffree grew more and more frustrated. Boyd, it seemed, was determined to lead "her children" in daily prayer.[7]

Jaffree had not been raised an agnostic. Like Charlene Boyd and so many of her colleagues in the Mobile County school system, he grew up in an environment where Christian symbols and messages were ubiquitous. Jaffree was born Frederick Hobbs, to an unwed mother, in Cleveland, Ohio, in 1944. His mother was a fervent Christian who sought to imbue piety in her only son. All around him, friends, family, teachers, and neighbors reinforced his mother's message that life was to be lived in service to Christ. Hobbs and his mother had little money but were awash in devotion.[8]

Rather than sharing with her son a Christian devotion of humility and love, Hobbs's mother indoctrinated her son with a harsh Christianity that condemned sinners. Although she lied and stole, she considered herself "a Baptist missionary" and "went out and preached ... in churches and people's homes," thereby planting in his mind the connection between faith, dishonesty, and manipulation. She was not a patient woman, he recalled, not generous of spirit. Self-righteous, she lacked tolerance for beliefs that diverged from her own. In her eyes, evangelical Christianity alone bespoke the will of God. Years later, Charlene Boyd's religious fervor struck old, unpleasant chords inside Jaffree.[9]

Growing up, Hobbs felt ambivalent. He aspired to fulfill his mother's Christian ideals, even as he rebelled against his community's expectation of clean, Christian living. Those ideals were engrained deeply inside his head by a mother and schoolteachers who presented their worldview as absolute truth that he dared not examine too closely. "When I would attempt to question it in my mind," he recalled, "I would be fearful, fearful that I would meet damnation if I allow[ed] myself the thought processes of believing that a deity does not exist." At the same time, Hobbs acted out. He stopped attending school and got in trouble with the law. He cultivated a "nonconformist" persona and adopted "an independent pattern of behavior." Obedience and defiance melded into a strident yet confused mentality.[10]

Upon graduating high school and attending college, Hobbs found himself confronted with alien ideas that jolted him from the religious certitude imbred by his mother. He learned to doubt. He became a critic of not only Christian dogma but also racial injustice. Challenging his old religious framework became bound up with challenging the white supremacy that, he believed, he had internalized. As he took courses in comparative religion and black consciousness, his "philosophy then became that Jesus Christ was black." He became an Afrocentric Christian and sought to convert other black students to his view.[11]

As Hobbs's conception of blackness continued to evolve, so too did his appreciation for the moral and intellectual autonomy of the individual. More and more, he aspired to direct his own life. He never became a member of any black radical organizations, despite his sympathies. Following the directions of another person was anathema to Hobbs. He refused "to have somebody tell me what I should do, what I should believe, how I should think." The domination of white people over black people, as he saw it, reflected the inequalities plaguing human relations more generally, the arbitrary authority of some people over others. Inequalities between groups of people should in no way be accepted as "natural." Social order now seemed to him nothing other than domination by the powerful over the powerless.[12]

His radical questioning of social relations led Hobbs to an ever deepening skepticism toward all human belief systems. He could no longer tolerate viewpoints held mindlessly, without scrutiny. Knowledge, freedom, and self-empowerment became paramount to him. He now determined that adherence to religious worldviews emerged sheerly out of social conditioning. To the skeptical Hobbs, belief in God appeared irrational, absurd. Dedicated to controlling his own life, he could no longer fathom why human beings would choose to have faith in God, especially a God who "maintained control" over the universe and "expect[ed] blind obedience to a will as articulated in some book." Lacking proof of a supreme being, he now declared himself an agnostic.[13]

As he entered the Cleveland-Marshall College of Law at age twenty-eight, Hobbs legally changed his name, in an attempt further to own himself and his destiny. Like many other black men and women of his generation drawn to their African roots, he yearned to assert an authentic self untainted by white treachery. Just as in his departure from Christianity, Hobbs sought to deprogram his mind and determine his own life path. He took the last name Jaffree, the name of a college professor whom he had held in high regard; for a first name, he adopted "Ishmael" for its biblical implication of "outcast." In changing his name to reject the history of black enslavement in the United States, Hobbs was influenced by Malcolm X, whose chosen surname "symbolized the true African family name that [the Black American] could never know." At once, Jaffree's new name "was a matter of personal pride" and a reflection of his bitterness toward a social environment that made no room for his authentic, deepest self.[14]

Two years later, Jaffree fell in love with Mozelle Horst. The couple were united not only by race but also by a shared religious marginality. Horst belonged to the Behá'í faith and was sensitive to the persecution that the Behá'ís endured in their homeland Iran, and to their virtual invisibility in the United States. Upon graduating law school and marrying Horst the following year, Jaffree committed himself to serving victims of oppression. He determined that the deep South was becoming a hub of black legal activism; soon, he learned that in Mobile, down on the Gulf Coast, a significant voting rights case was being fought with vigorous participation from the local black legal community. A year later, the couple moved south to Mobile.[15]

The Jaffrees soon started a family. They resolved to raise their children free of religious and ideological indoctrination. Convinced that children absorb their parents' belief systems – whether religious, agnostic, or atheistic – the Jaffrees sought to cultivate ideological neutrality in their home, to support their children's speculation into all matters that crossed their minds, to inspire them "to examine, to explore, to ponder, to think about, to be exposed to different philosophies, all types of ideologies." As their children developed intellectually, the Jaffrees exposed them "to a multiplicity of worldviews and then ultimately let them choose for themselves" how and what to believe.[16]

Jaffree – father, lawyer, Mobile transplant – had chiseled for himself a pointed ideology whose primary element was dissent. He asserted the inalienable right to make life choices untainted by custom. He placed a premium on following logical trains of thought, regardless of where they pointed. If his logic led him to take an unpopular stance, then all the better. Jaffree's ideology was political. He believed that the law should protect minorities; the more unpopular the minority, the more crucial its protection. His worldview prioritized religious agnosticism, intellectual skepticism, African American dignity, and civil rights for the politically powerless. And he hoped, in his adopted home state, to find others who shared his political values.

After learning that teachers were leading prayer activities in Mobile public schools, Jaffree claimed to be shocked. Yet he could hardly have expected his new neighbors – African Americans included – to share his particular sociopolitical commitments. He surely recognized the profound role played by Christianity in the southern black community. The Christian church had famously been central to the black struggle, including the civil rights movement. Mobilians, black and white, could hardly have been expected to prize the skeptical, debunking mentality that Jaffree valued so dearly. This may actually have pleased him. His palpable antireligious animus, burning inside him at least since college, drove him to contest the rituals and prejudices of his adopted hometown. In all likelihood, he anticipated and welcomed Boyd's unreceptiveness. Jaffree was a man spoiling for a fight, eager to seethe in righteous indignation. In that respect, he had chosen an optimal place to live, one where he would soon encounter as great a lack of sympathy and understanding as any location could possibly have yielded.[17]

TEACHING AND PRAYING

As Boyd continued to lead her children in grace, Jaffree became angrier and angrier. At first, he resisted confronting her, reluctant to make trouble for a fellow African American. Yet he became increasingly frustrated that Boyd, a black woman, would be oblivious to what he considered the larger struggle on behalf of the rights of all minorities. Jaffree's mounting anger eventually surpassed his reluctance, and, in December, he visited his son's teacher at school. He went up to her classroom and asked her to come to the door, which she did. Thus began a protracted struggle between Jaffree and the Mobile public schools.[18]

Boyd experienced Jaffree, standing at her door, as threatening and mean-spirited. In the conversation that ensued between them, Boyd denied forcing any of the children to sing grace. Jaffree, she later recalled, told her "that it doesn't matter whether it is voluntary or not," and that "there were lawsuits all over the country" trying to prohibit teachers from doing what she was doing. She recalled Jaffree's warning that she "could go to jail for what [she] was doing." Jaffree disavowed ever saying "that she could go to jail." Admittedly, he did inform her that, in leading her class in prayer, she was violating the U.S. Constitution.[19]

Ignoring Jaffree's warning about the constitutional issue, Boyd instead complained that Chioke had been "telling some of his fellow classmates that Santa Claus was a fantasy." This riled Boyd. It seemed to Jaffree that she considered traditional Christmas narratives, like religious narratives generally, as things to be preserved and not debunked. Jaffree could not have disagreed more. Chioke had already learned from his father that Santa Claus did not exist, and that their Christmas presents came from Mozelle and him, not from some "figure that flies in the air on a sleigh and comes down the chimney." Jaffree had little sympathy for Boyd's remonstration. "I told her that, while she may desire to allow children to continue to believe in myths, I didn't desire that." As far as he was concerned, Chioke "could tell the children anything he wanted to tell them," just "as long as Chioke was not disrupting the class."[20]

Chioke was indeed disrupting the class, Boyd maintained. She would recall that the boy initially remained quiet during grace but, around February, began "punching children and hitting [his classmates] and talking real loud." Boyd increasingly chafed at the boy's obstructive behavior. Finding him loud and opinionated, she grew more and more irritated. The young boy, it seemed, was making his father's cause his own.[21]

When the daily grace continued, Jaffree asked Boyd for another meeting. He threatened to contact her principal, Betty Lee. He warned that, if he were not accommodated, then he would "initiate a civil lawsuit via the A.C.L.U. serving a restraining order enjoining the above referenced activity naming [Boyd] as well as others as party defendants."[22] It would be Boyd who sought out Lee's advice. Soon after, Lee was assured by the deputy superintendent of schools that the activity was legal as long as it was voluntary, and so Lee advised Boyd to continue. Boyd never responded to Jaffree. She had no wish to meet with him, nor was she inclined to honor his request that she stop saying grace, a request that she found nonsensical and undeserving of compliance. And because Lee did not direct her to adjust her practice, Boyd felt no obligation to do so. She took instructions from the school principal, not from Jaffree.[23]

When Lee received a phone call from Jaffree, she suggested they excuse Chioke from class during grace. Jaffree "advised her" against that solution, insisting that it "would be embarrassing for Chioke to be leaving the class." It seemed outrageous to Chioke's parents that the burden of remaining free from indoctrination would be placed on the shoulders of a kindergartener. "I don't think that giving students a chance to opt out of participating in prayers in school is helpful," Mozelle maintained, "because the child who opts out is still pointing to himself and saying 'look at me I'm different.' He has to leave the classroom." Ishmael agreed. He contended that, when teachers lead their classes in prayer, students from nonreligious families are placed at a severe disadvantage. "Those children are forced to make a decision," he asserted, "either to sit there and participate, perhaps even against their will or against their parents' will, or leave the class and become visible." Asking a young child to make that decision was unfair, especially given children's tendencies to be cruel toward one another. And, "for students in a class to know that a child does not believe in prayer or does not want to participate, that child will be ostracized." The burden of ensuring religious neutrality in the classroom ought to rest with the school, the Jaffrees believed, not with its students.[24]

Several months after prayer in the classroom became a frequent family topic, Aakki, the oldest Jaffree child, told his parents that his class, too, said grace every day prior to eating lunch. According to Aakki's teacher, Julia Green, the boy had always participated enthusiastically in the activity. Singing grace and engaging in religious exercises had helped to make Aakki more communicative and comfortable, easing some of the difficulties associated with his emotional and motor-skills disabilities. Indeed, Jaffree admitted that, until learning about the religious activities in Green's classroom, he had concluded that she "had done a good job with Aakki with respect to helping him come out of his shell."[25]

But Jaffree didn't see any connection between Green's ability to ease Aakki's developmental struggles and the religious activities taking place in her classroom. Yes, Green had performed well as a teacher. In Jaffree's eyes, though, preaching was a separate job. Public institutions were not meant to accommodate ministry and worship. If such actions helped children with their problems, then parents perhaps ought to take their children to church. Jaffree had never, until then, asked Green whether she led prayer activities because, in his account, he didn't believe that they were widespread in Mobile schools. Once disabused of his supposed ignorance, Jaffree determined that exposure to religious exercises had caused Aakki to "suffer emotional harm." Already fragile, the boy was forced to make choices he was incapable of making. Jaffree described the boy as "torn between a parent that told him that" religious activities "should not go on [in school] and that he does not have to participate and he should not be even subtly forced to participate," and "a teacher who continued to engage in these activities." However, neither Aakki nor his father ever claimed that Aakki didn't want to pray in class. Nor did Green ever ask Aakki how he felt about the matter. Although both teacher and father felt sure about their own strategies for treating the boy, neither ever asked Aakki what he himself wanted.[26]

More than Aakki's seeming contentment with praying caused Green not to consult the boy. The twelfth-year teacher did not seriously consider that Aakki – or any other child – might feel troubled by prayer. Like her colleague Boyd, Green had been born and bred in an environment in which prayer was a ubiquitous, essential part of daily life. She was raised in Mobile, attended county public schools, and, by first grade, had learned the grace that she would continue to recite, as a student and then as a teacher. Christianity was the backdrop against which Green lived her entire life. Her religious beliefs required her to say grace before eating. Green "pray[ed] without ceasing." Although she had occasionally accommodated non-Christian students by excusing them from class or simply letting them remain silent during grace, Green was certain that every student she had ever taught evinced an inherent need to pray.[27]

When Green led grace, she was not proselytizing, she insisted, but exercising her religious freedom. That she served as an agent of the state apparently did not figure in her calculation. Green took for granted that "children say grace all the time," and that it was her job "to instill" in them the need to be "thankful to God ... for giving them their daily bread." She needed to lead her students in prayer, as prayer pleased God. Not to do so was virtually impossible. She had no doubt whatsoever that the classroom was "a proper place" in which for children to pray, since praying is a "part of their everyday life." Never did she imagine that Aakki or any other student might be offended by such a basic, essential part of the school day. Nor did she wish to indulge any such reluctance that might actually surface.[28]

Ella (Pixie) Alexander, who taught Jaffree's daughter Makeba, had no more interest than Green or Boyd in accommodating dissenters from the

Christianity of her understanding. Throughout her nearly thirteen years as a public-school teacher, Alexander had aimed to fill her students with the same deference to God that filled her own life. She held strong Christian values, and she felt obligated to instruct children in accord with her Christianity. Throughout her time teaching in Mobile, Alexander had led her students daily in reciting grace and the Lord's Prayer, carefully "teaching the children to learn to pray, to thank God for their food." While denying that she forced students to pray, she conceded that she never informed students of their right to abstain. Nor did she notify parents that her curriculum included religious content. Such caution seemed unnecessary to Alexander, who claimed not to have considered that students or parents might be offended by prayer. Although she admitted lacking familiarity with religions other than Christianity, she insisted that classroom prayer constituted neither proselytization nor a governmental establishment of religion. Quite simply, her faith demanded that, wherever she was, she worship God freely and help others to do the same.[29]

Only toward the end of the school year did Jaffree learn of Makeba's exposure to the recitation of grace. By that time, he found himself in a conflict that, all at once, infuriated him and whetted his appetite for battle against the forces of religious orthodoxy. Predictably, Alexander, like Boyd and Green, could not understand or feel sympathy for his plea on behalf of his right to raise his children free from religious indoctrination by the state. None of these teachers could imagine that, in singing God's praises, she might possibly disserve any child's interests. Christianity grounded and oriented the teachers' everyday lives. They and their superiors viewed classroom prayer, Bible reading, and other religious activities as necessary dimensions of education, not as curricular options. Cultivating honorable, Christian character in students was, for them, a paramount function of public schooling.[30]

Like those teachers, Jaffree knew that children were stamped indelibly by their education, which made it a realm of danger as well as fortuity. For him, the real danger facing impressionable children came from Christian brainwashing. The power wielded by proselytizing Christian schoolteachers anguished him, even as it sanctioned his rage. A man of fervent principle, Jaffree felt justified in contesting these teachers' apparent disregard for the habits of free thinking that he and his wife were trying to instill in their children. He would fight for his principle. If that troubled the devout Christian schoolteachers, then he was ready – eager, even – to challenge their tidy, faith-driven routine. Publicly, he presented himself as protecting his and his family's constitutional rights. As he put it, he "simply wanted [his] children to be free from the coercive effects of teacher-initiated religious activities in the public schools."[31]

NO RESPONSE

Convinced that the schools wouldn't readily comply with his requests, Jaffree sought out legal assistance in early May 1982. The Alabama Civil Liberties Union (ACLU) lacked the resources to get involved. Local civil-rights attorneys assured him that the law was on his side, but almost none would engage a cause so likely to infuriate local blacks as well as whites. Frustrated but undeterred, Jaffree turned to Ronnie Williams, an African American and former colleague at a local firm dedicated to serving poor clients. Williams agreed that "the law was so clear" that any legal action "would be an open-and-shut thing, no big deal." To be sure, Williams had no desire to incur public wrath. Friends and associates warned him not to get involved, lest he turn himself into a local pariah. In the end, though, the constitutional soundness of Jaffree's argument – its concurrence with case law – prompted Williams to offer his services to his former coworker.[32]

On May 10, Jaffree wrote to Abraham Lincoln Hammons, superintendent of county schools. Jaffree's letter complained that religious exercises in the classroom necessarily coerced dissenting students. "Acting *in locus parenti*," the teacher became a "coercive presence," with her authority bolstered by the pressure of "group dynamics at play." Amid those forces, "there can be no such creature as 'voluntary prayer' or the voluntary observance of or recognition of a deity." Jaffree spelled out what, for him, was obvious. "The urge to conform to expected behavior is overwhelming. It would be asking too much of any child (especially one of tender years) to overcome or subdue such pressure." Hence, he told the superintendent, "the voluntariness of the program does not save it from the constitutional defect."[33]

Jaffree laid out his argument in constitutional terms. The Mobile public schools, he told the superintendent, had run roughshod over both religion clauses of the First Amendment – the schools had at once violated his free exercise of religion and established a religion that they forced on his children and himself. "An unbroken line of cases decided by the U.S. Supreme Court" had demonstrated the unconstitutionality of organized religious activities in public schools, even if those activities might appear voluntary. His rights abridged, Jaffree stood ready to pursue his complaint. "I am looking forward to hearing from you soon concerning this matter," he told Hammons, assuring him he was "hopeful that this issue can be resolved informally." However, he continued, "I am prepared to provide my children with the full panoply of rights granted to them by the United States Constitution."[34]

The following the day, May 11, the letter was received by the school system and made its way to the principal of Aakki's school, who immediately showed it to Green, Aakki's teacher. Only at that moment did Green fathom the degree of Jaffree's unhappiness. Jaffree's complaint shocked and confused her. Although she was willing to let the children say grace quietly to themselves, she seriously doubted whether silently thanking God for their food could work as effectively as singing thanks aloud. The prospect of silencing the children was nearly too much to bear, and Green could not bring herself to show up for school that Thursday or Friday. Green finally decided to comply with the wishes of the disgruntled parent, at least for the time being. When she returned on Monday, she informed her students that they would no longer be singing grace out loud together. As she later recalled, "the children questioned me, 'Mrs. Green, why not, why not?'" Green instructed them to say grace quietly to themselves, and, for the remainder of the school year, the children did just that. The children's reaction confirmed Green's belief that thanking God for food was appropriate and natural for the children – even for Jaffree's son. "I watched to see what would happen. All the children at the table, including Aakki, they bowed their heads and, to themselves, said their little prayer." Green suspected that Aakki had never objected to saying grace. She blamed Jaffree for starting trouble and, for some strange reason, trying to deprive her students – including his own son – of the grace that so thoroughly contented and nourished them.[35]

Several days later, Jaffree was still waiting for Hammons's response. None was immediately forthcoming. He repeatedly called the superintendent's secretary, who told him she had no information to pass on. Frustrated, he telephoned Lee, principle of the school where Boyd taught kindergarten. After debating Jaffree over the rights and wrongs of classroom prayer, Lee informed him that she had been advised that the classroom prayer was unobjectionable as long as it was voluntary. Rebuffed, Jaffree hung the phone and continued his vigil for a letter from Hammons. The letter didn't come. Nor would Hammons return his calls. On about May 19, the secretary told him that a response was in the mail but that she knew nothing more. Still, he waited.[36]

Local resistance to his civil-libertarian politics, it seemed, ran deeper than he had anticipated. Gradually, he was recognizing how stupefied and offended these Mobilians were at his attempt to silence religious devotion inside their classrooms. Jaffree considered it generous and decent of him to pursue resolution through private conversation rather than litigation, but his children's teachers, principals, and school superintendent appeared not to see it that way. To the contrary, they seemed to see in him a parent bent on imposing his strange, perplexing inclinations on an entire town.[37]

An exasperated Jaffree, grabbing at straws, called Emma Reed, the principal of Makeba's school. Reed told him she was busy. She directed him back to Hammons. She hung up. Soon afterward, on May 24, Reed showed Alexander the letter but issued no directive. Alexander then continued the activities for the remainder of the school year. The whole matter didn't terribly concern her principal. "I did not see this as a problem, because [the letter] was not addressed to me," Reed explained. Nor did either she or Alexander believe that simple classroom devotionals could really be much cause for alarm, notwithstanding Jaffree's complaint. Alexander knew nothing of the illegality of school prayer. Reed knew only that children had always prayed in Mobile schools.[38]

Jaffree was riled that none of these teachers or principals cared a whit for his interests as a non-Christian, that all portrayed the influence of Christianity in the classroom as natural, unobjectionable, inevitable. None appeared the least bit concerned. Alexander vigorously denied proselytizing or "encourag[ing] the establishment of a religion." She was simply acting in accord with her Christian values, and so she could not, in good conscience, teach schoolchildren in any manner other than the one that so offended Jaffree. Green believed her religious freedom to be threatened by Jaffree's demand. By leading her class in grace, she was honoring her deepest convictions, not proselytizing. It was she, and not Jaffree, who was exercising religious freedom. Jaffree's protest shocked Boyd, who remained convinced that she had not violated anyone's interests. She couldn't imagine that Jaffree had a legitimate basis for complaint, and, despite his letters and his visit to her class, she expected him eventually to cease his nastiness. Nor, according to Boyd, could most of her colleagues at E. R. Dixon fathom why someone would complain about lunchtime grace. Green found that Jaffree's actions outraged the parents of her students. "I had several parents ask me why the children didn't do it anymore. I explained to them what happened, and they said, 'My God, what's wrong with that man?'"[39]

More and more aware of the full measure of his opponents' intransigence, Jaffree prepared to file a lawsuit. The ACLU, which reviewed his letter to Hammons, advised him to take court action. Of course, Jaffree knew that bringing suit would not make life easy for him. The hostility that he might incur made him a bit nervous. "I realize this is a very conservative area and people have grown up with the Bible from Day One, and that I would not be the best-liked person in the city by bringing this lawsuit." Still, Jaffree believed passionately in his cause. He knew that case law was on his side, and he hoped for a quick victory. The colleagues he consulted confirmed his optimism. As each passing day brought no response from Hammons or the Mobile County school board, Jaffree became more consumed with the urge to act. He implored Williams: "I sent my letters; they ignored my letters. I made my requests; they ignored those. Maybe if we file something, that will get their attention that I'm serious."[40]

On May 21, having heard and received nothing from Hammons, Jaffree again called the superintendent's secretary. This time, she read him Hammons's response. According to Jaffree, the letter effectively said nothing. Not only had Hammons indefinitely delayed responding; now that he had responded, his statement was, in Jaffree's words, an egregiously "ambivalent ... noncommittal response." It appeared that the superintendent "didn't consider [Jaffree's complaint] important enough to even do anything about it." At "wit's end," Jaffree instructed Williams to draw up a legal complaint.[41]

ALTERNATIVE MEASURES

On May 28, 1982, Jaffree filed suit in U.S. District Court for the Southern District of Alabama. His complaint sought to enjoin the three teachers, their principals, and the Mobile school board from permitting any teacher-led religious exercises. Because the primary purpose behind any teacher-led religious activities was nonsecular in nature, the suit alleged, such activities violated the Establishment Clause of the First Amendment, which prohibited Congress from establishing any religion. The First Amendment did not specifically refer to the governments of the individual states, but Jaffree's complaint held what several suits since the 1940s had claimed, that the Fourteenth Amendment's requirement that states guarantee citizens' equal protection under the law implied that those same states were bound as well by the Bill of Rights, the first ten amendments to the Constitution. That is, the First Amendment was extended to state governments through the Fourteenth Amendment. The complaint charged that, "by engaging in activities designed to foster a belief in religion," the three teachers and their superiors had "willfully, maliciously and wantonly disregarded Plaintiffs' constitutional rights" and caused them "to suffer great mental and emotional distress."[42]

Jaffree claimed to be defending two vulnerable and all-important goods – his children's ability to think for themselves and the Constitution's prohibition against religious establishment. He saw state-sponsored, teacher-organized prayer activities as deleterious toward both ends. "I want to try to ensure that my children have an opportunity to be free thinkers and not be conditioned to the Christian faith or to any faith at a young age," he insisted. Because children as young as his could not "understand the difference between a belief and a fact," the two would likely meld together in their impressionable minds. Jaffree longed, retroactively, to save his own impressionable mind from years of brainwashing by his evangelical mother. He refused to suffer old indignities anew through his children's experiences at school.[43]

To Jaffree, the Constitution's separation of church and state safeguarded children's right to learn to think clearly and freely, against encroachment by the state and the benighted popular majority. He wanted to ensure that public-school teachers – officers of the state – not trample over the right of politically vulnerable groups by forcing them either to embrace or repudiate religion. "Enacted in the Constitution," he pointed out, "are laws to protect minorities, to protect the individuals." As an agnostic, he saw himself and his children as members of a minority group. Their right not to be molded by a state-established religion was the sort of right that the Constitution was meant to protect. This was exactly the point of the Establishment Clause. He and his children deserved to be spared from the tyranny of majority-imposed, state-sanctioned religion. He hoped that his suit would protect their right to think freely as well as help "preserv[e] the integrity of the Constitution."[44]

While keeping her distance from her husband's efforts, Mozelle Jaffree quietly supported them. Her husband, she believed, was demonstrating to their children that problems ought to be solved not through authoritarian demand and mindless obedience but through civil procedures that preserved the right to dissent. She sought to impress upon them the paramount importance of stating one's beliefs and trusting that the rule of law would offer protection. Filing a lawsuit was not an act of antagonism but an appeal to rational adjudication. She explained to them that, "because we couldn't arrive at a solution the way we tried, by talking to the people involved, that we would go to court for it, and whatever happened, we would abide by the ruling of the court." As a Behá'í, she was especially committed to civil laws protecting the religious rights of minorities. Although she did not play an active role in the lawsuit, she shared her husband's conviction that defending free thought and defending the Constitution went hand-in-hand.[45]

Jaffree seemed to assume that the line between his needs and his children's was faint at best. His complaint suggested that, by violating his constitutional rights, the schools had trampled over his children's rights as well. In fact, it remained unclear how exactly his children felt about the matter. His suit charged that the classroom prayers had anguished him and them alike – that, like their father, they, too, had been aggrieved. Yet, although the suit alleged that the three children had "on numerous occasions ... complained" about the prayers, only Chioke had expressed any objection, either to his teacher or his father. Indeed, the suit claimed that the religious exercises clashed not with the children's stated beliefs but with their *possible* beliefs, along with their father's insistence "that prayer in school is unlawful." Given the intense peer pressure in the classroom environment, the complaint reasoned, they had been forced either to "acquiesce in something in which they *may* not believe" or else endure humiliation at the hands of their classmates. Jaffree thus assumed that, because he had been aggrieved, his children had also been aggrieved – even though neither Makeba nor Aakki had expressed such grievances to their father or their teachers.[46]

It was Jaffree's moral convictions, more than his children's, that had been violated. When an interviewer suggested that his children may have suffered less if he had simply instructed them to remain quiet in class during grace, passed on his beliefs to them at home, and avoided dragging them into a lawsuit, Jaffree countered that the blatant violation of his own constitutional rights demanded redress. He was determined to honor his convictions and "endure this ... hardship." The interviewer pressed the matter. "It's one thing for you to go through it based on the principle.

It's another thing for your children to go through it based on your principles." For Jaffree, his own interests were his children's interests; the risk he felt compelled to take necessarily had to be shared by his family. "I really have no choice," he contended. "If you're going to challenge a practice, then ... you recognize the risks that it causes your family to suffer. ... Fortunately, I talked to my children, and I think I made them feel they're doing something very important." The Jaffree children were thus enlisted in their father's battle against what he denounced as Christian mind control – a battle against the brainwashing that he had suffered in his own past.[47]

Jaffree's most assertive lawyerly instincts now took over. On June 4, he and Ronnie Williams amended their complaint to a class-action suit on behalf of all present and future students exposed to religious activities in Mobile public schools. Not only would Jaffree protect his children; He would also fight to stop the Mobile schools from brainwashing all vulnerable students. Knowing that his children had already transferred schools within the county system and might do so again, Jaffree wanted to guarantee that they would encounter no further devotional exercises anywhere in Mobile. Further, he asserted, "the claims of the Plaintiffs are typical of the claims of the Class." He would see to it that the rights of Mobile schoolchildren in general suffered no violation similar to that being endured by his children. On June 30, Jaffree and Williams issued a second amended complaint, which named as defendants Alabama governor Forrest H. (Fob) James Jr., the state's attorney general, and the Alabama Board of Education. The plaintiffs sought to enjoin these new defendants "and anyone acting in concert with them from implementing and enforcing certain state laws which provide for prayer in schools in violation of the Constitution of the United States of America." Family in tow, Jaffree prepared to take on the state of Alabama.[48]

STATE OF DENIAL

With this last change to his lawsuit, Jaffree was reacting to a bill, currently before the state legislature, that would institute spoken prayer in Alabama public schools. Governor James had learned of Jaffree's legal action against the teachers and principals through Mobile's two major daily newspapers, the *Press* and the *Register*, which had run stories about the lawsuit in early June. James recognized in the case an opportunity to encode school prayer into law, a popular position throughout the state. He decided to launch an "extraordinary" session in the Alabama Senate and House, an extended period of debate held while the legislature was normally at recess. The governor called on lawmakers to pass a bill that he had championed earlier in the year, one that permitted teachers to lead "willing students" in a specific prayer included as part of the legislation. Addressing the legislature, he gave an account of Jaffree's complaint and threw "the full authority of [the governor's] office ... behind those three brave teachers in Mobile." Once lawmakers turned his bill into law, Jaffree might challenge it, he hoped, and thereby provide Alabama the chance to defend school prayer in court.[49]

The governor was every bit as ideologically driven as Jaffree and just as eager to do political battle over school prayer. James came to office as part of the New Right of the late 1970s and early 1980s, a movement that defined itself in great part through its moral conservatism.[50] Ronald Reagan's election as president in 1980 was accompanied by the first Republican takeover of the Senate in nearly thirty years. Republicans and conservative Democrats attempted to roll back years of liberal government by aggressively seeking to outlaw abortion, legalize school prayer, abolish busing meant to achieve racial desegregation, and stiffen procedures and penalties against convicted criminals. In the battle against liberalism, some on the right looked to strip the Supreme Court of its power to review legislation related to many of those issues. Conservatives also advocated for states' rights, the doctrine historically evoked to defend white supremacy. The effort to enhance the power of the states vis-à-vis the federal government, and to limit the power of the Supreme Court, was more than a battle against liberal policies. It was a battle against the secularism, permissiveness, and egalitarianism associated with the Sixties.[51]

Like many in the New Right, James believed that public schools needed to incorporate religious and patriotic content. He played a key role in removing, from Alabama classrooms, four social studies textbooks that purportedly used vulgar language and showed sympathy toward communism. He championed a bill that would have guaranteed equal treatment to creationism and evolution in textbooks and in classroom discussion. Another measure supported by James would have required all textbooks used in Alabama schools to speak respectfully of religion and the free-market system, teach children to respect authority figures and the "work-ethic," and avoid "promot[ing] sadistic or degrading behavior." Most of these measures failed to win legislative approval. One that did increased the number of state textbook-committee members from fourteen to twenty-three, with the additional nine members to be selected by the governor. When James made his selections, he chose only laypersons, whom he hoped would counter the influence of the professional educators on the committee – liberals all, supposedly.[52]

James's moral agenda had been strongly informed by the crusading urges of his wife, Bobbie James. Although the governor's wife considered her life's priorities to be a good wife and mother, she doggedly pursued political activism toward conservative Christian goals. Having long been "interested in seeing prayer put back in public schools," as she put it, Bobbie James had run unsuccessfully in 1970 as a Republican candidate for the Opelika, Alabama, school board. She opposed the Equal Rights Amendment; while admitting that women did experience discrimination, she diagnosed this as "a spiritual problem" not repairable through legislation. In 1980, at her urging, the governor prohibited members of his administration from participating in the White House Conference on Families, which, she charged, was promoting liberal values repugnant to Christianity. So, too, were schoolteachers who advanced the theory of evolution while ignoring "scientific creationism." Lobbying hard for a law mandating equal treatment in the classroom for both theories, Bobbie James insisted that God didn't want students "brainwashed by liberal, pseudo-intellectual, atheistic educators, who know neither the God they speak of, nor have the fear of God that is the beginning of wisdom." Reagan's election as president prompted her to proclaim, "It was Jesus that gave us this victory. ... God in his mercy heard the prayers of Christians all over this country." During debate over Alabama's textbook bill, the first lady crowed "that the time has come for God-fearing people to speak up" in politics. It was unacceptable, she declared, for Alabama teachers to continue using books that caused children to "question our patriotism, our love of country, to say nothing for an attitude which promotes promiscuity."[53]

In the summer of 1982, the governor dug in his heels. He won passage of several bills that he considered his way of "getting tough," making government do the business of the people. One bill criminalized the illegal possession of food stamps. James convinced the legislature to abolish the insanity defense in criminal cases, arguing that "criminals had abused the insanity defense" and "used it to stop justice." Lawmakers, at his urging, passed laws criminalizing prostitution; creating stiffer penalties for child pornography; allowing defendants testifying in their own behalf to be charged with perjury; denying parole and work release to class-A felons; and requiring that minors charged with murder, rape, sodomy, robbery, kidnapping, or drug trafficking be charged as adults. "Without any question," the governor beamed, "soft spots in the Criminal Code have been eliminated."[54]

The crowning achievement in James's crusade to toughen Alabama's moral character lay in signing a new school prayer law. No issue was more important to James – or his wife – than securing the place of religion in the public schools. All along, Bobbie James had remained confident that prayer would eventually be returned to the schools. Her dream moved one step closer to reality in April 1981, when the governor won legislation meant to "restore sanity to public policy" by passing a bill allowing silent prayer in public-school classrooms. The bill's sponsor, Senator Donald Holmes, declared that "by passage of this bill . . . the children in this state will have the opportunity of sharing in the spiritual heritage of this state and this country." Eight days later, the governor signed the bill into law, telling the press corps, "I wish Bobbie could be here."[55]

Elsewhere in the United States, as in Alabama, opponents of church-state separation were attempting to return "voluntary" prayer to the public schools. In fall 1979, Massachusetts legislators passed a school prayer law tailored to pass constitutional muster by specifying that prayers had to be student led. The Massachusetts Supreme Court determined that the safeguard did not spare the law from constitutional defect. Oklahoma similarly sanctioned "voluntary" classroom prayer in 1980. Federal courts struck down similar statutes from New York, Louisiana, and Texas during the winter of 1981–1982. Federal judges believed themselves bound by *Engel* and *Schempp*. But popular majorities consistently opposed those decisions, and state legislatures continued to register that opposition.[56]

Undeterred by the federal courts, James won passage of the April 1981 silent prayer bill. Yet the Jameses sought to craft a still further-reaching law, one that could provoke a court challenge and ultimately force the Supreme Court to revisit *Engel* and *Schempp*. Early in 1982, the Alabama governor sent lawmakers a measure authorizing teachers to lead "willing students" in prayer – and providing the precise contents of that prayer. The prayer's author was none other than the governor's eldest son, Fob James III, a recent graduate of Duke University Law School, practicing Mobile attorney, and right-wing evangelical. Throughout the spring, the bill languished in the legislature. When the governor learned of

Jaffree's battle against school prayer, he envisioned a vehicle that he and the state could ride to the Supreme Court. Jaffree's lawsuit was a gift to the governor, who promptly "saluted" the Mobile teachers "and every other teacher in the state who wants to pray or lead willing students in prayer to the God who made us all."[57]

On June 16, 1982, the governor requested that the legislature resuscitate the prayer bill submitted earlier that year. His request came only five weeks after Reagan had called for a federal amendment protecting the right of students to pray voluntarily in public schools. Although the Alabama governor concurred with the president's goal of protecting school prayer, he disapproved of Reagan's method. James wanted altogether to remove the matter from federal government oversight. The First Amendment's religion clauses did not actually apply to the states, he believed, and the Supreme Court had misinterpreted the Constitution when it declared otherwise. The president's amendment gave him "great concern" because it "would give the federal government, for the first time, constitutional power over school prayer in the states, thereby setting a dangerous precedent." Rather than amend the Constitution and thereby enlarge its scope, James wanted the courts to interpret it correctly by asserting the right of states to manage their own religious affairs. He sought to get the federal government out of Alabama classrooms, not drag it further in.[58]

The James prayer bill was a family effort. The governor's son, who wrote both the bill and its appended prayer, had signed up for a war supposedly between a Christian people asserting self-rule and a federal judiciary imposing tyranny by a small atheist minority. The Supreme Court, he insisted, had thwarted the will of the American people when it "allowed a few atheists to deprive our people of the God who created them." The Court had abrogated unto itself undue power. "Unless people have God above government, then government is God." With the James prayer bill, Alabama stood poised to "confront the Supreme Court of the United States." Should the legislature pass the bill, the governor's son promised, it would effectively say "No sir, Supreme Court, you are not our God. God is our God." His words were echoed by his mother, who, before the joint committee debating the bill, spoke of the "need to acknowledge God as sovereign over our public schools," lest heathen forces continue to determine curricular policy. Neither she, her son, nor the governor would allow federal judges to infringe on the right of the people – the Christian conservative people – to carry out their moral obligations through the making of civil law.[59]

During full debate in both houses, several legislators opposed the bill on account of the all-too-intimate involvement of the governor's family. Even some supporters worried that the included prayer would diminish the bill's chances of surviving constitutional scrutiny. "If we prescribe a prayer by legislative action, one representative warned, we'll be teaching the students to pray." The governor's son reassured lawmakers that the bill did not prescribe, but merely suggested, that teachers recite the attached prayer. The legislature ultimately agreed. As one newspaper columnist quipped, it substituted it rejected "a prayer written by the Son of God in favor of one drafted by the Son of Fob." On July 1, the Senate president delivered the approved bill to the governor, who signed it into law on July 12.[60]

The governor predicted that Alabama would not have long to wait before the new law was challenged in court. And a court case might just overturn *Engel* and *Schempp*. He was hopeful, telling Alabaminans, "We think that there's a reasonable possibility of a reversal," given that the prayer bill had been "designed to stand the test of the courts in the days ahead." James looked to instigate a thoroughgoing reinterpretation of the Constitution. "It's time to address the '62 decision [*Engel*], not by trying to find a loophole, but by contesting the grounds" on which the ruling rested. His lawyers would show that "our founding fathers never intended that you couldn't acknowledge God in a public institution."[61]

The Alabama Board of Education did not agree that the governor's bill would withstand judicial scrutiny. On a 4–3 vote, the state board voted not to endorse the new bill. Instead, it passed a resolution "support[ing] voluntary, *non-prescribed* prayer in the public schools of Alabama," hoping to reflect Alabamians' strong support for school prayer without taking a legally indefensible stance. Meanwhile, the Board of School Commissioners of Mobile County considered fighting Jaffree's lawsuit without weighing in on the prayer law. Robert Campbell, attorney for the Mobile school board, the teachers, and the principals, denied the validity of Jaffree's charges. In a brief sent to the federal district court in the first week of July, Campbell pointed out that the board had no policy regarding prayer or religious activities. The board thus stood in compliance with the Establishment Clause, Campbell maintained – it exhibited the religious neutrality required by law. As for Boyd and the other teachers, their actions presumably did not constitute state policy and so did not violate federal law.[62]

The governor, now a party to the *Jaffree* case, disputed the district court's jurisdiction over the matter. Unlike the Mobile school board, James made no attempt to portray the state's actions as neutral toward religion. He asserted that Alabama public-school policy – regardless of religious content – lay beyond the purview of federal law. Only a body more august than the federal courts could exercise sovereignty over the matter. The governor's attorney of record, his son, informed the court that, "by the authority of Most High God, Whose authority is recognized by the Declaration of Independence, the Constitution of the United States of America, ... and the Alabama Law respecting prayer in the schools, neither this Court nor any court has jurisdiction over the prayers of the people of God."[63]

Williams asked the court on July 15 to issue a temporary order restraining the defendants from acting in accord with the recently signed bill. Williams argued that the law would surely be found unconstitutional, especially given that its suggested prayer, in all important respects, was equivalent to the "Regents' Prayer" struck down by the Supreme Court in *Engel.* Beyond doubt, the new law violated the Establishment Clause because, as in the earlier case, the prayer in question had been "composed by government officials as part of a governmental program to further religious beliefs." Moreover, Williams held, the bill could not pass judicial scrutiny by virtue of its sponsors' stated design "to provide for a prayer that may be given in the public schools." Given the statute's unlikely chance of surviving on its merits, Williams asked the court to enjoin it until a trial could be convened.[64]

Williams persuaded the judge assigned to the case, W. Brevard Hand, to consider his application for an injunction. On July 21, the judge's office telephoned attorneys for all of the parties, to inform them that the injunction hearing would take place imminently. Counsel for the governor requested extra time for considering his answer to the judge's order. Hand denied that request, giving him exactly one week to respond. The judge announced that he would hear arguments on August 2.[65]

DIGGING IN THEIR HEELS

Like Alabama's first family, most members of the Mobile school board evinced the Christianizing political impulses of the New Right. Those impulses drove board president Dan Alexander, founder and director of Save Our Schools (SOS), a national organization dedicated to dismantling the U.S. Department of Education and reversing liberal trends in public schooling. At the board's July 28 meeting, Alexander implored fellow members to defend themselves against Jaffree's charges. He assured them that the Establishment Clause did not prohibit the free expression of people's religious convictions, at any time or in any place. Even officials of state-run schools enjoyed the right to express their faith openly and publicly. By ruling otherwise, Alexander insisted, the Supreme Court had misapplied the First Amendment, which *protected* religious expression. The presence of a single atheist in a classroom did not justify depriving the remaining students and their teachers of the right to pray where and when they chose. He read a telegram he had received from a coalition of religious right organizations encouraging public educators in Mobile "to continue to stand up for the rights of children to pray voluntarily." The telegram was signed by several of America's most prominent Christian conservatives, including Paul Weyrich, Connie Marshner, Gary Jarmin, and Robert Grant. Alexander suggested that, should the board stand behind the schoolteachers being sued, it could expect financial assistance from religious right organizations.[66]

Attorney Campbell told the board members that they would need to testify in court either that they supported the teachers or that they opposed them and would ensure that the devotional exercises ceased. Most of the five members agreed with Alexander. A resolution declaring full support for the teachers passed on a vote of 3–1 with one abstention. Unlike the state board of education, the Mobile school board threw itself into the legal contest, fueled by the board president's hunger to fight for all citizens' unconditional right to pray aloud wherever they chose.[67]

The enthusiasm of the Mobile school board paled next to the intensity of the first family's defense of the new prayer law. At Hand's deadline of July 28, the governor's son petitioned the court to dismiss the case. His brief staked out drastic rhetorical ground. By "sanctioning public prayer," the brief said, the state of Alabama was simply "proclaiming" its "dependency on God." Public-school students, like the children of Israel, were surely free to call out to God in holy supplication. "The people of Alabama wish to pray to their God," roared the governor's son, "and no court on earth has jurisdiction over their prayers." The younger James warned that "any person or power standing against [Alabama's prayer] law interposes human government as an idol in the place of God," an act in direct violation of God's expressed will.[68]

Two days after James had petitioned for a dismissal, another actor entered the stage. A group of seven Alabamians submitted a motion to intervene in the *Jaffree* case on behalf of the defendants. The seven prospective intervenors were parents of children enrolled in public schools; five had children in the Mobile school system. Most notable among them was Paul McHenry, pastor at Mobile's Ridgewood Presbyterian Church and one of the city's best-known religious conservatives. In its motion to intervene, prepared and submitted by Mobile attorney Barber (Bob) Sherling, the group asserted its right to free religious expression, which, it claimed, was threatened by the lawsuit. Should the court bar religious activity from the public schools, the motion argued, it would violate the Free Exercise Clause. The court would do the same if it overturned either the state's 1982 prayer law or its 1981 statute permitting silent prayer. The right of students and teachers to pray, affirmed by local practice and state law, constituted the right to the free exercise of religion.[69]

Sherling contended that his clients' admission into the case was justified by the spuriousness of Jaffree's class-action claims. Attempting to attain class-action status for his suit, Jaffree had asserted that all Mobile public-school students shared the interests of his children, and that "the claims of the ... Plaintiffs will fairly and adequately protect the interests of the Class" of all students in the county public schools. This, said the intervenors, was absolutely untrue. "Not only is [the plaintiffs'] interest not adequately represented by the existing parties," Sherling asserted; in fact, the plaintiffs were seeking "to deny Intervenors certain inalienable rights that have been guaranteed to Intervenors by the First Amendment."[70]

INJUNCTION HEARING

On Monday morning, August 2, 1982, in the U.S. District Court for the Southern District of Alabama in Mobile, Hand commenced proceedings in *Jaffree* v. *James*. A crowd of about seventy-five spectators, some carrying Bibles, filled the courtroom. Present were Jaffree and Williams, Mobile school board attorney Campbell, Alabama Board of Education lawyer Charles Coody, intervenors' attorney Sherling, and governor's counsel and son, James III. Governor James, choosing to remain in the state capital, Montgomery, did not attend. Hand's first order of business was to bifurcate the suit into two separate cases. The first case, beginning that day, would address whether the state should be enjoined from enforcing the 1981 and 1982 prayer laws, statues 16–1–20.1 and 16–1–20.2. The case against the teachers, the Mobile County Board of School Commissioners, the Mobile schools superintendent, and the Alabama Board of Education would be severed from the case against the governor and tried at a later date.[71]

Over the objection of Williams, Hand granted Sherling's clients permission to intervene in both cases. Sherling successfully argued that the group needed to intervene because it did not share in the plaintiff's grievances and so could not properly be considered part of the class for whom the plaintiff spoke. Indeed, the parties' interests were opposed, given that Jaffree was "seeking to deny the intervenors of a Constitutional right, the right to exercise their religion whenever and wherever they choose." Sherling maintained that the state's new prayer law "merely sanctions something that the intervenors already have a right to do," to worship God freely, so "that if this preliminary injunction is granted, then by implication there will be denied a right which they already have."[72]

Refusing to countenance an illegitimate trial, the governor's son told the court he "was hoping the case would be dismissed in about ten minutes." The younger James reiterated that no court of civil law had jurisdiction over Alabamians' prayers to God. The people's religious liberty was at stake in this case, and the only authority fully equipped to guard that liberty was the ruler in heaven. Williams responded that the issue of the court's sovereignty over God was not relevant to the case. God was not on trial, Williams argued; only those public servants named as defendants were on trial. Hand agreed. "The Lord is not the defendant in this case, the state is," he maintained. "I do not conceive [this case] to be a suit against the Almighty. It is a suit against the named parties." Hand assured the parties that he would continue to preside over the case and that the governor's motion for dismissal was denied. James offered no further arguments. Promising an appeal, he rose and left the courtroom.[73]

Williams urged Hand to enjoin both statutes, the 1981 law allowing teachers to lead students in silent prayer and the 1982 law allowing teachers to conduct spoken prayer. The statutes violated federal case law, Williams explained, because they had not been intended to serve any secular purpose. To make his point, Williams called to the stand Holmes, Senate sponsor of Alabama's 1981 silent prayer bill and supporter of the more recent measure. Holmes freely admitted that, in writing and sponsoring the former, he had acted on his lifelong religious convictions. Williams handed Holmes the comments he had made in the Alabama Senate when his bill was being debated, and Holmes now read those comments to the court. "By passage of this bill," he had promised legislators, "our children ... will have the opportunity of sharing in the spiritual heritage of this state and this country. The United States as well as the State of Alabama was founded by people who believe in God." Holmes had plainly revealed his nonsecular designs in reminding his colleagues, "I have worked hard on this legislation to accomplish the return of voluntary prayer in our public schools and return to the basic moral fiber."[74]

Williams also looked to establish that Jaffree's children might suffer "irreparable injury" if an injunction were not granted. Jaffree elaborated. Were teachers to abide by either of the two statutes, he testified, they would create a coercive classroom atmosphere. "For children to be in a class and to raise their hand and say they want to opt out" would be "to admit they are non-conformers and atheists or worse," Jaffree reasoned. And that "would be so difficult that in essence you would not have any voluntary behavior whatsoever." When surrounded by classmates and teacher praying, children "simply participat[e] because of the fear, however subtle, however indirect, that if they opt out they will be forever stigmatized in the eyes of their classmates." Jaffree wanted his children to learn to think critically, not to be indoctrinated with a religious worldview. He had no problem exposing them to religious ideas, he insisted; it was only indoctrination that concerned him. "I don't want my children," like Pavlov's dogs, "salivating at the mouth every time they hear a bell." In his view, routine immersion in devotional exercises was a kind of conditioning harmful to children's intellectual development.[75]

Counsel for the intervenors flatly rejected Jaffree's assertions. Both of Alabama's prayer laws, Sherling averred, fell far short of establishing a state religion. It was his clients and not the Jaffrees who were being threatened with harm. Sherling sought to demonstrate that an injunction order by the judge would suppress his clients' free exercise of religion. The Constitution guaranteed all citizens the right to pray how, where, and when they chose, Sherling maintained. Any infringement on that right would injure his clients egregiously, intolerably.[76]

Sherling's witnesses told of being obligated to pray at all times and in all places. McHenry testified that he had taught his kindergarten-age son that he was required to pray – not "that he is allowed to do it, but he must do it," that it "is a requirement of the Lord." Accordingly, the boy prayed several times a day. Another of the intervenors, Jean Sullivan of Mobile, insisted "that God requires that we ... pray at all times and ... pray in regard to every aspect of our lives." No matter where they went, these witnesses were commanded to praise God openly, without restriction. In this regard, the classroom was no different from the home or church and the school day was no different from the Sabbath. Intervenor Douglas Smith, an eighth-grade teacher, made the point firmly, insisting that he could not possibly suspend his open devotion to God for any part of the day. "I'm totally consumed by my allegiance to God," he insisted, "and I cannot leave that at the door when I walk in the school building." Again and again, Sherling's witnesses described their entire waking day as permeated by worship.[77]

Nor was it sufficient to protect silent prayer but not verbal prayer, Sherling and the intervenors argued. God required Christians to praise him aloud. McHenry maintained that the classroom was a setting where his son would expect to pray out loud and, if prevented from doing so, would be harmed. Sullivan agreed. "Children need guidance," and self-directed silent prayer would not provide that guidance. Were Smith prohibited from praying aloud in the classroom, he maintained, the government would be "telling me God cannot be a part of my life when I'm a teacher." Fred Wolfe, pastor of Cottage Hill Baptist Church, Mobile's largest congregation, argued that silent prayer was wholly inadequate for a Christian. "Most of the prayer that I see in the New Testament was offered ... not silently but verbally," Wolfe told the court. He believed it essential that people communicate their faith openly among others because God "said that 'you are the light of the world' and must 'let your light shine before men.'" Williams asked him, on cross-examination, whether laws limiting religious activity to silent meditation were not a means of accommodating students' religious needs without imposing religion on others. Wolfe rejected this reasoning. Laws permitting only silent worship, he maintained, were no more than "a way of silencing people from expressing their faith." To the intervenors, it was those who needed to pray verbally – and not those who wished to abstain – whose rights were at stake in this trial.[78]

The intervenors expounded a theory of religious freedom quite different from the plaintiff's conception. Williams opined that, in a public space such as a classroom, children exposed to religious devotion would either be coerced into adopting the practice or be turned into pariahs by their peers. Guaranteeing the religious freedom of children meant shielding them from state-sanctioned pressures to conform. The intervenors, in contrast, championed a classroom environment in which all individuals were free to express their religious beliefs and free to affirm or ignore the religious beliefs of others. In Wolfe's view, it was "the right to pray" that deserved protection in the public schools. Shielding children from exposure to prayer was a luxury; guaranteeing them the freedom to pray was a necessity. If "it would be an offense to [someone else] for me to communicate to my God," he argued, then "it would be [a bigger] offense to me not to communicate with my God." Smith made sure that, in his classroom, all children were free to express their religious beliefs, even if those diverged from the beliefs of the other students. "I will not allow under any circumstances any student to ridicule any other student because of a different religious viewpoint," he testified. In turn, his students had granted him that same courtesy. Although "I believe what I believe is correct," Smith asserted, "another person may have a different view, and they are allowed the freedom to share that, and I would not do anything to prohibit that freedom."[79]

The intervenors promoted a "free market" exercise of religion in which all students and teachers were free to express themselves as they saw fit, to ignore the prayers of others, and to be excused from unbearable activities. Sullivan did not want her children saying Buddhist prayers, practicing witchcraft, using Ouiga boards, or referring to God as a woman. But, she insisted, exposure to non-Christian prayer would not hurt them because they knew they "had the right not to pray." Wolfe explained that the onus was on the offended party, especially if their views did not predominate. "When you are in a minority faith," he contended, "you must accept the reality that religious majorities may speak more audibly than you and drown out your voice. Christians in many countries are in a minority and experience exactly that." If, "in a given situation," one finds oneself in the religious minority, one should "sit there and listen or excuse [one]self," Wolfe contended. Religious freedom dictated that each individual be at liberty to worship as he or she chose. The Constitution did not silence any person's religious expression.[80]

Because the Jaffree children were free to ignore or opt out of practices that they found intolerable, the intervenors argued, the prayer laws remained voluntary and thus unobjectionable. Like any other students, the Jaffrees could leave the room if they were so offended by prayer. Smith told Sherling that, if at any time he offended any students by expressing his Christian convictions, then he would "make arrangements for them to leave." Sullivan likewise opined that children always "had the right not to pray." In his closing arguments, Sherling reminded Hand that "these Plaintiffs have the right to leave the classroom ... or tune out their minds if the religion of Christianity is being preached." Contrary to what Jaffree believed, the state's public schools were not establishing a religion because they were not forcing students to participate in any religious activities whatsoever.[81]

If the schools were advancing any religion at all, Sherling posited, it was "what has been described by the courts as the religion of humanism." This line of reasoning would prove vital to the intervenors' case. They claimed that public education was permeated by a liberal, atheistic worldview known as secular humanism. Among many teachers and authors of textbooks, this worldview manifested as "an expression of a conviction or a belief on the part of [a] particular person." So comprehensive was this worldview that it functioned as a religion. In fact, as the Supreme Court had at times suggested, it was a religion. According to the intervenors, the religion of secular humanism was advanced whenever textbooks included sexually explicit material or took God's name in vain. It was promoted by mere inattention to Christianity's historical role in American history. So widespread was the promotion of secular humanism in the schools, Sherling insisted, that Christian public-school students, every bit as much as Jaffree's children, faced an established religion contrary to the values that they were taught at home.[82]

Byron Tabor, an intervenor and the parent of three children attending Mobile public schools, testified to the harm his family withstood as a result of secular humanism's promotion. Tabor's children had encountered, in the classroom and in their schoolbooks, "the teaching of humanism and the teaching of God's name in vain," lessons at odds with the Christian belief system given to them by their parents. Tabor and his wife constantly had to "re-educate" their children and instill into them knowledge of absolute right and absolute wrong. They instructed their children to exit the classroom "if the teacher begins to teach evolution as a fact," if "Planned Parenthood comes in and brings their contraceptives," or if "a Buddhist or homosexual was allowed to come in and start talking about his lifestyle." So exasperated had they become that they felt forced to enter their children in private Christian schools. Given the steep tuition, this imposed a hardship on the family. They had little choice but to endure the burden, Tabor believed, in order to escape the secular humanism being forced on them.[83]

After similar sentiments were conveyed by Wolfe, Hand initiated his own line of questioning, suggesting that the correct definition of religion might be a matter for debate. Hand asked Wolfe if he considered "a belief in God [to be] a requisite to religion." "No," it was not, Wolfe responded. "Because the Supreme Court declared that humanism is a religion, and [because] humanism expresses no belief in a higher power," he contended, religion "does not have to be belief in a God as such." Rather, religion was indicated by any "set of values and views to which a person adheres." Agnosticism, communism, and socialism all constituted religions. Grasping the implications in his statements, Hand queried: "If the government is allowed to prescribe a course of education that in essence teaches socialism, are they engaging in teaching a religion?" "It is my deep conviction that they are," Wolfe replied.[84]

Although the judge intermittently asked questions and offered observations throughout the hearing, his thinking could not be conclusively discerned. At one moment, he appeared supportive toward the plaintiffs. Suggesting the inappropriateness of verbalizing prayer in public settings, he quoted the sixth chapter of the New Testament's Book of Matthew. "When you pray, do not be like the hypocrites, who love to pray standing up in synagogue and at the street corners, for everyone to see. ... When you pray, go into a closet, shut the door, [and] pray to your Father in secret." At other moments, Hand seemed to favor the intervenors' position. His comments indicated that he might consider humanism a religion. And he entertained the notion that the classroom might function best when it accommodated all religious expression, even if that disadvantaged students adhering to a minority religion. Hand compared such religious freedom to freedom of speech. While "it is improper to use vulgar language on the television," he pointed out, such language still gets used. And, when it does, "you don't have to listen to it, you can turn [the television] off." Clearly, Hand grasped – and perhaps shared – the intervenors' belief that the free exercise of religion demanded that all parties be allowed to express themselves.[85]

Hand's apparent sympathy with the intervenors' position was striking, given its divergence from Supreme Court jurisprudence regarding prayer in public schools. In fact, he let the parties know that Court precedent, while very important, would not determine his ruling.

"The Intervenor wants an opportunity to build a record in order to attack the present condition of the law," he announced, "and I'm not supposed to deny him that right." The far-ranging testimony permitted by the judge opened up all kinds of possibilities. As the injunction hearing drew to a finish, Hand signaled that his decision might contain surprising elements and perhaps accommodate ambitious challenges to existing law.[86]

MIXED SIGNALS

On the morning of August 9, 1982, in the matter of *Jaffree* v. *James*, Hand enjoined any implementation of Alabama's 1981 and 1982 school prayer laws. In so doing he affirmed the arguments of Williams. Hand ruled that the plaintiffs had met their burden by demonstrating that enforcement of the laws might harm Jaffree irreparably, that such harm would outweigh any harm caused by an injunction, that an injunction served the public interest, and that the plaintiffs were likely to succeed at trial based on the merits of the case. Hand determined that the two statutes' failure to pass the *Lemon* Establishment Clause test had rendered likely the plaintiffs' eventual success on the merits. He needed look no further than *Lemon*'s first prong, which required all statutes to have a secular purpose. The author of the 1981 bill, Senator Holmes, had admitted that his purposes were religious, while the 1982 bill's own language demonstrated its authors' religious designs. "Since these statutes do not reflect a clearly secular purpose," Hand opined, "no consideration of the remaining two-parts of the *Lemon* test is necessary."[87]

"This Court adheres to the philosophy of *stare decisis*," or precedent established through high-court rulings, the judge announced. He would not indulge "the modern trend of handling matters on a case-by-case basis," as such ad hoc decision-making was "destructive of the judicial system and precludes the citizens of this country from their right to know what the law is and how to follow consistent patterns of conduct in their day-to-day activities." Because he had taken "an oath before God that he would uphold the laws of the United States," he was "obligated to follow the decision law on this sensitive question." Hand knew well that *stare decisis* required the First Amendment's application to the individual states, through incorporation by the Fourteenth Amendment. In keeping with that dictate, he determined that the state of Alabama could pass no law that respected an establishment of religion or prohibited citizens' free exercise of religion. "Any governmental activity ... that prescribes or proscribes the conduct of religion is offensive to all citizens and the Constitution."[88]

Hand's declaration of adherence to *stare decisis* conflicted with his earlier insistence that Court precedent would not determine his ruling. In fact, his injunction ruling indicated both that he would adhere to precedent *and* that he would consider all matters without prejudice. He seemed especially to appreciate the intervenors' argument on humanism, which he called "a fresh approach [relative] to that now found in the annals of case law." The courts, in their previous applications of the Establishment Clause, had not defined religion with sufficient clarity and thoroughness, Hand suggested. It seemed to him that religion did not require belief in God. Rather, any "concept" or "value held to be of supreme importance" by an individual in effect constituted that individual's religion. "The religions of atheism, materialism, agnosticism, communism and socialism have escaped the scrutiny of the courts throughout the years," Hand complained. To their adherents, they unquestionably were religions. Their tenets were "ardently adhered to," he insisted, and were "advanced in the teachings and literature that is presented to the fertile minds of the students in the various school systems." He declared it "time to recognize that the constitutional definition of religion encompasses more than Christianity and encompasses as well the establishment of a secular religion."[89]

For the time being, Hand was content to rule that Alabama's prayer laws likely enough violated the Establishment Clause to require an injunction. Yet his ruling raised more questions than it answered. Because he had defined religion functionally, as any comprehensive worldview that provided answers to life's ultimate questions, his assertion that "the state of Alabama must remain neutral in respect to establishing a religion" took on a curious meaning. Might the public schools need to refrain from advancing any and all coherent lenses for viewing the world? Hand wondered as much. "If the state cannot teach or advance Christianity," he asked, then "how can it teach or advance the Antichrist?" An aggressive application of the Establishment Clause – should the court carry it out – would be quite a complicated undertaking.[90]

Hand intimated the sort of painstaking operations that might become necessary were he ultimately to strike down the prayer laws for running afoul of the Establishment Clause. "If the courts are to involve themselves in the proscription of religious activities in the schools," he warned, then "we are going to have to involve ourselves in a whole host of areas, such as censoring, that we have heretofore overlooked." Hand did not relish an aggressive role for the courts. Although he believed it prudent for schools to prohibit disruptive religious exercises, he wished to tread as lightly as possible over citizens' free religious expression. As he saw it, the Establishment Clause directed the state to avoid religion, not monitor it. It was not his job to shield children from exposure to unfamiliar religions. He suggested that Jaffree was unrealistic in seeking to guard his children against religious expression, since even the youngest of children must begin to decide what values they accept and what values they reject. It certainly was not the place of the courts, he contended, to decide when citizens "must commence accepting or rejecting ideas and in what areas we are to be protected and for how long." To Hand it was far better to permit a free range of religious expression than to proscribe such expression.

Hand's mixed message was not apparent to everyone. Some observers saw only an injunction. Williams and Jaffree concluded that Hand had ruled in their favor. For Williams, the decision affirmed the separation of church and state. Jaffree expressed "hope that this decision will deter other people in other jurisdictions from engaging in the same type of religiously-based behavior" as the state of Alabama had. Buoyed by Hand's ruling, he called on people of faith to "leave the practice of religion in the homes and churches, where it belongs, and leave it out of the schools." The ACLU, which would submit a brief on Jaffree's behalf for the upcoming trial, praised Hand's flawless legal analysis.[91]

Some conservatives drew the same conclusion. According to Jaffree, the Moral Majority got in touch with Hand and asked him to reconsider his stance. Nor was the governor much pleased. While he did find "some consolation in certain passages [of the ruling] which appeared to endorse the right of voluntary prayer in schools," his aide reported, James generally struck a defiant stance toward Hand and his injunction against the laws the governor had done so much to create. In historian Joseph Newman's estimation, the governor failed to discern the ruling's subtext. "Both the supporters and detractors of Judge Hand should have read his injunction more carefully," Newman writes, "for it contained ample clues to the final judgment he would render in the case."[92]

Only Sherling expressed confidence that defenders of school prayer had scored a victory. The ruling gave him hope that his clients would "gain new legal ground" when the matter was decided at trial. He noted Hand's criticism of earlier court decisions that had "overlooked the totality of what is religion." Sherling applauded Hand's willingness not to equate religion solely with Christianity. "We don't think we should be denied the right to pray or foster our religion," he maintained. While conceding that non-Christians ought to be accorded that same right, Sherling insisted that if the right to exercise religion openly were denied to Christians, it ought to be denied to everyone else as well. If "no establishment" meant "no religion," then that proscription ought to apply to non-Christians such as Jaffree.[93]

Notes

1 *Dare We Defend Our Rights?* (1992: L. Wade Black and the Alabama Center for Law and Civic Education), narrated by Wayne Flynt; Transcript, *Ishmael Jaffree et al.* v. *Board of School Commissioners of Mobile County et al.*, Civil case no. 82–0554–H, box no. 1, accession no. 021–93–0423, location no. C0681974 SAN (Federal Records Center, East Point, Ga.), November 15–18, 1982, p. 144; Joyce Leviton, "A Former Child Evangelist Wins a Supreme Court Fight against Prayer in Public Schools," *People*, June 24, 1985, p. 36.

2 Joseph Newman, "Interview with Jaffree," *Harbinger*, October 15, 1985, p. 11; *One Nation under God: School Prayer and the First Amendment* (Alexandria, Va.: Close Up Publishing, 1995); Transcript, *Jaffree* v. *Board*, 108, 212, 234; "A Conversation with Ishmael Jaffree," *Azalea City News & Review*, February 17, 1983, pp. 1, 4; "An Interview with Ishmael Jaffree," *Azalea City News & Review*, February 24, 1983, p. 5; Sandra Baxley Taylor, "Jaffree: Anti-Prayer Suit Aimed at Choice," *Birmingham News*, Sun., September 5, 1982, p. B1; Leviton, "Former Child Evangelist Wins a Supreme Court Fight against Prayer in Public Schools," 36.

3 Transcript, *Jaffree* v. *Board*, 111, 121, 126–28, 133–34; Deposition of Charlene Boyd, *Ishmael Jaffree et al.* v. *Board of School Commissioners of Mobile County et al.*, August 17, 1982, Wallace File, SG 5012, Legal Case Files, Alabama Department of Archives and History (624 Washington Ave., Montgomery, Ala.), p. 26.

4 Transcript, *Jaffree* v. *Board*, 144–45, 233–34; *Dare We Defend Our Rights? Engel* v. *Vitale*, 370 U.S. 421 (1962); *School District of Abington, Pa.* v. *Schempp*, 374 U.S. 203 (1963).

5 *Dare We Defend Our Rights?* Deposition of Boyd, 10, 26; *One Nation under God;* Transcript, *Jaffree* v. *Board*, 111, 121.

6 Deposition of Boyd, 8, 13, 31, 46–47, 13, 31; Transcript, *Jaffree* v. *Board*, 109–12, 121, 133.

7 *Ibid.*, 145; *One Nation under God;* Taylor, "Jaffree," B1.

8 Peter Irons, *The Courage of their Convictions: Sixteen Americans Who Fought Their Way to the Supreme Court* (New York: Penguin, 1990), 368; Transcript, *Jaffree* v. *Board*, 208–9, 233–34; "Conversation with Ishmael Jaffree."

9 Leviton, "Former Child Evangelist Wins a Supreme Court Fight against Prayer in Public Schools," 36; "Conversation with Ishmael Jaffree," 1; Transcript, *Jaffree* v. *Board*, 209, 234.

10 *Dare We Defend Out Rights?* ; "Conversation with Ishmael Jaffree," 4; Transcript, *Jaffree* v. *Board*, 208–9; "Interview with Ishmael Jaffree," 5; Irons, *Courage of Their Convictions*, 368.

11 Leviton, "Former Child Evangelist Wins a Supreme Court Fight against Prayer in Public Schools," 38; Taylor, "Jaffree," B1; Irons, *Courage of Their Convictions*, 370–71; "Interview with Ishmael Jaffree," 5.

12 Irons, *Courage of Their Convictions*, 370–71; "Interview with Ishmael Jaffree," 5.

13 Transcript, *Jaffree* v. *Board*, 211–12, 230–32; "Interview with Ishmael Jaffree," 5.

14 Irons, *Courage of Their Convictions*, 371–72; "Conversation with Ishmael Jaffree," 1; Alex Haley and Malcolm X, *The Autobiography of Malcolm X* (1965; New York: Ballantine, 1992), 216.

15 Leviton, "Former Child Evangelist Wins a Supreme Court Fight against Prayer in Public Schools," 38; "Conversation with Ishmael Jaffree," 4; Transcript, *Jaffree* v. *Board*, 208, 234; Irons, *Courage of Their Convictions*, 372.

16 *One Nation under God;* Newman, "Interview with Jaffree," 11; *Dare We Defend Our Rights?* Transcript, *Jaffree* v. *Board*, 212.

17 Paul Harvey, *Freedom's Coming: Religious Culture and the Shaping of the South from the Civil War through the Civil Rights Era* (Chapel Hill: University of North Carolina Press, 2005); David L. Chappell, *A Stone of Hope: Prophetic Religion and the Death of Jim Crow* (Chapel Hill: University of North Carolina Press, 2004); Wayne Flynt, *Alabama Baptists: Southern Baptists in the Heart of Dixie* (Tuscaloosa: University of Alabama Press, 1999); O. Kendall White Jr. and Daryl White, eds., *Religion in the Contemporary South* (Athens: University of Georgia Press, 1995), 34–45, 79–88, 106–23; Eric C. Lincoln, *Race, Religion, and the Continuing American Dilemma* (1984; New York: Hill and Wang, 1999); James H. Cone, *God of the Oppressed* (1975; Maryknoll, N.Y.: Orbis, 1997).

18 Taylor, "Jaffree," B1; Transcript, *Jaffree* v. *Board*, 145–46.

19 *Ibid.*, 112–13, 123–24, 146–48.

20 *Ibid.*, 146–48; "Conversation with Ishmael Jaffree," 4.

21 Transcript, *Jaffree* v. *Board*, 125–28.

22 *Ibid.*, 149; *One Nation under God*; Ishmael Jaffree to Charlene Boyd, March 11, 1982. (Plaintiff's exhibit 1, trial records of *Jaffree* v. *Board.*)

23 Transcript, *Jaffree* v. *Board*, 114–15, 149, 171–72; *One Nation under God;* Jaffree to Boyd, March 11, 1982; Deposition of Boyd, 56, 59.

24 *Dare We Defend Our Rights?* Newman, "Interview with Jaffree," 11.

25 Transcript, *Jaffree* v. *Board*, 176–78, 180, 191–99, 214–15.

26 *Ibid.*, 145, 214, 242; "Conversation with Ishmael Jaffree," 4.

27 Transcript, *Jaffree* v. *Board*, 176, 180, 186, 194–95.

28 *Ibid.*, 179, 186, 191–93, 200–206.

29 *Ibid.*, 66–76, 82–83, 228–29.

30 *Ibid.*, 74, 79, 81, 242–43.

31 *Dare We Defend Our Rights?* Newman, "Interview with Jaffree," 11.

32 Transcript, *Jaffree* v. *Board*, 218, 284, 282; Irons, *Courage of Their Convictions*, 374; Ron Williams interview by Robert Daniel Rubin, March 19, 2002, Mobile, Ala., 1 (in Robert Daniel Rubin's possession); *Dare We Defend Our*

Rights?; "Interview with Ishmael Jaffree," p. 5. The Supreme Court established the unconstitutionality of organized religious exercises in the public schools in *McCollum* v. *Board of Education*, 333 U.S. 203 (1948); *Engel* v. *Vitale;* and *Abington.* v. *Schempp.*

33 Transcript, *Jaffree* v. *Board*, 214, 216; Ishmael Jaffree to Abraham Lincoln Hammons, May 10, 1982 (Plaintiff's exhibit 2, trial records of *Jaffree* v. *Board*).

34 *Ibid.* The two most important Supreme Court rulings on religious activity in the classroom specified that voluntarism did not spare such activity from constitutional defect. In *Engel* v. *Vitale*, Justice Hugo Black wrote that a violation of "the Establishment Clause ... does not depend upon any showing of direct governmental compulsion and is violated by the enactment of laws which establish an official religion whether those laws operate directly to coerce nonobserving individuals or not." *Engel* v. *Vitale*, 430. Justice Tom Clark reiterated this point a year later in *School District of Abington Township* v. *Schempp*, which declared classroom Bible reading a violation of the Establishment Clause. Unconstitutionality, said Clark, was in no way "mitigated by the fact that individual students may absent themselves upon parental request." *Abington* v. *Schempp*, 224–25.

35 Transcript, *Jaffree* v. *Board*, 181–89.

36 *Ibid.*, 216–17, 282.

37 "Interview with Ishmael Jaffree," 5.

38 Transcript, *Jaffree* v. *Board*, 67, 72, 101–2, 105, 216–17.

39 *Ibid.*, 76, 83, 188, 200–206; Deposition of Boyd, 18, 64.

40 Transcript, *Jaffree* v. *Board*, 216, 220, 284; *Dare We Defend Our Rights?* ; Williams interview, 1.

41 Transcript, *Jaffree* v. *Board*, 217–18, 281–82.

42 [Initial] verified complaint, *Jaffree* v. *Board*, May 28, 1982, 1–2, 7. The Supreme Court first incorporated the Free Exercise Clause into the Fourteenth Amendment in *Cantwell* v. *Connecticut*, 310 U.S. 296 (1940). The Establishment Clause was first incorporated in *Everson* v. *Board of Education*, 330 U.S. 1 (1947).

43 "Conversation with Ishmael Jaffree," 4; Transcript, *Jaffree* v. *Board*, 208.

44 "Conversation with Ishmael Jaffree," 4; *Dare We Defend Our Rights?*.

45 *Dare We Defend Our Rights?*.

46 [Initial] verified complaint, *Jaffree* v. *Board*, 5, 7, emphasis added.

47 "Conversation with Ishmael Jaffree," 4.

48 Amended complaint, *Jaffree* v. *Board*, June 4, 1982, pp. 1–2; Transcript, *Jaffree* v. *Board*, 219–20; Second amended complaint, *Jaffree* v. *Board*, June 30, 1982, pp. 1–2.

49 *Montgomery Advertiser*, June 3, 1982, p. 9; *Mobile Register*, June 4, 1982, p. B1; *Mobile Press*, June 4, 1982, p. A2; *Birmingham News*, May 4, 1981, p. A6; *Montgomery Advertiser and Alabama Journal*, June 13, 1982, p. B3; *Mobile Register*, June 17, 1982, p. 10; *Montgomery Advertiser*, June 17, 1982, p. 13; *Montgomery Advertiser and Alabama Journal*, July 11, 1982, p. A2; Leviton, "Former Child Evangelist Wins a Supreme Court Fight against Prayer in Public Schools," 36; *Journal of the Senate of the State of Alabama: Second Extraordinary Session of 1982*, June 21–July 5, 1982, p.3.

50 The literature on the New Right's moral conservatism is extensive. Notable works from recent years include Andrew Hartman, *A War for the Soul of America: A History of the Culture Wars* (Chicago: University of Chicago Press, 2015); Darren Dochuk, *From Bible Belt to Sun Belt: Plain-Folk Religion, Grassroots Politics, and the Rise of Conservative Evangelicalism* (New York: Norton, 2011); Daniel K. Williams, *God's Own Party: The Making of the Christian Right* (New York: Oxford University Press, 2010); Kevin M. Kruse, "Beyond the Southern Cross: The National Origins of the Religious Right," in *The Myth of Southern Exceptionalism*, ed. by Matthew D. Lassiter and Joseph Crespino (New York: Oxford University Press, 2010), 286–307; Steven P. Miller, *Billy Graham and the Rise of the Republican South* (Philadelphia: University of Pennsylvania Press, 2009); Paul Boyer, "The Evangelical Resurgence in 1970s American Protestantism," in *Rightward Bound: Making America Conservative in the 1970s*, ed. by Bruce J. Schulman and Julian E. Zelizer (Cambridge, Mass.: Harvard University Press, 2008), 29–51; Joseph Crespino, "Civil Rights and the Religious Right," in *Rightward Bound*, ed. by Schulman and Zelizer, 90–105; Allan J. Lichtman, *White Protestant Nation: The Rise of the American Conservative Movement* (New York: Atlantic Monthly, 2008), 330–78; and Donald Critchlow, *Phyllis Schlafly and Grassroots Conservatism: A Woman's Crusade* (Princeton: Princeton University Press, 2005), 243–95.

51 *Washington Post*, December 1, 1980, pp. A1, 8–9; *New York Times*, May 24, 1981, sec. 4, p. 19; Mike Shanahan, "Popsicle Brigade Tries to Get in Step with the Senate," *Associated Press*, December 18, 1981, AM cycle; *Washington Post*, January 17, 1982, p. A2.

52 *Birmingham News*, September 27, 1978, pp. 1, 6; *Birmingham News*, October 1, 1978, p. A2; *Birmingham News*, January 16, 1979, p. 9; *Mobile Register*, January 16, 1979, p. 6; *Montgomery Advertiser and Alabama Journal*, January 15, 1979, p. 13; "Inauguration of Fob James: Governor of Alabama, Fifty-fifth Inauguration," Montgomery, Alabama, January 15, 1979. File: Governors-James-AL1, Local History and Genealogy Division, Mobile Public Library, Mobile, Ala.; William H. Stewart, "Forrest ('Fob') James Jr.," in *Alabama Governors: A Political History of the State*, ed. by Samuel L. Webb and Margaret E. Armbrester (Tuscaloosa: University of Alabama Press, 2001), 244.

53 *Birmingham News*, October 1, 1978, pp. 15–16, 18; *Washington Post*, January 30, 1981, p. C14; *Mobile Press*, March 19, 1981, pp. 1, 6; *Montgomery Advertiser*, June 30, 1982, p. 13; *Mobile Press Register*, September 19, 1982, p. E8; Stewart, "Forrest ('Fob') James Jr.," 244. Sandra Baxley Taylor, *Fob: The Incredible Story of Fob James Jr.* (Mobile: Greenberry, 1990), 338. On the White House Conference on Families, see Edward J. Lynch, "The White House Family Feud," *Policy Review*, no. 13 (Summer 1980), 121; *New York Times*, February 12, 1980, sec. 2, p. 6; and William Martin, *With God on Our Side: The Rise of the Religious Right in America* (New York: Broadway, 1996), 174–89.

54 *Montgomery Advertiser*, June 3, 1982, pp. 9, 15; *Montgomery Advertiser and Alabama Journal*, June 13, 1982, p. B3; *Montgomery Advertiser and Alabama*

Journal, July 11, 1982, p. A2; *Montgomery Advertiser*, August 11, 1982, p. 18; *Mobile Register*, August 11, 1982, p. B8; *Montgomery Advertiser*, August 13, 1982, p. 1; *Mobile Press Register*, August 14, 1982, p. B2; *Montgomery Advertiser and Alabama Journal*, August 14, 1982, pp. A1–2; *Mobile Register*, August 25, 1982, p. C2.

55 Taylor, *Fob*, 343; *Mobile Press*, March 19, 1981, p. 6; *Montgomery Advertiser*, April 22, 1981, p. 1; *Birmingham News*, April 22, 1981, p. A2; *Montgomery Advertiser*, April 30, 1981, p. 47; *Birmingham News*, April 30, 1981, p. F2; *Mobile Register*, June 17, 1982, p. 10; *Journal of the Senate of the State of Alabama: Regular Session of 1981*, p. 921.

56 *Christian Science Monitor*, April 4, 1980, p. 5; *Washington Post*, January 26, 1982, p. A6. *Ibid.*, February 17, 1982, p. A6. *Ibid.*, March 12, 1982, p. A3. John W. Swomley, "Public Schools Embattled over Prayer," *Christian Century*, July 20–27, 1983, p. 681. *Engel* v. *Vitale; Abington* v. *Schempp*. Bruce J. Dierenfield, "'Somebody Is Tampering with America's Soul': Congress and the School Prayer Debate," *Congress and the Presidency*, 24 (Autumn 1997), 167–204.

57 *Mobile Register*, June 17, 1982, p. 10; *Montgomery Advertiser*, June 23, 1982, pp. 1–2; *Mobile Press*, June 23, 1982, p. 10; *Mobile Register*, June 30, 1982, p. A8; *Montgomery Advertiser*, July 22, 1982, p. 23; "Fob James III Mixes Law with Religious Vocation," *Mobile Press*, July 4, 1985; Newman, "New Right and Education," 12.

58 *Mobile Register*, June 17, 1982, p. 10; *Montgomery Advertiser*, June 17, 1982, p. 13; Taylor, *Fob*, 341; *Washington Post*, September 16, 1982, p. A3.

59 *Montgomery Advertiser*, June 23, 1982, pp. 1–2; *Mobile Press*, June 23, 1982, p. 10.

60 Taylor, *Fob*, 242, 344–45; *Mobile Press*, June 23, 1982, p. 10; *Montgomery Advertiser*, June 23, 1982 p. 2; *Mobile Register*, June 30, 1982, p. A8. *Montgomery Advertiser and Alabama Journal*, July 4, 1982, p. B3; *Montgomery Advertiser*, July 13, 1982, p. 1; *Journal of the Senate of the State of Alabama: Second Extraordinary Session of 1982*, June 21–July 5, 1982, p. 253.

61 *Montgomery Advertiser*, June 23, 1982, p. 2; *Montgomery Advertiser*, June 24, 1982, p. 2; *Montgomery Advertiser*, July 13, 1982, p. 1; *Mobile Register*, July 13, 1982, p. 1.

62 *Montgomery Advertiser*, June 23, 1982, pp. 1–2; *Montgomery Advertiser*, June 25, 1982, p. 13; Minutes of the State of Alabama Board of Education, 1980–1982, July 13, 1982, p. 1; emphasis in original. Defendants' response to amended complaint, *Jaffree* v. *Board*, June 6, 1982, p. 2. Minutes of the Regular Meeting of the Board of School Commissioners of Mobile County, Alabama, Central Administrative Office of the Mobile County Public School System, Barton Academy (504 Government Street, Mobile, Ala.), August 11, 1982, pp. 397–98.

63 Defendant Fob James's response to complaint, *Jaffree* v. *Board*, [approx.] July 9–12, 1982, p. 5.

64 Plaintiffs' motion for a temporary restraining order at *Jaffree* v. *Board*, July 15, 1982; Memorandum of law in support of plaintiffs' motion for a temporary restraining order at *Jaffree* v. *Board*, July 15, 1982, pp. 4–8; *Engel* v. *Vitale*, 425; *Journal of the Senate of the State of Alabama: Second Extraordinary Session of 1982*, p. 8.

65 Announcement of hearing on plaintiffs' application for preliminary injunction at *Jaffree* v. *Board*, July 19, 1982 (trial records of *Jaffree* v. *Board*); Order to consolidate the hearing on the preliminary injunction with the trial on the merits, at *Jaffree* v. *Board*, July 23, 1982 (trial records of *Jaffree* v. *Board*).

66 Minutes of the Regular Meeting of the Board of School Commissioners of Mobile County, Alabama, July 28, 1982, pp. 369–71. S. Lloyd and R. Tremaine, "Dan Alexander," (Mobile) *Harbinger*, November 26, 1985, pp. 11–12; "Education Elitists Want Your Children," *Blackboard* (published by Save Our Schools, a division of the Taxpayers Educational Lobby, Washington, D.C.), December 1982, pp. 1–2.

67 Minutes of the Regular Meeting of the Board of School Commissioners of Mobile County, Alabama, July 28, 1982, pp. 369–71. *Mobile Register*, July 29, 1982, p. B1; *Mobile Press*, July 29, 1982, p. A1; *Montgomery Advertiser*, July 30, 1982, p. 10.

68 Defendant Fob James's motion to dismiss, at *Jaffree* v. *Board*, July 28, 1982. Order to consolidate the hearing on the preliminary injunction with the trial on the merits, at *Jaffree* v. *Board*, July 23, 1982 (trial records of *Jaffree* v. *Board*); Defendant Fob James's brief in support of motion to dismiss, at *Jaffree* v. *Board*, July 28, 1982; Order to consolidate the hearing on the preliminary injunction with the trial on the merits, at *Jaffree* v. *Board*, July 23, 1982 (trial records of *Jaffree* v. *Board*), pp. 2–3; *Mobile Press Register*, July 31, 1982, p. B1.

69 Motion to intervene, at *Jaffree* v. *Board*, July 30, 1982 (trial records of *Jaffree* v. *Board*); Order to consolidate the hearing on the preliminary injunction with the trial on the merits, at *Jaffree* v. *Board*, July 23, 1982 (trial records of *Jaffree* v. *Board*); *Mobile Press Register*, November 6, 1982, p. A12.

70 Second amended complaint, at *Jaffree* v. *Board*, p. 2; Plaintiffs' motion for an order of class certification, at *Jaffree* v. *Board*, July 20, 1982 (trial records of *Jaffree* v. *Board*), pp. 10–12; *Montgomery Advertiser*, July 30, 1982, p. 10; "Lord Is Not a Defendant in Prayer Suit, Says Hand," *Mobile Press*, August 2, 1982.

71 *Montgomery Advertiser*, August 3, 1982, p. 2; *Mobile Register*, August 3, 1982, p. A6; Transcript, *Ishmael Jaffree et al.* v. *Gov. Fob James et al.*, Civil case no. 82–0792–H, box no. 7, accession no. 021–93–0423, location no. C0681974 SAN (Federal Records Center), August 2 and 5, 1982, pp. 1–5, 11.

72 *Ibid.*, 10, 49–50.

73 *Ibid.*, 14–25, 29, 32–33, 37, 51; "Lord Is Not a Defendant in Prayer Suit, Says Hand,"; *Montgomery Advertiser*, August 5, 1982, p. 16.

74 Transcript, *Jaffree* v. *James*, 51–59, 176–77, 249–53. The three-pronged test for compliance with the Establishment Clause was laid out in *Walz* v. *Tax Commission of the City of New York*, 397 U.S. 664 (1970); and *Lemon* v. *Kurtzman*, 403 U.S. 602 (1971).
75 Transcript, *Jaffree* v. *James*, 77–79, 94–98, 265–66.
76 *Ibid.*, 6–11, 265–66.
77 Motion to intervene, records of *Jaffree* v. *Board*, 2. Transcript, 136, 153, 165, 246.
78 *Ibid.*, 156–57, 172–73, 188–89, 198, 209, 246–48.
79 *Ibid.*, 198–209, 229–40.
80 *Ibid.*, 165–68, 203–5. According to Michael McConnell, "the pluralist state thus affirms the equality of all citizens by allowing all to participate in public affairs without privileging any particular ideology or mode of persuasion." Michael W. McConnell, "Believers as Equal Citizens," in *Obligations of Citizenship and Demands of Faith: Religious Accommodation in Pluralist Democracies*, ed. by Nancy L. Rosenblum (Princeton: Princeton University Press, 2000), 105.
81 Transcript, *Jaffree* v. *James*, 173, 238, 263.
82 *Ibid.*, 263–64. In three Establishment Clause cases, the Supreme Court suggested that secular humanism was a religion. *Zorach* v. *Clauson*, 343 U.S. 306 (1952), 313–14; *Torcaso* v. *Watkins*, 367 U.S. 488 (1961), 495; and *Abington* v. *Schempp*, 374 U.S. 203 (1963), (Stewart, J., dissenting), 313. Two rulings based on free exercise found likewise. *United States* v. *Seeger*, 380 U.S. 163 (1965), 165–66; and *Welsh* v. *United States*, 398 U.S. 333 (1970), 342–43.
83 Transcript, *Jaffree* v. *James*, 224–29.
84 *Ibid.*, 212–13.
85 *Ibid.*, 199–200. Matthew 6: 5–6, *The New English Bible with the Apocrypha* (New York: Oxford University Press, 1970), New Testament, p. 9.
86 Transcript, *Jaffree* v. *James*, 176–78.
87 *Jaffree by and through Ishmael Jaffree et al.* v. *Fob James et al.*, 544 F.Supp. 727 (1982), 727–31. *Lemon* v. *Kurtzman*.
88 *Jaffree* v. *James*, 730–31.
89 *Ibid.*, 729, 732.
90 *Ibid.*, 732–33. A functional definition of religion is advanced in James Davison Hunter, "Religious Freedom and the Challenge of Modern Pluralism," in *The Religious Liberty Clauses and the American Public Philosophy*, ed. by James Davison Hunter and Os Guiness (Washington: Brookings, 1990), 54–73; and Richard A. Baer Jr., "Why a Functional Definition of Religion Is Necessary If Justice Is to Be Achieved in Public Education," in *Curriculum, Religion, and Public Education: Conversations for an Enlarging Public Square*, ed. by James T. Sears and James C. Carper (New York: Columbia University Press, 1998), 105–15. "A doctrine is fully comprehensive when it covers all recognized values and virtues within one rather precisely articulated scheme of thought." John Rawls, *Political Liberalism* (New York: Columbia University Press, 1996), 175.

91 Williams interview by Rubin, 1; *Mobile Register*, August 10, 1982, p. A1; Joseph W. Newman, "Organized Prayer and Secular Humanism in Mobile, Alabama's, Public Schools," in *Curriculum as Social Psychoanalysis: The Significance of Place*, ed. by Joe L. Kincheloe and William F. Pinar (Albany: State University of New York Press, 1991), 52.
92 Newman, "Organized Prayer and Secular Humanism in Mobile, Alabama's, Public Schools," 52; *Mobile Press*, August 10, 1982, pp. 1, 4; *Montgomery Advertiser*, August 11, 1982, p. 13; Joseph Newman, "The Injunction," *Harbinger*, October 15, 1985, pp. 3, 9.
93 *Mobile Register*, August 11, 1982, p. B8; *Montgomery Advertiser*, August 10, 1982, p. 1.

2

The Moral Majority of Alabamians

LITIGATING THE GOOD NEWS

Returning to Alabama in 1980 after several years of living overseas, Tom Kotouc was a man on a Christian mission. Kotouc saw around him a society that demeaned religion by prohibiting its public expression. America seemed to him repressive compared with Lebanon and Jordan, where he had been working as a tax lawyer. The Lebanese people he met – in particular Muslims and Christians – had exchanged religious ideas freely, without inhibition. "Even though they were killing each other after hours," Kotouc later recalled, "they were still very respectful of each other's ideas." In this war-torn society, "it was not 'wrong' to become a Christian or 'wrong' to become a Muslim." Kotouc found that the people living in Lebanon neither hid their own religious values nor disdained the religious values of their neighbors, whatever those values might be. Far from being suppressed, religion, he observed, was openly embraced in Lebanese and Jordanian society. Back on his home terrain, he was startled by what seemed to him intolerance toward religious expression.[1]

His impressions reinforced a suspicion growing in him for some time. Americans, he feared, were losing the "freedom of religion similar to what I think we experienced in this country in times past." Surrounding him, he saw a society stripped of its characteristic openness and vigor toward expression of Bible-based morality. Kotouc believed that the 1960s – and especially the Supreme Court's decisions in *Engel* and *Schempp* – had ushered in an era of religious repression. Since the Sixties, Christians in the United States, he found, had routinely suffered indignities and faced intolerance in the public sphere, where inclusivity had given way to the silencing of Christianity.[2]

At the same time that the Supreme Court was acknowledging a wall of separation between church and state, young Kotouc was running headfirst into that wall. While attending college at the University of Nebraska, he and friends were forced to move their Bible study sessions from their dormitory rooms to a special house dedicated for religious study. This made no sense to Kotouc. "You can read *Playboy* and sit around and discuss that and have card games," he thought. "Why can't you discuss the Bible?" Later, at Harvard Law School, he remained plagued by the seeming inconsistency and injustice of that policy, concluding that the university's stance "was not a constitutionally tenable position." Three thousand miles away, at the University of California, Berkeley, students participating in the Free Speech Movement had recently won the right to express themselves publicly. Like those activists, Kotouc sought to ensure that "free access to ideas be available on a university campus."[3]

Years later, at the start of the 1980s, Kotouc moved to Montgomery and became friends with someone who worked directly for Governor Fob James. The friend suggested to the governor that Kotouc might be willing and able to help assist with the school prayer bill. Soon after, the governor asked Kotouc to serve as his legislative lobbyist for the reform of state education laws. Kotouc agreed. He was also given a special assignment: to represent a group of Alabama citizens seeking to intervene in the *Jaffree* case. Like him, his new clients advocated free access to and expression of religious ideas among students attending public schools. He later recalled that his clients "were very concerned about the fact that, if the petition of Jaffree was granted, then there would be no prayer, no religious exercise, in public school." Kotouc considered their aims reasonable, as they sought only to "coexist in the public arena" alongside people not committed to praying openly and regularly. Their objectives akin to his own, he agreed to coordinate their legal efforts.[4]

James played a key role in setting the intervenors into motion. His legal assistant, Kotouc, remained on the state payroll throughout the summer. According to the state comptroller's office, the state paid Kotouc for expenses rendered June through August, including the interviewing of witnesses in Mobile. These were intervenors' witnesses. They testified only for the intervenors and not for the state, despite being interviewed by a state employee. In August 1982, the governor's office was paying Kotouc to research and prepare the intervenors' case.

James tethered civil government to ambitious evangelical pursuits outside of official state business.[5]

Months later, during preparations for the *Jaffree* appeal, James asked Kotouc to join forces with Tom Parker, a lawyer in the state attorney general's office. Parker was the husband of the governor's niece, Dottie James Parker, whom Kotouc described as "very strong in her faith." Dottie Parker encouraged her husband to get involved. With Parker's entry into the case, Alabama's first family expanded its influence over the intervenors. The intervenors' efforts became a cornerstone in the governor's attack against the prohibition of prayer from public-school classrooms.[6]

Prior to Parker's involvement, Kotouc set about finding another lawyer to help him. Recognizing that the case would likely be tried in Mobile, Kotouc "began enquiring about what attorneys in Mobile would be good in trial." Fellow Christians referred him to Mobile lawyer Bob Sherling, who, according to Kotouc, "was very willing to help." The two counselors had complementary needs. In Sherling's words, Kotouc "had no experience in litigation" and needed someone with Sherling's courtroom skills, while he himself "had no experience in constitutional law" and "had never heard of secular humanism," so that he needed Kotouc's tutoring on the jurisprudence of church and state. As fortune would have it, "things fell into place together" and their joint effort "worked out well."[7]

Both attorneys described their investments in the case as much more than professional or financial. Kotouc saw his efforts as Christian advocacy. Defending the intervenors was a labor of love. If he were paid for his services, he maintained, then "that was great"; if not, then "we still were interested in volunteering our time." Sherling recounted that when Kotouc "called me up and asked me if I would be interested in getting involved in this case," he quickly "recognized it as a cause" and became eager to jump in. Through his engagement with the cause, Sherling "got more out of it than most other people."[8]

Kotouc, Sherling, and Parker epitomized what Stuart Scheingold and Austin Sarat refer to as "cause lawyers." Most lawyers consider their own moral convictions irrelevant to their legal practice, personal matters to be bracketed out and left at home. Most see themselves as neutral professionals who apply their expertise to whatever issues concern their clients. Others, however, buck this tendency. By prioritizing their own moral and political inclinations rather than an unbiased professionalism, cause lawyers turn their work into "a deeply moral or political activity, a kind of work that encourages pursuit of their vision of the right, the good, or the just. Cause lawyers have *something to believe in* and bring their beliefs to bear in their work lives." They serve first and foremost as advocates for public issues that they care about, and they choose clients who also pursue such causes. "Not only are they eager to take sides in social conflict and to identify themselves with the sides they take, but they are determined to construct their legal practice around this taking of sides."[9]

Until the late 1970s, Christian conservatives rarely performed such legal advocacy. Civil-rights lawyering had, to them, indicated society's state of decline. Many had lamented that Americans in general had grown enamored with their own autonomy as individuals – abandoning family, church, and country – and that political lawyering bore some culpability. Yet, as the Christian Right took stock of its own relative lack of success in advancing political causes, it began to consider the benefits of bringing lawsuits. Slowly, it recognized that, by using the courts, it could further its own goals. Leveraging liberals' strategies for conservative purposes came to make sense.[10]

In the late 1970s, religious legal advocacy groups emerged. Although these organizations championed "individual freedom," their conception differed significantly from how liberals understood the idea. Christian-conservative legal activists appropriated the discourse of rights and set about to secure religious rights by using strategies like those used by African Americans, women, and other constituencies seeking progressive reform. Yet they continued to oppose what they considered the secularist concept of individual moral autonomy, and they remained committed to Christianizing government, law, and society. Their right to worship and evangelize openly rested, as they saw it, not on civil law, but on God's law – thus making their commitment to civil liberties and civil rights problematic. They touted the virtue of religious pluralism, but only as a political strategy. As evangelicals began to engage in political activism, some became willing to enter the courts and assert their rights to worship publicly, as Christians, alongside citizens acting on the basis of non-Christian identities. The United States may have been a nation populated mostly by citizens of Christian heritage, but for these evangelicals, their rights needed to be reclaimed from the hostile forces who exercised political power.[11]

Waging court battles became, in their eyes, a necessary evil. The intellectual climate among Christian conservatives shifted, prompting many to think of cause lawyering as a religious calling. They were inspired by the writing of Francis Schaeffer, who exhorted Christian lawyers to emulate their liberal counterparts, but to pursue the opposite goal of Christianizing the law. Beginning in 1979, Christian book companies published many more books on church-state law than during the preceding decades. Evangelical legal organizations formed and issued amicus briefs in Supreme Court cases addressing education and abortion. According to Kevin den Dulk, "intellectuals and other elites within the broader world of evangelicalism became convinced that 'secular forces' must be confronted in terms of a theology of activist politics." Motivated by those writers, numbers of evangelical lawyers experienced a "calling to law."[12]

Litigation – and politics in general – became, for these Christians, a matter of protecting an imperiled way of life. Christianity, they believed, was being held hostage by liberal judges who blithely disregarded the will of the Christian majority. Perhaps those judges' minds could be changed. A cadre of evangelical cause lawyers began to reverse a tradition of passivity in the legal arena. They entered courtrooms and spurred litigation efforts to secure individual rights – the rights of individuals to live in accordance with and to express traditional religious precepts.[13]

The Christian Right's ambivalence toward the federal courts was demonstrated by James and the group he set in motion. While continuing to decry the effects of "judicial activism," he and the intervenors employed the same methods used by church-state separationists: they went to court. The intervenors staked claims to their civil rights by inserting themselves into a trial in which they were not directly implicated. They did not need to get involved in *Jaffree.* Their involvement surprised all the other parties, including the Mobile school board. To be sure, their posture was defensive insofar as they looked to protect an age-old practice, school prayer. Still, they seized a political opportunity and went on the attack. Now was the era of asserting one's constitutional rights, and the moment had arrived for religious conservatives to assert theirs. The intervenors, deliberately and determinedly, asserted a Christian influence on constitutional politics.

Sherling's work on the group's behalf epitomized cause lawyering. Enthusiastically, he placed his skills as a litigator at the service of his new clients, whose attempt to secure their rights as Christians attracted him on a personal level. Sherling understood his professional work as a product of his evangelicalism. "If I decide that I don't want to do something or I do want to do something, it's going to be based on my interpretation of scripture. That's the only thing that I have to order my life on." From that flowed his eagerness to help parents secure for their children a public-school environment that was, at the very least, not corrosive to their lives as Christians. The secularization of the classroom infringed, he believed, on the rights of Christians such as himself to raise children not brainwashed by the secular state. Beyond offering the intervenors his professional services, Sherling became an important member of the group, one who contributed skills that the group badly needed and highly valued.[14]

Like Sherling, Kotouc was determined that his child be able to maintain her moral compass within the public-school environment. Kotouc cared about his clients and their religious rights. His resolve to rectify their marginalization intensified during his involvement with the Rutherford Institute, a conservative Christian think tank concerned with legal issues. Kotouc believed that the secular classroom, far from honoring students of all religious orientations, discriminated against those who believed in moral absolutes – even though the Constitution entitled them, always and everywhere, to speak their conscience. Christian teachers were likewise entitled. And Christian parents deserved not to be undermined by having their children reprogrammed by the secular-humanist schools. Kotouc understood himself first and foremost as a Christian obligated to bear witness for Christ. Working on the *Jaffree* case gave him an opportunity to serve a cause not only bigger than his career but bigger than the law itself.[15]

Sherling and Kotouc recognized "the potential of the law, as interpreted by judges, to promote a political and moral vision for America that would persist long after the elected officials who championed those same views left office." Judicial activism, they saw, could cut in a variety of directions and yield opportunities to all who availed themselves of it. The intervenors' attorneys were the new face of cause lawyering, "young, politically engaged, and unfettered by evangelicalism's traditional hostility to book learning." They were as convinced of their cause and prepared to argue in its behalf as were Jaffree and Ronnie Williams.[16]

ASSEMBLING GOD'S ARMY

Kotouc's first recruit was a friend from church, Doug Smith, whose name would appear atop the motion to intervene. A teacher of eighth-grade science and a serious-minded evangelical concerned about children's moral education, Smith was an ideal candidate to join the intervenors and testify at trial. He knew little about the governor's prayer law or Jaffree's complaint until Kotouc filled him in. He and his daughter quickly signed on. Kotouc called Smith "a particularly fascinating person for me to work with." Besides finding him "extremely articulate," Kotouc appreciated the difficulty that Smith encountered being a science teacher and a devout Christian. "He was always coming . . . up against the need to teach two perspectives rather than just one if he was going to be able to protect the Christian perspective." Kotouc correctly surmised that Smith felt strongly enough to join the cause.[17]

The greatest enthusiasm for the intervenors' cause came from down in Mobile, site of the original conflict. Mobile's religious temperament disposed its residents to resent and resist Jaffree. Traditionally, it had been a tolerant city with a large Catholic population and a yearly Mardi Gras celebration, but over recent decades its character had changed. During World War II, Mobile's recently rebuilt ports and transportation routes made it an ideal site for the defense-related manufacturing plants that the federal government built there. Poor whites and blacks poured in to work at those plants. The city's population grew 64 percent between 1940 and 1944. This huge sudden growth left Mobile without adequate public schools, housing, and other services and added to the stress of depression and war. The poor sharecroppers who arrived brought with them a Manichean, fundamentalist worldview that, according to Wayne Flynt, transformed Mobile "from the state's most culturally diverse and tolerant city to a center of racial and religious conflict." George Wallace's strident antiliberalism found greater support in Mobile than in any other Alabama city. Jaffree's actions were bound to be seen there as a threat to a set way of living.[18]

According to Joseph Newman, the 1980s New Right "found especially fertile ground in Mobile." Given Jaffree's propensity toward playing the role of outsider and agitator, and given Mobile's identity as a "place under attack," bitter conflict was inevitable. Local newspapers and television stations routinely identified Jaffree as an agnostic and a Muslim, marking him as alien and threatening. Jaffree quickly became the ultimate "other" in Mobile's distinctively conservative Christian culture. An unabashed freethinker and religious skeptic, Jaffree violated his neighbors' desire to maintain a homogeneous and stable environment adhering to a fundamentalist understanding of Christianity.[19]

It didn't take long for Mobilians to organize in resistance to Jaffree. One of the people whom Sherling approached was Sue Webster, who had formerly attended Sherling's church. Webster and her husband John began telling friends about the intervenors' plans and became two of the group's key organizers. Word quickly spread among members of the Websters' current congregation, Cottage Hill Baptist Church. With more than 8,000 members, Cottage Hill was one of Alabama's two largest Baptist churches. Built in 1944, in the throes of the city's demographic shift, the church came to emblemize conservative Protestantism in post–World War II Mobile. In 1970, church members constructed an elaborate new building featuring a dome roof and a "sanctuary in the round" that seated more than 1,600 worshipers and stood out as the largest church sanctuary on the Gulf Coast. Cottage Hill's size, resources, location atop one of the city's highest elevations, and televised weekly services made the church "the bright shining beacon light of conservative Christianity" in Mobile. Its zealous congregants took great interest in the *Jaffree* case, and several joined the Websters in lending assistance to Sherling and Kotouc. By September, a groundswell of support built up throughout the city, with Cottage Hill the epicenter of the movement to contest Jaffree's actions.[20]

No intervenor showed greater zeal than Fred Wolfe, pastor of Cottage Hill. Wolfe arrived at the church in 1972 having already established himself as a strong theological conservative. Between 1979 and 1985, when fundamentalists broke off from moderates within the Southern Baptist Convention (SBC) and seized control over the denomination, Wolfe became one of the leading spokesmen for the fundamentalists. The former University of South Carolina football star carved out a name for himself by preaching Biblical inerrancy, denouncing abortion, and condemning the so-called debauchery associated with Mobile's annual Mardi Gras celebration. Articulate and charismatic, Wolfe attained a large, faithful following among Mobile Christians.[21]

Wolfe assumed a leadership role in the resistance to Jaffree. Along with Pastor Paul McHenry, Wolfe attempted to convince Mobilians that if Jaffree were to win his suit, their own religious freedom would be suppressed. "The Constitution," he maintained, "provided freedom of religion, not freedom from religion." He charged that Jaffree, like other proponents of church-state separation, was aiming to complete a process already under way: the removal of God from every inch of public life. This, according to Wolfe, was taking place even in Mobile, where the vast majority of citizens wanted to pray openly to God. "If you're not careful," he warned, "you protect the rights of the minority to the exclusion of the majority." The intervenors' campaign gave Wolfe the "chance to be personally involved" in protecting the Christian majority's "freedom of public expression."[22]

Wolfe's and McHenry's testimony at the August 1982 injunction hearing intensified their ardor. Soon after, they and several other local ministers met in Mobile and scheduled a rally for September 23. To drum up support, the group named a steering committee comprised of three members: Wolfe, McHenry, and Samuel Phillips, pastor of Bay View Church. The steering committee was charged with setting up a Religious Freedom Defense Fund, which would raise money to defray the intervenors' legal expenses.[23]

Reiterating the intervenors' arguments at the injunction hearing, McHenry insisted that Christian students and teachers be guaranteed the right to express their authentic selves in the classroom. He advocated, not for censorship, but for a robust and inclusive religious atmosphere. McHenry maintained that he and his allies were merely "trying to keep people from being inhibited from expressing themselves in a reasonable manner." The intervenors did not wish to establish "mini churches" inside the classroom, he insisted; what they wanted was to ensure that teachers and students be permitted to think and speak from their own, genuine perspective. Adults and children alike needed not "to be so restrained they can't answer questions from a [Christian] world and life view."[24]

During a September 17 news conference at Cottage Hill, Wolfe and McHenry exhorted local Christians to join this fight to defend their liberties. Money donated would enable the intervenors to carry the fight "all the way to the Supreme Court if necessary." The issue at hand, Wolfe warned, went "far beyond the matter of voluntary prayer." Were Jaffree successful, "then all mention of God will be stopped in Mobile County public schools." McHenry decried that the lawsuit "infringes on our rights as individuals." It now fell to the intervenors to make sure that Christians "be able to express their religious and cultural heritage without being sued."[25]

Between 2,500 and 3,000 people packed into Cottage Hill Baptist Church on September 23. The crowd learned from Wolfe and McHenry that the constitutional rights of Christians were under attack by a liberal culture and a liberal federal judiciary. And those, in turn, were dominated by the religion of secular humanism. The crowd was far too big for the church auditorium; many people sat in the chapel, where they watched the program on a large screen. Julia Green, Charlene Boyd, and Pixie Alexander – the schoolteachers named in Jaffree's complaint – were in attendance and received a long standing ovation.[26]

Wolfe and McHenry explained to the eager throng why it behooved them to get involved. While stressing that the lawsuit imperiled free religious exercise, the speakers expressed even greater concern about its potential to establish a state religion. They reiterated Sherling's claim that the Constitution's proscription against the establishment of religion ought to extend to "secular humanism," a nontheistic worldview that functioned as a religion just as much as did Christianity. Wolfe referred to the Supreme Court's 1961 *Torcaso* v. *Watkins* decision, which, he explained, "specifically defined secular humanism as a religion equivalent to theistic and other non-theistic religions." McHenry pointed out that the Court's *Engel* ruling, issued the following year, was "unequal in the application of the law" because it considered only Christian establishments of religion and not humanistic ones. To function adequately, *Engel* needed to be applied equitably and consistently.[27]

Wolfe ended by beseeching the crowd to defend the rights of Christians – to go "all the way to the Supreme Court if necessary." He called for volunteers to read textbooks being used in Mobile schools in order to find passages proselytizing the religion of secular humanism. Information gathered would be used in the upcoming trial. The pastors implored those in attendance to sign a petition pledging their support to the intervenors. Almost fourteen thousand dollars was collected at the rally. Three hundred and twenty-three people signed the petition that night, with another three hundred adding their names by the time the trial began.[28]

Exhibiting the Manichean ideology described by Flynt, the intervenors portrayed the absence of devotional expression as implying its polar opposite – atheism. Not to worship God openly was to worship all that was not God. Their stark moral dualism rendered them unable and unwilling to compromise with citizens advancing alternative ideologies. By challenging devotional exercises in the classroom, Jaffree had painted himself as more than just "alien" or "other" in the eyes of Cottage Hill members and most other Mobilians. According to Jaffree's lawyer, Williams, "they saw Jaffree as the Devil" and Williams himself as "somebody who's representing the Devil."[29]

The intervenors' sense of their own moral superiority was bolstered by their standing as religious majority. As Jaffree was irregular so they were normal. Their schools belonged to them, and they deserved to run them however they, the majority, saw fit. It was their right. Jaffree may have wrapped himself in "the Constitution['s] laws to protect minorities," but Wolfe and the intervenors could not have understood the First Amendment more differently. "I don't think it was the intent of the Constitution to take away the rights of the majority to ensure the rights of the minority," Wolfe insisted. "When you are in a minority faith," he opined, "you must accept the reality that religious majorities may speak more audibly than you and drown out your voice." The minority had simply to "sit there and listen." Mobile's moral majority would not sit by idly while its civil rights were usurped by a tiny, alien minority.[30]

THE LOCAL CZAR OF CLASSROOM MORALITY

Dan Alexander, president of the Mobile County Board of School Commissioners, likewise dug in his heels to defend Mobile's Christian majority from the intruding infidel. One of the city's most controversial public figures, Alexander seized upon the *Jaffree* case and incorporated it into his arsenal of hot-button issues. An ambitious lawyer, Alexander had been advocating for right-wing causes with zeal since he joined the board in 1974. Defending schoolchildren's right to pray became, for him, yet another opportunity for public provocation. Alexander added his loud voice to the chorus rising against Jaffree and in support of "the people."[31]

Alexander and fellow board candidate Ruth Drago had won election in 1974 running as populists, representatives of Mobile's white lower-middle class trying to unseat the city's traditional business elite. Alexander modeled himself on the legendary Huey Long of Louisiana. He was brash and egotistical, an outspoken politician on a school board traditionally marked by civility. To maintain his base of support among "ordinary" Mobilians, he battled against the professional teachers' associations, the federal courts, and the board's first two black commissioners, elected in 1978. "Right from the start," writes Richard Pride, Alexander "wanted the board, and particularly him, to have direct power over the schools and what was done in them." In so doing Alexander became a renegade. "Over time, he challenged the independent authority of superintendents, senior staff, and principals, and he threatened the security of teachers." By the end of his reign in 1983, Alexander's exploits had made him the most notorious local figure.[32]

Alexander's aggressive promotion of schoolteacher competency testing got him into hot water with educators' associations; it also enraged the board's two black commissioners, Robert Gilliard and Norman Cox, and African Americans throughout the county, who saw him as determined to purge the schools of black teachers (who, presumably, might score lower on such tests). Alexander framed the issue as a nonracial matter. He argued that he was responding to parents' concerns that their children were being taught by underqualified teachers. Alexander emphasized merit, contending that weak teachers, regardless of race, ought not be rewarded for their incompetence. His meritocratic vision resonated with many white Mobilians, who believed competency testing would spur good old-fashioned competition favorable to whites.[33]

Typical of New Right politicians, Alexander accused educational elites of ignoring the needs and values of ordinary, hardworking people and imposing their own liberal agendas on vulnerable students. Those who made education policy, he charged, were a tiny minority whose vision conflicted with the values held by the majority of citizens – the same majority whose tax dollars paid for the public schools. On educational matters, "no one was out there speaking for the average taxpayer or parents." The professional educators who ran the National Education Association and the U.S. Department of Education became, in Alexander's public pronouncements, corrupt, sinister forces out to destroy American society.[34]

In September 1979, Alexander formed the Taxpayers' Education Lobby (TEL), whose mandate was to wrest control over public education away from teachers and place it in the hands of local citizens. Alexander convinced prominent political operative Richard Viguerie that TEL had a vital mission to execute. Viguerie introduced his new associate to Paul Weyrich, Howard Phillips, and people at the Heritage Foundation – all central players in the New Right. TEL's newsletter was incorporated into Viguerie's far-reaching direct-mail empire. Alexander soon changed the organization's name to Save Our Schools (SOS), opened a DC office, and purportedly attracted more than 50,000 members and contributors. He became a national political player, all the while advancing an anti-elitist vision of education reform.[35]

Alexander's conservative allies broadened his political agenda and gave him new language to explain his worldview. By summer 1982, Alexander was blaming secular humanism for the public schools' supposed failure. To combat America's "permissive and mobile society," he called on schools to inculcate "traditional American values which we have gotten away from like love of God, neighborhood and country." SOS followed its attack on the Department of Education by urging public schools to facilitate prayer, teach the biblical account of human origins, and emphasize "traditional values about the differences between men and women." Alexander began appearing regularly on cable television. The "Moral Majority Report" radio program featured a piece on SOS. Most notably, Alexander was invited to meet with President Reagan and give a speech on the Capitol Mall on National Prayer Day in May 1982.[36]

It is possible to dismiss Alexander's "moral" turn as opportunism, and to conclude that religious conservatives joined with him in a marriage of convenience. By reckoning with George Lakoff's conception of conservative worldview, we can reach a different conclusion: that the full package of New Right positions fit squarely together, and that Alexander's education agenda was a perfect match with his allies' wider vision. Lakoff sees conflicting conservative and liberal worldviews at the heart of American politics. Each worldview advances a moral interpretation of what education, economics, politics, religion, and family relations ought to be. Lakoff finds, at the center of conservatives' worldview, a "strict father" Christianity stressing self-discipline and self-reliance. According to this worldview, everyone's interests are protected when moral order is preserved, and moral order is preserved only when children grow into economically self-reliant, upright adults. Conservatives believe that public education tends to produce "postmodern humanists who deny the existence of any absolute values" and threaten the moral order.[37]

To fortify the moral order it considers as so vulnerable, the conservative worldview embraces a version of Christianity that prioritizes the development of moral character, self-discipline, and the ability to function well in a hierarchy. This religious impulse is inherently political. As Lakoff writes, "Strict Father Christianity requires that the world be competitive and survival difficult if the right kind of people (strong people) are to be produced and rewarded." The Strict Father Christian believes that society cannot afford to raise children unable to thrive on their own, abide by established moral norms, submit to rightful authority, and compete economically. If our government and schools do not produce such citizens, then society's moral order – the common good – becomes imperiled. Strict Father Christianity depends on conservatively oriented public institutions, and such institutions depend on Strict Father Christianity.[38]

Alexander's politics derived from this conservative worldview. Affirmative action and lax educational standards were bad, Alexander argued, because they rewarded laziness and mediocrity, failed to inculcate self-discipline, eviscerated moral character, weakened economic competition, and threatened the public good. Alexander adopted an explicitly Christian rhetoric because it meshed with his political values, not because New Right bigwigs in DC changed his thinking. Indeed, Alexander and other local operatives throughout America anticipated the broad conservative ideology so successfully articulated by Reagan. The Mobile conflict enabled Alexander to express what he already believed.[39]

Alexander's involvement in the conflict began in earnest on July 28, 1982. At the school board meeting that evening, he urged the other commissioners to throw their full support behind the teachers and principals in charge of Jaffree's children. Once again, Alexander argued that the will of the popular majority ought to be sovereign. Taxpayers, he insisted, needed to speak with "one unified single voice." Diversity was divisive; dissenters had no right to influence policy. "We're a nation founded under one God, and the majority of us believe it," he told television reporters. "The majority has always ruled in this country," and they would continue to rule Mobile schools. Alexander implored that children in a classroom not "be kept from praying" simply "because there might be one atheist in that class." Like the intervenors, Alexander positioned himself as a defender of Mobile's God-fearing majority.[40]

At the July 28 meeting, the board voted to support the teachers and principals being challenged by Jaffree. Two weeks later, it considered whether to adopt a formal policy regarding classroom prayer. Board attorney Robert Campbell urged caution, emphasizing that the board historically had remained neutral regarding religion in the schools. If the board were now to adopt a policy on the matter, Campbell maintained, it would abandon its neutrality. And that would weaken its position in court. Campbell convinced board members not to pass a formal school prayer policy, in order to avoid "entangling" the public schools with religion.[41]

The school board's purported neutrality failed to constrain Alexander, who flooded the airwaves and plastered the newspapers with declarations trumpeting the right of students and teachers to pray in school. Alexander appeared nationally on "Crossfire" and "The Charlie Rose Show." On "The Last Word," an ABC news program, he appeared with Williams and John East, a freshman U.S. senator from North Carolina and protégé of Jesse Helms. He even debated Jaffree on television and radio. Almost single-handedly, Alexander turned the Jaffree case into a national story.[42]

The issue allowed Alexander to blur the lines between his positions in SOS and on the school board. He marshaled financial support for the board's legal efforts by featuring stories about the *Jaffree* case in the SOS newsletter, which Viguerie was now circulating through his mailing list of 100,000. At the same time, Alexander raised funds for SOS by promoting his actions as Mobile school board president. In its newsletter, SOS puffed *Jaffree* as "the best test case in the country on this issue." A consummate politician, he promoted his career through the case and bolstered the board's legal resources through his increased personal connections.[43]

Alexander spoke directly to Mobile schoolteachers at the annual teachers' meeting on August 30. "Do whatever you have been doing in the past," he promised teachers, "and you will have the support of the board." Although many of them assumed that Hand's injunction applied to all religious activities, Alexander insisted that this was not the judge's intent at all. In telling them to carry on as usual, Alexander claimed actually to be implementing the judge's instructions. "The status quo is obviously what the court meant to maintain," Alexander maintained, and, if teachers changed their practices, then that would "undo" the status quo. Hand's order prohibited only the 1981 and 1982 Alabama prayer laws and the "God is Good" jingle; it made no reference at all to prayer "in general" and thereby sanctioned the vast majority of practices being conducted in the schools.[44]

Alexander's statements outraged Jaffree, who felt that the school board president was attempting to circumvent the ruling. The day after Alexander issued his instructions, Jaffree and Williams filed a motion asking Hand to hold him in contempt of court. Hand had clearly enjoined all agents and servants of the state and local boards of education from conducting voluntary prayer in the classroom, the plaintiffs' motion stated. By encouraging teachers to disregard the injunction, Alexander was "mak[ing] a mockery of this court." He was insulting the court and all parties to the trial.[45]

Unfortunately for Jaffree, Hand did not see Alexander's actions that way. During a half-hour contempt hearing on September 17, Alexander claimed to have understood the injunction as merely upholding the status quo, and to have adhered to that order. Jaffree countered by accusing Alexander of failing to give teachers clear and appropriate directions for abiding by the judge's order. Indeed, Jaffree said, Alexander had flouted the order. Jaffree's argument failed to persuade Hand, who did not find, in Alexander's comments, contempt of court. Hand ruled quickly and without much comment. Jaffree's concerns once again fell on deaf ears.[46]

Issuing public declarations on the constitutionality and morality of school prayer would be Alexander's most significant accomplishment. His reign on the Mobile school board would end in a little more than a year. In September 1984, he would lose in his bid to win a seat in Congress; in December 1986, he would be convicted of extorting kickbacks on school-related contracts and would spend four years in prison. Although he briefly resurrected his political career in Washington, DC after his release, he soon drifted into political obscurity. Nevertheless, for ten years Alexander exerted more influence over public-school policy – and perhaps over public life – than anyone else in Mobile. His campaign to preserve individual achievement, conservative Christian morality, and the rights of the popular majority resonated powerfully with many people. The conservative majoritarianism that Alexander tapped into ran deeply through Mobile's political culture. It made it all but inevitable that, when Jaffree issued his complaint, his neighbors would oppose him bitterly.[47]

THE PEOPLE'S CHAMPION AGAINST JUDICIAL TYRANNY

Alexander wasn't the only public figure turning *Jaffree* into a personal crusade. Nor was he the only official brought before Judge Hand on contempt charges. Governor James – creator of the Alabama prayer statutes, catalyst for the intervenors – rode the case as his prize political issue. No one reflected the Christian Right's ambivalence toward the courts as thoroughly as the governor. While instructing Kotouc to organize a group to intervene voluntarily in the case – to go to court and invoke their constitutional rights as a religious majority – James insisted that the federal courts lacked the jurisdiction to overturn his prayer laws or regulate the religious practices of public-school teachers and students. The governor denounced the courts even as he used them. From July 1982 through January 1983, he remained in the news, encouraging citizens to resist the heathen federal courts and urging the Supreme Court to repent its wicked ways.

Immediately after learning of Hand's August 9 injunction, an aide to the governor called the ruling "the beginning of the court challenge [James] was looking for." Nothing would stop the governor from taking this matter all the way to the U.S. Supreme Court, James promised. When the Court ruled against school prayer in 1962, he insisted, it "overrode 180 years of legal precedent." Since then, the federal courts had "played with loopholes and technicalities" instead of trying to correct *Engel.* The governor vowed to do better and to do it now. He would bring Hand's errant ruling to the attention of the Court and permit the justices, at long last, to rectify the egregious mistake committed twenty years earlier.[48]

What made James believe that he could convince the justices to invalidate twenty years of case law? On what pretense could he demand the Court's attention? *Jaffree* hadn't even gone to trial yet, much less been appealed in Circuit Court. One newspaper concluded that, "with only four months remaining in office, James apparently surmised that the standard appellate process would not serve his political needs," since an opinion coming out of that process "would likely come long after James had lost his political base." Perhaps his inspiration to act precipitously came in a letter from former Justice Department lawyer Hermine Meyer, who saw an opportunity to demonstrate, once and for all, that the courts had gotten it wrong for the last twenty years. Surely he was influenced by his son, Fob James III, who sought to issue "an unabashed challenge to the Supreme Court's 1962 and 1963 school prayer decisions." So moved, the governor hired Meyer to write a petition for a writ of mandamus that, he hoped, would compel the Court to overturn Hand's injunction as well as the Court's own *Engel* and *Schempp* rulings. The governor planned, in two days, to arrive at the Supreme Court and file his petition, to "make the most fundamental legal challenge in this century to the Supreme Court's unconstitutional usurpations of power over the states and the people." He hoped that the Court would "correct immediately its own unconstitutional usurpation of power" and order Hand "to dismiss the present case and to never again exercise jurisdiction in a case involving school prayer in Alabama." Until that happened, James declared, "I will not consider myself bound by the lower court decree."[49]

The governor arrived in Washington, DC, on September 14, 1982, with his wife, son, bodyguard, and petition. His brief was thorough and ambitious. It claimed that the Constitution's framers had intended the Establishment Clause as a prohibition against the creation of a national church, not against any mention of religion in public institutions. Had the *Engel* and *Schempp* Courts looked closely at the history and language of the First Amendment, they would have recognized this fact. The petition looked selectively at Supreme Court rulings commenting on the doctrine of incorporation – the notion that the Fourteenth Amendment was intended to incorporate the liberties guaranteed in the Bill of Rights and apply them to the individual states. In the Court's own case law, James contended, "there is no constitutional provision which has made the religious clause of the First Amendment applicable to the States." The governor had virtually nothing to say about *Gitlow* v. *New York* or *Cantwell* v. *Connecticut* and completely ignored *Everson* v. *Board of Education* – three of the most relevant cases. Had the petition addressed those opinions, it probably would have attributed them, as it attributed *Engel* and *Schempp*, to an overzealous Court bent on "extending federal jurisdiction over powers reserved to the States in order to bring them under federal control."[50]

James portrayed himself as a mouthpiece for the people's grievances against the elitist Court. With his clean-cut, good-ole-boy, political-outsider image, James looked the part. Brimming with populist indignation, he warned the federal judiciary that Americans were not happy. "The people have been prevented from making their own laws," his petition complained. They had "lost control over their local affairs, their schools, their children and their families." Fortunately, "they ha[d] begun to recognize that this prohibition" against school prayer came "from the judges, not from the Constitution." Feeling violated by their own servants, the people had "begun to ask why judges whom they ha[d] not elected [we]re permitted to make the laws for them." Americans would not passively surrender their democratic government, as evidenced by statutes such as the Alabama prayer laws. The governor put the justices on notice. "The many efforts all through the land to resurrect prayers in the public schools reflect the growing skepticism of the American people with this Court." All was not lost, however. With his petition, James now offered the justices a chance to restore popular sovereignty.[51]

James invited one hundred reporters to a ten o'clock news conference on the morning of his arrival. His first stop, however, was the Supreme Court, to submit his petition to the Court clerk. To the governor's dismay, the clerk refused to accept the document. The courts had a well-established appellate process, it turned out. James would first have to obtain either a ruling from the Eleventh Circuit Court in Atlanta or a directive from the Supreme Court instructing the clerk to accept the petition. James then scampered off for his press conference, where he explained to reporters that he had been detained by excess paperwork. He laid out for reporters the contents of his petition and then issued his own personal order against Hand's injunction. "I am today encouraging all Alabama school officials, as well as the people of Alabama," he declared, "to stand on their constitutional rights, to ignore this federal court injunction, and to proceed with prayer in the classroom, with blessings at mealtimes, and with any other heartfelt prayer which the citizens of Alabama may wish to say." James dared the courts to fine him. Then, he and his son were off again, back to confront their other nemesis, the Supreme Court clerk.[52]

A few reporters caught word of the roadblock James had encountered and followed him back to the courthouse. Again he tried to submit his petition; again the clerk refused to accept it. James insisted that he had met all the requirements; the clerk assured him that he had not. James pulled out his bound copy of the "Rules of the Supreme Court of the United States" and began reading it to the clerk, who patiently explained that the clerk's role – unwritten but well established through custom – was to use his discretion to screen petitioners and instruct them on the procedures they needed to follow. He reiterated that the governor was free to submit a motion asking the justices to direct him to accept the petition, although no such motion had ever been submitted. Fob James III huffed, "I can't believe this," and stomped out of the room, only to return a moment later to warn his father, "It's a trap. They're trying to evade the issue. They're trying to dismiss this issue on a technicality." The governor and his son held court with reporters outside the clerk's office. "When the justices learn what happened," the younger James scolded, "I would hope they would send us an apology."[53]

Word of James's audacity quickly reached Mobile, where an aghast Jaffree instructed Williams to ask Hand to hold the governor in contempt of court. Later that afternoon – the same day on which the governor made his remarks – Williams filed a motion at the District Court in Mobile, charging James with "expressly, publicly and unequivocally violating" Hand's injunction. The motion characterized James's comments as "flagrantly contemptuous." It alleged that the governor had used "the full weight, power, and prestige of his office to urge and encourage school officials, teachers and others to completely disregard the [injunction's] express provisions." Such demagoguery constituted, if anything, an even "more blatant example of contempt than [that] of Alexander."[54]

Returning home, James continued to paint himself as the people's defender against judicial tyranny. Since the *Engel* ruling in 1962, he complained, the "federal courts ha[d] frustrated the efforts of school board members, legislators, and other state officials trying to find a legal way to allow teachers and students to say a blessing, pray to God, or have Bible reading while at school." At the same time, the governor held out an olive branch to the federal judge whom he held most responsible for frustrating the will of Alabamians. Perhaps, James suggested, Hand was as much a victim of the system as were the American people. Perhaps Hand had been forced, against his will, to issue the injunction. After all, Hand had noted that the First Amendment barred the establishment of religions such as atheism, socialism, and materialism. The governor surmised that Hand was "caught in a conflict between following the Supreme Court's ruling of 1962 ... and his conscience." All along, James had refused to acknowledge the silver lining surrounding the injunction ruling. Now, faced with contempt charges, he portrayed his erstwhile adversary as an ally.[55]

With *Jaffree* v. *Board* scheduled to begin in ten days, Hand held a hearing on November 5 to determine whether he would bring the governor up on contempt charges. At the hearing's start, Hand told James that he need not remain in attendance. The governor left the hearing. His attorney assured the judge that "Governor James has taken heart from what you said in your Aug. 9 order" and that he in no way intended to defy the court. Williams protested that James had never shown even one bit of remorse for his statements. After playing a videotape of the September 14 news conference, the judge admitted that the governor "was less than circumspect in what he did." Still, he insisted, James's remarks did not warrant censure. "Only in the case of raw disregard should federal courts interfere with state authority," Hand told the court. The governor's comments warranted prudence, not vigilance. And prudence required that he "not ... slap the governor over the head with this." Hand dismissed the charges.[56]

Williams expressed dismay and "total disappointment" with Hand's decision. Jaffree claimed to be shocked. The governor dared the judge to stop him, and the judge did nothing. It now became clear to Jaffree "that Judge Hand wasn't serious about the enforceability of his [injunction]." The one person who had seemed like Jaffree's single ray of hope in this entire saga now appeared to be just another brick in the wall against which Jaffree was banging his head. Meanwhile, the governor's attorney called the decision "splendid." And Hand revealed a bit more of his true intentions when he wondered whether "the governor read the [injunction] opinion before he made the statements that he did."[57]

RACE, RELIGION, AND THE WILL OF THE LOCAL MAJORITY

Jaffree and Williams continued to believe that the clear validity of their claims would spark broad public support for their position. They expected at least some local people to recognize that the state and county had denied the Jaffree family its rights as a religious minority, and that nothing deserved people's full support as much as did the efforts of law-abiding citizens standing up for their constitutional rights. Jaffree and Williams felt confident that many Mobilians – especially black Mobilians – would appreciate and honor the plaintiffs' effort to compel government not to tread on a member of a politically powerless group. By speaking out as a besieged minority, Jaffree believed, he was staking out a legal identity that would resonate with others who saw their own plight in similar terms.

Jaffree still considered the case clear cut and expected to win it squarely on its merits. Relevant case law promised all-but-certain victory, as "there was nothing to distinguish the present case from the evils to be avoided as articulated in *Engel.*" All along – from his correspondence with school administrators and teachers, continuing through his courtroom testimony – Jaffree maintained that Court precedent certified the constitutional correctness of his position. The First Amendment guaranteed his right to spare his children the compulsive effects of classroom prayer. Surely, at least some observers of the case would recognize the validity of his stance, even (or especially) if the local school system and the state legislature had not.[58]

Jaffree and Williams were emboldened by Hand's injunction order, which underscored the importance of honoring Supreme Court rulings. "The modern trend of handling matters on a case-by-case basis," the judge proclaimed, was "destructive of the judicial system and preclude[d] the citizens of this country from their right to know what the law is and how to follow consistent patterns of conduct in their day-to-day activities." Because he had sworn "an oath before God that he would uphold the laws of the United States," he was now "obligated to follow the decision law on this sensitive question." Hand's declared commitment to *stare decisis*, or Supreme Court precedent, echoed Williams's personal conviction that democracy in America rested with the Court's ultimate legal authority. Success at trial seemed to await the plaintiffs.[59]

For Jaffree, the unquestionable rightness of his position derived from more than its conformity with case law. Spoken, organized prayer needed to be kept out of the public schools, he believed, because constitutional principles required it. Even people with unpopular views were entitled to fundamental rights and liberties. "Enacted in the Constitution are laws to protect minorities, to protect the individuals," he insisted. Central to the American dream was a promise to religious dissenters that government shall not promote religion. As Jaffree understood it, his lawsuit aimed only to make good on that promise. By preserving the rights of religious minorities, he was protecting the interests of all citizens, because free government required universal religious freedom. His suit was necessary for "preserving the integrity of the Constitution."[60]

By speaking out as a minority, Jaffree and Williams longed in particular to attract Mobile's African American community. They hoped that African Americans might sympathize if they framed the issue as one in which the civil rights of minorities were once again being frustrated by the dominant, white legal regime. "This is what the civil rights movement was all about," Williams would tell black audiences. "The same Constitution, the same freedoms that Jaffree is talking about, are the freedoms you were talking about when you were seeking ... fair housing, voting, equal treatment on the jobs." If black Mobilians could be persuaded that the *Jaffree* case was yet another scene in a long-running battle to protect minority rights, perhaps they would line up behind the two black attorneys.[61]

Jaffree tried to reach this same audience with a letter to the editor of the *New Times*, a weekly newspaper serving Mobile's African American community. He portrayed his struggle as typical of the black struggle in white America. "This case," he argued, "is all about what Black people in this country are all about – minority right versus majority might. We, as a minority, have often sought the protection of the Constitution when our rights were being threatened by the White, insensitive majority. I did no less." Whereas a letter he wrote to the *Mobile Press Register* connected minority rights to the interests of all citizens, his letter to the *New Times* tied them specifically to the interests of black people. He hoped that the connection would seem as obvious to others as it did to him.[62]

The history of interracial mistrust in Mobile did, in fact, affect the situation. To a great extent, race determined which groups actively opposed Jaffree's efforts and which did not. Few people of color banded together with the forces opposing Jaffree. Other than the schoolteachers and principals being sued, none of the central school prayer advocates in the case was black. African Americans, by and large, kept their distance from the intervenors and their campaign against secular humanism. When Mobile school board president Dan Alexander got the board to declare its support for the teachers conducting religious exercises, the only commissioners not to vote for his motion were the board's only two black members, Robert Gilliard and Norman Cox. The movement to resist Jaffree was an almost entirely white effort, carried out by New Right activists.[63]

Mistrust caused black Christians in Mobile to avoid cooperating actively with their white neighbors. According to Flynt, African Americans "have long memories about some of these [white Christian conservatives] and their role in the segregationist movement. And, as a consequence of that, they tend not to support churches like Cottage Hill," the epicenter of the antihumanism campaign, "even when Cottage Hill is supporting the same issues, like school prayer, that they believe in." That lack of cooperation became apparent to Wolfe, whom, according to Williams, African Americans saw less as a religious leader than as a political activist, "more like Dan Alexander than a truly religious person." And, of course, no one evoked more hostility among black Mobilians than the school board president, who waged his fight for classroom prayer at the very same time that he was attempting to fire black teachers for speaking "sub-standard" English. Whatever its merits on religious grounds, the intervenors' project began as and remained a white effort.[64]

Longtime school board commissioner and Mobile native David Thomas agreed with this assessment. African Americans didn't oppose the intervenors' mission – they mistrusted the intervenors. To Thomas, Black Mobilians saw "issues like abortion and prayer in school" as "cosmetic issues" covering up more important issues such as affirmative action, school vouchers, and state assistance to the poor. Alexander's biggest nemesis on the board, Gilliard, characterized the antihumanism campaign as a "publicity stunt ... intended to generate greater support in the community for private schools." The intervenors were simply looking to ruin the reputation of the public schools, Gilliard believed, and to attract whites to private schools less susceptible to governmental oversight. Racial segregation was their goal. "And they chose that vehicle of 'secular humanism' to help get them there."[65]

Of course, it wasn't that religious issues didn't matter to black Mobilians. It was because religious devotion was so central to their lives that they felt no need to turn to state-run institutions to safeguard it. Although he considered himself a cultural "traditionalist," Thomas believed that no state employee was entitled to impose her personal religious attitudes on her students. The experience of slavery and Jim Crow, he maintained, had caused blacks to mistrust government when it tried to prescribe morality. Fellow school board commissioner Hazel Fournier agreed. Black history and culture had instilled in her a deep faith in God and love of prayer – so deep that it required no government sanction. Gilliard, "a profoundly religious man," considered the intervenors' actions detrimental to the all-important teaching of open-mindedness. The board had "an obligation to expose children to as much of the thinking process as possible," he believed, and could not allow teachers to impose a particular religious viewpoint. The religious orientation of every student deserved to be tolerated. Religious worship, for Gilliard and the others, remained a free, personal act – not one to be mandated by the state.[66]

The history of black suffering and black faith swung like a double-edged sword. Government, black Mobilians believed, had no right to promote any particular form of religion or to sanction the prayers of schoolchildren. At the same time, history made local African Americans equally sensitive to any attempt to prohibit classroom prayer. Their profound religiosity and generally conservative cultural orientation and morality disposed them to support religious expression freely occurring within public institutions. Black Mobilians no more wanted Jaffree and Williams to determine the place of religion in the classroom than they wanted the governor or the school board to decide it. When the "profoundly religious" Gilliard opposed Alexander's pro-prayer resolution, he did so by suggesting an alternative motion permitting silent prayer. Fournier and Thomas felt comfortable with classroom prayer that was sufficiently ecumenical. Their concern was with religious inclusivity. Notwithstanding Jaffree's assertions to the contrary, classroom prayer did not infringe on the rights of secularists, Fournier maintained, because tolerance required respecting the right of people to pray as well as their right not to pray. Thomas likewise favored a pluralistic approach that made room for prayer and discussion about God. Free religious expression, they held, remained the fairest and best means of accommodating difference in the classroom.[67]

Jaffree confronted more than lack of sympathy from fellow blacks. Throughout the conflict, he was castigated by the local African American community as an enemy of Christianity, an obstacle to people's open worship of God. Jaffree became "other" to Mobile blacks as much as to members of Cottage Hill Baptist Church. His isolation was total and harsh. "I had no one," he said, "no group, no individual, even, within [the black] community that I could look upon for support." Jaffree reported "getting all kinds of nasty letters, threatening phone calls, eggs thrown at my windows, air let out of my tires." He became "*persona non grata* in the black community."[68]

Most Mobilians, black and white alike, were so offended by Jaffree's suit that they treated his attorney with the same disdain they leveled at him. Some of Williams's black clients informed him that "they could not, in good conscience, use the services of somebody who's representing the Devil." Williams asked several black attorneys if they would help him with the case; not one agreed. One black colleague told Williams that "she couldn't go home if she got involved in this case," so vehemently did her friends and family loathe Jaffree. Over the phone and through the mail, Williams routinely received death threats. He found himself isolated from fellow African Americans, his law practice and professional reputation damaged badly.[69]

African Americans saw Williams and Jaffree as disloyal to their own people. Not only did black Mobilians fail to sympathize with Jaffree and Williams as embattled minority activists up against the system; most condemned them as enemies of Christianity – and, thus, enemies of the African American community. "To have a black person and a black attorney" attempt "to determine what existence religion can have in schools," Thomas insisted, "was just a slap in the face to the black community." Those sentiments were shared by other local African Americans, including Pastor Wesley James, who compared Williams to a black lawyer representing the Ku Klux Klan. "Even though the Ku Klux Klan had a right to be defended," black lawyers "shouldn't have been the ones who defended them," at least not "if they . . . were looking for most of their career to come from the African American community."[70]

Religion, not race, determined African Americans' attitudes toward Jaffree's efforts. His and Williams's comparisons between this case and efforts at racial desegregation persuaded few Mobilians, either black or white. Much to Jaffree's chagrin, African Americans reacted to his lawsuit not as members of a minority, but as part of the majority – as Christians wanting to preserve their right to pray in school. Mobile's racial divide did keep the black community from joining forces with the intervenors, whose overall political inclinations placed them squarely in a New Right movement with little appeal to most African Americans. Nonetheless, black Mobilians regarded regarded Jaffree's lawsuit no differently from how the intervenors did. Not unlike their white neighbors, most local blacks understood Jaffree's complaint as an attack on the rights of Christians.[71]

It made sense for Jaffree and Williams to frame the conflict in constitutional terms. For twenty years the Supreme Court had prohibited spoken, collective prayer in public schools. But church-state separation was not honored in Mobile, where the conservative Christian majority jealously guarded its customs and its power. The situation confirmed Jaffree's preconceptions and fears. Again, as in his childhood, a community clung tightly to its mores; again, strident Christians imposed their will. His frustration aside, Jaffree succeeded in instigating the fight that he wanted – against the tyranny of Alabama's Christian majority.[72]

FREEDOM AND ORDER

If there seemed one party nearly certain to support Jaffree, it was the federal judiciary. As *Jaffree* v. *Board of School Commissioners of Mobile County* commenced on November 15, 1982, the plaintiff imagined that, at long last, his complaint would be seen for what it was – a simple request to implement federal law. The presiding judge, Hand, knew as well as Jaffree that precedent came down clearly on the plaintiff's side. Although Jaffree had felt frustrated over Hand's refusal to hold Alexander and James in contempt, Jaffree remained confident that Hand would rule in his favor, as in the earlier injunction order. Even if other Mobilians had not defended Jaffree's rights, it stood to reason, the federal judge would.[73]

Jaffree did not know Hand personally or even by reputation. Nor did Williams, who had opened his local law practice only one year earlier. Had they been familiar with him, they would have entertained reservations about the reliability of the judge's support. Not unlike the defendants and intervenors, Hand was a staunch conservative who believed that social institutions demanded grounding in Christian morality. He saw it as a primary mission of schools to instill in children a sense of right and wrong. To provide moral guidance, he believed, educators need to provide children with a shared understanding of God's requirements from human beings. For Hand, American society was fundamentally a religious society. Impairing that foundation could only weaken its edifice.[74]

Hand was no religious fanatic, no firebrand. He did not read the Bible frequently; he aimed not to impose his particular religious convictions on other people. His public addresses repeatedly stressed the salutary effect of religious pluralism on culture and society. America, he maintained, thrives from the variety of its citizens' religious affiliations and styles. Hand greatly valued his half-century membership and regular attendance at Dauphin Way Methodist, known as a somewhat liberal church, and he was well-liked by fellow members – even those who disagreed with his political and judicial views. He especially prized the warm and engaging relationship he had with the congregation's longtime pastor, whose progressive ideals challenged the judge's own conservatism. Hand never considered leaving the church because of its liberalism. He stayed on, enthusiastically believing that "you learn something when you listen to people who might not have your same view."[75]

Notwithstanding his appreciation for religious diversity, Hand advocated inculcating "Judeo-Christian morality" into children. Honoring freedom of conscience did not, for him, mean banishing religion from the public life. Quite the contrary. Hand insisted that a free and tolerant society could not possibly flourish if its citizens lacked a traditional moral grounding. "Immorality," he told a congregation, was nowadays "spreading throughout our society," threatening our liberties and eroding our civility. It could be resisted only if citizens carefully taught their young to love and honor God. Just laws and secure institutions derived from "our religious heritage," America's "fundamental morality." If our laws were to "represent the true meaning of freedom as conceived by our Founding Fathers," he insisted, Americans needed to demand that those laws be informed by "a profound belief in God and the teachings of our Judeo-Christian heritage." In order to accommodate religious dissent, society needed affirmatively to embrace and strengthen its religious core.[76]

In the 1970s, Hand began to construct a subtle argument regarding the free exchange of ideas and the religious foundations of American society. On one level, his argument glistens with the ideals of pluralism. Hand warned that a "community is already in the process of dissolution where ... nonconformity with the accepted creed, political as well as religious, is a mark of disaffection," where "orthodoxy chokes freedom of dissent and where faith in the eventual supremacy of reason has become so timid." But Hand did not urge Americans simply to tolerate nonconformity and employ reason. In fact, he believed, citizens could not reason or dissent effectively if they lacked a solid religious background. Only by trusting in God could citizens be secure enough to compare ideas, to think broadly, to act generously. A solid moral foundation gave rise to the "spirit of liberty." It allowed individuals to feel secure, to trust diversity, to "seek to understand the minds of other men," to judge their fellows "without any bias."[77]

Hand would develop this notion of morally grounded freedom of thought – an ideal that espoused not skepticism toward tradition or debunking of background culture, but firm yet freely chosen moral conviction. Even if one marches to the beat of a different drummer, one need not endlessly debate the merits of the beat. One should march freely. At the same time, one should remain open and attuned to the beat of God, the rhythm that steadied all marchers. One's metronome must sound a dual, complex rhythm, free yet contained. Disciplined by Christian morality, a citizen became strong enough to act freely and sustain a free society. Hand's vision of intellectual diversity had little in common with Jaffree's wish to shield his children from society's prejudices. Hand did not want to dissolve society's reigning myths; rather, he sought to firm them up, that they might guide future generations of free-thinking citizens.[78]

Like his attitudes toward religion and social custom, Hand's attitudes toward government and law distanced him widely from Jaffree. Foremost, Hand considered himself an advocate of republicanism. The U.S. government historically had been great, he held, because it had functioned as a system in which free, virtuous people, through their elected representatives, ruled themselves and determined their own laws. The tenet most central to Hand's political thinking was that citizens, bolstered by strong moral values, ought to be in charge of their own lives and own government. Government should not serve as their overlord or caretaker.

Throughout the twentieth century, Hand believed, the federal government had gradually deprived Americans of self-rule, and many Americans had been happy to surrender that control in return for the promise of security. Pledging to make everyone feel comfortable, the federal government had gained the people's approval to do just about anything. And when citizens did complain, the government and its appendages redoubled their control. This, according to Hand, was the case with the nation's public schools, where "it's what the *government* thinks the people ought to be taught that's being taught." Backed by the power of its courts, the U.S. government had forced the states to impose secularism and collectivism on the people, even when local majorities held entirely different values. Discouraged by those trends, Hand concluded that "the United States is no longer a republic – it's a socialist state" in which "government runs everything."[79]

This did not bode well for Jaffree, who was expecting Hand to restrain the local Christian majority and its representatives in the Alabama legislature. Jaffree assumed that Hand would honor the precedents set by the Warren Court, which had assiduously defended the rights of minorities against the tyranny of the majority. But Hand was, first and foremost, a defender of "the people" and their right to self-rule, and for him "the people" referred to the popular majority and the lawmakers it elected. His republicanism did not predispose him to sympathize with Jaffree's complaint, any more than did his commitments to states' rights and strict constitutional construction. In all of these ways, the judge's attitudes epitomized the conservative legal movement's efforts to rein in an out-of-control judiciary.

Hand had long embraced the twin concepts of states' rights and strict construction. These had prompted his active support for the presidential campaign of Barry Goldwater – and in particular, for the candidate's stance against court-ordered desegregation. In 1971, Richard Nixon appointed Hand to the federal bench, and, from that time forward, Hand issued rulings that infuriated blacks and liberals. *Brown* v. *Board of Education*, he believed, had been "decided rightly for the wrong reasons" and had turned the Supreme Court into a Big Brother in robes. As ugly and unjust as racism might be, it was not the place of the courts to eradicate it. Only "the people" could render just laws and create a good society, Hand contended. The Warren Court and the lower-court judges who carried out its edicts had arrogated unto themselves far more power than the Constitution granted them. They had not understood that the Constitution meant precisely what it said, and not a word more.[80]

Hand's record on voting rights, desegregation, and affirmative action registered his reluctance to overrule state law and local practice. In two voting rights cases in which he declined to overturn at-large procedures for electing country officials, Hand insisted that it was the place of government to be color blind – to guarantee merely that all adults be able to vote – and that it was not the government's business to eradicate the racism that exists within and between human beings. "The Constitution speaks not to the manner in which individuals are treated by others, but rather to the manner in which individuals are treated by government," he wrote. "It is likely that the law can change men's ways but not their minds." Those opinions and others like them earned Hand widespread contempt. The National Association for the Advancement of Colored People tried unsuccessfully in 1976 to get Hand removed from the *Birdie Mae Davis* case, Mobile's thirteen-year-old school desegregation battle. Eight years later, black Mobilians recoiled once again as Hand, seeking assistance with the case, appointed a "special master" with extremely conservative views on desegregation and affirmative action. Hand continued to preside over *Davis* until 1997, when he finally dismissed the case and yet again angered many local African Americans. His constitutional philosophy did not, on the whole, sit well with Mobile's black community.[81]

Jaffree's case would be tried by a judge on an admitted mission to render decisions "based on the real law" – according to what the Constitution said precisely and what its authors presumably intended it to say. Hand combined strict constructionism with the jurisprudence of original intent. He looked to history to reveal the understandings of those who wrote the text, in order that those understandings regain their authority. This, for Hand, necessitated reversing the liberalism that had dominated the courts since the Warren Court era. "Activist" liberal judges, he complained, had for years been ruling based on what they "want the law to be." That tendency needed "to be counterbalanced by letting the law be the law." "To that extent," he confessed, "I was an activist" as much as them.[82]

In fact, Hand strove to do more than simply "let the law be the law." Hand was willing to use his authority to resist prevailing liberal trends in the law. Conservative jurisprudence since the 1970s had registered an ambivalence toward judicial activism. While continuing to pay homage to the notion that judges should leave lawmaking to legislators, conservative judges had also advocated using the courts to strike down liberal laws and elicit reversals of liberal rulings. During the 1970s, Justice Rehnquist had shown a great willingness to overturn acts of Congress not expressly sanctioned by the Constitution's precise text and its authors' clear intent. Hand promised that he, too, "would not hesitate to alter what may have been the direction in which the law was going at the time, to put it on a track that I thought was the intent of the law." Hand felt aggrieved that his beloved Constitution had been misinterpreted and misapplied. He was set to proffer judicial activism in defense of conservative principle.[83]

In light of Hand's attitudes toward moral education, social custom, rule by popular majorities, states' rights, strict construction, and constitutional originalism, it was not obvious that he would decide again in Jaffree's favor. His injunction ruling offered less assurance than Jaffree and Williams originally thought – a matter not lost on Sherling. Hand had appeared willing to consider the intervenors' arguments, even though they cut against the grain of religion clause jurisprudence since World War II. He stated, during the hearing, "the Intervenor wants an opportunity to build a record in order to attack the present condition of the law, and I'm not supposed to deny him that right." In his ruling, he seemed especially to appreciate the intervenors' contention that secular humanism, like Christianity, constituted a religion – an argument he considered "a fresh approach [relative] to that now found in the annals of case law." Although he had committed himself to abiding by case law, he had also complained that it had "overlooked the totality of what is religion." Moreover, his injunction ruling had addressed only the state prayer law; the actions of the schoolteachers had been severed from the case against the state and would now be considered for the first time. How Hand would rule on the latter issue was not the near-certainty imagined by Jaffree and Williams.[84]

CHURCH-STATE SEPARATION ON TRIAL

Hand heard opening statements in *Jaffree* v. *Board of School Commissioners* on November 15, 1982. Neither he nor most of the participants could have imagined the various directions that the trial would travel. Witnesses for the Mobile school board and the intervenors would advance bold, audacious arguments. The two parties would construct cases so different from one another so as virtually to create two distinct trials. In the end, the plaintiffs would encounter a multifaceted resistance that they had hardly anticipated.[85]

Williams opened by reiterating that the First Amendment requires a wall of separation between church and state and that prayer activities in

Mobile classrooms had breached that wall. He reminded the court that the non-denominationalism and voluntarism of those prayers did not render them constitutional. Anticipating the arguments of the intervenors as well as the school board, he also maintained that, in prohibiting classroom prayer, the court would not be denying any citizens the right to practice their religion. No one's free exercise would be impeded by the application of Supreme Court precedent to this case.[86]

Williams laid out a straightforward case, and Jaffree built on his lawyer's assertions. His children had been denied their right not to be indoctrinated by the state, Jaffree testified; the religious exercises they endured explicitly violated the Establishment Clause. Nor did Williams surprise anyone with his questions to the schoolteachers and principals. All admitted that they had done nothing to accommodate Jaffree. Each of the teachers confirmed that she had sought to instill love of God into schoolchildren. Boyd told Williams that she considered it necessary to teach students to thank God for food "because that's who ... I thank"; likewise, Julia Green reported that she taught children to thank God because "it is part of my religion to be thankful." Going a step further, Alexander admitted not only to "teaching the children to learn to pray" but to "instilling Christian values in the children." None of the teachers disputed promoting religious values. Williams tried to demonstrate that, as public servants, they had entangled government with religion. By virtue of the teachers' direct affiliation with the state, Williams charged, their proselytizing constituted a state establishment of religion.[87]

Robert Campbell and Robert Mudd, the lawyers for the Mobile school board, the teachers, and the principals, did not disagree with Williams on the facts. They asserted that Williams completely misunderstood what the First Amendment required of the state and guaranteed to its employees. Yes, the teachers had acted in accord with their most deeply held values – and this was in keeping with what the constitutional text permitted and its authors intended. It was the teachers, and not Jaffree, whose fundamental liberties were at stake. Whereas Williams treated them as government officials prohibited from advancing any religion, defense counsel depicted them as citizens entitled to act according to their religious convictions. Individual schoolteachers were not the government. They could not possibly establish a religion.[88]

Campbell and Mudd did more than deny that the schoolteachers represented the state. The defense lawyers launched an ambitious assault on the entire notion that the Establishment Clause bars prayer in state-run schools. To accomplish this they called to the stand James McClellan, a highly regarded scholar at the forefront of New Right constitutional politics. Catapulted by the testimony of this one expert witness, the defense expanded the scope of the trial beyond the parameters of most Establishment Clause cases. Campbell's and Mudd's argument challenged Hand to think outside the wall-of-separation paradigm.[89]

For more than a decade, McClellan had been arguing that liberal judicial activism had butchered the Constitution and trampled democracy. McClellan viewed the Constitution, as did Hand, through an originalist lens, believing that the Constitution is no more than what its words say and what its authors said about the words they had written. McClellan believed that, throughout recent decades, the Court had neglected to read the document in its most important context, the history of its adoption. Rather than understanding the First and Fourteenth amendments in terms of the amendments' histories, the justices had invented new meanings for them based on the justices' own predilections. Most troubling to McClellan was the "living Constitution" championed most famously by Justice William Brennan. McClellan feared the discarding of the actual Constitution, and with that the disappearance of the people's right to self-rule.[90]

McClellan had promoted his ideas in numerous ways. He had taught political science at several universities and published works laying out his constitutional vision. After the trial, he would go on to found and direct a prominent conservative think tank, the Center for Judicial Studies, and edit its flagship journal, *Benchmark*, from whose pages he would decry the federal judiciary's disregard for the two principles dearest to his heart: states' rights and judicial restraint. McClellan also exerted a more direct influence on federal law. From 1974 to 1983, he served as a high-ranking assistant to senators Helms, East, and Orrin Hatch – lawmakers central to the New Right. McClellan crafted legislation through which Helms and East would try to strip the Court of its jurisdiction over matters such as school prayer. Only months before *Jaffree*, McClellan had written in the *Villanova Law Review* that "jurisdiction-limiting bills ... are essential to protect the rights of people," which they will accomplish by reversing judicial supremacy and "return[ing] power over civil rights to the states." Throughout his repertoire of scholarship and public service ran two themes: division of sovereignty between the levels of government and separation of power between the branches.[91]

Alarmed by the status quo in American law and ready to transform it, McClellan was an ideal expert witness for the school board. He sought nothing less than to instigate "a conservative constitutional revolution."

This included providing assistance to conservative cause lawyers, whom he urged to pursue fundamental constitutional change rather than short-term courtroom victories. He encouraged them especially to scrutinize the incorporation doctrine. None of the Bill of Rights, he insisted, properly attached to the states. Conservatives needed to show that the Establishment Clause was never intended to restrict state governments – that, to the contrary, it confirmed for "each state that it was free to define the meaning of religious establishment under its own state constitution and laws." Unabashedly, McClellan declared that the entire Bill of Rights provided "a guarantee to the states that they were free to *deny* civil liberties to their citizens."[92]

McClellan was the Mobile school board's only expert witness. The board needed no one else, as he brought all of his intellectual weight to bear on his testimony. Through it, McClellan made the defense's case that the Establishment Clause did not restrain the Mobile teachers and schools because it did not apply to state-run institutions. His argument rested on his own examination of the Establishment Clause in light of its writing and adopting. Jurisprudence since World War II was not a cornerstone, for McClellan, but an aberration in constitutional history. The incorporation doctrine had no justification. The Establishment Clause protected states' rights. It did not limit them.[93]

McClellan's testimony tied his defense of states' rights to his other favorite cause, the separation of powers. America's system of checks and balances, he asserted, guaranteed all three branches of the federal government a say in how the Constitution is interpreted. Flatly rejecting the notion of "judicial supremacy," McClellan held that Congress was duty-bound to check the Court. He applauded, as an example of such vigilance, the Senate's recent attempt to retract the Court's jurisdiction over school prayer – although he did not, at trial, acknowledge his own role in that effort. For McClellan, judicial supremacy over the people's elected representatives obstructed popular rule. The Court's prohibition against religious expression in public schools was "undemocratic," he maintained, because it allowed "a small, select minority" to "impose their view on the people." Democracy required the right of the people to "encourage morality," and the courts had no business standing in the way.[94]

McClellan was determined to turn recent case law on its head. Hand had a chance to instigate Supreme Court reconsideration of the Establishment Clause, he believed, and he would convince the judge to seize the opportunity. He offered the radical suggestion that Hand defy precedent since *Everson* and restore religion to Alabama schools. Hand heard from McClellan that a district court judge must remain open to ruling against Supreme Court decisions. Federal judges were duty-bound to uphold the Constitution, McClellan asserted, but not the Supreme Court's interpretation of it. If a judge "felt under his conscience that an unconstitutional decision had been made" by the Court, then "certainly it would be consistent with his oath of office ... to challenge it." The Court itself had admitted that it makes mistakes, McClellan pointed out, and "it is certainly our obligation as members of the legal profession to alert it to the fact that it may have made a grievous mistake in 1947." Under extraordinary circumstances, a judge could "attempt to overrule a precedent of long standing." A judge needed to bear in mind his right – and even obligation – occasionally to countermand the Supreme Court.[95]

Williams had not prepared for the defense's far-reaching argument, appearing either unfamiliar with McClellan's thinking or surprised that the witness would stake such bold, audacious claims. Williams was so caught off guard by McClellan's arguments that he could only dismiss them as irrelevant to the case. He had little to ask or say about the history of the Establishment Clause, the doctrine of incorporation, or the supremacy of the courts. He compounded his problem by calling, as his sole expert witness, Delos McKown, a philosopher with no background in constitutional history or law. McKown did nothing to undermine McClellan's claims. He could not, under cross-examination, even identify the *Everson* case. Williams could not convincingly respond to the defense's central line of argument.[96]

NEUTRALITY AND INCLUSIVITY

Reeling from the blow delivered by McClellan, Williams was blindsided by the unusual claims made by the intervenors. Unlike the board, the intervenors called many witnesses, further drowning out the plaintiff's voice. Their attack diverged completely from McClellan's. The intervenors said little about political theory or the structure of government, focusing instead on the definition of religion. Through their witnesses they questioned whether ideas can ever be religiously neutral, whether America's public schools treated the interests of Christians and non-Christians evenhandedly, and whether prayer could justifiably be removed from the classroom while expressions of secular "faith" enjoyed free reign. The intervenors reaffirmed that secular humanism constituted a religion and deserved no preferential treatment over other religions. Examining textbook after textbook used in Mobile schools, their witnesses tried to show that secular humanism – and not Christianity – exerted undue influence over the nation's educational establishment. Christianity, they argued, had been all but expelled from the classroom. And rigorous, evenhanded application of the Establishment Clause required that if the theistic morality were purged, then human-centered morality needed also to be eliminated. Since such a purge was not practical, or really even possible, Christian prayers deserved a place alongside expressions of secular "religion."

The intervenors' case amounted to an attack on the American system of public education. To spearhead that attack they called an expert witness who exerted significant impact on the Christian Right. Rousas John Rushdoony was the founder of Christian Reconstructionism and a prolific writer on education, law, religion, and history. Since the 1960s, Rushdoony had tried to change the political behaviors of Christian conservatives. He argued that a culture's fundamental values comprised the culture's religion, and that education always functioned to advance that religion. No education system could ever be religiously neutral – either Christianity or some other faith would necessarily be advanced. Present-day American public schools, he said, served as organs of an Enlightenment-based, humanistic religion incompatible with Christianity. He considered this situation intolerable, and he called on American Christians to change society by reasserting the dominance of Christianity over the human-centered religion that had been established by the federal government.[97]

Rushdoony sought to build a Christian theocracy in the United States. His prescriptions were severe. He looked to eliminate the welfare state and the public-school system, and he prescribed capital punishment for blasphemy, adultery, acts of homosexuality, and incorrigibility in teenagers. Religious pluralism was anathema to Rushdoony's theocracy, in which true believers would no longer be bound "in the name of toleration ... to associate on a common level of total acceptance with the atheist, the pervert, the criminal and the adherents of other religions." Likewise, he believed that "Christianity is completely and radically antidemocratic." Democracy needed to fall victim to the new order.[98]

Notwithstanding their harshness and fanaticism, Rushdoony's views had influenced key New Right thinkers such as Francis Schaeffer and Howard Phillips, as well as televangelists such as Pat Robertson and James Kennedy, who frequently hosted Rushdoony on their programs. His most direct impact was on First Amendment scholar John Whitehead, whose Rutherford Institute had been launched with Rushdoony's assistance. In his introduction to Whitehead's *The Separation Illusion*, Rushdoony advanced his novel theory of the Establishment Clause. The religion clauses, he asserted, were intended only to protect Christianity from the state, in order that Christianity could dominate all of society. The Framers did not intend to protect state or society from religion. Informed by his mentor's essay, Whitehead published an important article suggesting that the Establishment Clause barred a state establishment of secular humanism. Rushdoony's agenda to eradicate secularism in America profoundly influenced a wide array of fundamentalists, evangelicals, and charismatics. Although "Reconstructionist name recognition is minimal," according to John Richard Neuhaus, the movement's ideas have "touched inestimable numbers of conservative Christians at the grassroots level of society."[99]

In his *Jaffree* testimony, Rushdoony betrayed none of his theocratic designs – nor did opposing counsel compel him to do so. Not once did Rushdoony denounce democracy or religious pluralism. To the contrary, he portrayed himself as a religious pluralist who wished merely to see Christianity provided equal treatment with humanism. He did not attack the First Amendment but contended that it had been misapplied. He complained that government schools had established the religion of humanism, thereby denying religious liberty to Christians. Controlled by humanists, government had trodden over the pluralism that had once made America great. "If there were freedom for a variety of groups," Rushdoony maintained, "there would be more understanding and a greater ability to live together in appreciation of what each group contributes to a pluralistic society." It fell to schoolteachers to act "as fairly as possible," to accord "respect for varying positions," to nurture "a free market of ideas."[100]

Disguised as a broad-minded Christian, Rushdoony delivered the intervenors' most piercing attack. What Jaffree was seeking, he asserted, could not exist. The public schools could not possibly maintain religious neutrality in the classroom, for simply to teach was necessarily to advance a religion. According to Rushdoony, secular humanists were governed by pre-theoretical suppositions that functioned fully as a religion. He held that, inevitably, "we view the world in terms of where we are positioned, what our faith is." We "know" to be true what our worldview, our faith, requires us to believe. Through its control of public education the humanistic worldview had become America's dominant faith, fulfilling the vision of public education pioneer Horace Mann as well as the many influential thinkers who signed the *Humanist Manifestos*, which presented humanism as the only religion appropriate for modern life. In his view, this evidence compelled the court to treat secular humanism as a religion.[101]

Rushdoony charged the Mobile public schools with instituting secular humanism as a state establishment of religion. With Rushdoony's testimony on this point, the intervenors adopted their central tactic of directing witnesses to discuss particular textbooks used in Mobile schools and assess their religious content. Rushdoony opined that the textbooks he examined advanced the humanistic worldview while ignoring or disparaging the Christian worldview. Two psychology books, he complained, presented the humanistic notion that sex roles were culturally learned but not the Christian idea that sex roles were assigned by God. A science book explaining human evolution made no reference to the corresponding Christian account of human origins. In a short story where a character lied, the author did not reproach him for doing so and thus endorsed the moral relativism typical of humanism. Especially crucial, for Rushdoony, was a social-studies book proclaiming that "morals are rules made by people." That assertion, in his estimation, blatantly promoted the humanistic view that morality has no transcendental basis – a religious view in direct conflict with the Christian perspective.[102]

The intervenors' next star witness, James Kennedy, seconded Rushdoony's assessment. Co-founder of the Moral Majority and one of the New Right's most influential figures, Kennedy had made a name for himself denouncing secular humanism, public education, and the federal courts. His church, Fort Lauderdale's enormous Coral Ridge Presbyterian, hosted Richard Nixon whenever the former president stayed in Florida. Kennedy had spread his influence largely through his "Coral Ridge Hour," one of the nation's most-watched television programs. In his televangelism and public speaking, he warned audiences that "secular humanists ha[d] declared war on Christianity" and had turned their worldview into "the established religion of America." Kennedy exhorted "Christian fellow Americans" to "reconstruct America in accordance with the Biblical guidelines which God has given us." This meant directing schools to instill biblical morality rather than impart secular knowledge. Kennedy called on his followers to take "drastic action," to open up the schools to "the Holy Spirit working through the atonement of Jesus Christ," which alone could "regenerate and renew the hearts and minds of children."[103]

While testifying, Kennedy, like Rushdoony, kept quiet about Christian theocracy. Rather than call for a Christ-oriented curriculum in the public schools, Kennedy championed the same inclusive religious pluralism that Rushdoony did, a pluralism that would make room for Christianity *alongside* secular humanism. The classroom, he insisted, needed to accommodate more than "only one view of reality," more than one religion. Kennedy defined "religion" much as Rushdoony did – as any fundamental worldview that "defines one's ultimate concerns in life." Because religion provided the basis for all that people thought and said, he posited, "all education ha[d] to have a religious foundation." Although the "free marketplace of ideas" required schools to present secular humanism as just one among multiple religions, it now enjoyed exclusive influence in the classroom. Kennedy called it "virtually an established religion in America, in contradiction to the First Amendment." This seemed certainly to be true in Mobile schools, he reported, as evidenced by their textbooks. Throughout America, the establishment of secular humanism was causing countless Christian children to suffer discrimination in public-school classrooms, where they routinely endured humiliation on account of their religion. Christian children, he charged, were the real victims of religious discrimination.[104]

The intervenors' case was advanced most cogently by Richard Baer, a professor of ethics at Cornell University. For several years, Baer had been writing about "values clarification," a widely used teaching method that aimed to help children discover their own personal values and that strove not to impose external values on them. Baer had charged that proponents of values clarification were mistaken in characterizing their practice and theory as value-neutral. In fact, he said, proponents advanced a particular worldview, based on ethical subjectivism and ethical relativism, that conflicted with the traditional religious worldview held by many Americans. Baer's writing brought academic credence to the intervenors' vision.[105]

On the stand, Baer supported Rushdoony's and Kennedy's testimonies. He defined religion broadly, as "that set of views and commitments which determine your life's direction." Any set of views and commitments that functioned as a religion, he asserted, was a religion, regardless of its substance. Secular humanism's moral theory, based on subjectivity and relativity, could not be reconciled with theistic morality. Baer maintained that the public schools presented only humanistic worldviews, when, in fact, they were obligated to present both theistic and humanistic orientations. "If we make the kind of judgment that it is improper for children to pray in school . . . but at the same time permit a range of other [practices] that are religious in nature . . . then we have a very serious question of evenhandedness." Baer charged that liberals had "been so blind to the fact that secularism is not religiously neutral that" they had "pushed for a very one-sided victory." In so doing they stepped all over the rights of believers in God.[106]

If at some moments Baer advocated for fairness and inclusivity for all viewpoints, at other moments he sought the removal of secular humanism from the public schools and the promotion of only theistic religion. Indeed, he seemed unsure whether he really wanted the schools to reach "messy compromises" and "equitable solutions" after all. Baer asserted what Rushdoony and Kennedy implied: that the problem wasn't simply that secular humanism enjoyed a monopoly in the classroom, but that it was a flawed and dangerous worldview that shouldn't even be allowed in the classroom. Its radical subjectivity threatened the nation's social and political order, Baer told the court. The view "that all things are a matter of personal preferences and tastes" could dissolve people's absolute adherence to "freedom, justice, [and] democracy." This was unacceptable. Children needed to be taught life's verities, and secular humanism's moral relativity undermined that process. Its "constant inculcating of doubt and skepticism . . . created a mood of doubt in the child . . . towards the kind of things that many of us are trying to teach our children at home." Baer's testimony revealed an ambiguity at the heart of the intervenors' case. At moments, they defended Christianity's place in the classroom; at other moments, they clamored to eradicate all non-Christian ways of thinking about the world.[107]

TRIANGULATION

In refuting Jaffree's complaint, the intervenors' case complemented the position taken by the school board. Even if Hand rejected McClellan's remonstration that the federal courts had no rightful say over the individual states' religious policies and practices, the judge could still accept the intervenors' reasoning that Christian exercises could not fairly be prohibited unless the court also purged the schools of all traces of humanism. Jaffree's quest now lay vulnerable to a states' rights challenge conjoined with a Christians' rights challenge.

Nevertheless, tensions between Jaffree's opponents had mounted. Prior to the trial, the intervenors had been designated "defendant intervenors," partners with the school board. That designation seemed logical, given their support for schoolteachers' right to lead students in prayer. Ever since the intervenors' first public rallies, they had vociferously defended the teachers and principals being sued. Over the course of the trial, however, the intervenors aimed most of their criticism at the board, which, it claimed, had defied the Constitution and injured Christians by advancing the religion of secular humanism. Ironically, the intervenors issued accusations against their codefendants similar to Jaffree's complaints – accusations that the schools were establishing a religion and were harming children who did not subscribe to it. As the trial progressed, the board came to see itself as the intervenors' primary target.

On the morning of November 18, prior to the fourth and final day of hearings, the parties met in Hand's chambers. There, Campbell and Mudd asked the judge if he would convert the intervenors into plaintiffs. The board's objectives, according to its lawyers, were so dissimilar to those of the intervenors that the two parties could hardly be considered collaborators. Campbell and Mudd pointed out that their clients had the narrow agenda of demonstrating that the actions of the teachers, principals, and board members did not breach the Constitution. The intervenors, they claimed, had broader objectives that were, at best, immaterial to their own.[108]

Sherling and Kotouc wished to remain defendants, insisting that their designs only strengthened the board's case. The intervenors' attack on humanism in the classroom, according to their lawyers, in no way dampened their resolve to protect classroom prayer. Of course, the court might still proscribe classroom prayer; in that case, they would ask Hand also to purge the schools of humanism. And that, they conceded, would burden the schools. Still, matters would probably not come to that, as humanism could not be removed from the curriculum without utterly disrupting the entire educational process. Both humanism and Christianity would need to be accommodated. The intervenors portrayed themselves as defending the teachers' right to lead prayers, not as asking the schools to redesign their entire curriculum. This persuaded Hand to leave the parties in their present alignment for the time being. But it did not placate Campbell and Mudd.[109]

The board's attorneys registered ringing objections throughout the remainder of testimony by the intervenors' witnesses. Gone was the mutual support marking the codefendants' earlier interactions. Mudd and Campbell complained that the schools were under siege on all sides, while Sherling and Kotouc insisted that they were condemning "the current thought among educators" rather than the actions of this board and these teachers. Hand now acknowledged that the intervenors were waging "a direct attack" on the board. He warned Sherling and Kotouc that their case would more likely hamper the school system than bolster its ability to continue its current practices. If the intervenors' case were successful, and if the court abided by the Supreme Court's prohibition against organized, vocal prayer in the public schools, then Hand would be compelled somehow to remove all "religion" from the classroom. This scenario failed to disturb Sherling, who admitted that, "at the outset," he and Kotouc had considered "fil[ing] suit against the School Board and say [ing], 'take religion out of'" the classroom altogether.[110]

Hand essentially presided over two distinct trials. Neither resembled the trial that Jaffree and Williams had imagined when they first brought suit against the Mobile public schools. Campbell and Mudd contested not the plaintiff's account of the facts, but the constitutional theory underlying his complaint. They did nothing less than challenge the jurisdiction of the Supreme Court. Meanwhile, the intervenors – with equal audacity – attempted to redefine "religion." With their truckload of textbooks and parade of witnesses, they assaulted the common sense underlying church-state separation. Kotouc and Sherling did not question whether the U.S. Constitution properly restrained Alabama public schools; they did not try to shield the Mobile teachers and principals from the federal government's gaze. But the extremity of their claims, alongside the defendants' constitutional revisionism, made the latter seem not quite as outrageous as it otherwise would have. And the intervenors' case equipped Hand with an additional set of reasons for possibly finding against the plaintiff.[111]

Notes

1 Website for the Law Offices of Thomas O. Kotouc, P.C. www.qa3.com/pageq/1,2278,118,00.html?action=about&bid=bio1; Thomas Kotouc interview by Robert Daniel Rubin, March 22, 2002, Montgomery, Ala., 2.
2 *Ibid.*, 2, 11.
3 *Ibid.*, 2.
4 *Ibid.*, 2–3, 5; Website for the Law Offices of Kotouc.
5 *Mobile Press Register*, September 25, 1982, p. B2.
6 Kotouc interview, 5; "Textbook Case Lawyer Says Victory Is More Important Than Lost Money," *Alabama Journal*, March 11, 1987; Kotouc interview, 6.
7 *Ibid.*, 7; Bob Sherling interview by Robert Daniel Rubin, November 14, 2000 Mobile, Ala., 6.
8 Kotouc interview, 7; Sherling interview, 6.
9 Stuart A. Scheingold and Austin Sarat, *Something to Believe In: Politics, Professionalism, and Cause Lawyering* (Stanford: Stanford University Press, 2004), 2, 9, emphasis in original.

10 Gerald N. Rosenberg, *The Hollow Hope: Can Courts Bring About Social Change?* (Chicago: University of Chicago Press, 1991), 5; Steven P. Brown, *Trumping Religion: The New Christian Right, the Free Speech Clause, and the Courts* (Tuscaloosa: University of Alabama Press, 2002), 23.

11 Kevin R. den Dulk, "In Legal Culture, but Not of It: The Role of Cause Lawyers in Evangelical Legal Mobilization," paper delivered at conference on cause lawyers and social movements, University of California, Los Angeles, March 2005 (in Robert Daniel Rubin's possession).

12 Francis A. Schaeffer, *A Christian Manifesto* (Wheaton, Ill: Crossway, 1981), 47–51, 103, 118, 132–33; den Dulk, "In Legal Culture, but Not of It," 10, 13.

13 den Dulk, "In Legal Culture, but Not of It," 8–14; Scheingold and Sarat, *Something to Believe In*, 112–17; Brown, *Trumping Religion*, 26.

14 Francis Wilkinson, "Judge Hand's Holy War," *American Lawyer*, 9 (May 1987), 112; Sherling interview, 9–10, 19.

15 Kotouc interview, 4–5, 9–10. On Rutherford, see R. Jonathan Moore, *Suing for America's Soul: John Whitehead, the Rutherford Institute, and Conservative Christians in the Courts* (Grand Rapids, Mich.: Eerdmans, 2007); Gilbert T. Sewall, "Religion and the Textbooks," in *Curriculum, Religion, and Public Education: Conversations for an Enlarging Public Square*, ed. by James T. Sears and James C. Carper (New York: Columbia University Press, 1998), 77–79; *Wall Street Journal*, February 17, 1994, sec. B, p. 1; and Frederick Clarkson, "Radical Reconstruction," *In These Times*, March 8, 1998, p. 16.

16 Brown, *Trumping Religion*, 7–9, 23; Wilkinson, "Judge Hand's Holy War," 112.

17 Smith interview 6–7; Transcript, *Ishmael Jaffree et al.* v. *Gov. Fob James et al.*, Civil case no. 82-0792-H, box no. 7, accession no. 021-93-0423, location no. C0681974 SAN (Federal Records Center, East Point, Ga.), August 5, 1982, pp. 235–36. Kotouc interview, 8.

18 Allen Cronenberg, "Mobile and World War II, 1940–1945," in *Mobile: The New History of Alabama's First City*, ed. by Michael V. R., Thomason (Tuscaloosa: University of Alabama Press, 2001), 209–10, 215; Wayne Flynt interview by Robert Daniel Rubin, August 24, 2004 (conducted by telephone), 3, 7–8; Wayne Flynt, *Alabama Baptists: Southern Baptists in the Heart of Dixie* (Tuscaloosa: University of Alabama Press, 1998), 566–67; Joseph W. Newman, "Organized Prayer and Secular Humanism in Mobile, Alabama's, Public Schools," in *Curriculum as Social Psychoanalysis: The Significance of Place*, ed. by Joe L. Kincheloe and William F. Pinar (Albany: SUNY Press, 1991), 48.

19 Newman, "Organized Prayer and Secular Humanism," 48; Joseph Newman interview by Robert Daniel Rubin, March 14, 2002, Mobile, Ala., 18–20; Flynt interview, 8, 11; "A Conversation with Ishmael Jaffree," *Azalea City News & Review*, February 17, 1983, p. 4; "An Interview with Ishmael Jaffree," *Azalea City News & Review*, February 24, 1983, p. 5; *One Nation under God: School Prayer and the First Amendment* (Alexandria, Va.: Close Up Publishing, 1995).

20 John Webster and Sue Webster interview by Robert Daniel Rubin, October 22, 2002, Mobile, Ala., 10; Fred Wolfe interview by Robert Daniel Rubin,

December 4, 2000, Jackson, Miss., 3, 5–6; Wilkinson, "Judge Hand's Holy War," 111–42; Newman interview, 25; Flynt, *Alabama Baptists*, 567; Flynt interview, 3, 7; *Mobile Press Register*, January 8, 1989, sec. G, p. 2. Burt Rieff, "Conflicting Rights and Religious Liberty: The School-Prayer Controversy in Alabama, 1962–1985," *Alabama Review*, 54 (July 2001), 192–93. Quotation from Newman interview, 25.

21 Flynt, *Alabama Baptists*, 567; Wolfe interview, 4; *Mobile Press Register*, June 14, 1994, sec. B, p. 2. On the SBC conflict, see David T. Morgan, *The New Crusades, the New Holy Land: Conflict in the Southern Baptist Convention, 1969–1991* (Tuscaloosa: University of Alabama Press, 1996); Barry Hankins, *Uneasy in Babylon: Southern Baptist Conservatives and American Culture* (Tuscaloosa: University of Alabama Press, 2002); and Flynt, *Alabama Baptists*, 563–624.

22 Wolfe interview, 4, 13; *One Nation under God;* Rieff, "Conflicting Rights and Religious Liberty," 192–93.

23 *Mobile Press Register*, September 11, 1982, p. B8.

24 *Ibid.*

25 *Ibid.*, September 18, 1982, p. B1.

26 *Mobile Register*, September 24, 1982, p. A10.

27 *Ibid. Torcaso* v. *Watkins*, 367 U.S. 488 (1961), 495 n11. For the history of the concept of secular humanism as a religion, see Chapter 6.

28 *Mobile Register*, September 24, 1982, p. A10; Newman, "Organized Prayer and Secular Humanism," 54; *Mobile Press*, September 24, 1982, pp. A1, A6.

29 Flynt interview, 8, 11–12; Newman interview; Ron Williams interview by Robert Daniel Rubin, March 19, 2002, Mobile, Ala., 15.

30 "Conversation with Ishmael Jaffree," pp. 1, 4; Wolfe interview, 14; Transcript, *Jaffree* v. *James*, 205. The term "moral majority" derives from the organization of that same name begun by Jerry Falwell. Susan Friend Harding, *The Book of Jerry Falwell: Fundamentalist Language and Politics* (Princeton: Princeton University Press, 2000).

31 Richard A. Pride, *The Political Use of Racial Narratives: School Desegregation in Mobile, Alabama, 1954–1997* (Urbana: University of Illinois Press, 2002), 126–27; S. Lloyd and R. Tremaine, "Dan Alexander," (Mobile) *Harbinger*, November 26, 1985, pp. 11–12.

32 Pride, *Political Use of Racial Narratives*, 126–28, 133–34, 148, 184–85, 202, 213.

33 *Ibid.*, 138–44, 148, 166, 178–79, 184–85, 215, 225, 237, 265. Alexander played on a standard theme among post-Sixties conservatives, that affirmative-action policies disregarded fairness and personal accountability. See J. Harvie Wilkinson, *From Brown to Bakke: The Supreme Court and School Integration, 1954–1978* (New York: Oxford University Press, 1981); Jonathan Rieder, "Rise of the Silent Majority," in *Rise and Fall of the New Deal Order, 1930–1980*, ed. by Steve Fraser and Gary Gerstle (Princeton: Princeton University Press, 1989), 254–58; Matthew D. Lassiter, *The Silent Majority: Suburban Politics in the Sunbelt South* (Princeton: Princeton University Press, 2006); and Thomas J. Sugrue and John D. Skrentny, "The White Ethnic Strategy," in *Rightward Bound: Making America Conservative in the*

1970s, ed. by Bruce J. Schulman and Julian E. Zelizer (Cambridge, Mass.: Harvard University Press, 2008), 171–92.

34 Pride, *Political Use of Racial Narratives*, 138–44, 148.

35 *Ibid.*, 187, 207, 225; Lloyd and Tremaine, "Dan Alexander," 11; "Education Elitists Want Your Children," *Blackboard* (Published by Save Our Schools, a division of the Taxpayers Educational Lobby, Washington, D.C.), December 1982, p. 2 (Records of *Jaffree* v. *Board*, United States District Court, Southern District of Alabama, Southern Division, 113 St. Joseph St., Room 518, Mobile, Ala.); "From the Desk of Dan C. Alexander Jr." *Blackboard*, December 1982, p. 2; *Mobile Register*, July 29, 1982, sec. A, p. 1. Viguerie outlines his blueprint for political activism in Richard A. Viguerie, *The New Right: We're Ready to Lead* (Falls Church, Va.: Viguerie Company, 1981). On Viguerie's impact on conservative politics, see Godfrey Hodgson, *The World Turned Right Side Up: A History of the Conservative Ascendancy in America* (Boston: Houghton Mifflin, 1996), 109–14, 228–29; Steve Bruce, *The Rise and Fall of the New Christian Right: Conservative Protestant Politics in America, 1978–1988* (New York: Clarendon, 1988), 54–59; and Bruce J. Schulman, *The Seventies: The Great Shift in American Culture, Society, and Politics* (New York: Free Press, 2001), 193–98.

36 *Mobile Register*, July 29, 1982, p. A1; Pride, *Political Use of Racial Narratives*, 188, 203, 207; "Education Elitists Want Your Children," p. 2; "SOS on the Move," *Blackboard* (Published by Save Our Schools, a division of the Taxpayers Educational Lobby, Washington, D.C.), December 1982, pp. 1, 4; "Alexander, Jaffree, and Others: Mobilians Set for ABC Show," *Mobile Press*, October 25, 1982; Newman, "Organized Prayer and Secular Humanism," 63.

37 George Lakoff, *Moral Politics: How Liberals and Conservatives Think* (Chicago: University of Chicago Press, 2001), 3, 12–14, 35, 163, 170, 229–36.

38 *Ibid.*, 249–54, 261. See also Jonathan Haidt, *The Righteous Mind: Why Good People are Divided by Politics and Religion* (New York: Pantheon, 2012), 128–54.

39 Pride, *Political Use of Racial Narratives*, 215, 185, 197.

40 *Mobile Register*, July 29, 1982, p. A1; *Mobile Register*, July 29, 1982, p. B1; *One Nation under God;* Minutes of the Regular Meeting of the Board of School Commissioners of Mobile County, Alabama, Central Administrative Office of the Mobile County Public School System, Barton Academy (504 Government Street, Mobile, Ala.), July 28, 1982, p. 370; Lloyd and Tremaine, "Dan Alexander," 11–12.

41 Minutes of the Regular Meeting of the Board of School Commissioners of Mobile County, August 11, 1982, pp. 397–98. Robert Campbell interview by Robert Daniel Rubin, November 10, 2000, Mobile, Ala., 12, 24.

42 Lloyd and Tremaine, "Dan Alexander," 11; "Alexander, Jaffree, and Others."

43 "SOS on the Move," 1, 4; Newman, "Organized Prayer and Secular Humanism," 63; Minutes of the Regular Meeting of the Board of School Commissioners of Mobile County, July 28, 1982, p. 371; *Mobile Press*, July 29, 1982, p. A1; "SOS President Sued for Allowing Children to Pray," *Blackboard*,

December 1982, p. 2; Lloyd and Tremaine, "Dan Alexander," 11–12; "Alexander Denies 'Using' Prayer Issue," *Mobile Register*, August 19, 1983, p. B1; *Mobile Press Register*, September 12, 1982, p. A9.

44 *Mobile Register*, September 2, 1982, p. B1; *Mobile Press Register*, September 18, 1982, p. B1; Deposition of Dan Alexander, Mobile, Ala., November 4, 1983, records of *Jaffree* v. *Board*.

45 "Interview with Ishmael Jaffree"; *Mobile Register*, September 2, 1982, p. B1.

46 *Mobile Press Register*, September 18, 1982, p. B1; (Mobile) *Beacon*, September 25, 1982, pp. 1–2.

47 Pride, *Political Use of Racial Narratives*, 212–15, 225–26; (Mobile) *Beacon*, September 15, 1984, p. 4.

48 *Mobile Press*, August 10, 1982, pp. 1, 4; *Mobile Register*, August. 11, 1982, p. B8; *Montgomery Advertiser*, August 11, 1982, p. 13; *Montgomery Advertiser and Alabama Journal*, August 15, 1982, p. B15.

49 *Mobile Press Register*, September 19, 1982, p. E8; Sandra Baxley Taylor, *Fob: The Incredible Story of Fob James Jr.* (Mobile, Ala.: Greenberry, 1990), 345; "Alabama to Fight School Prayer Ban," *Washington Times*, September 13, 1982; Fob James, "Constitutional Question of Voluntary Prayer in School to Be Taken Directly to Supreme Court," governor's weekly newspaper column, 1979–1983: James File, SG 5074, Legal Case Files, Alabama Department of Archives and History (ADAH) (624 Washington Ave., Montgomery, Ala.), September 13, 1982.

50 *Mobile Register*, September 14, 1982, p. A12. Defendant Fob James's petition for a writ of mandamus (never filed), *Jaffree* v. *James*, 1983–1987: Wallace File, SG 5012, Legal Case Files, ADAH, 12, 14–16, 18, 20. James based his conclusion on *Bartkus* v. *Illinois*, 359 U.S. 121 (1959). *Gitlow* v. *New York*, 268 U.S. 652 (1925); *Cantwell* v. *Connecticut*, 310 U.S. 296 (1940); *Everson* v. *Board of Education*, 330 U.S. 1 (1947).

51 *Birmingham News*, September 27, 1978, pp. 1, 6; James's petition for a writ of mandamus, 24, 27.

52 Joseph Newman, "The Injunction," *Harbinger*, October 15, 1985, p. 3; *Washington Post*, September 16, 1982, p. A3; *Mobile Register*, September 16, 1982, p. A1; *Mobile Press Register*, September 19, 1982, p. E8; *New York Times*, September 16, 1982, p. B10. Fob James, "Statement of the Governor of Alabama," national press release distributed at news conference, September 15, 1982, Wallace File, 1–2; Taylor, *Fob*, 349.

53 *Mobile Register*, September 16, 1982, p. A1; *Mobile Register*, September 17, 1982, p. B2; *Mobile Press Register*, September 19, 1982, p. E8.

54 Newman, "Injunction," 1; *Mobile Press Register*, September 26, 1982, p. A1.

55 Fob James, "Prayer in Public Schools: This Issue Will Not Fade Away," governor's weekly newspaper column, September 20, 1982, James File, 1–2.

56 *Mobile Register*, November 6, 1982, pp. A1, A6; Taylor, *Fob*, 349; Newman, "Injunction," 9; *Washington Post*, November 6, 1982, p. A12.

57 *Mobile Register*, November 6, 1982, p. A6; Taylor, *Fob*, 349; Newman, "Injunction," 9.

58 Memorandum of law in support of plaintiffs' motion for a temporary restraining order, *Jaffree et al.* v. *Board of School Commissioner of Mobile County et al.*, July 15, 1982, Wallace File, 4–5; Letter from Ishmael Jaffree to Abraham Lincoln Hammons, May 10, 1982 (Plaintiff's exhibit 2, trial records of *Jaffree* v. *Board*), emphasis in the original; Transcript, *Jaffree* v. *Board*, 217–18; *Dare We Defend Our Rights?*, narr. Wayne Flynt (1992: L. Wade Black and the Alabama Center for Law and Civic Education); "Conversation with Ishmael Jaffree," 4.
59 *Jaffree by and through* Jaffree v. James, 544 F.Supp. 727 (1982), 730–31; Williams interview, 33–34; *Dare We Defend Our Rights?*
60 *Ibid.*; "Conversation with Ishmael Jaffree," 4; Ishmael Jaffree, letter to the editor, *Mobile Press Register*, February 14, 1983.
61 Williams interview, 20.
62 Ishmael Jaffree, letter to the editor, (Mobile) *New Times*, June 6, 1985; Ishmael Jaffree, letter to the editor, *Mobile Press Register*, February 14, 1983.
63 Flynt interview, 4; Williams interview, 18, 23; Wolfe interview, 17. A notable exception was Wesley James, pastor at Mobile's Franklin Street Baptist Church. Wesley James interview by Robert Daniel Rubin, March 13, 2002, Mobile, Ala. Minutes of the Regular Meeting of the Board of School Commissioners of Mobile County, July 28, 1982, p. 371.
64 Flynt interview, 4; Wolfe interview, 17–18; Williams interview, 17, 20–23; Pride, *Political Use of Racial Narratives*, 64, 126–215.
65 David Thomas interview by Robert Daniel Rubin, November 20, 2000, Mobile, Ala., 1, 12–14. Minutes of the Regular Meeting of the Board of School Commissioners of Mobile County, 371. Robert Gilliard interview by Robert Daniel Rubin, December 1, 2000, Mobile, Ala., audio recording, side 1. On black mistrust of white religious initiatives, see James interview, 3–4; Flynt interview, 4; and Michael O. Emerson and Christian Smith, *Divided by Faith: Evangelical Religion and the Problem of Race in America* (New York: Oxford University Press, 2000), 93–113.
66 Thomas interview, 5–7, 13; Hazel Fournier interview by Robert Daniel Rubin, November 29, 2000, Mobile, Ala., audio recording, side 1; Minutes of the Regular Meeting of the Board of School Commissioners of Mobile County, February 26, 1986, pp. 100–01.
67 Flynt interview, 3–4; Minutes of the Regular Meeting of the Board of School Commissioners of Mobile County, July 28, 1982, p. 371; Fournier interview, side 2; Thomas interview, 6.
68 *Dare We Defend Our Rights?*; Newman interview, 24; Flynt interview, 12; Fournier interview, side 1; Joyce Leviton, "A Former Child Evangelist Wins a Supreme Court Fight against Prayer in Public Schools," *People*, June 24, 1985, p. 36; Rieff, "Conflicting Rights and Religious Liberty," 194.
69 Williams interview, 3–4, 9, 14–15.
70 Thomas interview, 15–16; James interview, 6–7.
71 Rieff, "Conflicting Rights and Religious Liberty," 193–94; Flynt interview, 11–12.
72 *Engel* v. *Vitale*, 370 U.S. 421 (1962); *School District of Abington, Pa.* v. *Schempp*, 374 U.S. 203 (1963).

73 Ken Englade, "A Twist of Faith: How an Alabama Judge Turned a Fight over Religion in the Classroom into a Battle over Secular Humanism in the Textbooks," *Student Lawyer*, 16 (September 1987), 16–17.
74 "Judge Hand Talks about Christianity," *Mobile Register*, April 30, 1987; *Mobile Register*, October 6, 1986, p. B3; W. Brevard Hand interview by Robert Daniel Rubin, October 10, 2002, Mobile, Ala., 9–10.
75 W. Brevard Hand interview by Robert Daniel Rubin, April 11, 2000, Mobile, Ala., 4–5, 12–13, 37–38; *Montgomery Advertiser and Alabama Journal*, November 26, 1987, p. A1; W. Brevard Hand, speech delivered at Mobile Rotary Club, Mobile, Alabama, April 25, 1974, pp. 12–13, Speech file 1, W. Brevard Hand Papers (United States District Courthouse, Southern District of Alabama, Mobile, Ala.); W. Brevard Hand, "The Religious Foundation of Good Government," speech delivered at the Government Street Methodist Church, Mobile, Alabama, June 27, 1976, p. 4, Speech file 1, Hand Papers; W. Brevard Hand, "A Different Drummer," *Notre Dame Journal of Law, Ethics, and Public Policy*, 3 (Summer 1988), 569–90; *Birmingham News*, June 28, 1987, p. A4; Hand interview, October 10, 2002, 3–5.
76 "Judge Hand Talks about Christianity"; *Mobile Register*, October 6, 1986, p. B3; Hand interview, October 10, 2002, pp. 9–10; Hand, "Religious Foundation of Good Government," 1–2; Hand, speech at Mobile Rotary Club, 4.
77 Hand, speech at Mobile Rotary Club, 4, 12–13; Hand, "Religious Foundation of Good Government," 4.
78 W. Brevard Hand, "Constitutional Construction and the Educational Process," speech before the Committee for the Bicentennial of the Signing of the U.S. Constitution, delivered at Grove Hill Elementary School, Mobile, Alabama, November 17, 1987, Speech file 2, Hand Papers; Hand, "Different Drummer." Hand's connection between religion and intellectual freedom recalls the thinking of William F. Buckley and Willmoore Kendall. See William F. Buckley, *God and Man at Yale: The Superstitions of Academic Freedom* (Chicago: Regnery, 1951); and Willmoore Kendall, "The Bill of Rights and American Freedom," in *What Is Conservatism*, ed. by Frank S. Meyer (New York: Holt, Rinehart, Winston, 1964), 41–64.
79 W. Brevard Hand interview by Robert Daniel Rubin, April 13, 2000, Mobile, Ala., 5–8; *Ibid.*, April 11, 2000, 11, 18; Hand, speech at Mobile Rotary Club, 2–5, 8–11; Hand interview, October 10, 2002, 8, emphasis in original; W. Brevard Hand interview by Robert Daniel Rubin, December 5, 2000, Mobile, Ala., 9.
80 *Ibid.*, 2–3, 5–10; *Montgomery Advertiser and Alabama Journal*, November 26, 1987, p. A2. *Birmingham News*, June 28, 1987, p. A4; "High Court Declines NAACP Demand," *Mobile Register*, April 20, 1976; *Mobile Beacon*, June 16, 1984, pp. 4, 8; "Judicial Hubris and Double Standards: The Unhappy Story of Federal Judge W. Brevard Hand," *Bedeviled Advocate*, November 24, 1987, pp. 1, 6, 8; *Los Angeles Times*, March 16, 1987, sec. 1, p. 1; *Los Angeles Times*, March 29, 1987, sec. 5, p. 3; Alan Dershowitz, "A Disgrace to the Federal Judiciary," *St. Petersburg Times*, March 14, 1987; Gilliard interview, side 1; Thomas interview, 9–12; Hand interview, October 10, 2002, pp. 18–19.

81 *Clark* v. *Marengo*, 469 F.Supp. 1150 (1979), 1173 n31; *F. D. Reese* v. *Dallas County*, civil case no. 7503-73-H, accession no. 021–78-8297, location no. 181963 SAN (Federal Records Center); High Court Declines NAACP Demand," *Mobile Register*, April 20, 1976; "Master Appointed in School Suit," *Mobile Register*, May 24, 1984; "Court Keeps Expert in Segregation Case," *Mobile Press Register*, September 12, 1984; *Mobile Beacon*, June 16, 1984, pp. 4, 8; *Los Angeles Times*, March 29, 1987, sec. 5, p. 3; *Mobile Press Register*, January 7, 1996, p. A1; *Ibid.*, March 28, 1997, pp. A1, A4. Two black Mobilians whom I interviewed, James and Williams, insisted that Judge Hand was a principled and decent man, even though they disagreed strongly with his politics. James interview, side 2; Williams interview, 4, 35–37. Two other black interviewees offered drastically different assessments. Thomas characterized Hand as "the last bastion of white supremacy," a man "who believes that people 'have places' in society." According to Thomas, "the feeling in the black community is that, if you go before Judge Hand, you know you're gonna lose if you're black." In Gilliard's opinion, Hand's ideas had "always been based on a racist platform" and were marked by their lack of objectivity. Thomas interview, 9, 11; Gilliard interview, side 1.

82 Hand interview, April 11, 2000, 34; *Montgomery Advertiser and Alabama Journal*, November 26, 1987, p. A2.

83 Raoul Berger to Brevard Hand, February 1, 1983, *Jaffree* case files, Hand Papers; Brevard Hand to Raoul Berger, February 16, 1983, *Jaffree* case files, Hand Papers; Hand interview, October 10, 2002, p. 23; "Interview with W. Brevard Hand," *Southern Partisan*, 7 (Summer 1987), p. 35. Thomas M. Keck, *The Most Activist Supreme Court in History: The Road to Modern Judicial Conservatism* (Chicago: University of Chicago Press, 2004), 6, 10, 109, 148–59. Hand interview, April 11, 2000, p. 35.

84 Transcript, *Jaffree* v. *James*, 178; *Jaffree* v. *James*, 729–32.

85 Rieff, "Conflicting Rights and Religious Liberty," 197; Peter Irons, *The Courage of their Convictions: Sixteen Americans Who Fought Their Way to the Supreme Court* (New York: Penguin, 1990), 361, 363.

86 Transcript, *Ishmael Jaffree et al.* v. *Board of School Commissioners of Mobile County et al.*, Civil case no. 82–0554–H, box no. 1, accession no. 021–93–0423, location no. C0681974 SAN (Federal Records Center), November 15 1982, pp. 2–7.

87 *Ibid.*, 62–102, 108–14, 133–37, 172–73, 179–81, 208–15, 223, 250–51.

88 *Ibid.*, 71–72, 77, 95, 126–30, 174–75, 200–04.

89 The defense essentially sought a reversal of the twentieth-century case law resting on *Everson* v. *Board; McCollum* v. *Board of Education*, 333 U.S. 203 (1948); *Engel* v. *Vitale;* and *Abington* v. *Schempp.*

90 James McClellan interview by Robert Daniel Rubin, October 14, 2004 (conducted by telephone), 5; James McClellan, "The Making and Unmaking of the Establishment Clause," in *A Blueprint for Judicial Reform*, ed. by Patrick B. McGuigan and Randall R. Rader (Washington, D.C.: Free Congress Research and Education Foundation, 1981), 295–325; James McClellan, *Joseph Story and the American Constitution: A Study in Political and Legal Thought* (Norman: University of Oklahoma Press, 1971), esp. 147–49; James

McClellan, "Congressional Retraction of Federal Court Jurisdiction to Protect the Reserved Powers of the States: The Helms Prayer Bill and Return to First Principles," *Villanova Law Review*, 27 (May 1982), 1019–29. William J. Brennan, "The Constitution of the United States: Contemporary Ratification," *South Texas Law Review*, 27 (Fall 1986), 433–45.

91 McClellan interview, 1, 4, 7; Richard B. Bernstein, "R. I. P. James McClellan, 1937–2005," H-Net, June 16, 2005. http://h-net.msu.edu/cgi-bin/logbrowse.pl?trx=vx&list=HLaw&month=0506&week=c&msg=0e8YPO%2bFvZ4DsPYBV07XsQ&user=&pw; McClellan, "Congressional Retraction of Federal Court Jurisdiction to Protect the Reserved Powers of the States," 1029.

92 James McClellan, "A Lawyer Looks at Rex Lee," *Benchmark*, 1 (March–April 1984), 5, 10; James McClellan, "When Prayer Fell in Alabama: Reflections on the *Jaffree* Case," *Southern Partisan*, 4 (Spring 1984); McClellan interview, 26–27; McClellan, "Making and Unmaking of the Establishment Clause," 295; McClellan, *Joseph Story and the American Constitution*, 147, emphasis in the original.

93 Transcript, *Jaffree* v. *Board*, 525–33, 544–49.

94 *Ibid.*, 589–600.

95 *Ibid.*, 556, 603.

96 *Ibid.*, 424–32, 505–09, 578, 584–85.

97 Rousas John Rushdoony, "Religion and the State," Chalcedon Report No. 152 (Apr. 1978), in *The Roots of Reconstruction* (Vallecito, Calif.: Ross House, 1991), 985–87; Rousas John *Rushdoony, Intellectual Schizophrenia: Culture, Crisis, and Education* (Philadelphia: Presbyterian and Reformed Publishing, 1961); Rousas John Rushdoony, *The Messianic Character of American Education: Studies in the History of the Philosophy of Education* (Vallecito, Calif.: Ross House, 1963); Rousas John Rushdoony, *The Philosophy of the Christian Curriculum* (Vallecito, Calif.: Ross House, 1981).

98 Rushdoony's theocratic vision is captured in Rousas John Rushdoony, "The Meaning of Theocracy," Chalcedon Position Paper No. 15 (August 1979), in *Roots of Reconstruction*, 63–68; Rousas John Rushdoony, *The Institutes of Biblical Law*, vols. 1 and 2 (Phillipsburg, N.J.: Presbyterian and Reformed Publishing, 1973); *Washington Post*, December 23, 1987, p. D3; and Rousas John Rushdoony, "The Heresy of Democracy with God," Chalcedon Position Paper No. 6 (August 1979), in *Roots of Reconstruction*, 25–29. Rushdoony quoted in Anson Shupe, "The Reconstructionist Movement and the New Christian Right," *Christian Century*, October 4, 1989, p. 881; and Boston, "Thy Kingdom Come," 175. See also William Martin, *With God on Our Side: The Rise of the Religious Right in America* (New York: Broadway, 1996), 353–55; and Chip Berlet and Matthew N. Lyons, *Right-Wing Populism in America: Too Close for Comfort* (New York: Guilford, 2000), 247–54.

99 William Edgar, "The Passing of R. J. Rushdoony," *First Things*, no. 115 (August–September 2001), 24–25; Peter J. Liethart, "Old Geneva and the New World: The Reverend Rousas J. Rushdoony, 1916–2001," *Weekly Standard*, March 26, 2001, p. 36; Walter Olson, "Invitation to a

Stoning: Getting Cozy with Theocrats," *Reason* (November 1998), http://reason.com/9811/col.olson.shtml; Michael D. Gabbert, "An Historical Overview of Christian Reconstructionism," *Criswell Theological Review*, 6 (Spring 1993), 281–301; Shupe, "Reconstructionist Movement and the New Christian Right," 882; Rodney Clapp, "Democracy as Heresy," *Christianity Today*, February 20, 1987, pp. 17–23. John W. Whitehead, *The Separation Illusion: A Lawyer Examines the First Amendment* (Milford, Mich.: Mott, 1977), 9–10; Rushdoony, "State as an Establishment of Religion"; John W. Whitehead and John Conlan, "The Establishment of the Religion of Secular Humanism and Its First Amendment Implications," *Texas Tech Law Review*, 10 (Winter 1978), 1–66; Brief amicus curiae of the National Association of Evangelicals, *Widmar* v. *Vincent*, 454 U.S. 263 (1981), June 1, 1981. Richard John Neuhaus, "Why Wait for the Kingdom? The Theonomist Temptation," *First Things*, no. 3 (May 1990), 13–21. Many additional works confirming Rushdoony's profound influence on the Christian Right are cited in Chapter 6.

100 Transcript, *Jaffree* v. *Board*, 331–33, 361.

101 *Ibid.*, 310–16, 322, 360–61.

102 *Ibid.*, 344–60.

103 *St. Petersburg Times*, June 12, 1989, p. A1; Rob Boston, "D. James Kennedy: Who Is He and What Does He Want?" *Church & State*, 52 (April 1999), 12; Michelle Cottle, "Of God and Gays," *New Republic*, May 10, 1999, p. 23; John W. Swomley, "Who Is D. James Kennedy and Why Should We Fear Him?" *Humanist*, 57 (May–June 1997), 28–29. "Dr. Kennedy's Profile," website of Coral Ridge Ministries www.coralridge.org/about_djk.htm; *New York Times*, January 27, 1981, p. A12; *Washington Post*, January 30, 1981, p. C14; D. James Kennedy, *Reconstruction: Biblical Guidelines for a Nation in Peril* (Fort Lauderdale: Coral Ridge Ministries, 1982), i–ii, 16–20.

104 Transcript, *Jaffree* v. *Board*, 612–14, 620–23, 632–37.

105 Richard A. Baer Jr., "Teaching Values in the Schools: Clarification or Indoctrination?," *Principal* (Reston, Va.), 61 (January 1982), 16–21; Richard A. Baer Jr., "A Critique of the Use of Values Clarification in Environmental Education," *Journal of Environmental Education*, 12 (Fall 1980), 13–16; Richard A. Baer Jr., "Values Clarification as Indoctrination," *Educational Forum*, 41 (January 1977), 155–65. Values clarification was most famously championed in Louis E. Raths, Merrill Harmin, and Sidney B. Simon, *Values and Teaching: Working with Values in the Classroom* (Columbus: Merrill, 1978).

106 Transcript, *Jaffree* v. *Board*, 781–83, 786–88, 795–96, 805–08.

107 *Ibid.*, 788–91, 801, 809–10.

108 *Ibid.*, 656–57, 713.

109 *Ibid.*, 747–48.

110 *Ibid.*, 640, 683–86, 691–94, 712–16. *Jaffree* v. *Board of School Commissioners of Mobile County*, 554 F.Supp. 1104 (1983), 748–49.

111 Rieff, "Conflicting Rights and Religious Liberty," 197; Irons, *Courage of their Convictions*, 361, 363.

3

Justice Made Political

CORRECTING THE SUPREME COURT'S ERRORS

On January 14, 1983, two months after the conclusion of testimony in *Jaffree* v. *Board of School Commissioners,* Brevard Hand found against the plaintiff. The Establishment Clause had not been violated, he ruled; the teachers' religious activities had not violated the Constitution. Hand "therefore ordered that the complaint" against them and the school board "be dismissed with prejudice." He issued the briefest of opinions regarding Jaffree's lawsuit against the state, which, since the August injunction, had lain unaddressed. "In light of the reasoning in" *Jaffree* v. *Board,* Hand summarily found, "the Court holds that the claims in this case [*Jaffree* v. *James*] fail to state any claim for which relief could be granted under the federal Constitution." Without further ado, the judge dissolved his own injunction and sanctioned Alabama's 1981 and 1982 prayer laws. Case closed.[1]

Hand did more than strike down Ishmael Jaffree's entire complaint. The judge's ruling in *Jaffree* v. *Board* confronted the American legal and political establishments with a brazen set of claims about the nature of American government and the way the Constitution ought to be understood. No narrow opinion, *Jaffree* v. *Board* was a broadside for numerous causes central to the New Right: the need to read the Constitution's text strictly, place it in the historical context of its authors' supposed intentions, protect public expressions of religion, defend states' rights, assure popular majorities of their right to determine the laws by which they lived, and resist the dissolution of the Constitution's republican principles.

The *Jaffree* decision thrust Hand into a debate surrounding perhaps the era's most important constitutional question – whether, when interpreting the Constitution, federal judges ought to rely exclusively on the words of the text and the intentions of its authors, or whether they should think of the text's meaning as unsettled and evolving, understandable only in light of society's changeable circumstances. These were years in which many politicians, lawyers, and intellectuals widely attacked what they labeled liberal "judicial activism," or policymaking by liberal judges. Hand left no doubt where he stood. Judges had to choose among two distinct methods of interpretation, he wrote. They could treat the Constitution either as its creators intended it be treated, or "as a living document, chameleon-like in its complexion, which changes to suit the needs of the times and the whims of the interpreters." Hand chose the former. As he plainly admitted, he hoped through his ruling to build support for the "originalist" understanding, that the Constitution means today exactly what it meant when originally written and ratified. "The paramount consideration in defining the scope of any constitutional provision," he maintained, is "to ascertain the intent of the legislature" that generated it. And intent could best "be evidenced by statements of the leading proponents." Therein lay the key to understanding the First and Fourteenth amendments. "If statements of the leading proponents are found, those statements are to be regarded as good as if they were written into the enactment."[2]

Regardless of how much Hand considered himself an originalist seeking only to understand and implement the Constitution, his *Jaffree* opinion performed political work. Through it he tried to ensure that judges not use the Constitution to usurp the people's right to legislate through their elected representatives. Hand maintained that the living Constitution effectively amended the document, which could rightly be done only according to the procedures mandated in the document itself and not according to the whims of judicial activists. "Amendment through judicial fiat is both unconstitutional and illegal," he asserted. "It undermines the very basic notion that this country is governed by laws and not by men." Hand argued that judicial activism, far more than just being wrongheaded, was terribly dangerous, as it set an example by which reckless judges could bend the law to their will. He beseeched his fellow citizens: "We must give no future generation an excuse to use this same tactic to further [the] ends which they think proper under the then political climate as for instance did Adolph Hitler when he used the court system to further his goals." To preserve the public's trust in the courts, and to halt the republic's slide into tyranny, judges had to ground themselves in the clear "teachings of history," which counseled judicial restraint.[3]

Hand admitted his "indebtedness to several constitutional scholars" whose work informed the designs behind his ruling. Two he mentioned by name. "If this opinion will accomplish its intent, which is to take us back to our original historical roots, then much of the credit for the vision lies with Professor James McClellan and Professor Robert L. Cord." McClellan – chief witness for the Mobile school board and author of an intervenors' exhibit – was cited frequently throughout the decision. So, too, was Cord, from whose seminal work, *Separation of Church and State,* the intervenors drew directly in their questioning. Hand similarly relied on the work of Raoul Berger, a close friend of McClellan and the era's most noted articulator of the originalist position. Hand had seized the opportunity that McClellan had laid down before him – to instigate a conservative constitutional counterrevolution rolling back decades of supposedly unsound, illegitimate rulings. He, as much as the parties to the case, had become personally invested in his ruling.[4]

Hand's historical investigation began with the Establishment Clause, its authors, and their immediate historical context. Hand made no pretense of detachment. McClellan's position simply became his position. Quoting McClellan's essay "The Making and Unmaking of the Establishment Clause," Hand found that the Establishment Clause was intended, not to forbid government advancement of Christianity, but rather "to exclude all rivalry among *Christian* sects and to prevent any *national* ecclesiastical establishment." Hand used the same essay in asserting that the Founders never intended to apply the Establishment Clause to the states. Paraphrasing McClellan's trial testimony, he concluded that "the first amendment in large part was a guarantee to the states which insured that the states would be able to continue whatever church-state relations existed in 1791." Hand condemned recent Establishment Clause jurisprudence and called for its undoing. "Enough is enough," he declared. Now was the time to resuscitate the true historical record, and he was resolved to do the job.[5]

Hand likewise positioned himself in a debate, then going on among some politically inclined lawyers, about whether the Fourteenth Amendment truly incorporates the Bill of Rights. Although for practical purposes the question had been decided by the Supreme Court by the 1950s, some conservatives wished to reopen the matter. *Jaffree* allowed Hand to join the fray. He found that McClellan had presented convincing evidence against incorporation. Hand did not mention the plaintiffs' evidence because there was no evidence to mention – Ronnie Williams had assumed the matter long settled and so had said nothing about it. Based on a selective reading of constitutional scholarship, Hand pronounced judgment against the Court's entire practice of extending the Bill of Rights to the states. "The historical record," he concluded, "shows without equivocation that ... the fourteenth amendment did not incorporate the establishment clause of the first amendment against the states."[6]

Hand's advocacy of states' rights and judicial restraint reinforced his majoritarian convictions. Religious minorities needed to endure the indignities and inconveniences that went along with being different from the majority, he believed. The Jaffree children's suffering of ostracism did not entitle them to legal redress. "Since the states were historically free to establish a religion," he reasoned, "some irritation by non-believers or those in the religious minority was a necessary consequence of establishment." It could not be prevented. "Psychological pressure naturally flows anytime a state takes an official position on an issue"; that in itself did "not make an establishment unconstitutional." Whenever the majority determined laws, Hand wrote, minorities had to endure constraint, even compulsion. The Constitution did "not protect people from feeling uncomfortable. A member of a religious minority will have to develop a thicker skin if a state establishment offends him." And "tender years are no exception," he added, with the plaintiff's children in mind.[7]

Hand's majoritarianism spoke to his republicanism. By protecting the majority's right to legislate, Hand claimed, we preserve popular sovereignty. If we "have faith in the rightness of our charter," he wrote, "then all will have input into change and not just a few." For Hand, it was the Constitution's republican nature that the justices had most egregiously contravened. In its haste to do good, the Court had usurped the people's fundamental right and responsibility to choose their laws freely and wisely. "The judiciary has, in fact, amended the Constitution to the consternation of the republic," Hand warned. No matter how pure their motives, judicial activists were baldly "denying to the people their right to express themselves. It is not what we, the judiciary, want," he maintained; "it is what the people want translated into law pursuant to the plan established in the Constitution as the framers intended. This is the bedrock and genius of our republic." The "mantle of office gives us no power to fix the moral direction that this nation will take," he insisted. When judges legislated, they destroyed the republican fabric from which America was woven. Hand refused to be party to such treachery.[8]

By emphasizing his obligation to the Constitution's text rather than the Court's rulings, Hand justified his most radical assertion: that a lower-court judge such as himself was not bound to uphold federal case law that he found unconstitutional. Hand once more walked the path laid out for him by McClellan. To validate his violation of *stare decisis*, Hand cited legal authorities who suggested that the automatic affirming of precedent could have deleterious consequences. He implied that judicial custom required – and certainly permitted – a federal judge sometimes to violate case law. "In cases involving the federal constitution," Hand asserted, "a court should be willing to examine earlier precedent and overrule it if the court is persuaded that the earlier precedent was wrongly decided." This was especially so when that court determined that the justices had failed to account for the historical context in which the constitutional provisions in question had originally been adopted. Because "the United States Supreme Court has erred in its reading of history," he felt compelled to countermand First Amendment jurisprudence.[9]

Given how drastically his *Jaffree* decision disturbed existing doctrine, Hand suspected that it might go unheeded – or worse. Most of the legal establishment and the national media, he recognized, would assume that he had acted with recklessness and contempt. Yet Hand was unfazed. "Perhaps," he imagined, "this opinion will be no more than a voice crying in the wilderness." Perhaps his "attempt to right ... a misreading of history" would "come to nothing more than blowing in the hurricane." But, for Hand, crying in the wilderness was a small price to pay for preserving the Constitution. It had to be done.[10]

Although the judge considered himself properly stationed to reverse erroneous Supreme Court decisions, the passages he quoted called on "the Court" rather than "a court" to resist blind adherence to precedent. "The Court" would seem to refer to the Supreme Court, not to any and all federal courts. Only McClellan appeared to sanction the kind of pioneering course Hand trod. Not even those critics of the Supreme Court who urged it to revisit certain areas of case law recommended that lower-court judges reverse High Court precedent. Hand did not acknowledge the radicalism of his action. He failed to recognize the irony that, in disregarding *stare decisis*, he himself could be accused of the very recklessness and disregard for history with which he charged others. His criticism of judicial activism – the tendency of judges to abrogate so much power unto themselves that they effectively amended the Constitution by "judicial fiat" – could easily be redirected back against him.

Hand did not intend his political efforts to be stymied by the reversal that likely awaited his *Jaffree* ruling. If *Jaffree* were reversed, he did "not desire to be precluded from a further recitation of appropriate fact as may be essential to further conclusions in the case." His processing of the facts and law in the case may have been sufficient for rendering a decision, but the process had not been exhaustive. Further resolution might be necessary. He warned that, "if the appellate courts disagree with this Court in its examination of history and conclusion of constitutional interpretation thereof, then this Court will look again at the record in this case and reach conclusions which it is not now forced to reach."[11]

"Should [his] judgment be reversed" and the case be remanded back to him, what issues would compel his further attention? Hand pledged to address those matters raised by the intervenors. He would be forced to consider whether secular humanism was a religion and whether it had been systematically promoted in Mobile schools. He may not have based his ruling on the intervenors' arguments, but he had been persuaded by them. "If this Court is compelled to purge [daily prayer] from the classroom," Hand promised, "then this Court must also purge from the classroom those things that serve to teach that salvation is through one's self rather than through a deity." Establishment Clause jurisprudence had not resolved the issue, he maintained. As it now stood, "case law deals generally with removing the teachings of the Christian ethic from the scholastic effort but totally ignores the teaching of the secular humanist ethic." Case law did not address the situation in Mobile public schools, which, the intervenors had shown, were "rife with efforts at teaching or encouraging secular humanism – all without opposition from any other ethic – to such an extent that it [had become] a brainwashing effort." Hand warned his superiors: If forced to implement the Establishment Clause, he would view it more comprehensively than it had yet been viewed.[12]

Hand surmised how all this might look. He confirmed the school board's contention that the intervenors had positioned themselves analogously to Ishmael Jaffree. "The advocacy of the intervenors," he acknowledged, required that they be realigned as plaintiffs. They, like Jaffree, had charged Mobile schools with violating the Establishment Clause. Should the clause be enforced against the Mobile schools, then Sherling's and Kotouc's clients would have as much of a claim as Jaffree. What exactly this might entail remained unclear. But Hand warned of the great difficulties that would be unleashed were he forced to deny the state of Alabama the right to religious establishment. A continued "blind adherence" by the

Court to church-state doctrine would "result in an engulfing flood of other cases addressed to the same point raised by intervenors." To reverse Hand would be to open a can of worms so big it could not be contained. The implications were unfathomable. Courts thereafter would "be called upon to determine whether each [school] book or any statement therein advances secular humanism in a religious sense, a never-ending task." This was the judge's greatest fear – or hope.[13]

UP AND DOWN THE LADDER

Prior to the *Jaffree* trial, the key actors in the conflict had been motivated by a variety of factors. The attorney for the Mobile school board, Bob Campbell, had pragmatically defended the right of local educators to conduct classes as they saw fit. Board president Dan Alexander had been concerned primarily with the rights of local taxpayers, and with his own reputation. Governor Fob James had sought somehow to convince the Supreme Court to reverse its 1962 and 1963 rulings against prayer in public schools. The lawyers for the intervenors, Tom Kotouc and Bob Sherling, had cared most about protecting the rights of Christians. And Hand had set out, as he always did, to limit the federal government's ability to impose its will on Alabama. Although each of those men would have identified as a conservative, only the governor had aimed to spark constitutional counterrevolution.

With the handing down of Hand's *Jaffree* opinion on January 14, 1983, each of the key conservative actors in the case came to embrace and adopt the testimony and writings of McClellan. Hand validated McClellan's majoritarian vision and encouraged the others to tie their own arguments to it. Each, scrambling to position himself and represent his stance in the best possible light, now identified his own objectives with the constitutional counterrevolution being advanced not only by McClellan but also by conservatives at the upper echelons of government. The constitutional theory that McClellan had so convincingly delivered before the court came to shape the post-trial legal machinations of most of the key *Jaffree* players.[14]

McClellan's and Hand's positions squared perfectly with James's views. The governor lauded Hand's decision as an important victory in the emerging battle to defend the right of states to resist encroachment by the federal government. The day of the verdict was "a historic day," in James' estimation, and Hand was a "courageous and brilliant" man. Throughout the entire affair, James had looked for *Jaffree* to trigger a full-scale reversal of *Engel* and *Schempp*. Now, he declared, that reversal had begun. The governor called on the administration of President Ronald Reagan actively to assist the *Jaffree* defendants in their legal travails. More than defending religion in schools motivated the governor. In the weeks since the trial, he had become consumed with advancing constitutional federalism. Speaking to a group of law students, James emphasized the importance of the states' rights cause, which his own administration had served by passing the prayer statutes and defending them in court. In the near future, he predicted, constitutional conservatives would carry the fight to the Supreme Court, to appeal the Eleventh Circuit's all-but-certain reversal of Hand's ruling.[15]

Local support for the ruling was abundant. The *Mobile Press-Register* praised Hand's opinion while denouncing the Court and its *Engel* and *Schempp* rulings. Stuart Gaines, executive director of the Moral Majority of Alabama, called the decision "fantastic" and predicted it would send "a few tremors out of Mobile across the map." Two of the teachers who had sparked the controversy, Charlene Boyd and Julia Green, voiced great satisfaction with the ruling; the third teacher, Ella Alexander, labeled it the product of God's will. The principal of Mobile's Murphy High School called the ruling proper and inevitable. In Alabama, he declared, "you can no more keep prayer and Bible-reading down than you can keep black people segregated in 1983. Prayer is as much a part of our culture as the turnip greens and cornbread we serve in the cafeteria."[16]

The most widely publicized local reaction came from Alexander. Like James, Alexander applauded the ruling's clear defense of the right of states to determine their own policies on religion. Immediately after the decision was announced, the board president held a televised press conference at Hall Elementary School, where he reported that Hand had just given his okay to saying grace in class. All at once, the schoolchildren in attendance broke into applause and recited grace in unison. This confirmed for Alexander that Hand's interpretation of the Constitution echoed the longtime thinking of Alabamians. "When we used to say 'states' rights,' that's what we were talking about," Alexander explained. Hopefully, the concept might now be resuscitated, stripped free of the arch segregationist uses to which it historically had been put.[17]

The very aspects of Hand's opinion that so pleased James and Alexander – its protection of the popular majority's right to promote its morality under law, its defense of the doctrine of states' rights, and its audacious strike against Supreme Court jurisprudence – stunned Ishmael Jaffree.

He could only marvel at what seemed to him the decision's groundlessness and absurdity. It made no more sense to Jaffree than "the president calling a news conference to say he's discovered the world is flat." Immediately, he promised to challenge the ruling, insisting that he would "be boiled in oil" if he did not.[18]

Before filing an appeal, Jaffree and Williams tried, once again, to gain some relief from the trial judge. They asked Hand to reinstate his initial injunction and to reverse his judgment assessing trial costs to the plaintiffs – arguing, in essence, that they shouldn't be forced to pay for a trial that by all rights they deserved to win. "Plaintiffs," they wrote, "would be the prevailing parties, but for the Court's decision to decline to follow *stare decisis*." In all fairness, they should not be required to fund a trial judge's adventures in bald judicial activism. In no way, they insisted, could they have anticipated the judge's startling refusal to acknowledge his own jurisdiction over a state government's entanglement with religion. It was reckless, Williams suggested, for the court to reverse itself and violate established practice.[19]

Hand would have none of this. Promptly and without comment, he denied Williams's motion. The Eleventh Circuit Court of Appeals turned down a similar request, days later, to enjoin Hand's *Jaffree* v. *Board* and *Jaffree* v. *James* rulings. A frustrated Williams determined that he would have to go even further up the judicial ladder to find relief from the unrelenting religious proselytization practiced by the state and its servants. His search to win an injunction set into motion a two-month-long game of mutual recrimination between the plaintiffs and the Mobile school system, with each side accusing the other of acting unreasonably and unlawfully. Throughout, the board would invoke the authority of the trial court, which stood at the bottom of the power chain in the federal judiciary. Williams, knowing he would find little sympathy there, would travel up the ladder of judicial authority in search of relief.[20]

On February 1, 1983, Williams submitted an emergency request to Justice Lewis F. Powell, the member of the U.S. Supreme Court in charge of emergency motions for the Eleventh Circuit. Williams asked Powell to stay and enjoin Hand's two rulings until the Eleventh Circuit could review the case. In Williams's estimation, the current situation constituted an emergency and required immediate intervention. "The extraordinary relief sought in this application," Williams told Powell, was "extremely necessary, because, as of the date of the district court's ruling (January 14, 1983), prayer activity ha[d] resumed in Alabama public schools." Marked as "'different' than their peers," the Jaffree children were "being made to suffer," in violation of their First Amendment rights. The plaintiffs hoped that Powell would understand and honor their claims. They reminded him that, "with one stroke of [Hand's] pen the district court reversed over thirty-five years of Supreme Court precedent," and that, "if this ruling is allowed to stand the economic, political and social consequences will be *devastating*."[21]

By turning to the top of the federal judiciary, to a member of the same judicial body that had forged the nation's First Amendment case law, the plaintiffs attained a measure of success. Only hours after Williams had filed his motion, Powell granted a temporary stay against the district court's judgments. Nine days later, after reviewing the case, Powell concluded that "the District Court was obligated to follow ... this Court's decisions" in *Engel* and *Schempp*. Bound by *stare decisis*, Powell saw himself with no choice but to enforce the Supreme Court's determination that "conducting prayers as part of a school program is unconstitutional," even when "participation in those exercises was voluntary." He therefore felt "compelled to grant the requested stay."[22]

Determined not to let a Supreme Court justice undo its recent achievements, the school board attempted to minimize the impact of Powell's order. On February 3, the day after Powell had issued his preliminary stay, Campbell and Alexander sent every Mobile public-school principal a letter instructing her to direct her teachers not to decease from organized, outloud religious exercises but to "do what their convictions tell them to do." Because "Justice Powell did not enjoin all prayer activities" in explicit language, but had merely reinstituted Judge Hand's earlier injunction against the 1982 prayer law, the letter claimed, "Powell ha[d] put the case in the exact same posture it was in before Judge Hand ruled" on January 15. That is, Powell wanted teachers to decide for themselves whether or not to conduct religious exercises. Campbell and Alexander announced that "children and teachers can continue the activities they ha[d] been accustomed to prior to Mr. Jaffree's filing of the lawsuit against the board" as long as they steered clear of reciting the prayer provided by the 1982 prayer law. The board would not enforce any particular policy on prayer activities. In so doing it would abide by Powell's order.[23]

In fact, Powell's order did more than reinstitute Hand's original injunction. Powell's order stayed Hand's entire judgment. It applied to Jaffree's case against the school board and teachers as much as his case against the governor; it equally precluded any and all recitation of classroom prayer and implementation of the prayer statutes. The promptness of Powell's response, which came down within a few hours, indicated a strong and direct affirmation of the appellant's motion. With his swift affirmation, Powell approved Jaffree's request that Hand's ruling be stayed specifically in order to spare Jaffree's children the agonizing indignity of enduring classroom prayer. The Alabama statutes were not at issue, as they did not practically affect the situation in Mobile classrooms, where teachers conducted religious exercises on their own accord and in the manner of their own choosing. Quelling all religious exercises was the goal of Jaffree's request. It was the point of Powell's order.[24]

For Campbell and Alexander to interpret Powell's order as an injunction against only the Alabama prayer laws was to ignore the context in which the order had been sought and issued. But Campbell and Alexander were less interested in observing legal directives than in waging constitutional counterrevolution of the sort championed by McClellan. That Powell had intended to squelch religious classroom exercises only hardened their resolve. Their refusal to cease all prayer activities constituted a willful act of disobedience. Intentionally and blatantly, they challenged the Court's authority. Buoyed by Hand's brazen judicial activism, they followed the judge's lead in declaring that church-state policy was for local majorities to determine.[25]

Alexander painted the Supreme Court's intervention as antidemocratic. He expressed shock "that a single justice would take action interrupting 65,000 youngsters because of three" dissatisfied children. As per usual, he said, the Court had ignored the people's wishes. It was now up to the people to voice their disgust. "If someone doesn't give [the justices] the finger every now and then," Alexander sneered, "nothing ever changes." He promised that teachers in the Mobile schools would "do the same as in the past" and "go ahead" with their prayers as always. The school system would not cave in to Jaffree's "blatant attempt ... to halt the desires and rights of 65,000 schoolchildren and approximately 3,100 school teachers." After all, the vast majority had rights, too.[26]

Over the next six weeks, the plaintiffs and the school board struggled with each other to exert control over the situation. Jaffree would continue sending letters to the school system and the individuals involved with it, hoping somehow to cajole or coerce them into ceasing all religious classroom activities. Alexander and Campbell dug in their heels in defiance – against church-state separation, minority religious rights, and federal-court jurisdiction over school prayer. While Jaffree accused them of flaunting a direct order of the Supreme Court, they accused him of disregarding the judgment handed down by the district court. Just as Jaffree and Williams went up the judicial ladder to elicit the support of an authority who would tend to their interests, so did Alexander and Campbell climb back down the ladder and appeal to Hand, the one federal judge on whose sympathy they could count. Throughout, Jaffree's opponents would paint him – and not the school board – as the party running afoul of the courts. It was he, they insisted, who remained determined to impose his unpopular, idiosyncratic values on a law-abiding, God-worshipping community.

Jaffree's letters reiterated his complaint that the schools were denying his and his children's constitutional rights. He threatened to seek penalties against the school system in the event it continued allowing prayer. After Powell issued his preliminary order, Jaffree sent Makeba's teacher a letter asserting, yet again, that the Constitution permits government-run schools to transmit only secular values to children. The board's failure to comply with Powell's order prompted him to ask that Alexander issue "a notice to every school within this system advising all teachers to temporarily halt any and all sponsoring, initiating, organizing or approving of group prayer activities pending this appeal." In the event that his request was refused, he suggested that serious legal consequences would ensue.[27]

In his letter of March 11, Jaffree explained that his "obligations to members of Mobile's minority religious and non-religious communities" compelled his continued effort to stop the religious exercises. Jaffree portrayed himself as an outsider defending other outsiders, a member of a religious minority acting on behalf of all minorities. "Mine is a plea from another 'voice in the wilderness,'" he declared, borrowing an image from Hand's trial opinion. Beckoning from Mobile's remote cultural fringe, Jaffree told board members that he was "seeking [their] help with what is both a moral and legal dilemma" regarding whether or not to publicize the privately held sentiments of his allies. Another religious minority group, Mobile's Jewish community, had confided to him that they supported his mission. They admitted that they hadn't spoken out, according to Jaffree, because they didn't wish to anger Mobile's Christian majority. Like him, Mobile's Jews knew that the Constitution required church-state separation. Like him, they saw that freedom and democracy were threatened by the policies of the school board. "It is rather tragic that in this Country any member of any minority must fear reprisals if they speak out on controversial and politically sensitive issues."[28]

The board flat-out rejected Jaffree's claim to be a defender of the Constitution and the democratic values it embodied. The reality, Campbell suggested, was quite the opposite. On March 14, three days after Jaffree's final letter to the board, Campbell filed a motion with the district court asking that the plaintiff "be restrained and enjoined" from contacting or threatening the defendants or from "willfully ... interfering with the appeal of this case." The brief accused Jaffree of being a menace to – rather than a protector of – the public interest. Jaffree's demands constituted nothing less than "extortion and blackmail," a "campaign of harassment against the defendants," with the "intent of intimidating and coercing the[m]." What made Jaffree's behavior most offensive, according to the brief, was his standing as a civil servant, a Legal Services employee whose "salary is paid by the taxpayers of this country." Obligated to the people and bound to honor their decent sensibilities, Jaffree had instead offended them.[29]

To win sole legitimacy for its interpretation of the plaintiff's actions, the board sought to change the context surrounding them. While Jaffree portrayed himself as a beleaguered parent trying to secure for himself and his children the protection guaranteed by a direct order of a Supreme Court justice, Campbell painted him as a reckless attorney unwilling to abide by a district judge's ruling. Campbell charged Jaffree with mocking Hand's authority. This, and not the board's disrespect for the Supreme Court, was, for Campbell, the relevant background. Campbell's account virtually ignored Powell's order, thereby stripping Jaffree's actions of the context that most rendered them reasonable. Campbell requested that Hand "reiterate and confirm" his trial order dismissing Jaffree's complaint, in order to prevent Jaffree from "usurping this Court's power" with his demands on the school board. According to the board's brief, Jaffree had attempted effectively to retry the case through his inflammatory letters. His "actions represent[ed] a direct attack on this Court's decision." By suggesting that Jaffree had slighted Hand personally, Campbell played on the ego as well as the ideology of the one judge on whose assistance he could count – the one federal-court insider whom he knew to be a proponent of constitutional counterrevolution.[30]

Williams remained as determined to lift the case back up the judicial ladder as Campbell was to push it back down. One week later, Williams made good on Jaffree's threat to bring contempt charges against the board, asking Powell "to order appellees ... to show cause why they should not be held in contempt for violating Your Order of February 11, 1983." Just as Campbell had emphasized Jaffree's disregard for Hand's ruling, so did Williams emphasize the board's reckless disregard for Powell's injunction against Hand's ruling. "In an act of dogged defiance," Williams alleged, "the Board of School Commissioners of Mobile County, through its agents, servants, and employees, has disobeyed an

Order of a Justice of the United States Supreme Court." In so doing they threatened "to render courts and the judges who preside over them impotent," and to turn "the judicial power of the United States" into "a mere mockery."[31]

TEAM MCCLELLAN

Campbell and his clients weren't the only party aiming to thwart Jaffree's pursuit of minority rights. The intervenors, still involved in the case, had come on board with McClellan's constitutional interpretation. This constituted a shift. To be sure, their argument retained its civil-libertarian slant. The intervenors' lawyers urged the Eleventh Circuit, in the event it overturned Hand, to remand the case back to him and permit him to conduct a finding of fact to determine if secular humanism was being established in the schools, and if their own clients' right to free exercise was being violated. However, at this juncture, their argument's superior premise became that Hand had ruled correctly and that the appellate court should not reverse him. They framed their February 28 brief, as Hand had framed his January 14 decision, with McClellan's constitutionalism. In accord with what they identified as the Founders' intentions, Sherling and Kotouc proclaimed that the Establishment Clause did only two things: It prohibited creation of an official national religion, and it protected the right of individual states to establish religions free from congressional interference. Like Hand, the intervenors' lawyers relied on McClellan and Cord to substantiate this claim. And, like Hand, they relied on Berger and Charles Fairman in asserting the illegitimacy of the incorporation doctrine. Finally, they retread McClellan's steps when they declared that Hand was justified in disregarding *stare decisis*. Their exposure to McClellan's ideas had opened these two evangelical cause lawyers to the New Right's anti-judge, states' rights constitutionalism. Kotouc and Sherling now chose – at least for the time being – to align themselves with their fellow appellees in calling for a rollback of federal judicial review over state laws concerning religion.[32]

The new governor of Alabama, George C. Wallace, required no recruitment to the counterrevolution. During his earlier tenures as governor, 1963–1967 and 1971–1979, Wallace had angrily objected as the federal courts struck down law after law in the southern states. The courts' rulings against segregation and school prayer had especially enraged Wallace, who publicly denounced federal judges as Godless traitors against the United States and its people. Upon returning to office in January 1983, Wallace resumed his diatribe against the federal courts and their alleged usurpation of sovereignty rightfully belonging to the people and their elected state officials. The incoming governor picked up where the departing one left off, defending the right of the Alabama legislature to pass laws sanctioning prayer in public schools – laws desired, Wallace maintained, by the vast majority of Alabamians. The brief he submitted to the Eleventh Circuit in February expressed in more virulent language the same constitutional principles that McClellan had asserted and Hand had affirmed, the same constitutional principles being promoted by New Right politicians in Washington and throughout the United States in 1983.[33]

In his appellate brief, Wallace relied on his predecessor's constitutional interpretation, which had emphasized both the text itself and the history behind its creation. The new governor's brief also included, as an appendix, the petition for a writ of mandamus that James and his son had tried to submit to the Supreme Court back in October. Wallace, like McClellan, approached the First and Fourteenth amendments as an originalist and strict constructionist. The governor argued that, because the *Engel* and *Schempp* decisions were based neither on the plain text nor on the Framers' intent, they lacked constitutional legitimacy and demanded reversal.[34]

Hand had ruled properly, Wallace believed – in contrast to the Supreme Court, with its cult of constitutional interpretation. For Wallace, the question at the heart of *Jaffree* was "whether a judge of an inferior federal court must blindly follow precedents of the Supreme Court or is bound by his oath to follow the U.S. Constitution." The governor applauded Hand for recognizing that his only obligation was to the written Constitution, that "there is no constitutional provision that forces a judge to follow precedents of the Supreme Court." Hand had set into motion fundamental constitutional change, and it was now up to the Eleventh Circuit to advance the cause yet further. Wallace encouraged the court of appeals to capitalize on its "opportunity to join Judge Hand in pointing the way for other federal courts, including the Supreme Court, to correct previous rulings by which, under the leadership of the Supreme Court, federal courts have assumed powers which were not given to them by this Constitution."[35]

Wallace's brief captured the New Right's moral majoritarianism. The governor declared that the Supreme Court, through its church-state decisions, had disregarded the people's wishes and thereby forfeited their support. "It was obvious … that the people were losing confidence in the highest court of the land." Most Americans, he reported, felt strongly that the Constitution protected school prayer. "They could not believe that a Constitution, under whose protection schoolchildren had prayed in their classroom for 174 years, should suddenly have made this practice unconstitutional." "The people" had insisted that it was not the Supreme Court's place to "fix the moral direction that this nation will take," and they had "begun to ask why judges whom they have not elected can make the laws for them." Wallace accused the Supreme Court of misusing the Fourteenth Amendment. Under the guise of "substantive due process," the Court had usurped the people's right to self-rule. "The real Constitution," he charged, was "based on the principles of sovereignty and self-government of the people. In such a system, the decision as to what is 'implicit in the concept of ordered liberty,' is a policy decision and belongs to the people who make their will known through their elected representatives."[36]

The new governor urged the judges of the Eleventh Circuit to join himself, Hand, and other conservatives in restoring "the real Constitution," which rested on popular sovereignty. Wallace tied his defense of school prayer, states' rights, and legislative supremacy to the prominent New Right claim that a "Constitution in exile," discredited during the New Deal and the Warren Court, lay waiting to be restored to its rightful authority. He hitched his case to a growing nationwide movement aiming to peel back a half-century of liberal governance and to strip activist federal judges of the lawmaking authority that they had stolen from the people. As he had done earlier in his career, Wallace dug in his heels and waged "massive resistance" against the forces of liberalism and the authority of the federal courts.[37]

UP TOWARD WASHINGTON

When Hand placed the imprimatur of the federal judiciary on the constitutional vision advanced by McClellan, he did more than frustrate Jaffree's complaint, more even than declare school prayer consistent with the U.S. Constitution. Hand – along with Campbell, Alexander, Kotouc, Sherling, and James – had enlisted in a constitutional counterrevolution led by men at the center of American government during the early-to-mid 1980s. That effort was spearheaded by a cadre of prominent legal scholars and activists, members of the Reagan Justice Department, several far-right Republican senators, and a conservative minority on the Supreme Court. Their impassioned advocacy kept constitutional issues at the forefront of the New Right agenda throughout the Reagan presidency. The ensuing struggle to preserve Hand's *Jaffree* ruling was part of a larger struggle to create a majoritarian form of republican democracy, one capable of promoting the sort of "traditional" moral worldview that, its proponents believed, the majority of Americans wanted to see promoted under law.

It made sense for the appellees to turn for support to the Reagan administration. Throughout the 1980 campaign and his first two years in office, President Reagan had repeatedly spoken out in favor of school prayer and against activist judges who ruled it unconstitutional. He gave the Alabama governor and the Mobile school board reason for hoping that the Department of Justice might write an amicus brief (a friend-of-the-court memorandum) or even argue on their behalf at the appellate hearing. And hope they did. James wanted "to see President Reagan file a brief through the Department of Justice." Alexander wanted the same. Noting that "Reagan has consistently pledged support for school prayer," Alexander believed that the president had now been handed an opportunity to act on that support, and he called for him to do so.[38]

The *Jaffree* defendants gained a boost when their cause was taken up by Jeremiah Denton, U.S. senator from Alabama since 1981 and champion of myriad conservative moral causes. Born and raised in Mobile, Denton achieved fame in 1966 as a prisoner of war in Hanoi, North Vietnam, when, during a televised interview with a Japanese correspondent, he blinked T-O-R-T-U-R-E in Morse code. At a time when many soldiers were questioning the mission and tactics of the armed forces of the United States, Denton stood out for his undiminished love of country and faith in God. Commander Denton spent seven and a half years in prison camps. After returning to the United States in 1973, he continued to defend the nation's war effort, which, he insisted, had been thwarted only by bad decisions made in Washington. His years in battle and in prison left him, above all, with a deep faith. "I'm a changed man," Denton told a reporter in 1978. "I know God." His experience had "remove[d] all doubt" in his mind that God had special plans for his country and for him. "I am now unafraid to ... protest against those things which He sees [as] wrong."[39]

The society and culture that Denton found upon his return seemed to him far more sordid and sick than the one he had known before going off to war in 1964. Returning home "was an unbelievable culture shock." The former navy commander found an American people besieged by immorality. "Divorces were incredibly high, the family was breaking up. . . . This nation [wa]s not being true to what [had] brought us to our greatness." Confronted with "the destruction of the family as an institution," American society faced "immediate danger." Denton lamented that his government had turned its back on the Ten Commandments, "the values on which it was founded and by which it was great." By ignoring those values, America was endangering its future. In late October 1977, he became executive assistant to the president of a local college. Soon after, Denton went to work for the Christian Broadcasting Network, believing that such work would allow him better to serve God and country. His quest led him in 1980 to seek the office of U.S. senator. Bolstered by the energetic grassroots assistance of Jerry Falwell's Moral Majority and the support of stalwart senator Jesse Helms, Denton bested his Democratic opponent in November 1980 and became Alabama's first Republican senator since Reconstruction.[40]

Denton quickly became one of the most active and outspoken members of an incoming group of New Right senators seeking to remake government. Throughout his Senate career, from 1981 to 1986, he promoted issues central to the Reagan revolution. Denton railed against "big government" and in favor of free enterprise; he blasted the newspapers and the television networks for their alleged liberal bias; he fervently opposed gun control, supported increases in defense spending, and defended restrictions on the civil liberties of criminal suspects. As chair of the Subcommittee on Security and Terrorism, he announced that "the national good is best served by a limited relinquishment of some individual rights." Threatening, un-American forces evoked his bitter ire. These included peace advocates, violent criminals, and "federal judges [who] show[ed] more compassion for rapists and murderers than for the innocent citizens who are their victims." The society that the senator had known and loved – American society of the 1950s – had been turned inside out by the liberalism of the 1960s. His quest now was to rescue America from decadence and permissiveness.[41]

Denton's "morals" agenda, like that of the *Jaffree* intervenors, featured a call to self-restraint and self-discipline – a central tenet of American conservatism. Perhaps his biggest cause, trying to curb the sexual appetites of teenagers, embodied this value. Only by practicing sexual abstinence, he believed, could teenagers internalize the discipline on which a free society rested. "Freedom is the luxury of self-discipline, and we're blowing it," he declared. In spring 1981, Denton won passage of a bill derisively known as the "Chastity Law," whose essential purpose was to "discourage teenagers from engaging in sexual activity, while encouraging those who did become pregnant to carry their pregnancies to term." He became one of the most ardent advocates in Washington for what was becoming widely promoted as "family values." "In order to have a family, you've got to have some kind of self-discipline effort with respect to the control of your sexual drive," he opined again and again. Denton spoke out against abortion, pornography, and married women working at paid jobs. He implored his followers not to lose hope. "As a United States senator, I am working to pass laws and policies in the U.S. Congress which are morally good for your family and our society," Denton promised. His work did not go unnoticed, as conservative organizations repeatedly honored him as one of their most admired and appreciated members of Congress.[42]

Denton called Hand's *Jaffree* decision an important "step in our struggle to restore constitutional rights," to put America "back on the right track of re-establishing our proud heritage as a nation which respects and protects religious freedom." The senator "commended the U.S. District Court for the Southern District of Alabama for its courage in standing up for the right of the States to make and implement their own laws in accordance with their constitutional powers." He set out, prior to the appellate hearing, to convince the Reagan administration to submit an amicus brief in support of the Mobile school board and the Alabama governor. Along with fellow Republican senators Helms of North Carolina and Charles Grassley of Iowa, as well as Falwell, Denton met at the White House on February 16, 1983, with the administration's two most powerful legal advisors, Attorney General William French Smith and presidential counselor Edwin Meese III. Denton urged the administration to enter the case. After the meeting, he reported feeling "extremely optimistic" that the *Jaffree* defendants would win the backing of the Department of Justice.[43]

The senator's optimism was misplaced. While continuing to pledge support for school prayer, the administration decided that, for the time being, it would not utilize *Jaffree* as a vehicle for that support. Although some department officials favored the idea, the attorney general chose not, at this time, to submit an amicus brief to the Eleventh Circuit. Right-wing hardliners within Justice, led by William Bradford Reynolds, were rebuked by more moderate conservatives such as Solicitor General Rex Lee and his assistant, Paul Bator, who considered Hand's ruling reckless and indefensible. The department determined it could not line up behind a district judge who would disregard his judicial superiors. "We don't want to encourage lower courts to overrule Supreme Court precedents," a spokesperson for the attorney general said. "The place for that is in the Supreme Court."[44]

Back in Mobile, Alexander expressed anger and frustration at the administration's decision. He belittled the president's frequent promises to protect school prayer as "only symbolic words that won't be backed up by constructive action." By declining to submit an amicus brief, the administration had reneged on its promises, he said. It had turned its back on the people who had elected the president. Alexander argued that, rather than keeping its distance from the case, the administration ought to lend its "total support" to prayer advocates. Still, he held out hope for a change of heart. In the eventuality that the Eleventh Circuit's ruling was appealed to the Supreme Court, Alexander promised vigorously to solicit the Justice Department's participation in the next phase of the case.[45]

Denton expressed his frustration, too. And, like Alexander, he remained optimistic in spite of his disappointment – largely on the basis of the attorney general's stated openness to filing a brief at a future time. Denton, according to his spokesperson, was "hopeful that the Justice Department will get involved in this case when it is reversed and remanded to Judge Hand's court, as every one expects it will be." He pledged to continue soliciting the administration's support. "Anxious to protect the right of young Americans to the free exercise of religion in our public schools," he would do what he could to win a reversal of *Engel*, "a palpably erroneous decision."[46]

COUNTER-ESTABLISHMENT

It was not unreasonable for Denton, Alexander, and their allies to solicit the administration's active support. Under Reagan, the Justice Department moved more sharply to the right than under any other administration in recent history. Although Richard Nixon had selected judges whom he considered "strict constructionists," no president prior to Reagan had more systematically nominated conservative judges or more comprehensively sided with conservative litigants. Attorney General Smith embodied the old-boy conservatism the president so admired; the man in charge of the department's Civil Rights Division, Reynolds, battled the minority rights legacy of the Warren Court with unmatched single-mindedness; Meese, the president's closest personal advisor and, later, attorney general, denounced judicial liberals more vociferously than any other official in U.S. government. On issues from school prayer and abortion to criminal prosecution, affirmative action, and busing, the minority rights revolution of the mid-twentieth century lay fat in the crosshairs of the Reagan Justice Department. Notwithstanding the department's refusal to submit a brief during the circuit court phase of *Jaffree,* a number of its officials sought to roll back the minority rights revolution as fully as did McClellan and Hand.[47]

The sharp right turn of the Justice Department can be seen in the transformation of the role of the solicitor general. Although solicitors general tend roughly to share the political views of sitting presidents, the office traditionally had remained beyond politics, a domain of consummate professionalism. Historically, solicitors general retained a distance from the president and his staff, in order to reach constitutionally sound, impeccably reasoned judgments. The administration of Ronald Reagan transformed the character of the office. That transformation, according to Lincoln Caplan, "went considerably beyond the normal, unexceptional differences in policy and approach that can naturally be expected to occur from one SG to the next." Through Meese, Reynolds, and others, the administration assumed unprecedented control over the solicitor general. This helped create a Justice Department more dogmatically conservative than any other in recent memory.[48]

The department's rightward turn was also demonstrated by the man directing it throughout Reagan's first term, Attorney General Smith. Reagan's personal lawyer back home in California, Smith was one of three cabinet officers who enjoyed nearly unfettered access to the president. The attorney general was marked by his extraordinarily conservative pedigree. A hallmark of his tenure was his readiness to enforce the law according to the president's conservative philosophy. By 1984, the American legal establishment would conclude that Smith's policy changes had effectively redesigned the Justice Department, which, in the words of one local director with the American Civil Liberties Union, had "done a complete about-face on civil rights enforcement" and civil-liberties protection.[49]

In an October 1981 speech, Smith publicly declared his own judicial philosophy and his department's commitment to translating it into public policy. That philosophy was the same as the one advanced by Hand and McClellan in *Jaffree.* Over the past several decades, Smith complained, the "federal courts ha[d] engaged in ... judicial policy-making." He promised that his department would "focus upon the doctrines that have led to the courts' activism" and would "attempt to reverse this unhealthy flow of power from state and Federal legislatures to Federal courts, and the concomitant flow of power from state and local governments to the Federal level." This meant, quite simply, that Justice would continue "to select appointees to the Federal bench who understand the meaning of judicial restraint," and to make arguments in the Supreme Court that reflected that same philosophy.[50]

Smith maintained that it was not the Justice Department, but federal judges themselves, who threatened the independence of the courts. By involving themselves in creating laws – a political area not properly part of their function – the courts had abandoned their perch of constitutional objectivity. Activist federal judges entered the political arena and assumed the role of legislators, even though those judges were not "directly responsible to the electorate." Smith insisted that he was prescribing a nonpolitical role for the federal judiciary, the role for which the courts were mandated and best fitted. "The courts were insulated from popular pressure," according to Smith, "precisely because their function was not conceived to embrace policy making. Responsibility for policy making in a democratic republic must reside in those who are directly accountable to the electorate." Voted into office, the president and Congress – and not the courts – spoke for the people and were charged with making laws on their behalf.[51]

More than rhetoric went into the administration's campaign against judicial activism. With its record on appointing federal judges, the administration reversed a policy followed by presidents since Lyndon Johnson, whose 1964 Civil Right Act had spurred within the federal government a commitment to appointing an increased number of women, Latinos, and African Americans to civil-service positions. The percentage of minority and female nominations to the bench trended upward through the administration of Jimmy Carter. The Reagan administration decisively reversed this trend by basing its judicial appointments not on sex, race, or ethnicity but on judicial philosophy and judicial record – thereby asserting its commitment to so-called color-blind meritocracy. Reagan stood by the 1980 Republican Party platform, which had promised that a Republican president would appoint judges committed to "the decentralization of the federal government and efforts to return decision-making power to state and local elected officials." Although only one of the Justice Department's forty-one selections in 1981 was black and only one a woman, Deputy Attorney General Edward C. Schmults denied that the department was considering only white men for the bench. Rather, he insisted, he and Smith were looking strictly at applicants' qualifications. If white men were the most qualified, then white men would be nominated. Justice under Reagan would overwhelmingly nominate white male judges opposed to liberal judicial activism, engineering what *Congressional Quarterly* called "an ideological transformation of the federal judiciary."[52]

An ethos of unswerving loyalty to the president and his populist conservatism shaped the administration from its inception. To be considered for an appointment to the executive or judicial branch, individuals had to pass an ideological litmus test. As the administration's personnel director explained, his office required that nominees demonstrate their "adherence to the philosophy, policies, and objectives" of the president. It was counselor Meese, more than any of his colleagues, who fought to ensure that administration officials exhibited loyalty to the president. Meese functioned as Reagan's chief loyalty officer, denouncing anyone he considered apostate to the president's political program. Meese ensured that nominations to the federal judiciary passed through the same ideological screening process, with a candidate's judicial philosophy determining his or her eligibility for nomination. Determined to counterbalance decades worth of liberal appointments, presidential advisors insisted that nominees evince strong commitment to implementing the president's conservative ideology into policy.[53]

If sociologist Daniel Bell was correct that the post–World War II years registered an "end to ideology," then the Reagan era heralded the return of ideologically driven government. This was evidenced by the Washington, DC, legal "counter-establishment" that surrounded, pervaded, and relentlessly pressured the Justice Department. The counter-establishment was comprised of arch-conservatives who hounded government officials to reverse policies born out of the New Deal, Warren Court, and the Great Society. In the enforcement of ideological loyalty, the counter-establishment played a powerful role. By translating obscure constitutional theory into broad principles easily adaptable to the political process, it provided the president and his advisors with guidelines for sizing up judicial- and executive-branch applicants, as well as for choosing policies to pursue. Three organizations exercised the greatest influence on the Justice Department: the Washington Legal Foundation, the Free Congress Research and Education Foundation, and the Center for Judicial Studies – created and directed by McClellan. Among the demands of these groups was that the solicitor general's office engage in aggressive constitutional advocacy. As Patrick McGuigan, head of the Free Congress Foundation's judicial revision project, put it, the counter-establishment functioned as "part of the team." Its influence was profound. It strong-armed an already ideologically inclined department even further into remaking the courts and refashioning department policy.[54]

No group pulled the Justice Department further rightward than McClellan's Center for Judicial Studies and its flagship journal, *Benchmark*. From its inception in 1983, *Benchmark* published article after article excoriating the courts for their liberalism and demanding that the president minimize their influence over public policy. The journal and the Justice Department affected one another symbiotically, with numerous *Benchmark* editors and contributors at some point either working with Republican politicians or serving as public advocates for the Reagan administration. Editor-in-Chief McClellan served as a legal counsel to senators Jesse Helms, John East, and Orrin Hatch; Supreme Court editor Bruce Fein worked as assistant deputy attorney general and chief counsel for the Federal Communication Commission; book review editor Gary McDowell served as associate director of the Office of Public Affairs and as Attorney General Meese's chief speech writer; regular contributor Daniel Popeo directed the Washington Legal Foundation, which regularly submitted amicus briefs defending administration positions; one senior editor, Grover Rees, oversaw the selecting of judicial nominees at Justice, while another, William Kristol, was special assistant to the secretary of education. The department routinely sought the advice and approval of these individuals, who effectively became its legal conscience.[55]

The counter-establishment generally approved of the president's efforts to transform government – efforts it believed mandated by the 1980 election. Still, the administration came under a good deal of heat from its right flank for failing to execute the transformation with sufficient vigor and determination. The journal *Human Events* complained that, within Justice, "radical holdover elements" from previous administrations were obstructing conservative projects such as winning legislation to restrict the jurisdiction of the federal courts. When Director of the Office of Legal Counsel Theodore B. Olson objected that these issues raised "some fairly difficult constitutional questions" that resisted easy resolution, Free Congress Foundation Director Paul Weyrich dismissed Olson's protest as equivocation. The Justice Department, Weyrich claimed, was capitulating to the legal establishment and clinging to a view of the Constitution that was utterly "perverted by the courts" and "by governmental regulations." One year later, *Conservative Digest*, published by Richard Viguerie, leveled similar charges against the administration, asking, "Has Ronald Reagan's Presidency Been Captured by Wall Street-Big Business-Corporate-Executive-Big New York/Houston

Law Firm-Eastern Liberal-And/Or Establishment-Non-Reaganite Republicans?"[56]

Smith's longtime friendship with the president and staunch Republican partisanship did not spare him from the counter-establishment's ire. His patrician background and refined demeanor made him appear out of touch with the party's populist base and turned him into a favorite target. Smith was "surrounded by people who may be registered Republicans, but they're not conservatives or even Reagan Republicans," charged one prominent lobbyist, who called the attorney general a "country-club" Republican. Other critics assailed Smith for adhering to established policies rather than implementing a bold, new right-wing program at every available opportunity. When he called a school prayer bill sponsored by Helms and written by McClellan "unwise" insofar as it would deprive the federal courts of their rightful authority to review legislation, Smith's standing on the right fell even further. Although he denounced the judiciary for its alleged "usurpation of the popular authority," Smith refused to condone, as an appropriate and constitutional response, legislation that would restrict the courts' authority over matters such as school prayer, abortion, and busing. "A lot of people," he complained, "don't recognize that there are laws on the books that we are sworn to enforce which we may not agree with and which may be inconsistent with the administration's current policy." The Justice Department was obligated "to enforce the laws as they are on the books, not as we wish they were." Smith's circumspection angered the firebrands who eschewed compromise. For his conservative caution, he was roundly condemned as an out-of-touch elitist disloyal to the Reagan revolution.[57]

SQUEEZING THE SG

The counter-establishment saw a likely ally in the president's choice for solicitor general, Rex Lee – dean of Brigham Young University's J. Reuben Clark Law School, practicing Mormon, and advocate for the constitutional positions staked out by the administration. Lee's opposition to the Equal Right Amendment earned him the enmity of women's groups, who came out strongly against his nomination. So strong was his support for states' rights that he struggled internally whenever required to defend the federal government's interests over those of the states'. Like Reagan, he mistrusted "judicial activism" and believed that the federal judiciary had encroached on the territory of the other governmental branches. Because "there are no elected federal judges," he wrote in his 1981 *A Lawyer Looks at the Constitution,* the judiciary had "the least requirement to be responsive to the people" and therefore had no business making laws. "Policymaking under our separation-of-powers system is the primary domain of the legislature," Lee insisted. "The courts should upset such legislative policy judgments only under extraordinary circumstances."[58]

Lee expressed support for every policy item on the president's agenda. Unlike previous solicitors general, he did not shrink from the prospect of political advocacy. "One of the purposes of the solicitor general," Lee held, was "to represent his client, the president of the United States" by "implement[ing] the president's policies ... through positions taken in court. When I have that opportunity, I'm going to take it." He would not waste the power of his position by neglecting to advance the Reagan agenda. "What's the point in having the engine at your disposal," he wondered, "if you don't take it out and drive it in the direction you really want when the chance comes?" Promoting a political program, he believed, was "one of the reasons [the people] elect a president and one of the reasons a president appoints a solicitor general."[59]

As solicitor general, Lee worked to foster judicial restraint. His office made a point of not filing lawsuits on matters it thought best decided by legislatures, believing that it could "do a great deal by urging the courts not to go too far." When Lee did argue cases before the Supreme Court, he urged the justices to avoid the sort of judicial activism that, in his opinion, stifled popular moral sentiment. In *Lawyer Looks at the Constitution,* he faulted the Court's rulings on contraception and abortion for "vest[ing] in the judiciary the license to roam at will through the territory of legislative policymaking," and entitling it to manufacture fundamental rights "out of bits and scraps that bear some resemblance to a variety of other provisions in the Constitution." If rights continued to be created anew with that much ease, Lee warned, "then there is little limit to the extent to which judges can substitute their own judgment for that of the legislature." Those concerns were echoed in Justice William Rehnquist's majority opinion in the first major case Lee argued before the Court. Popular suspicions "that the Government has violated the Establishment Clause," Rehnquist insisted, did not give judges "a special license to roam the country in search of governmental wrongdoing ... The federal courts were simply not constituted as ombudsmen of the general welfare."[60]

Lee was especially driven to reverse *Roe* v. *Wade,* which, for him, combined judicial overreach with the creation of extra-constitutional rights. In an amicus brief submitted to the Court in *Akron* v. *Akron,*

Lee defended a local anti-abortion ordinance by appealing to the basic democratic values of political deliberation and viewpoint tolerance. Lee pointed out – with logic like that employed by the *Jaffree* intervenors – that "competing views on [abortion] are deeply held by large numbers of American citizens." Only legislatures could give those views the extensive debate they deserved and required. When legislatures had taken up the issue, they had "considered the people's competing viewpoints and ha[d] made the difficult choices required by the legislative process." Precisely this sort difficult choice-making was now called for, Lee insisted, and the propensity of legislatures to carry it out responsibly made them – rather than courts – the appropriate venue for deciding government abortion policy. Unlike judges, "legislators must periodically account to the people for the way they have carried out their public responsibilities." Investing "lawmaking authority in the legislature rather than the judiciary renders the government accountable for the exercise of that authority." Consideration of abortion policy would be rendered most "effective if the ultimate resolution of the issue [were] not removed from the realm of public debate and resolution through constitutional determination."[61]

Lee's majoritarian stance on abortion policy – and his willingness to insist on the adoption of that stance, notwithstanding the Court's contrary conclusions – painted him, for liberals, as a constitutional counterrevolutionary. His *Akron* brief antagonized the general counsel to Planned Parenthood and the American Civil Liberties Union, who rejected what she considered the solicitor general's brute disregard for minority rights. The *Washington Post* reminded readers that that "the Bill of Rights was designed to protect against the excesses of political majorities that might use the strength of the state to trample unpopular views and interests," and that "turning over to the political branches the most difficult and controversial subjects, involving conflict between individual liberties and the power of government, stands the Constitution on its head." Lee's argument, delivered before the Court in November 1982, especially offended Justice Harry Blackmun. The author of *Roe,* Blackmun chastised the solicitor general for suggesting to the Court that it overturn that ruling – or, as Blackmun saw it, that it overturn *Marbury* v. *Madison,* the case that established judicial review. Justice Powell's majority opinion in *Akron* was blunt, asserting that "*stare decisis* ... is a doctrine that demands respect in a society governed by the rule of law."[62]

Still, however assertively he advocated for the administration's positions, Lee did revere the traditions of his office. As eager as he was to advocate for positions he supported, he would advance such positions in court only if he believed them credible, with at least the possibility of being accepted by the justices. Over the course of Lee's tenure, his methods became more and more moderate. His evolution was notable in a 1985 speech in which he lauded the "restraint traditionally exercised by Solicitors General," which, by protecting their reputation among the justices, became "the single most important factor contributing to the success of a President's litigating objectives." Increasingly, he would view his role as an advocate for the broad views of the nation – a position that traditionally had earned the solicitor general great authority before the Court. While it was "proper for the Solicitor General to use [his] adversarial advantages," Lee held, "it must be done with discretion, with discrimination, and with sensitivity, lest the reservoir of credibility which is the source of this special advantage be diminished, with adverse consequences not only to the government's ability to win cases, but also to an important institution of government itself."[63]

Lee's ambivalence about his role as advocate distinguished him from the more strident advisors in and around the Justice Department. Their attempt to force an aggressive "judicial retrenchment" made his own call for judicial restraint seem pallid. Lee's wish to honor executive restraint as much as judicial restraint created detractors inside and outside the administration. To his critics on the right he became a pariah, an obstacle to their campaign to rein in the federal judiciary. Before long, he reported, those detractors were accusing him "of disloyalty to the administration." According to the *Washington Post,* Lee "found himself pressured from all sides, accused alternately of being too political and not political enough, attacked from the right for not being a part of the Reagan team and from the left for being too much a part." He reported enduring such "enormous pressure" to advocate aggressively for school prayer and against abortion that those issues became "an albatross around my neck."[64]

By 1983, Lee became seen throughout the counter-establishment as part of the problem rather than the solution. *Human Events* reported that he had "disappointed conservatives time and again over the past two years by taking positions completely at odds with those of President Reagan." Resentment ran especially strong at *Benchmark,* where Supreme Court editor Fein accused Lee of betraying the administration. The fiercest denunciation came from Editor-in-Chief McClellan, who blamed Lee for the "conspicuous ... failure of the Reagan Administration to halt the expansion of Federal judicial power and return the nation to the principles of limited government." According to McClellan, Lee had deliberately promoted a liberal, activist agenda. He had "regularly advanced points of law ... calculated to preserve intact existing case law and the doctrines of the Supreme Court." Worse yet, for these critics, he had betrayed the president out of self-interest. *Human Events* charged Lee with "cowardice" that could only be attributed "to a reluctance by Lee to jeopardize his standing in the academic world by being too closely associated with conservative issues." McClellan similarly condemned Lee as a sycophant bent on scoring personal victories while neglecting the objectives of the administration whose revolution he was assigned to carry out. In McClellan's eyes, Lee's "real accomplishment" had been "the perpetuation of erroneous law, liberal values, and judicial supremacy."[65]

By 1984, the *Wall Street Journal* reported, "administration conservatives" had begun "planning ways to replace Mr. Lee." A group of prominent counter-establishment figures – including Weyrich, McGuigan, and the Moral Majority's Richard Dingman – wrote the president excoriating Lee and demanding his ouster. "It really is a shame Mr. Lee feels he has been placed under 'enormous pressure' to fulfill his constitutional duties and, not coincidentally, the Republican platform of 1980," the letter's authors quipped. "It really is a shame that this man feels that principled efforts to restore legal protection for unborn children are somehow 'an albatross' around his neck." It was his neck that the counter-establishment now called for. "Rex Lee should resign," the authors insisted, and "if he will not resign, he should be fired." And if he were not fired, then the president would pay the price. "Your Administration," they warned the president, "should not expect to retain the support of its closest friends when" it insults "those same friends." As McClellan explained, Lee had become an enemy in the "struggle for men's minds," in the "war of ideas and jurisprudential values" that the New Right had launched. In this war, no prisoners would be taken.[66]

Ideological opposition to Lee reached deep into the administration itself. Meese did not consider Lee a reliable part of the team. Even more strongly at odds with the solicitor general was the head of the Justice Department's Civil Rights Division, Reynolds, who consistently challenged Lee's positions. Labeled the "shadow solicitor" by Caplan, Reynolds enjoyed the support of Meese and the counter-establishment, despite – or because of – the controversy generated by his uncompromising stances. Reynolds first gained notoriety in early 1982, when he urged the administration to preserve the tax exemptions long granted to racially segregated religious colleges. Determined, along with Meese, to reverse the civil-rights orthodoxy guiding the Justice Department since the 1960s, Reynolds grew furious at the solicitor general's office for its failure to support him in cases involving desegregation, affirmative action, and busing. He was, temperamentally, Lee's antithesis. Reynolds pursued the president's agenda with unswerving zealousness, evincing little concern for legal precedent or for compromise. He saw it as his role to ensure that the administration "not slavishly adhere to the constitutional reasoning advanced by prior Administrations." This won him the support of the president, who declared "that Mr. Reynolds's civil rights views reflect my own," and that "the policies he pursued are the policies of this Administration, and they will remain our policies as long as I am President." McClellan came to think of Reynolds as his chief ally in the department, the man who would carry out his constitutional mission.[67]

THE BATTLE OVER *JAFFREE*

On church-state matters, the Reagan Justice Department sounded a strident conservatism. In *Lynch* v. *Donnelly,* where a group of Pawtucket, Rhode Island, residents tried to force the city to remove a nativity scene from its annual downtown Christmas display, Deputy Solicitor General Paul Bator and his assistant, Michael W. McConnell, generated an innovative and effective amicus brief. Rather than invoking the requirement, found in *Lemon* v. *Kurtzman,* that every church-state law contain a secular purpose, produce a religious effect, and avoid entangling government with religion, Bator and McConnell posited that the city should be held to a lesser burden. Government had long accommodated America's religious heritage, they claimed; therefore, displays such as Pawtucket's nativity scene should not "wholly and rigidly" be excluded from the public square. The brief appealed to America's "tradition of toleration" in insisting that government "be allowed to give some recognition to the belief of many of our people that religion should continue to play some role in our public occasions." Strict separation of church and state represented a breach of that tolerance, Bator and McConnell asserted, a disregard for the values of many Americans. It "betoken[ed] a systematic hostility to religion – in effect, the establishment of irreligion" – that was "as prohibited by the Constitution as is governmental establishment of religion." Rather than enforcing strict separation, government needed to strike a stance of "benevolent neutrality" toward religion.[68]

The argument's implications were startling. If hostility to religion were as much a religion as religion itself, then *Lemon*'s requirement that a statute or practice be secular made little sense. A number of department lawyers found Bator's and McConnell's call for "accommodation" of religion quite radical. By applying the argument's logic, they warned, government might justify all kinds of entanglements between itself and religion. Four Supreme Court justices shared their concern, although they lost out to the five who joined the majority opinion defending Pawtucket's nativity display using logic akin to Bator's and McConnell's. Apparently, Lee's office was not the bastion of liberalism that its detractors alleged.[69]

The office's most outspoken detractor hardly saw matters that way. McClellan roundly condemned the administration's stance in *Lynch* as a blunder, an inexcusable failure to impugn the federal judiciary's entire lawmaking enterprise. McClellan had hoped that Lee's office would use *Lynch,* much as McClellan had used *Jaffree,* to attack the incorporation doctrine and defend local communities from the iron hand of the Supreme Court. Because the First Amendment did not extend to state governments, McClellan believed, the appropriateness of the Christmas display remained for the people of Rhode Island alone to decide. The federal courts had no more business accommodating religion than squelching it. In McClellan's eyes, the *Lynch* case had provided the solicitor general's office a golden opportunity to demonstrate the travesty that was the federal courts' assumption of jurisdiction over the popular majority's religious practices. The solicitor general forsook that opportunity when he opted to dispute how – rather than whether at all – the federal courts should apply the Establishment Clause to the individual states. The crèche rather than the Constitution had become the issue. "Because the Solicitor General's brief did not question any of the Court's prior interpretations of the Establishment Clause, which emerged unscathed to haunt future generations," McClellan complained, "the Justices were not compelled to re-examine their holdings or defend their position."[70]

Whereas the department's response to *Lynch* irked McClellan, its stance on *Jaffree* infuriated him. In his estimation, Hand's decision signaled a momentous turn in the twentieth-century history of the U.S. Constitution. Hand had triggered "a reexamination of the Supreme Court's 'doctrine of incorporation,'" the strictly "judge-made rule of interpretation" that had "succeeded in amending the Fourteenth Amendment" and had become "the great well-spring of judicial activism in our time." If the solicitor general had dropped the ball in *Lynch,* then Hand had provided a do-over with *Jaffree.* Nor was McClellan alone in that assumption. Key conservatives inside and outside the administration "saw the case as an opportunity to clarify and even overrule Supreme Court opinions prohibiting school prayer," which the administration considered "among the worst vestiges of the liberal Warren Court."

Jaffree offered up more issues from their wish list than simply school prayer. The many "states' rights advocates" among them remained eager "to challenge the Supreme Court's entire doctrine of incorporation."[71]

The arguments of McClellan and the counter-establishment were voiced stridently by Reynolds. In an early 1983 memorandum, he dismissed Court rulings barring school prayer as "unworthy of respect." "Such judicial wrong-headedness," he declared, "may be just the catalyst needed to put momentum behind the president's efforts for a constitutional amendment" in support of school prayer. When he became aware of Hand's ruling and its scheduled review by the Eleventh Circuit, Lee's rival saw before him a golden opportunity to challenge the Court's Establishment Clause jurisprudence. That the administration was not a party to the case was no matter to Reynolds, who led the campaign to issue a *Jaffree* brief. Bator, for his part, skeptically eyed *Jaffree* as an "extraordinary opinion" recklessly "repudiating Supreme Court precedent." According to Bator, an enthusiastic Reynolds, along with administration allies, "pressed us to file an amicus brief in the Court of Appeals arguing that Judge Hand had gotten the thing right" and to get the solicitor general's office behind the judge's arguments "because the President had said the same in speeches." Because Reagan had clearly made it "his policy to restore prayer in the public schools," Reynolds insisted, the solicitor general was obligated to make it his policy as well.[72]

Reynolds's eagerness to enter *Jaffree* was not shared by the more judicious lawyers in the solicitor general's office. Bator thought it improper for the solicitor general to defend Hand," who, "as a lower-court judge," remained "bound by Supreme Court precedent." Indeed, the department would be doing nothing less than "encourag[ing] lawlessness on the part of lower-court judges." For the deputy solicitor general, "the principle that district-court judges must obey the Supreme Court is one that every lawyer ought to be clear on," even though, at the moment, it seemed, the "issue was up for grabs." When Lee likewise grew alarmed, a rift opened up between his office and Reynolds. A contentious round of Justice Department meetings pitted the solicitor general's office against its far-right opponents, who conducted an internal campaign to force Lee's compliance. With Bator's support, Lee held his ground. The administration had no business endorsing Hand's "defiance" of the Court, he argued; to do so would be to act with a temerity inappropriate for top government officials. After much wrangling, Lee garnered the support of

Attorney General Smith. The Justice Department submitted no brief to the Eleventh Circuit.

"IF THE SUPREME COURT ERRS, NO OTHER COURT MAY CORRECT IT"

On March 23, 1983, a three-judge panel heard arguments on Jaffree's appeal of *Jaffree* v. *James* and *Jaffree* v. *Board*, which the court had combined back into a single case, restoring the complaint's unitary status. Campbell reiterated the arguments he made during trial – arguments provided by his expert witness, McClellan – that the Founders had never intended to purge the nation's schoolrooms of prayer, and that the courts were obligated only to honor the Constitution and not Supreme Court case law. Campbell sounded the Constitution-in-exile theme. He applauded Hand's decision for pointing the courts back toward an earlier body of case law more faithful to the Constitution itself, one dishonored over recent decades. One of the judges hearing the case, District Court Judge Charles R. Scott, questioned the appropriateness of an inferior judge discarding Supreme Court precedent. So did Williams. He argued that Hand had no business excavating early history when the Supreme Court had already performed the background work it considered necessary and had staked a clear stance on the matter, consigning "further discussion to the halls of academia." But Campbell continued to insist that federal judges swore only "an oath under God." None swore allegiance to the Supreme Court; none was bound by anything other than the text of the Constitution, regardless of case law.[73]

The Eleventh Circuit chose not to sign off on the counterrevolution. On May 12, the three-judge panel issued a unanimous reversal of Hand's two rulings. Basing their decision straightforwardly on Supreme Court precedent, the judges insisted that they were acting apolitically, not making law or engaging in judicial activism. "We are not called upon to determine whether prayer in public schools is desirable as a matter of policy," they wrote. Their task was simply to "decide whether the trial court correctly determined that the recitation of prayers in the Mobile County, Alabama, public schools and the implementation of two Alabama statutes permitting religious practices in those public schools do not violate the establishment clause of the first amendment to the Constitution of the United States." The judges wished to refute any assumptions that they had ruled according to their own policy preferences. "This court merely applies the principles established by the

Supreme Court. While many may disagree on the subject of prayer in public schools, our Constitution provides that the Supreme Court is the final arbiter of constitutional disputes."[74]

The trial court had been as bound by Supreme Court precedent as were they, the judges insisted. They would not sanction Hand's disregard for Court precedent. In "attempt[ing] to justify its actions by discussing the limited exceptions to the doctrine of stare decisis," the district court had misapplied that doctrine. "The doctrine of stare decisis pertains to the deference a court may give to its own prior decisions," the judges maintained. "The stare decisis doctrine and its exceptions do not apply where a lower court is compelled to apply the precedent of a higher court. Federal district courts and circuit courts are bound to adhere to the controlling decisions of the Supreme Court." Not himself a member of the Supreme Court, Hand had no business refusing to abide by its rulings. The matter was not a mere technicality, but was crucial to understanding and enforcing the Constitution. "Judicial precedence serves as the foundation of our federal judicial system," the judges insisted. "Adherence to it results in stability and predictability. If the Supreme Court errs, no other court may correct it."[75]

The Eleventh Circuit had no intention of going along with McClellan's and Hand's plan. The Court had already dealt with and rejected McClellan's and Hand's account of the historical record of the Bill of Rights's adoption, and that was all that mattered. The judges were emphatic: "*The Supreme Court has considered and decided the historical implications surrounding the establishment clause.*" In rulings stretching from the 1940s to recent times, "the Supreme Court has concluded that its present interpretation of the first and fourteenth amendments is consistent with the historical evidence." It had found, beyond doubt, that the purpose of the Establishment Clause "was not to strike merely at the official establishment of a single sect, creed or religion." Rather, its "object ... was to create a complete and permanent separation of the spheres of religious activity and civil authority by comprehensively forbidding every form of public aid or support for religion." Likewise, the judges asserted, the Court had already dealt with objections to the incorporation doctrine, determining that the Constitution required applying the Establishment Clause to the states. The district court had heard no issues not already heard and decided. Nothing more on the matter remained to be said. "Consequently," the judges announced in their May 12 ruling, "we reverse the district court's dismissal of these actions" and "remand the case to the district court. Upon remand the district court is directed to . . . issue and enforce an order enjoining the statutes and activities held in this opinion to be unconstitutional."[76]

This single setback would not deter McClellan and his allies. They would carry the fight over *Jaffree* beyond the Eleventh Circuit, and beyond even the federal courts. Theirs was a battle being waged within and around the federal government. The battle to institute a more majoritarian form of democratic republicanism – one capable of promoting the sort of "traditional" morality favored by the alleged majority of Americans – was now under way inside the corridors of American political power. Counterrevolution was afoot.

Notes

1 *Jaffree* v. *Board of School Commissioners of Mobile County*, 554 F.Supp. 1104 (1983), 1105, 1130; *Jaffree* v. *James*, 554 F. Supp. 1130 (1983).

2 Hand's valorization of the Framers' original intent relies directly on Raoul Berger, who opined that where "the intention of the framers [is] unmistakably expressed, that intention is as good as written into the text." Raoul Berger, *Government by Judiciary: The Transformation of the Fourteenth Amendment* (Cambridge, Mass.: Harvard University Press, 1977), 7. See also Edwin Meese III, "Toward a Jurisprudence of Original Intention," *Benchmark*, 2 (January–February 1986), 1–10; Walter Berns, "The Constitution as a Bill of Rights," in *How Does the Constitution Secure Rights*, ed. by Robert Goldwin and William A. Schambra (Washington, D.C.: American Enterprise Institute, 1985), 50–73; Terry Eastland, "The Burger Court and the Founding Fathers: Are We All Activists Now?," *Policy Review*, no 28 (Spring 1984), 14–19; Charles Rice, "The Bill of Rights and the Constitution (1983)," in *The Bill of Rights: Original Meaning and Current Understanding*, ed. by Eugene W. Hickok Jr. (Charlottesville: University Press of Virginia, 1991), 11–15; Earl M. Maltz, "Some New Thoughts on an Old Problem – The Role of the Intent of the Framers in Constitutional Theory," *Boston University Law Review*, 63 (July 1983), 811–51; Henry P. Monaghan, "Our Perfect Constitution," *New York University Law Review*, 56 (May–June 1981), 353–96; and Michael J. Malbin, *Religion and Politics; The Intentions of the Authors of the First Amendment* (Washington, D.C.: American Enterprise Institute, 1978).

3 *Jaffree* v. *Board*, 1126, 1129, 1129–30 n41.

4 *Ibid.*, 1113 n5, 1114. Transcript, *Ishmael Jaffree et al.* v. *Board of School Commissioners of Mobile County et al.*, November 15, 1982, Civil case no. 82–0554–H, box no. 1, accession no. 021–93–0423, location no. C0681974 SAN (Federal Records Center), pp. 556–71, 603. James McClellan, "The Making and Unmaking of the Establishment Clause," in *A Blueprint for Judicial Reform*, ed. by Patrick B. McGuigan and Randall R. Rader (Washington, D.C.: Free Congress Research and Education Foundation, 1981), 295–325;

Robert L. Cord, *Separation of Church and State: Historical Fact and Current Fiction* (New York: Lambeth, 1982); James McClellan interview by Robert Daniel Rubin, October 14, 2004 (interview conducted by telephone), 2, 10–11, 14, 26–27;. Raoul Berger, *The Fourteenth Amendment and the Bill of Rights* (Norman: University of Oklahoma Press, 1989); James McClellan, "When Prayer Fell in Alabama: Reflections on the Jaffree Case," *Southern Partisan*, 4 (Spring 1984); James McClellan, "Hand's Writing on the Wall of Separation: The Significance of *Jaffree* on Future Cases on Religious Establishment," in *How Does the Constitution Protect Religious Freedom?*, ed. by Robert A. Goldwin and Art Kaufman (Washington, D.C.: American Enterprise Institute, 1987), 62–64.

5 *Jaffree* v. *Board*, 1114–18, emphasis added by Hand.

6 *Ibid.*, 1113, 1119–25. The most public expression of opposition to the incorporation doctrine would come in a series of lectures given by Attorney General Edwin Meese in 1985. (See conclusion, pp. 321–25.) See especially Edwin Meese III, "Speech Before the American Bar Association, July 9, 1985," in *The Great Debate: Interpreting Our Written Constitution*, ed. by Paul G. Cassell (Washington, D.C.: Federalist Society, 1986).

7 *Jaffree* v. *Board*, 1118 n24.

8 *Ibid.*, 1126–29.

9 Transcript, *Jaffree* v. *Board*, 556, 603; *Jaffree* v. *Board*, 1126–28. Hand quotes Chief Justice Burger in *Coleman* v. *Alabama* (1970): "By placing a premium on 'recent cases' rather than the language of the Constitution, the Court makes it dangerously simple for future Courts using the technique of interpretation to operate as a 'continuing Constitutional Convention.'" *Ibid.*, 1127, emphasis added.

10 *Ibid.*, 1128.

11 *Ibid.*, 1108, 1129.

12 *Ibid.*, 1129–30 n41.

13 *Ibid.*, 1129–30 n41.

14 McClellan advanced his constitutional vision most fully in James McClellan, *Joseph Story and the American Constitution: A Study in Political and Legal Thought* (Norman: University of Oklahoma Press, 1971); McClellan, "Making and Unmaking of the Establishment Clause"; and James McClellan, "Congressional Retraction of Federal Court Jurisdiction to Protect the Reserved Powers of the States: The Helms Prayer Bill and Return to First Principles," *Villanova Law Review*, 27 (May 1982), 1019–29. An interesting expansion of the idea of counterrevolution comes from Andrew Hartman, who contends that Christian conservatives of this period saw themselves as "cultural counterrevolutionaries" who, like McClellan, wanted to return America to a time when their own ideas were purportedly dominant. Andrew Hartman, *A War for the Soul of America: A History of the Culture Wars* (Chicago: University of Chicago Press, 2015), 79.

15 *Mobile Press Register*, January 15, 1983, pp. A1, A6; *Mobile Register*, December 1, 1982, p. B2; *Ibid.* December 15, 1982, p. B2.

16 *Mobile Press Register*, February 6, 1983, p. A4; *Ibid.* January 15, 1983, p. A6; *Ibid.*, January 16, 1983, p. A9; *Washington Post*, February 5, 1983, p. A4.

17 *Mobile Press Register,* January 15, 1983, p. A6; *One Nation under God.*
18 *Mobile Press Register,* January 15, 1983, p. A1.
19 Plaintiffs' motion to alter judgment pursuant to F.R.C.P. 59, at *Jaffree* v. *James*, records of *Jaffree* v. *Board,* January 17, 1983.
20 Order denying motion for stay and injunction and alteration of judgment, at *Jaffree* v. *Board,* records of *Jaffree* v. *Board,* January 18, 1983; "Motions Denied in Prayer Suit," *Mobile Register,* January 19, 1983; Appellants' emergency motion to restore initial injunction, at *Jaffree* v. *James*, records of *Jaffree* v. *Board,* January 22, 1983; United States Court of Appeals for the Eleventh Circuit, order denying appellants' emergency motion for stay and injunction pending appeal, at *Jaffree* v. *Board*, records of *Jaffree* v. *Board,* January 27, 1983; Williams interview by Robert Daniel Rubin, March 19, 2002, Mobile, Ala., side 1.
21 *Mobile Register,* February 3, 1983, pp. A1, A6. Supreme Court of the United States, Appellants' application for stay and injunction pending final disposition in the Eleventh Circuit Court of Appeals, at *Jaffree* v. *Board,* records of *Jaffree* Order denying motion for stay and injunction and alteration of judgment, at *Jaffree* v. *Board,* records of *Jaffree* v. *Board,* January 18, 1983; "Motions Denied in Prayer Suit," *Mobile Register,* January 19, 1983; Appellants' emergency motion to restore initial injunction, at *Jaffree* v. *James*, records of *Jaffree* v. *Board,* January 22, 1983; United States Court of Appeals for the Eleventh Circuit, order denying appellants' emergency motion for stay and injunction pending appeal, at *Jaffree* v. *Board*, records of *Jaffree* v. *Board,* January 27, 1983; Williams interview by Robert Daniel Rubin, March 19, 2002, Mobile, Ala., February 2, 1983, pp. 4, 9–10, emphasis in original.
22 Supreme Court of the United States, Justice Powell, Circuit Justice, temporary order for stay, at *Jaffree* v. *Board*, trial records of *Jaffree* v. *Board,* February 2, 1983. *Mobile Register,* February 3, 1983, p. A1. Supreme Court of the United States, Justice Powell, Circuit Justice, on application for stay, at *Jaffree* v. *Board*, trial records of *Jaffree* v. *Board,* February 11, 1983, pp. 2–3.
23 "Act on Convictions, Alexander Advises," *Mobile Press,* February 4, 1983; "Alexander Says Teachers Free to Follow Beliefs about Prayer," *Mobile Register,* February 4, 1983.
24 Supreme Court, temporary order for stay, at *Jaffree* v. *Board*. Supreme Court of the United States, Appellants' application for stay and injunction pending final disposition in the Eleventh Circuit Court of Appeals, at *Jaffree* v. *Board,* February 2, 1983, trial records of *Jaffree* v. *Board,* pp. 4, 9–10.
25 "Act on Convictions, Alexander Advises."
26 "Alexander Says Teachers Free to Follow Beliefs about Prayer"; *Washington Post,* February 5, 1983, p. A4; Supreme Court, on application for stay, at *Jaffree* v. *Board,* 2–3; "Supreme Court Justice Rules Out State-Sponsored Prayers," *Mobile Press Register,* February 12, 1983.
27 Ishmael Jaffree to Abe Hammons, January 20, 1983, 1983–87: Wallace File, SG 5012, Legal Case Files, Alabama Department of Archives and History (624 Washington Ave., Montgomery, Ala.); Ronnie L. Williams to Robert

C. Campbell III, January 26, 1983, Wallace File; Ishmael Jaffree to Abe Hammons, January 26, 1983, Wallace File; Ishmael Jaffree to Ms. Huntsberry, February 4, 1983, Wallace File; "An Interview with Ishmael Jaffree," *Azalea City News & Review,* February 24, 1983, p. 5; "Supreme Court Justice Rules Out State-Sponsored Prayers," *Mobile Press Register,* February 12, 1983; Ronnie L. Williams to Robert C. Campbell, March 1, 1983, Wallace File.

28 Ishmael Jaffree to Board of School Commissioners, March 11, 1983, Wallace File, emphasis in original.

29 Defendants' motion for preliminary injunction pending appeal, at *Jaffree* v. *Board*, March 14, 1983, Wallace File, 2, 4, 7, 8. "Board Asks Judge to Muzzle Jaffree," *Mobile Press Register,* March 19, 1983.

30 Defendants' motion for preliminary injunction pending appeal, at *Jaffree* v. *Board*, 6–8.

31 Appellants' motion for show cause hearing and appropriate sanctions against appellees, at *Jaffree* v. *Board,* Wallace File, March 21, 1983, pp. 1, 4–5.

32 Brief for appellee intervenors, at *Jaffree* v. *Board*, February 28, 1983, pp. 12–34.

33 Dan T. Carter, *The Politics of Rage: George Wallace, the Origins of the New Conservatism, and the Transformation of American Politics* (New York: Simon and Schuster, 1995), 162; William M. Beaney and Edward N. Beiser, "Prayer and Politics: The Impact of *Engel* and *Schempp* on the Political Process," *Journal of Public Law*, 13 (1964), 486–87; Brief for appellee George C. Wallace, governor of Alabama, at *Jaffree* v. *Board*, February 28, 1983.

34 Defendant Fob James's petition for a writ of mandamus (never filed), *Jaffree* v. *James,* 1983–87: Wallace File, SG 5012, Legal Case Files, ADAH, 12, 14–16, 18, 20. Brief for appellee George C. Wallace, governor of Alabama, at *Jaffree* v. *Board*, trial records of *Jaffree* v. *Board,* February 28, 1983, pp.1, 14–15.

35 *Ibid.*, 1, 6, 30.

36 *Ibid.*, 3, 23, 29.

37 *Ibid.*, 23. On conservative attempts to restore the so-called Constitution in exile, see Cass R. Sunstein, *Radicals in Robes: Why Extreme Right-Wing Courts Are Wrong for America* (New York: BasicBooks, 2005), 1–19; and Jeffrey Rosen, "The Unregulated Offense," *New York Times Magazine,* April 17, 2005, www.nytimes.com/2005/04/17/magazine/the-unregulated-offensive.html. The term is commonly attributed to Supreme Court nominee Douglas Ginsburg. Douglas H. Ginsburg, "Delegation Running Riot," *Regulation*, 1 (1995), 84. See also Randy E. Barnett, *Restoring the Lost Constitution: The Presumption of Liberty* (Princeton: Princeton University Press, 2004). Carter, *Politics of Rage*, 156–94. The term "massive resistance" famously described southern white intransigence toward racial desegregation. Dewey W. Grantham, *The South in Modern America: A Region at Odds* (Fayetteville: University of Arkansas Press, 1994), 209–13, 221–23.

38 Bruce J. Dierenfield, "'A Nation under God': Ronald Reagan and the Crusade for School Prayer," in *Ronald Reagan's America*, vol. 1, ed. by Eric J. Schmertz, Natalie Datlof, and Alexej Ugrinsky (Westport, Conn.: Greenwood,

1997), 235–61; "Act on Convictions, Alexander Advises," *Mobile Press,* February 4, 1983; "Prayer Decision Criticized," *Mobile Press,* March 1, 1983.

39 Burr Ingram, "An Experience That Removes All Doubt," *Alabama Magazine,* March 1978, pp. 16–17; *Mobile Press,* May 10, 1966, p. B4; *Ibid.,* April 4, 1973, pp. A1, A4; *Washington Post,* November 6, 1980, p. A22; *U.S. News & World Report,* November 24, 1980, p. 11.

40 Ingram, "Experience That Removes All Doubt," 17; "Denton Sees U.S. at Crossroads," *Mobile Press Register,* November 11, 1979; *Azalea City News & Review,* August 14, 1980, p. 3; *Washington Post,* October 21, 1980, p. A3; *Washington Post,* November 5, 1980, p. A5; *Ibid.,* November 6, 1980, p. A22; *Mobile Press Register,* August 22, 1982, p. A10.

41 *Washington Post,* December 1, 1980, pp. A1, A8–A9; Peter Ross Range, "Thunder from the Right," *New York Times Magazine,* February 8, 1981, pp. 23, 64; *Birmingham News,* April 5, 1981, p. F4; *Mobile Press,* May 26, 1981, pp. 1, 7; Mike Shanahan, "Popsicle Brigade Tries to Get in Step with the Senate," *Associated Press,* December 18, 1981, AM cycle.; *Washington Post,* January 17, 1982, p. A2; *Mobile Register,* August 12, 1982, p. A2; *Montgomery Advertiser,* August 12, 1982, p. 11; *Ibid.,* August 19, 1982, p. 10; *Mobile Press Register,* August 22, 1982, p. A10; *Ibid.,* October 2, 1982, p. A8; *Mobile Register,* October 27, 1982, p. B1; *Mobile Press Register,* November 20, 1982, p. D4; *Mobile Beacon,* June 4, 1983, p. 4; *Ibid.,* August 13, 1983, p. 8; *Ibid.,* March 2, 1985.

42 *Birmingham News,* April 1, 1981, p. A10. *Ibid.,* May 6, 1981, p. A6; *Congressional Quarterly Almanac,* 40 (98th Cong., 2nd Session: 1984), 465; Beth Spring, "New Federal Law to Promote Chastity Is Set to Take Effect," *Christianity Today,* March 19, 1982, pp. 41, 46. *Mobile Register,* July 29, 1982, p. B2; *Mobile Press Register,* August 22, 1982, p. A10; *Montgomery Advertiser,* August 27, 1982, p. 4; *Mobile Beacon,* July 16, 1983, pp. 4, 8; *Mobile Register,* March 7, 1984, p. A3"; Denton Again Makes Conservative List," *Mobile Press Register,* April 21, 1984; *Mobile Beacon,* August 17, 1985, p. 2.

43 *Mobile Register,* March 1, 1983, p. A1; "Prayer Decision Criticized," *Mobile Press,* March 1, 1983; "Prayer Proponents Feel Betrayed by Reagan," *Mobile Press Register,* April 3, 1983; "Denton Says School Prayer Case First Step toward Restoring Rights," *Montgomery Advertiser,* December 5, 1984; *Mobile Beacon,* December 15, 1984, p. 2.

44 Lincoln Caplan, *The Tenth Justice: The Solicitor General and the Rule of Law* (New York: Knopf, 1987), 99–101; "Prayer Decision Criticized"; *Mobile Register,* March 1, 1983, pp. A1, A6.

45 *Ibid.*; "Prayer Proponents Feel Betrayed by Reagan."

46 *Mobile Register,* March 1, 1983, pp. A1, A6; *Mobile Beacon,* December 15, 1984, p. 2.

47 On Nixon's praise for strict constructionism, see Michael W. Flamm, *Law and Order: Street Crime, Civil Unrest, and the Crisis of Liberalism in the 1960s* (New York: Columbia University Press, 2005), 173–78; and John W. Dean, *The Rehnquist Choice* (New York: Free Press, 2001), 12–16.

48 Caplan, *Tenth Justice,* 1–50, 61–64.

49 *National Review,* July 24, 1981, p. 817; *New York Times,* January 23, 1984, p. A16; *Washington Post,* January 23, 1984, p. A1; *New York Times,* January 24, 1984, p. A14.

50 *New York Times,* October 30, 1981, p. A22.

51 *Washington Post,* November 30, 1981, p. A1; *New York Times,* January 26, 1982, p. B8. William French Smith, "Urging Judicial Restraint," *American Bar Association Journal,* 68 (January 1982), 60. For criticism of Smith's October 1981 speech, see *New York Times,* October 31, 1981, p. 15; *Christian Science Monitor,* November 2, 1981, p. 13; *New York Times,* November 7, 1981, p. 48; and *New York Times,* November 10, 1981, p. A23.

52 Hugh Davis Graham, *Civil Rights and the Presidency: Race and Gender in American Politics, 1960–1972* (New York: Oxford University Press, 1992), 67–68; John D. Skrentny, *The Minority Rights Revolution* (Cambridge, Mass.: Belknap, 2003), 85–142. Herman Schwartz, *Packing the Courts: The Conservative Campaign to Rewrite the Constitution* (New York: Scribner's, 1998). *Congressional Quarterly Almanac,* 37 (97th Cong., 1st Session: 1981), 411; 38 (97th Cong., 2nd Session: 1982), 372; 39 (98th Cong., 1st Session: 1983), 286; 40 (98th Cong., 2nd Session: 1984), 243–44; 41 (99th Cong., 1st Session: 1985), 246; 42 (99th Cong., 2nd Session: 1986), 59–73.

53 *Washington Post,* March 1, 1981, p. A1; *Congressional Quarterly Almanac,* 38 (97th Cong., 2nd Session: 1982), 417; *Washington Post,* January 23, 1984, p. A1.

54 Daniel Bell, *The End of Ideology: On the Exhaustion of Political Ideas in the Fifties* (Cambridge, Mass.: Harvard University Press, 1988). Sidney Blumenthal, *The Rise of the Counter-Establishment: From Conservative Ideology to Political Power* (New York: Times, 1986), 3, 301–02, 311–35; *Washington Post,* August 9, 1985, p. A1; *Congressional Quarterly Almanac,* 38 (97th Cong., 2nd Session: 1982), 417–18; 41 (99th Cong., 1st Session: 1985), 222, 246–47. "After decades of judicial activism," McGuigan and Randall Rader declared, "a movement is building that is not only disenchanted with the judiciary, but fully prepared to take steps to curb the powers of the courts." Patrick B. McGuigan and Randall R. Rader, "Judicial Oligarchy: Have the People Ceased to Be Their Own Rulers?," in A *Blueprint for Judicial Reform,* ed. by Patrick B. McGuigan and Randall R. Rader (Washington, D. C.: Free Congress Research and Education Foundation, 1981), 366.

55 *New York Times,* November 22, 1981, p. A3; *Congressional Quarterly Almanac,* 41 (99th Cong., 1st Session: 1985), 222, 247. Caplan, *Tenth Justice,* 97, 103–07; Blumenthal, *Rise of the Counter-Establishment,* 301–02; *Washington Post,* August 9, 1985, p. A1; Curriculum vitae, Gary L. McDowell, http://oncampus.richmond.edu/academics/leadership/faculty/mcdowellcv05.pdf.

56 *Washington Post,* August 24, 1981, p. A7; *New York Times,* January 24, 1984, p. A14; *Washington Post,* February 26, 1982, p. A3.

57 *Washington Post,* May 31, 1982, p. A1; *Ibid.*, January 23, 1984, p. A1; *New York Times,* January 24, 1984, p. A14; *Ibid.*, January 26, 1982, p. B8; *Washington Post,* February. 22, 1982, p. A2; *Congressional Quarterly Almanac,* 38 (97th Cong., 2nd Session: 1982), 404. William French Smith to Strom Thurmond, May 6, 1982, United States House of Representatives,

Committee on the Judiciary, Subcommittee on Courts, Civil Liberties, and the Administration of Justice, Hearings on Statutory Limitations on Federal Jurisdiction (June–July 1981), pp. 324–39. Su. Doc. Y4 .J89/1:97/104. *Washington Post,* November 30, 1981, p. A1.

58 Caplan, *Tenth Justice*, 65–80; *Los Angeles Times,* July 25, 1983, pp. 1, 10; *Washington Post,* August 11, 1983, p. A21; Rex E. Lee, *A Lawyer Looks at the Constitution* (Provo, Utah: Brigham Young University Press, 1981), 183, 187.

59 *ABA Journal,* 69 (June 1983), 71; *Washington Post,* August 11, 1983, p. A21.

60 *U.S. News & World Report,* February 15, 1982, p. 33; Brief for the United States as amicus curiae in support of petitioners, *Valley Forge Christian College* v. *Americans United for Separation of Church and State,* May 1981; Lee, *Lawyer Looks at the Constitution,* 188–89; *Washington Post,* March 8, 1982, p. A2. *Valley Forge Christian College* v. *Americans United for Separation of Church and State,* 454 U.S. 464 (1982), 487.

61 Lee, *Lawyer Looks at the Constitution,* 188; Brief for the United States as amicus curiae in support of petitioners, *City of Akron* v. *Akron Center for Reproductive Health,* July 1982.

62 Caplan, *Tenth Justice,* 105; *ABA Journal,* 69 (June 1983), 71; *New York Times,* August 13, 1982, p. A24; *Washington Post,* August 18, 1982, p. A22; *ABA Journal,* 69 (June 1983), 71; *City of Akron* v. *Akron Center for Reproductive Health,* 462 U.S. 416 (1983), 420–21.

63 *Washington Post,* March 8, 1982, p. A2; *Los Angeles Times,* July 25, 1983, p. 10; *Washington Post,* August 11, 1983, p. A21; Caplan, *Tenth Justice,* 76; Rex E. Lee, "Lawyering for the Government: Politics, Polemics, and Principle," *Ohio State Law Journal,* 47 (Summer 1986), 597, 599.

64 Caplan, *Tenth Justice,* 76–80; *Washington Post,* March 8, 1982, p. A2; *Los Angeles Times,* July 25, 1983, pp. 1, 10; *Washington Post,* August 11, 1983, p. A21; *Wall Street Journal,* September 6, 1984, p. 1; *Washington Post,* May 1, 1985, p. A4. *Los Angeles Herald-Examiner,* November 17, 1985, p. F1.

65 James McClellan, "A Lawyer Looks at Rex Lee," *Benchmark,* 1 (March–April 1984), 1–2, 14; *Human Events,* August 6, 1983, p. 4; *Wall Street Journal,* September 6, 1984, p. 1.

66 *Ibid.*; *Human Events,* August 6, 1983, p. 4; *ibid.*, August 20, 1983, pp. 3–4; McClellan, "Lawyer Looks at Rex Lee," 14.

67 Caplan, *Tenth Justice,* 80–94; *Washington Post,* January 14, 1982, p. A2; *New York Times,* June 28, 1985, p. A1.

68 Caplan, *Tenth Justice,* 61–64, 95–98. *Donnelly* v. *Lynch,* 525 F.Supp. 1150 (1981), 1153–54; *Lynch* v. *Donnelly,* 465 U.S. 668 (1984). For more than a decade prior to *Lynch, Lemon*'s tripartite test had served as the standard for adjudicating Establishment Clause cases. *Lemon* v. *Kurtzman,* 403 U.S. 602 (1971), 612–13. Brief for the United States as amicus curiae supporting petitioners, *Lynch* v. *Donnelly,* June 1983.

69 Caplan, *Tenth Justice,* 97; *Lynch* v. *Donnelly.*

70 McClellan, "Lawyer Looks at Rex Lee," 5.

71 McClellan, "When Prayer Fell in Alabama"; *Wall Street Journal,* September 6, 1984, p. 1.

72 *Ibid.*; *Washington Post,* June 6, 1985, p. A4; *New York Times,* June 23, 1985, sec. 1, p. 24; Caplan, *Tenth Justice*, 99–100.

73 United States Court of Appeals for the Eleventh Circuit, order denying appellants' emergency motion for stay and injunction pending appeal; "Founding Fathers' Aim on Prayer Argued," *Mobile Press,* March 23, 1983.

74 *Jaffree* v. *Wallace,* 705 F.2d 1526 (1983), at 1528, 1536.

75 *Ibid.*, 1532–33.

76 *Ibid.*, 1530–32, 1536–37, emphasis in the original.

4

Accommodation

COURTING ACCOMMODATION

In the wake of the Eleventh Circuit's May 1983 ruling, all parties assumed Supreme Court review of *Jaffree* to be forthcoming. Reynolds now renewed his struggle to get theReagan administration involved in the case. According to Reynolds, the solicitor general's earlier contention that a circuit court should not be asked to strike down Supreme Court rulings was irrelevant to the upcoming phase of the case. "We are now in the Supreme Court," he reminded Lee. The parties had reached the appropriate time and place to ask the Court to reconsider its prior rulings. But for Lee, the underlying issue had not changed at all. If he were to file a brief urging reversal of the Eleventh Circuit, he would still be asking the Court to strike down its own long-established jurisprudence on the Establishment Clause. At no point had it become the solicitor general's intention to ask this of the Court. At no point would it be appropriate for him to advocate for the "district judge [who] thumbed his nose at the Supreme Court."[1]

Somehow, the White House came to know and look favorably on Reynolds's position. One of Lee's allies in the solicitor general's office charged that Reynolds had been given a "back channel to the White House" and that, "more than once, our positions were shot down at the White House by people who shouldn't even have known what we were doing." This was confirmed by *Benchmark* editor and former Associate Deputy Attorney General Bruce Fein, who admitted that sources had been briefing Meese, a strong backer of Reynolds. Having secured the favor of the White House and its approval for submitting a *Jaffree* brief,

Reynolds pressed the solicitor general to take a stance uncompromising enough to reflect the president's strong support for school prayer and states' rights. In October, Reynolds told Lee that "it would be counter-productive for the Government to argue strenuously for a narrow exception to the Schempp and Engel doctrine ... if, in so doing, we effectively endorsed the existing school prayer precedents." Reynolds urged Lee not to repeat the timidity of the solicitor general's *Lynch* brief. "Our position in the Supreme Court must be crafted in such a way so to make abundantly clear that we view *Schempp* and *Engel* as wrong and unworthy of respect."[2]

Lee and Bator imagined producing a very different amicus brief. Bator attempted to sell the president and attorney general on a cautious strategy by emphasizing its greater likelihood of success compared with the bleak fate sure to befall Reynolds's planned assault on *stare decisis*. Bator wanted the solicitor general to defend, among all the practices and statutes contested in *Jaffree*, the one with the best chance of winning the Court's approval: Alabama's 1981 silent-prayer statute, which sanctioned a daily "period of silence not to exceed one minute in duration ... for meditation or voluntary prayer." Defending the other items originally challenged by Jaffree – the 1982 law sanctioning recited prayer and the devotional practices conducted in Mobile classrooms – "would have required the Solicitor General to tell the Court that *Schempp* and *Engel* were based on an erroneous principle," inviting a stinging rebuke. "You go to the Court [only] when there are lower-court decisions and law-review articles and other expressions in the legal culture showing serious and thoughtful controversy about a matter." Because such careful "intellectual preparation had not been done ... in the case of the prayer decisions," the justices were bound to interpret the Reynolds position as an attack on their authority. What did make sense, Bator claimed, was to advance the silent-prayer issue, given that the Court had never prohibited silent prayer. This alone might win a favorable ruling.[3]

Bator was once again able to break through Reynolds's influence and persuade Attorney General Smith that the cautious path was the best path. Bator and Lee were allowed to shape the administration's case. In a preliminary brief submitted December 1983, the solicitor general asked the Court to review only that part of the Eleventh Circuit's ruling that prohibited silent prayer, requesting that this specific issue not become subsumed into any broader church-state deliberations. The solicitor general depicted classroom moments of silence as fitting comfortably within the ethos of pluralism and tolerance prescribed by the religion clauses of the First Amendment. "The theme I wanted to stress," Bator maintained, "was that intolerant secularism is as out of harmony with the religion clauses of the Constitution as an official religion would be." Room needed to be made for all viewpoints.[4]

If the justices were unsure about which elements of the case to review, it didn't show in the two orders that they issued in April 1984. In the first of these, the Court refused to review the Eleventh Circuit's decision regarding prayer activities in the Mobile schools. In the second, it affirmed the appellate court's decision on the 1982 Alabama spoken-prayer law, which it called "repugnant to the Establishment Clause of the First Amendment, applicable to the States under the Fourteenth Amendment." Taking their cue from the solicitor general, the justices chose, with their second order, to review only the 1981 law, the one sanctioning silent prayer.[5]

The Lee-Bator team submitted a second brief in July, after the Court had granted certiorari. The new document reiterated the "accommodationist" position captured in the *Lynch* brief – that fairness required accommodating religious citizens as well as nonreligious ones. Once again, the solicitor general counterposed doctrinaire church-state separationism with a "benevolent neutrality" respectful of all worldviews and practices. Lee and Bator averred that "the purpose of the Establishment Clause is not to work an artificial secularization upon our public life and institutions, but to ensure that the force of government is not brought to bear to induce or to restrain voluntary religious exercise (or nonexercise)." Alabama's silent-prayer statute, they insisted, was "fully consistent with that purpose." It passed constitutional muster because it remained "neutral among religions and between religion and nonreligion." Taking for granted that Alabama was bound by the Establishment Clause, the brief posited that the Establishment Clause encouraged the adoption of laws precisely like the Alabama silent-prayer law. "Ours is a nation of great religious diversity," the solicitor general reminded the Court; to foster harmony amid such diversity, the people must "develop habits of mutual respect and toleration for the religious practices of others." Alabama's statute helped perform this work. "The moment of silence provides an opportunity for young people to learn that each individual is free to worship and believe (or not believe) according to the dictates of his own conscience, and that the religious practices of others do not threaten or interfere with their own," the brief asserted. "The moment of silence is uniquely suited to such a lesson in toleration because of its dual nature – as an opportunity for exercise of faith among those who believe, and a wholly secular occasion for those who do not."[6]

Lee and Bator paid a price for their pragmatism. Right-wing critics throughout the department lost faith in Bator, much as they had already lost faith in Lee, for being too motivated by law and not enough by politics. Several demanded Lee's dismissal and his replacement by Reynolds, who likely would attempt to push the increasingly conservative Court even further rightward in ways that Lee would not. The *Jaffree* brief was the breaking point. As one prominent department official complained, the solicitor general's brief "concedes defeat before the argument is made." Had the administration followed Reynolds's recommendation, the official insisted, then, "even if the Supreme Court rejected the government's position the case could be a political rallying point for the Reagan administration and would heighten pressure on the Supreme Court to bring its decisions into line with public opinion."[7]

Outside the administration, the call for Lee's head was led by McClellan, who complained that "the perplexing refusal of the Reagan Administration to come to Hand's defense" had "weakened the force of Judge Hand's ruling." The government's moderate stance had scuttled McClellan's own project, and he wasn't happy. In his 1984 article "A Lawyer Looks at Rex Lee," he excoriated the solicitor general for letting pass "an historic occasion ... to lay the foundation for a conservative constitutional revolution." Lee's conformity to existing canons of law galled McClellan, who accused the solicitor general of "misunderstand[ing] ... his own role" within the administration. Such a traitor to the counterrevolution could not be permitted to derail the Reagan agenda any longer, the *Benchmark* editor wrote. "To say that he is not suited for the task to which he has been assigned is to understate the case for his prompt removal."[8]

Lee announced that he was resigning as solicitor general on April 30, 1985, a victim of the New Right's ideological zealotry. Hounded relentlessly by Reaganites who eschewed the respect for tradition that Lee valued, he was not long for an administration poised to turn even further rightward during its second term. Upon departing, he defended the positions he had taken as practical in light of the Court's incremental rate of change. Lee denied that he lacked the political will to carry out the conservative agenda and maintained that employing restraint was the best long-term method of realizing that agenda. But the differences between him and his detractors were as much philosophical as tactical. Unlike McClellan, Paul Weyrich, and others in the counter-establishment, Lee fully understood that "stare decisis is an important part of American law." While his critics were forever demanding that he "press the

Administration's policies at every turn and announce true conservative principles through the pages of my briefs," Lee knew that that was not his job. Committed to working within the law and honoring the Court's record, Lee could not provide the administration with the service that its right flank demanded.[9]

Lee's victory in submitting a moderate *Jaffree* brief and subsequent fall within the administration spoke to the constitutional battles taking place in and around the federal courts. In the wake of the struggle over *Jaffree*, Lee's critics prevailed with the Justice Department, which moved even further to the right. The administration would continue its transformation of the solicitor general's office, which increasingly became a political subordinate executing the president's political agenda. Unfortunately for Meese, Reynolds, and the counter-establishment, their influence within the administration failed to generate the legal victories for which they longed. Meanwhile, the arguments made by Lee, Bator, and McConnell in their *Lynch* and *Jaffree* briefs would nudge the Court toward a more accommodationist position on church-state matters. In the mid-1980s, the Christian Right would aim to influence constitutional law primarily by accepting Supreme Court precedent, including the validity of the incorporation doctrine. Insisting that they were entitled to protection under the law equal to that of other citizens would, for the present time, be the movement's strategy for winning a bigger role for religious expression in the public sphere.[10]

CONSERVATIVE COALITION

Counterrevolution was afoot as well in the U.S. Senate. Here, too, constitutional conservatives made their mark during the early 1980s, when the Senate underwent its sharpest rightward turn in decades. McClellan influenced key Senate conservatives, just as he had influenced Hand and members of the Justice Department. At the height of deliberations over the proper role of the federal courts in America's republican system of government, influential conservatives rallied behind Hand's *Jaffree* ruling. Counterrevolutionaries in the Senate found themselves facing the same difficulties encountered by Reynolds and his allies. Immoderate changes proved hard to sell.

As far back as the early 1960s, *Congressional Quarterly* had begun to track what it labeled a "conservative coalition," an emerging congressional alliance of Dixiecrats, or southern Democrats, and conservative Republicans. The relatively liberal composition of the House of

Representatives made that chamber's conservative coalition far smaller than its Senate counterpart. Beginning in 1977, the size and power of the coalition in the Senate ascended, while its political orientation grew ever more radical. Now known widely as the New Right, the coalition became a vocal minority, instilling discomfort within the mainstream of both parties. The rise of the New Right foreshadowed the emergence of the Tea Party nearly thirty years later. Its members appeared as brash, ideologically driven upstarts intent on redesigning federal social policy.[11]

In November 1980, with Republicans gaining control of the Senate for the first time since 1955, the conservative coalition took a quantum leap forward. Sixteen new Republicans were elected that year; at least half of them enjoyed volunteer and financial support from far-right organizations, including groups with religious orientations and "family values" agendas. The election doubled the ranks of New Right senators, who were filled with raw passion and prepared to fight for what they believed to be the will of ordinary Americans. "The conservative Republican Senate freshmen came crashing onto the enemy shores of liberal Washington, riding the crest of the New Right wave, self-confident and even self-righteous, convinced that they held the new franchise on truth," wrote the *Washington Post.* In contrast to established conservatives such as Barry Goldwater and Howard Baker, the recent electees adopted a confrontational style. They were not terribly given to compromise, eager as they were to arrest decades-long liberal policies. Nor were they shy about it. Malcolm Wallop (R-Wyo.), elected in 1976, explained that "ours is an offensive battle," while recently elected William L. Armstrong (R-Colo.) eagerly anticipated "pursuing the peaceful overthrow of government" through the use of "confrontation politics." The chamber's customary decorum was anathema to these conservative radicals; political pragmatism was a wet blanket on their missionary fires.[12]

To their critics, the far-right senators were impetuous bullies. Some critics dubbed them the "popsicle brigade" on account of their childishness and refusal to observe protocol. Others, such as the executive director of Americans for Democratic Action, were harsher, calling them "new primitives" looking "to repeal the twentieth century." For columnist Nina Totenberg, history might have been in the making. "One hopes we haven't reached the point in this country where civility and caution go out the window. One hopes we are not being faced with a sort of right-wing Red Guard that is unswervingly bent on its own form of cultural and constitutional revolution." Liberal Republican senators recoiled from the New Right's fervor. Robert Packwood (R-Or.) complained of their

"Cotton Mather mentality," a "narrow, unforgiving ... feeling that 'God speaks to me [and] I will tell you what He says,'" while Lowell Weicker (R-Conn.) admonished opponents of legalized abortion that "we're not running this country on instructions from Mount Sinai." Another senator anonymously scolded his far-right colleagues, "The democratic process presupposes that you have differences of opinion, but you respect your opponent's point of view and the element of compromise that the process requires."[13]

However much it may have ruffled liberals' feathers, the conservative coalition enjoyed tremendous success beginning in 1981, as several New Right leaders, including James McClure (R-Id.), Jake Garn (R-Ut.), Orrin Hatch (R-Ut.), and Jesse Helms (R-N.C.), assumed important committee-leadership posts. *Congressional Quarterly* reported that, in 1981, the New Right "showed a strength unequaled in the 25 years *Congressional Quarterly* had measured the coalition's muscle." That year, the coalition defeated Northern Democrats in 95 percent of votes that reached the Senate floor. Although conservatives did not get the opportunity to pass "morals" legislation that year, they gained a great deal of momentum and grew sanguine about their prospects for ultimately turning their vision into law.[14]

The New Right drew its life force from one senator more than any other. Since his arrival in 1973, Republican Jesse Helms of North Carolina had stood out among his colleagues as a disciplined, driven right-wing ideologue. Helms's reputation was earned along the Senate's margins, where he remained throughout his early tenure. His persistence as a conservative standard-bearer paid off, as, by 1980, he ascended to the unofficial leadership of the congressional New Right. That year, he voted along with the conservative coalition on an unequaled 98 percent of floor votes. Helms would go on, throughout the decade, to vote along with the coalition at a clip matched only by Sen. Strom Thurmond (R-S.C.). Helms's voting record and performance as a leader among his right-wing colleagues earned him the adoration of super-activists such as Richard Viguerie and Howard Phillips, national director of the Conservative Caucus, who called him "our most valuable player."[15]

Helms made his mark early in his Senate career. He frequently cast the lone vote against popular programs, staking out what columnist George Will called "the outer limit of conservative activism." From the start, Helms anticipated the cultural conservatism of the 1980s by seeking to shift government policy on school prayer, abortion, and busing – issues on which the New Right would register some of its most vocal claims.

He caused much controversy in 1977 by waging a concerted but unsuccessful battle to end affirmative-action programs. He would later garner notoriety when he opposed the creation of a national holiday honoring Martin Luther King, whose personal character the senator impugned. Actions such as these made Helms anathema to moderates and liberals while enhancing his reputation on the right. Presaging groups such as the Moral Majority, he urged his party, in 1975, to recruit citizens "not presently part of the political process," to convert "the conservative majority" of Americans into loyal Republicans. The party would follow this precise strategy, as it reached out to religious conservatives and promised to counter the influence of liberal "cultural elites."[16]

Helms's prestige hit its heights with the 1980 presidential election, which journalist Peter Range called "Jesse Helms's personal moment of triumph after years as a senatorial lone wolf." So enormous was his impact on the party's platform that year that the *Washington Post* dubbed it the "Helmsian platform." Establishment Republicans acquiesced as Helms's stance on moral issues became official party positions. Bolstered by vocal and determined support from Christian conservatives, particularly Jerry Falwell and the Moral Majority, Helms and his allies secured planks calling for a constitutional ban on abortion and for the appointment of federal judges committed to overturning *Roe* v. *Wade.* A triumphant Helms declared, "I got ninety-nine percent of what I wanted." His victory at the Republican convention, along with the party's victory at the polls, brought him unprecedented power and confirmed him as the leader among Senate conservatives. As Range observed, "Helms and other New Rightists ... are convinced that the political tide is still surging to the right, and they are prepared and encouraged to ... test their principles against the voices of moderation and compromise."[17]

In 1980, Helms helped secure electoral victories for two first-time senators who would later spark his interest in *Jaffree.* One was Jeremiah Denton, the Mobile native and champion of family values who tried to persuade the Justice Department to submit a brief in the case. With Helms's support, Denton ran a strong campaign and established himself as a rising star in the Republican Party – a defender of school prayer, promoter of sexual abstinence, and crusader against abortion, student busing, and gun control. Helms also secured the election of his protégé, political scientist and fellow North Carolina Republican John East. So conservative was East, especially in his support for states' rights and judicial restraint, that Helms joked, "I'm now the liberal senator from North Carolina." Inspired by legislative advisor and longtime friend

James McClellan, East would submit an amicus brief to the Eleventh Circuit on behalf of Alabama and the Mobile school board in *Jaffree*. The senator's argument – like that of Judge Hand – derived straight from McClellan's trial testimony. "The establishment clause prohibits [any] federal action which jeopardizes the sovereignty of each state over its own religious affairs." The individual states were not barred from establishing religions – indeed, the First Amendment guaranteed their right to do so. Like Hand and McClellan, East defended the doctrine of states' rights and aimed to eliminate judicial activism.[18]

Helms, East, Denton, and many of their allies acted out of a worldview based partly on religious orthodoxy. Christian conservatives played a significant role in the 1980 election and the subsequent Republican-led government, although scholars disagree on the precise scope and nature of that role. During the early 1980s, Senate Republicans regularly sponsored "morals" legislation. Even as Reagan and congressional leaders prioritized economic and foreign policy initiatives, the New Right demanded that the Senate give equal attention to religious matters such as school prayer and abortion. Republicans Helms, East, Denton, Orrin Hatch (Utah), Roger Jepsen (Iowa), and others pressured their colleagues to enact laws honoring what they understood to be America's Christian heritage, effectively equating religious conservatism with love of country. Even though their efforts met with mixed success at best, they colored the Senate of the early 1980s with a conservative religious hue.[19]

COURT STRIPPING

Nowhere did conservatives make a bigger impact than on the Senate Judiciary Committee, whose chairmanship changed hands in 1981 from Ted Kennedy (D-Mass.) to Thurmond. This shift indicated far more than a new majority party. A man who had risen to power by fervently opposing racial desegregation now assumed the helm of the committee most responsible for the landmark civil-rights legislation of the 1960s. Thurmond, *Congressional Quarterly* pointed out, had "made his reputation as a states' rights activist and ... had voted against every major civil rights bill in Congress." To help shift the committee's agenda, the new chair added an eighteenth member, thereby giving his party a two-seat advantage over the Democrats. Thurmond recruited three extreme conservatives: East, Denton, and Charles Grassley (R-Iowa). Swayed by these moral traditionalists, the committee refocused its attention toward restricting the jurisdiction of the federal courts. Two Senate subcommittees, in particular, carried out those efforts – the Subcommittee on Separation of Powers, chaired by East, and the Subcommittee on the Constitution, chaired by Hatch. The Senate Judiciary Committee launched a three-year effort to reverse federal law on school prayer, abortion, and busing by attempting to remove those policy areas from the purview of the federal courts.[20]

New Right senators attempted to pass such bills – known by their opponents as "court-stripping" measures – partly because of expediency. Unlike a constitutional amendment, whose passage required a two-thirds majority in each house, a bill to contract the jurisdiction of the courts required only a simple majority. Moreover, conservatives had come, as fully as liberals, to recognize the influence wielded by the federal courts in determining religion's place within public institutions, and conservatives became determined to contain that influence. The majoritarian strain within conservatism since World War II now crystalized in an antijudicialism asserting that the federal judiciary, as much as liberalism, was a contagion needing to be quarantined. Many on the right clamored for government to assert the sovereignty of the individual states and the exclusive role for legislatures in the lawmaking process. Helms and East, in particular, aimed to reverse *Engel* and *Roe* by circumscribing the federal courts' authority and defending the right of popular majorities within each state to determine public policy.[21]

In 1954, with *Brown* v. *Board of Education* inaugurating a period of conflict between Congress and the Supreme Court, conservatives advanced the first court-stripping legislation since the nineteenth century. Congress would, in the years after *Brown*, entertain numerous bills to restrict the jurisdiction of the federal courts on a variety of matters, including government loyalty-security programs, school desegregation, legislative reapportionment, school prayer, and the rights of individuals accused of crimes. Following *Engel* and *Schempp* in 1962–1963, champions of school prayer introduced several court-stripping bills. Typical was Rep. Mendel Rivers (D.-S.C.), who announced that it was "time for Congress ... to drastically restrict and limit the appellate jurisdiction of this court which flaunts its authority in our very faces." Although the pace slowed down by the mid-Sixties, Congress continued occasionally to attempt to gerrymander the jurisdiction of the courts, particularly over school busing and abortion. Political scientist Edward Keynes contends that, for proponents of such legislation, "the objective was clear: namely, to reverse the justices' decisions, correct their extra-constitutional policy making, and prevent further judicial invasion of state and congressional authority."[22]

This strategy picked up steam again in 1974, when Helms – advised by McClellan – applied it to school prayer. Nearly every year over the next decade, Helms would introduce measures designed to restrict federal-court jurisdiction over school prayer, abortion, and busing. It was surrounding those issues, Helms told his colleagues, that the judiciary most blatantly robbed the people of their right to self-rule, as guaranteed by the Constitution. He explained that, "in anticipation of judicial usurpation of power, the framers of our Constitution wisely gave Congress the authority, by a simply majority of both Houses, to check the Supreme Court through regulation of its appellate jurisdiction." Responding to judicial tyranny by these means promised greater effectiveness than constitutional amendment, as efforts to reverse *Engel* through the latter had come to naught. Now, Helms declared, "the time has come to consider an alternative means of dealing with this problem." The repeated failures of these court-stripping bills to elicit a floor vote, or even a committee hearing, did not deter Helms and his occasional allies. The closest to success that they came was in 1979, when Helms got a jurisdictional bill on school prayer approved by the Judiciary Committee and the full Senate. The House, however, failed to act on the bill, and so, like every other year, the Helms proposal died.[23]

Jurisdictional gerrymandering squared nicely with a theory, gaining ground among conservatives, that judicial review constituted a "counter-majoritarian difficulty" within American democracy. Advocates of this theory suggested that, when the Court transgressed the (apparent) popular will, in a manner lacking clear directive within the Constitution's text, the Court violated the nation's democratic norms. The New Right's skepticism toward judicial review was stoked by a resurgence in popularity of Alexander Bickel's *The Least Dangerous Branch*, which depicted judicial review as an anomaly in a system where decision-making characteristically resides with the popular majority's chosen representatives. To establish the legitimacy of judicial review, Bickel maintained, government needed to confront, if not resolve, the counter-majoritarian difficulty posed by the practice.[24]

Addressing that difficulty became the project for two influential books published in 1980. In *Democracy and Distrust*, John Hart Ely echoed Bickel, claiming that "rule in accord with the consent of a majority of those governed is the core of the American governmental system," so that judicial review inevitably ran afoul of the nation's most fundamental political tenet. Yet, Ely, like Bickel, did not favor an unrestrained majoritarianism. In a democracy, he insisted, majority rule "cannot be the whole story, since a majority with untrammeled power to set governmental policy is in a position to deal itself benefits at the expense of the remaining minority." That same year, Jesse Choper published *Judicial Review and the National Political Process*, which also took seriously judicial review's tendency to cut "sharply against the grain of majority rule." More fully than either Ely or Bickel, Choper believed that this counter-majoritarian force was consistent with constitutional democracy. "The essential values of a democratic society," he argued, "assume the existence of certain inalienable minimums of personal freedom ... that guard the dignity and integrity of the individual." Those personal freedoms were protected by judicial review, which, despite its problematic place in our system, remained indispensable to that system.[25]

Among the many 1980s voices debating the proper place of judicial review in a constitutional democracy were staunch conservatives who would declare improper the courts' ability to check the will of majorities within individual states, particularly regarding civil liberties and civil rights. According to Stephen Macedo, "partisans of the New Right advocate[d] a new majoritarianism and a fundamental narrowing of judicial protections for individual rights," which, "if accepted by the nation's courts, would represent a decisive shift of power to legislative majorities and a basic revision of the nature of citizenship in America." Indeed, for conservatives such as Raoul Berger, Robert Bork, and Meese, true democracy required that the representatives elected by popular majorities determine public policies. Judicial review, Bork complained, had again and again "thwart[ed] democratic choice." After being named Ronald Reagan's attorney general in 1985, Meese would proclaim that "the Constitution is the fundamental will of the people." When we "allow the courts to govern simply by what it [sic] views at the time as fair and decent," he maintained, "the idea of democracy has suffered."[26]

McClellan defended Helms's court-stripping bills – which McClellan himself helped conceive and design – as catalysts for majoritarian democracy. Indeed, his root political assumption was that "democratic government is government by majority rule." He doubted that government could "honestly be called democratic if the interests of the minority, in the name of civil rights, are preferred to those of the majority, and [if] the people are governed by unelected judges." His friend East concurred. "If the United States stands for anything," he contended, "it stands for the idea of representative government and that the U.S. Congress shall be the fundamental policymaker, that it shall not be the primary function of the judiciary to do that." As Keynes noted, advocates of court stripping assumed that "the federal judiciary is a nondemocratic, irresponsible institution, which should refrain from interfering in the democratic process unless Congress and the state legislatures have clearly exceeded their constitutional authority."[27]

Because the Court had violated the basic precepts of democracy, New Right luminaries concluded, lawmakers were tasked to defend popular sovereignty. Thus, Berger urged Congress to heed the "widespread dissatisfaction with the judicial takeover of functions confided by the Constitution to the States and to the people." The primary architect of Helms's jurisdictional legislation agreed. "Without the power to regulate the Court's jurisdiction," McClellan feared, "Congress is helpless to limit the judicial power and the Court is exempted from the checks and balances system." Under such conditions, McClellan warned, the Court would surely continue to usurp the legislative function. "This is not only inconsistent with the basic principle of limited government, but makes judicial review intolerable in a democratic society." McClellan called on Congress to take the lead in preserving democracy. "Certainly no society can justly call itself democratic where as few as five appointed justices, who are beyond the control of the people and their elected representatives, can determine the meaning and substance of nearly all the freedoms that the people possess."[28]

Helms and East dug in their heels against judicial tyranny. Helms declared that he would no longer tolerate the Court's habit of "amend[ing] the Constitution by the simple expedient of judicial decree," which he pronounced "a severe long-term threat to the American Constitution and the rule of law itself." "By removing jurisdiction from the courts in areas where Federal judges have abused their authority," he assured fellow senators, "Congress will be acting to preserve the integrity of the Constitution." East agreed that the justices had "circumvented the legislative process" and had thereby acted "contrary to that fundamental tenet of democratic political theory that we, the Congress, ought to be making the fundamental policy judgments." The central question in court-stripping measures, East maintained, was not whether Congress was impinging on the judiciary's rightful function, but whether Congress would defend itself against justices who had impinged on its rightful function.[29]

Through 1980, Helms's efforts at curtailing the Court's jurisdiction had not gotten far. At no point could Helms procure the support of enough fellow senators to gain traction. Abortion, school prayer, and busing remained securely in the domain of the federal courts. But, again and again, he – with East's eventual help – positioned himself as spokesperson for a supposed silent majority of Americans being ignored and manipulated by the federal judiciary. His was a right-wing populist campaign to limit the impact of judicial review on American lawmaking and to resuscitate the democratic process.

COMPETING STRATEGIES

As the school prayer movement gathered momentum through 1981 and 1982, Helms and East found themselves fighting a battle similar to the one that Reynolds was waging in the Justice Department. The two senators carried the movement's majoritarianism to its logical conclusion. By cordoning off school prayer from "the least democratic branch" of government they hoped to preserve the right of local majorities to decide the matter for themselves. They found, much as Reynolds did, that many fellow conservatives eschewed their extremism. The well-established role of the federal courts was not something with which most Republicans wanted to tamper. Counterrevolution was not an easy sell.

From its beginning in the early Sixties, the movement to preserve school prayer was driven by majoritarian sentiment. The movement was born in the wake of *Engel*, which generated large-scale, visceral outrage at atheists and religious minorities for allegedly forcing their idiosyncratic preferences on the American people. The Court, too, endured condemnation, accused of favoring infidels over ordinary citizens. With little hope of changing the justices' minds, prayer supporters focused their efforts on amending the Constitution. In the quarter-century after *Engel*, Congress entertained more than six hundred proposals for a school prayer amendment. The testimony on behalf of these bills, along with the public commentary on them, registered much more than concern for children's moral instruction. Prayer supporters gave voice to a political critique of the Court, which they accused of violating democratic principles. Most proponents of the 1964 Becker Amendment to legalize classroom prayer echoed the witness who warned the House Judiciary Committee that "unless positive action is taken [to restore prayer in schools] it appears likely that in the name of religious freedom the will of the majority may very well be subjected to the will of the minority." Throughout the proceedings, the Court was identified as the tyrant forcibly recasting American society. Nowhere was this analysis articulated more clearly than in the testimony of Alabama governor George Wallace, who decried the

Court's "deliberate design to subordinate the American people, their faith, their customs, and their religious traditions to a godless state." Majoritarian critiques remained center stage at hearings on the Dirksen Amendment in 1966 and the Wylie Amendment in 1971, two further attempts at school-prayer amendments. Throughout, Congress was told that society's need to mold children and reproduce its own values was paramount. The rights of individuals – especially dissenters – mattered far less.[30]

When Helms took office in 1974, he assumed leadership of the movement within Congress. A constitutional amendment had proven elusive; jurisdictional gerrymandering, he and his advisor McClellan insisted, was the more promising strategy. Every year, for the remainder of the decade, Helms introduced court-stripping bills that downplayed free-exercise concerns and underscored the federal judiciary's usurpation of popular sovereignty. Helms's bills were far more radical than the amendment measures had been. The latter, notwithstanding the majoritarian rhetoric surrounding them, had looked to force the courts to protect school prayer, whereas Helms and McClellan looked to circumvent the courts altogether. Helms's 1980 bill attracted support from key Christian conservatives such as Moral Majority director Falwell, who lambasted President Carter for promising to veto the bill if it passed. Falwell reported asking Carter, on behalf of the supposed overwhelming number of Americans supporting school prayer, whether his veto would not constitute "discrimination against the majority."[31]

The Republican Party's ascendancy in 1981 signaled a watershed moment for prayer supporters in Congress. During that year alone, they introduced eleven different measures that would in some way restrict federal-court jurisdiction over school prayer. The only one seriously considered was the "Voluntary Prayer Act of 1981," Helms's and East's reissue of Helms's standard jurisdictional bill. On the Senate floor, Helms gave a McClellian defense of the prayer act. A primary defect of *Engel* and *Schempp*, he charged, was their dissonance with and disregard for popular will. The people, and not the justices of the Supreme Court, ought to determine the place of prayer in school; when the Court usurped the people's authority in this area, it ran roughshod over well-established popular customs. Helms maintained that the Court, through its decisions in *Engel* and *Schempp*, had performed a "sweeping condemnation of America's spiritual heritage," thereby squelching the voice of the people and "in effect g[iving] preference to the dissenters," who subscribed only to "the religion of secularism." Along with the will of the people, the history of the Constitution had been ignored. "An open historical inquiry,"

Helms concluded, "would have led to a result far different than that of the Court," which had "reached its holding in *Engel* and *Schempp* by way of a myopic and narrow view of the history of the Constitution."[32]

The justices' misreading of history had no more pernicious a consequence, Helms estimated, than their application of the Establishment Clause to the individual states. Like McClellan and Hand in *Jaffree*, he renounced the incorporation doctrine as a brazen act of judicial tyranny against the people of the states and their representatives – an act of callous disregard for the Constitution and the men who had written it. Had the Court rigorously examined the Establishment Clause's history, it could only have concluded, as had McClellan and Hand, that the Framers had "sought a division of power in which the States would retain their ability to establish or disestablish a religion." "There simply is no liberty contained in the establishment clause," Helms insisted, "to be 'incorporated' through the fourteenth amendment and applied to the States." In finding such a liberty, the Court had created a device through which elites in the federal government might impose their atheism onto ordinary citizens. That, he averred, would unconstitutionally restrict a state government from determining its own relationship with religion.[33]

Although the Helms-East bill remained caught in a filibuster for the remainder of 1981, the attention it received increased the momentum building in the legal counter-establishment. Weyrich's Free Congress Foundation helped promote Helms's and East's cause. In late November, the foundation held a press briefing in the Senate caucus room, where it unveiled a new collection of essays published through its recently launched Judicial Reform Project. *A Blueprint for Judicial Reform* contained essays by senators East, Hatch, and Grassley, former senator Sam Ervin, future attorney general John Ashcroft, and constitutional scholars McClellan, Patrick McGuigan, Charles Rice, and William Bentley Ball. Volume editor McGuigan declared that "after decades of judicial activism a movement is building that is not only disenchanted with the judiciary, but fully prepared to take steps to curb the powers of the courts." McClellan's essay rehearsed the arguments that he would advance one year later in Hand's courtroom. Among those highly receptive to the book were presidential advisor Meese and Attorney General Smith. While liberal organizations castigated it as an attack on the judiciary's independence, volume contributor Jules B. Gerard denounced those same organizations as enemies of democracy. And so the New Right war on "judicial excess" intensified.[34]

Helms and East continued to push their court-stripping bill into 1982. Opponents now sounded a more urgent alarm. The chief justices of the fifty states condemned the bill as "a hazardous experiment," while Senator Max Baucus (D-Mont.) proffered that it would permit Congress to "dismantle any part of the Constitution it wished and paralyze the courts from reviewing the conduct." Helms dismissed his critics as out of touch with ordinary American people. Among his critics was American Bar Association (ABA) President David Brink, who, back in November, had suggested that jurisdictional measures "challenge[d] our very form of government by threatening elimination of the third branch of Federal Government, the judicial." Helms countered, in March, that it was the ABA that was seeking to destroy the balance of power by making the judiciary sovereign. The organization's attempts to bring about judicial tyranny, he claimed, placed the ABA in conflict with the "overwhelming majority of American citizens."[35]

The counterrevolutionaries had put Reagan in a difficult position. The president had long believed in the propriety of school prayer and had publicly supported a prayer amendment, but in early 1982 he had not yet called for legislation of any kind protecting school prayer. Key conservatives pressured him and Senate Majority Leader Baker to commandeer passage of a prayer bill, along with a bill that would criminalize abortion. Reagan's characteristic pragmatism made him question the wisdom and viability of court stripping. On this matter, he was influenced by Smith, whose cautious nature and respect for judicial precedent tempered his dislike for judicial activism. Although Smith gave no public indication of his stance on court stripping throughout April 1982, he privately advised the president to pursue prayer legislation through alternative means. The Helms bill, he told the president, was "unwise" insofar as it would deprive the federal courts of their rightful authority to review statutory law.[36]

Finally, in May, the attorney general spoke out publicly, shedding doubt on the constitutional validity of jurisdictional gerrymandering. Smith sent letters to the House and Senate judiciary committees denying Congress's right to restrict the basic operation of the courts. "Congress may not," he declared, "make 'exceptions' to Supreme Court jurisdiction which would intrude upon the core functions of the Supreme Court as an independent and equal branch in our system of separation of powers." Key among those "core functions" was to ensure nationwide uniformity with constitutional doctrine. While it remained inappropriate for the federal courts "to intrude into areas that properly belong to the State legislatures," the proper "remedy for judicial overreaching," Smith insisted, was "not to restrict the Supreme Court's jurisdiction over those cases which are central to the core functions of the Court."[37]

Smith's statement enabled Reagan to frame the prayer issue distinctly in his own terms. On the same day that the attorney general undercut the Helms bill, the president told a gathering of religious conservatives that he was offering prayer legislation of his own. The one hundred twenty people gathered in the White House Rose Garden heard Reagan promise to submit a proposal for a constitutional amendment protecting voluntary prayer in public schools. The Reagan amendment, sponsored in the Senate by Thurmond, stated, "Nothing in this Constitution shall be construed to prohibit individual or group prayer in public schools or other public institutions. No person shall be required by the United States or any state to participate in prayer."[38]

Immediately afterward, and over the following months, the president held the rapt devotion of religious conservatives seeking government help in the social reproduction of traditional morality. Supporters understood his proposal as a defense of the majority's political prerogative to encode its moral preferences into law. Reagan captured the backing of the same forces backing Helms, and public statements promoting his amendment evinced a similarly majoritarian rhetoric. Freshman senator Steve Symms (R-Id.) insisted that, while "individuals or groups who are not religious and choose not to pray have a right to make that choice ... their views should not be imposed on the rest of the nation." Falwell announced that "the purpose of the constitutional amendment is to circumvent the Supreme Court." The amendment "will be passed," he predicted, simply "because the people want it." The president had grabbed the New Right trumpet out of Helms's hands, blown it loudly, and rallied the troops.[39]

The president's amendment never made it past the Senate Judiciary Committee in 1982. But throughout committee hearings that summer, proponents of the amendment continued their moral-majoritarian call. Even McClellan and Helms expressed their approval to the committee. The bill's sponsor, Thurmond, championed the amendment in much the same terms that Helms used to promote his bill. In his introductory remarks to the committee on July 29, Thurmond protested that the Court, in proscribing school prayer, had usurped "the constitutional authority of the States over church-state relations." The Reagan amendment "would reinstate ... the original intent of the Founding Fathers," Thurmond claimed, by restoring each state's right "to define the meaning of religious establishment under its own constitution and laws."[40]

By using McClellian arguments to endorse the amendment, conservatives were obscuring the vast difference between it and the Helms bill. In fact, the president's proposal did not embody the constitutionalism of the New Right. It did not roll back the incorporation doctrine or return to state governments all authority over religious establishment. It did not restrict the jurisdiction of the courts or sanction the passage of prayer laws. The amendment assumed a civil-libertarian premise – it extended the free exercise clause, so to speak – by specifying that the Constitution protected the right of groups and individuals to pray in public institutions, including schools, and that "no person shall be required by the United States or any *state* to participate in prayer." That is, the president's proposal sought to carve out an additional liberty, to restrain state governments from infringing on that liberty, and to set up the federal courts as its guarantor. All the sympathetic testimony in the world from Helms and McClellan couldn't deny that this proposal obstructed their plans for constitutional counterrevolution.[41]

THE CASE FOR COUNTERREVOLUTION

The Helms-East bill gained new life over the upcoming months. The two senators got a break when the president's amendment remained stuck in committee throughout 1982. The only prayer bill to gain attention on the Senate floor that year was theirs. Within months, their legislative mission would be buttressed by a crucial event. Hand's opinion in *Jaffree* would bring court stripping a measure of legitimacy that it had never before enjoyed, much as the opinion accorded Reynolds's efforts a patina of validity. A federal court ruling now suggested that Helms's and East's views were correct and their imagined law constitutional.

As summer arrived, Helms and East looked to distinguish their bill from the president's amendment. On June 30, East introduced into the *Congressional Record* a letter sent to him ten days earlier by Hermine Meyer, the former Justice Department official and now legal advisor to Alabama Governor Fob James (and, later, Governor George Wallace). As if written by McClellan, the letter argued that a prayer amendment would further distort First Amendment law by bestowing constitutionality on something unconstitutional – federal control over state religious matters. Soon afterward, Helms informed his colleagues of a letter he had received from Charles Rice, a Notre Dame law professor, contributor to the Free Congress Foundation's *Blueprint for Judicial Reform*, and author of the amicus brief sent to the Eleventh Circuit in *Jaffree* on behalf of

McClellan's Center for Judicial Studies. Rice's letter assured the senator that Smith's argument against jurisdictional legislation was "contrary to the clear language of the Exceptions Clause, the intent of the Framers, and the consistent indications given by the Supreme Court itself." His convictions confirmed, Helms accused the attorney general of promoting judicial activism and suggested he "consider revising [his] May 6 letter."[42]

When, on August 16, Helms tried to append court-stripping legislation to a bill addressing the public debt, he provoked opponents into dogged resistance. Senate liberals waged an extended filibuster led by Baucus, Packwood, and, at the helm, Weicker, a mercurial gadfly who had first come to prominence as a member of the Watergate Committee investigating President Richard Nixon. Throughout the Reagan era, the Connecticut Republican would remain the Senate's most tireless and effective champion for church-state separation. Weicker valued the Court for its protection of minorities, and he warned that the Helms bill would entirely deprive the Court of that vital capacity. Much as Ronnie Williams had recently remonstrated before Hand, Weicker posited that religious practices in the classroom "are never truly 'voluntary' and produce psychological pressures upon the children who do not wish to participate." The mission of the public schools, he maintained, was not to indoctrinate. "What the schools ought to be teaching our young people to believe is a respect for all beliefs, for differing beliefs, for minorities." His goal in opposing the Helms bill was to ensure that even a minority of one remained free from religious coercion in the classroom.[43]

The filibuster against the Helms bill lasted five weeks. While the *Jaffree* parties were preparing for trial, senators debated the proper role of the Court and the nature of its commitment to religious minorities. Baucus declared to his colleagues that "any democracy's quality is measured by the degree to which the rights of the minority are protected," and that his main goal was "to see that the majority does not misrule, that the minority is protected." Several other senators pledge similar commitments. Daniel Patrick Moynihan (D-N.Y.) waxed eloquent in describing how the Framers had "spoke[n] over and over again of a tyranny of the majority" and "devised the Courts as the institution in which minority rights would be protected." The Helms bill had to be defeated, he insisted, because, where minority rights were concerned, "it is emphatically the province of the Court to declare what the law is."[44]

Belief in the sanctity of individual rights and the legitimacy of judicial review remained so entrenched in American politics that even some school prayer advocates repudiated court-stripping measures. One was

Illinois Democrat Alan Dixon. While attesting that he "support[ed] voluntary prayer in the schools," he warned that the Helms bill "would impede the independence of the Federal judiciary." Another prayer backer, David Durenberger (R-Minn.), opined that "court stripping is a Pandora's box that can threaten all of our rights once it is opened up." Most damning of all were the pronouncements of Mark Hatfield (R-Or.), an influential Christian evangelical, who predicted that the bill would send the nation "heading down a reckless course." For Hatfield, "the roots of this great Nation" were "planted firmly in the Constitution and [we]re nourished by the freedoms protected in that document." It became obvious to Helms and East that even some committed Christians were wary of interfering with the Court's rights-protecting capacity.[45]

Jurisdictional gerrymandering also faced overwhelming disapproval from constitutional scholars. Three weighty petitions pressured senators to oppose the bill. One was sent by an august and diverse group including four former attorneys general, four former solicitors general, and former Supreme Court justice Arthur J. Goldberg. Although the group "as individuals" held "varying views on the [relevant] substantive policy issues," it unanimously found that Helms-East "pose[d] a dangerous threat to the integrity and independence of the federal judiciary in our constitutional system of government." That concern was echoed by the Library of Congress's Congressional Research Service, which warned that, "if Congress can insulate its own acts from review by the federal judiciary by simply denying the courts jurisdiction of their subject matter," then an "essential check on majoritarian excess would be eliminated." This was no trifling matter, senators were assured by deans of eight of the most prestigious American law schools. The deans apprised lawmakers that enforcement of minority rights would remain tenuous at best if not for the Court's solicitude. Fortunately, Americans enjoyed a constitution that wisely "limits the authority of political majorities." And nothing, they said, should be allowed to interfere with that function.[46]

It was precisely that function – insulation of minority rights from the reach of duly elected political representatives – that Helms and allies deemed problematic, in need of interruption. The real problem, they held, was not tyranny of the majority, but tyranny of the judiciary. East contrasted those senators "obstruct[ing] majority sentiment in the country" with Helms, who was "raising the broader question which every American senses in his political bones, that somehow or other we [the people] no longer make policy decisions in this country." That job, East claimed, had been hijacked by "the elite in the Supreme Court, the Federal judiciary, with lifetime appointments, no accountability, moving ever and ever into the policymaking role." Don Nickles (R-Okla.) concurred: "The proposed legislation would return to parents, teachers, and local school boards the right to decide for their children what policy on prayer is most appropriate in public schools."[47]

Although Helms and East would prove unable to end the filibuster and save their bill, they remained on the offensive through the following spring. Their high point came on January 14, with Hand's disquieting *Jaffree* decision. Finally, the counterrevolution could claim a victory. The ruling reignited Helms, who regaled colleagues with ringing testimonials to the Alabama judge. Helms crowed that Hand's opinion, issued "from within the lower echelons of the Federal judiciary itself ... represent[ed] a long overdue repudiation of judicial supremacy." represent[ed] a long overdue repudiation of judicial supremacy" *Jaffree* had changed history, Helms exclaimed. "Judge Hand has challenged the infallibility of the Supreme Court, and in so doing has delivered an opinion that will serve as a constant reminder that our judges take an oath to uphold the supremacy of the Constitution, not the supremacy of the Supreme Court or its interpretation of the Constitution." The author of *Jaffree* had handed down "a carefully reasoned and remarkably eloquent opinion," Helms contended, one "destined to go down in the annals of legal history as a landmark decision." Indeed, "the significance of Judge Hand's courageous decision is so far reaching as to suggest that we may be entering a new era of American constitutional development."[48]

Helms celebrated more than just Hand's challenge to judicial supremacy. According to the senator, *Jaffree* had performed vital work toward restoring power to the states and their popular majorities. "The opinion," he maintained, "demonstrates the unconstitutionality of the application of the first eight amendments in the Bill of Rights to the States, the so-called doctrine of incorporation, which has become the great wellspring of Federal judicial power in modern America." He hoped that Hand's ruling would strike a critical blow against federal court tyranny. "If the decision is upheld," Helms conjectured, "the States would be free, as they always were until a few years ago, to determine for themselves the nature of church-state relations within their jurisdictions, and the Federal Government would once again be prohibited from dictating such policies." The senator praised the individual who had informed and inspired Hand. "As Judge Hand generously acknowledges in his opinion, much of the credit for this dramatic new understanding of our Constitution goes to James McClellan," the expert witness whose influence had made the ruling "an augury of things to come." Helms applauded Hand's and McClellan's willingness to prioritize the intentions of the authors of the First and Fourteenth amendments. More than any other ruling of recent times, he concluded, *Jaffree* had reestablished the legitimacy of constitutional originalism, states' rights, and popular rule.[49]

Hand's ruling received additional exposure that spring at hearings in the Subcommittee on Separation of Powers, chaired by East. Under consideration was East's "Judicial Reform Act," a measure that more generally would restrict the jurisdiction of the federal courts. In the words of the subcommittee staff – presumably its chief counsel, McClellan – the bill "would withdraw from all federal courts the jurisdiction of cases claiming state abridgment of rights secured by the Bill of Rights." More comprehensive than any other court-stripping measure considered during these years, the East bill aimed explicitly to repeal the incorporation doctrine by legislative means. In introducing the bill, the subcommittee encapsulated its chief counsel's *Jaffree* testimony. Several weeks later, in a letter to the *Washington Times*, McClellan confirmed that the East bill was an extension of the *Jaffree* ruling. The new legislation's purpose, McClellan said simply, was "to withdraw major portions of Federal court jurisdiction over certain freedom that have been usurped from the states, and to restore the Bill of Rights to its initial purposes."[50]

Hearings on the Judicial Reform Act served as a constitutional convention of sorts. The subcommittee heard testimony from Rice, as well as from John S. Baker Jr., soon to become Alabama's lead attorney during the Supreme Court's hearing on *Jaffree.* Statements were submitted by McGuigan and Meyer. McGuigan roused the troops to action, warning that "our nation will not survive as a free democracy if we have a government run by judicial fiat," and promising that "the people of our country will not tolerate for much longer having their laws made by judicial decree by unelected, unaccountable judges." Rice identified Hand as "the point man" in this battle. This heartened Rice. "Even if [Hand] is reversed on appeal and ultimately the reversal is upheld by the Supreme Court, I think he has planted a seed." Now, "the educational process has begun and the work of this subcommittee will advance it."[51]

To East, Hand's most valuable service may have been his willingness to use his position to call attention to blatant errors in the Court's jurisprudence. East believed, as did Hand, that the Court's mistakes could be corrected if a lower-court judge such as Hand acted forthrightly, even though such actions would widely be characterized as reckless and improper. When one questions case law "in a public forum of this kind or in a court the way Judge Hand has done," East reflected, "people often will fault you simply because the issue has been a settled matter, at least as they see it, for some forty years. This, they claim, makes it inappropriate for discussion." But it was only through this sort of challenge that the people could check the judiciary's abuse of power. If he or Hand couldn't raise the issue in precisely this way, East inquired, then who would "guard the guardians"? "How do you ever evaluate the role of the courts when you must subscribe unquestioningly to the fictions they create, fictions like the doctrine of incorporation?"[52]

East recognized the huge odds that he and Hand were up against. The incorporation doctrine, he acknowledged, had become settled law. The states' rights doctrine, while not altogether obsolete, did not enjoy great legitimacy. Although law journals continued to scrutinize the concept of judicial review, only its harshest critics – mostly on the far-right wing of judicial politics – wished significantly to truncate its operation. In the Senate, the final blow to Helms-East had been delivered by no less a conservative stalwart than Goldwater, while, over at the Justice Department, cautious conservatives such as Lee and Bator convinced the Reagan administration to distance itself from Hand's judicial activism. The man on whom the New Right pinned its greatest hopes, Reagan, remained ambivalent at best toward court stripping. Lacking substantial backing among mainstream conservatives, the Judicial Reform Act never graduated from subcommittee, and the Helms-East prayer bills would never again garner support. This spelled the end of Senate measures to protect school prayer by restraining federal judges.[53]

PLURALISM AND PRAYER

The defeat of Helms-East and the failure of the Judicial Reform Act to reach the Senate floor signified that popular opinion favoring a school prayer amendment did not indicate a willingness among mainstream conservatives in Washington to restructure American government. To the bitter disappointment of the counter-establishment, Republican leaders failed, at this time, to pursue the counterrevolution sought by McClellan and Hand. Strident majoritarian rhetoric could not, at this moment in history, catalyze a successful movement to curtail judicial power or broaden the sovereignty of the individual states. So deeply engrained were individual and minority rights in American political culture that, even at the apex of Reagan's popularity, the counter-establishment could not win prayer legislation scaling back the Bill of Rights.[54]

Senate champions of school prayer took notice of the civil-libertarian arguments marshaled against the Helms and East bills, including those made by the evangelical Hatfield. Aiming to resuscitate the Reagan amendment, Hatch and Thurmond recognized that it would face defeat if it appeared in any way to sanction religious coercion by state government. In order to rally the broadest support possible, Thurmond convinced the president to add a sentence prohibiting federal and state governments from composing particular words to be recited by students. In late March 1983, Hatch and Thurmond resubmitted the president's 1982 school prayer amendment. One month later, the Subcommittee on the Constitution, chaired by Hatch, opened hearings on the measure. The hopes of prayer supporters were reignited.[55]

Hearings revealed a strategic shift among prayer advocates. Alongside the standard moral-majoritarian rhetoric emerged calls to protect the civil rights of religious Americans. Several witnesses testified quite differently from how they had the previous summer, shifting their emphasis toward citizens' rights to free exercise and free speech. Typical was Christian Voice director Gary Jarmin, who now demanded that tolerance be extended toward people of faith. Jarmin and others introduced into the prayer debate the idea that public institutions such as schools ought equally to honor the expression of religious and secular ideas. Robert P. Dugan Jr., director of the National Association of Evangelicals, abandoned his previous year's emphasis on promoting God's supremacy and instead asked the subcommittee, "Have we become so divided as a people that we cannot respect the beliefs of others? . . . Must we continue to instill in future generations of Americans the idea that something is so wrong with religious speech that it is not entitled to the protection afforded all other forms of speech?" Like the *Jaffree* intervenors, these witnesses presented religious conservatives as one among a plurality of groups wishing to speak publicly. Adopting the civil-libertarian logic that minorities had employed so effectively since the 1940s, they suggested that if society were truly to secure equality and diversity, then it needed to preserve the right to pray voluntarily in school.[56]

When discussion began on the Senate floor in March 1984, support for the amendment revealed inconsistent thinking on the matter. While a number of Republicans joined Helms and East in defending the proposal with the standard majoritarian arguments, some of those same conservatives also celebrated the amendment as a vehicle for ensuring religious liberties against infringement by any level of government, state or federal. Grassley reminded colleagues that "the first amendment was intended so that individuals would have the freedom to express their beliefs in every aspect of life." It was obvious to Symms that "American religious freedom ... allows for an unfettered and unthreatened choice between religion and no religion," so that state-run schools had to make both options available. McClure wished to ensure "that those children who wish to participate in prayer should have the right to do so." Free speech was hailed, alongside free exercise, as an essential good protected by the amendment. Thus did Jepsen hope that "the amendment under consideration today ... would stop the harassment and discrimination against students who are denied the right to religious free speech while their fellow students are guaranteed other forms of free speech."[57]

Those assertions were extraordinary. While some conservatives continued to assert that the states were under no obligation to protect the liberty of dissenters, more affirmed government's obligation to protect religious liberty in general. Their shift was made easier by their inventive redefinition of "religion." Like the *Jaffree* intervenors, amendment supporters argued that to give secularism a privileged place in the classroom was effectively to favor the secularist "religion" over theistic religion. God's absence from the classroom, they suggested, constituted a religion just as much as did God's presence. Denton complained that, because of the Court's insistence that religious neutrality required secular lawmaking guidelines, "our children ... are in essence being instructed that God is not relevant, or that religion is a lie," and that this had resulted in "State-fostered agnosticism." Symms, too, saw "a clear conflict of purpose between preventing established religion and the de facto establishment of functional atheism in the lives of our children." So, too, did East, who believed that enforcement of *Engel* and *Schempp* had led to the federal "Government establishing a national religion of secularism." Majority Leader Baker concurred, stressing that the amendment's goal was simply "to neutralize the antireligious bias in America's public schools."[58]

Although they called for the accommodation of both secular and theistic religion in the classroom, amendment supporters recommended the latter precisely for its capacity to promote tolerance. A liberal goal – fostering an acceptance of difference – could best be accomplished, they claimed, through traditional religious means. Conservatives refuted liberals' assumption that tolerance was most effectively fostered through the imparting of secular habits of thinking, in an environment where God was not worshipped. These conservatives suggested the opposite, that prayer broadened the mind and softened the heart, thereby promoting inclusivity and acceptance in the classroom. "If a child stands up and prays on

Monday and his or her classmates respect the prayer," Denton surmised, then "on Tuesday that same student will respect the prayer of another." Their minds would be broadened by the force of prayer. "Underlying all liberty must be a philosophy that understands and accepts variety in human behavior ... and that exemplifies the compassion of God."[59]

Amendment supporters faced objections by liberals who cited *Jaffree* to show that minority religious rights could flourish only in a nonreligious environment. Those liberals argued that a minority member surrounded by religious expression in the classroom would face unbearable pressure to conform to the dominant voice in the room. Patrick Leahy (D.-Vt.) agreed with Ishmael Jaffree that "peer pressure ... will guarantee that voluntary school prayer will never be voluntary." Howard Metzenbaum (D.-Oh.) predicted that the fate of Jaffree's children would reoccur everywhere school prayer was allowed. But conservatives dismissed these objections. The amendment, according to Hatch, "rejects the so-called implied coercion theory that some prayer opponents have raised to the effect that public-school prayer, by definition, violates the free exercise clause by exerting peer pressure upon minority-religion students to recite unwanted prayers." Denton concurred. He was "opposed to any school prayer approach that places undue pressure on a student to participate in a form of prayer that violates his or her conscience"; this amendment, he was sure, "would promote mutual understanding and tolerance among the students" rather than coercion.[60]

Defending liberty and pluralism didn't carry the proposal to victory. Only fifty-six senators voted affirmatively, eleven short of the two-thirds margin needed for victory. While Helms promised even fiercer battles yet to come, the defeat of the Reagan amendment convinced most Senate prayer supporters that they would gain no victory without more fully adopting the civil-libertarian premises crafted and employed historically by church-state separationists. They would need to forego trying to discredit the doctrine of incorporation, or even trying to "overturn" *Everson, Engel* and *Schempp*. Most prayer supporters now resolved to pursue legislation based squarely on the principle of accommodation, which demanded that government extend to religious expression the same protections as it gave to nonreligious expression. They would try to show that, to avoid entanglement with religion, government needed explicitly to cultivate an evenhanded stance toward religion, and that such a stance required government to accommodate religious speech within the public sphere as fully as it accommodated secular speech.[61]

Among the converts to accommodationism was the president. The day after his amendment went down in defeat, Reagan spoke publicly on the need to protect free religious speech. He was picking up on a theme gaining ground since December 1981, when the Supreme Court, in *Widmar* v. *Vincent*, ruled that a student religious organization was just as entitled as secular groups to use the facilities at the University of Missouri at Kansas City. The organization had argued that a university policy barring the use of its buildings "for purposes of religious worship or religious teaching" discriminated against the students' rights to free speech and free exercise. Writing for the majority, Justice Powell agreed. "Having created a forum generally open to student groups, the University seeks to enforce a content-based exclusion of religious speech," Powell charged. "Its exclusionary policy violates the fundamental principle that a state regulation of speech should be content-neutral." For the first time, the Court ruled that a public university could not refuse to accommodate religious speech if it accommodated nonreligious speech. It could not discriminate against student expression based on content.[62]

To Senate supporters of school prayer, *Widmar* offered hope that, on freedom-of-speech grounds, children might perhaps be granted the right to pray aloud in public schools. That hope rested on uncertain premises, as the Court had not extended its protection of free-speech rights to students younger than college age. But this did not deter prayer advocates. Soon there emerged a movement to pass legislation defending religious students' right of "equal access" to all public facilities. Two lawmakers, from the same party but with different political orientations, would become unlikely partners in this endeavor. One was Hatfield, an evangelical and political liberal who enjoyed the trust of colleagues across a broad swath of the ideological spectrum. In the spring of 1982, Hatfield first introduced on the Senate floor what he would later title the "Religious Speech Protection Act." He counterposed his bill with Helms-East. Not only was court stripping misguided, Hatfield argued; it also failed to acknowledge that students who were denied the right to discuss religious topics on school grounds were having their own civil rights violated. Congress didn't need to restrain the courts – it needed to direct the courts to protect the rights of religious citizens. Hatfield likewise opposed the president's voluntary prayer amendment, which he renounced as "not ... in line with our constitutional separation of church and state." Public schools, he insisted, had no business encouraging students to engage in religious activities of any sort. At the same time, neither they nor the federal government possessed the constitutional right to silence the religious speech of students meeting before or after class hours, as such speech was truly voluntary and unobtrusive upon the orderly and open process of secular learning.[63]

Weeks later, a nearly identical bill was submitted by Denton. While lambasting Powell for enjoining Hand's *Jaffree* ruling, Denton refrained from issuing moral-majoritarian declarations. On this occasion he offered up the "Equal Access Act," which would guarantee "equal access and opportunity to public-school students who wish to meet voluntarily for religious purposes." Denton's bill differed from Hatfield's in that the latter would apply only to high-school students; otherwise, the two measures were essentially identical. Denton had repositioned himself as a civil-libertarian. He assured opponents of the president's amendment that "the equal access bill does not mandate a teacher-led prayer or a State authored prayer, or even a moment of silence." To those alarmed by the Helms bill he emphasized "that the equal access approach does not interfere with Federal court jurisdiction." His bill, he promised colleagues, simply protected the free speech and free assembly rights of religious citizens. It was wholly in keeping with the Warren Court's affirmation that students "are possessed of fundamental rights which the State must respect."[64]

The liberal senator and his conservative counterpart moved forward independently of each other. After soliciting feedback from friends and foes of school prayer, Hatfield revised his bill to bar "discriminat[ion] against any meetings of students in public secondary schools," and not merely meetings of religious students. The First Amendment rights of students would be protected regardless of the content of those students' speech. Hatfield's measure explicitly "provide[d] the district courts with jurisdiction"; likewise, Denton revised his bill to specify that "the district courts of the United States shall have jurisdiction of actions brought under this Act." The Helms ally had abandoned the fight against the incorporation doctrine. Both senators emphasized the importance of governmental neutrality toward religion, a theme invoked repeatedly during Judiciary Committee hearings on the two bills in April 1983. That September, the committee approved the Denton bill without acting on the Hatfield bill. Equal access legislation won accolades at once from liberal Laurence Tribe and from Reagan's education secretary, Terrel Bell, who told the committee that "our public schools should mirror American pluralism," and that "by totally eliminating religious activities from public schools, society singles religion out and undermines it, thus destroying an important feature of our diversity."[65]

Immediately following the Reagan amendment's defeat in March 1984, Denton brought the Senate's attention back to the Equal Access Act. In this, an election year, many senators felt pressure somehow to affirm religious rights. Denton offered them a way. His bill, he warned, might be prayer supporters' last, best opportunity. Determining that Hatfield's alternative stood a greater chance of winning approval from both chambers, the two senators decided to collaborate on a single bill making it "unlawful to deny equal access to students in public secondary schools." The Alabama conservative conceded to his liberal partner's insistence that the bill protect the speech and assembly rights of all high-school students, rather than only religious students. The compromise legislation pleased American Civil Liberties Union counsel Barry Lynn, who surmised that it would bring "real benefit to many political and other student groups which seek ACLU assistance." Religion in schools had been transformed into a civil-liberties cause.[66]

The degree of that transformation became apparent in Hatfield's oratory of June 27, when the Senate considered the Equal Access Act. Hatfield reiterated his primary intention not to steer public schools toward any particular stance regarding religion. "I interpret the Government's [rightful] role in relation to religion to be neutral, to be neither an advocate nor to be hostile." His bill, he insisted, would require such neutrality. Its foremost concern was for civil rights and cultural diversity, with religion "a secondary consideration." It would evenhandedly prohibit all viewpoint discrimination. "All we are trying to do," he assured his colleagues, "is make equal the right of freedom of speech to any and all subject fields."[67]

The momentum accruing to equal access did not enthrall all Christian conservatives. Some saw Hatfield-Denton as an inadequate guarantee of the majority's ability to encode morality into law. During debate on the measure, several New Right senators – including Helms, East, Hatch, McClure, Garn, and Hollings – declined to speak at all. Senators who did speak, however, celebrated the federal government's role as watchdog against censorship and bias. Typical was Georgia Republican Mack Mattingly, who warned that, "when we suppress meetings where religious topics are discussed, we effectively censor speech. And when we censor speech, we come dangerously close to censoring ideas." Notwithstanding their ambivalence, the conservatives voted for the bill. So, too, did many liberals, whose support handed the Equal Access Act, at long last, a victory. The Democratically controlled House passed the bill without change on July 24, and the president signed it into law on August 11.[68]

Prayer supporters' first and only congressional triumph since *Engel* augured a mixed development. While protecting religious students' right to convene on high-school premises was no small matter, it hardly represented the sort of conquest long sought by Helms and his allies. The public schools were not converted into factories for creating devout young Christians; government was not reformed along majoritarian lines; the states'-rights doctrine did not attain newfound prominence. McClellan's hopes lay mired in frustration. The counterrevolution so ebulliently championed by him and others seemed not to be gaining traction. By instead appealing to minority rights, and by asking the federal courts to enforce those rights, the congressional New Right jettisoned its vision for transforming the Constitution – the vision that had triumphed in the courtroom of Judge Hand.

Notes

1 Lincoln Caplan, *The Tenth Justice: The Solicitor General and the Rule of Law* (New York: Knopf, 1987), 100–01. *Los Angeles Times*, July 25, 1983, p. 10.

2 *Wall Street Journal*, September 6, 1984, p. 1; Caplan, *Tenth Justice*, 101.

3 *Wall Street Journal*, September 6, 1984, p. 1; *Code of Alabama*, 1975, vol. 13, pp. 14–15; Caplan, *Tenth Justice*, 101–02.

4 *Washington Post*, December 14, 1983, p. A10; Caplan, *Tenth Justice*, 102.

5 *Wallace* v. *Jaffree*, 466 U.S. 926 (1984); *Ibid.*, 466 U.S. 924 (1984).

6 Brief for the United States as amicus curiae supporting petitioners, *Wallace et al.* v. *Jaffree et al.*, before the Supreme Court of the United States, on appeal from the United States Court of Appeal for the Eleventh Circuit, July 1984, pp. 9, 12, 20.

7 *Wall Street Journal*, September 6, 1984, p. 1; *Washington Post*, May 1, 1985, p. A4.

8 *Washington Post*, May 1, 1985, p. A4; James McClellan, "When Prayer Fell in Alabama: Reflections on the Jaffree Case," *Southern Partisan*, 4 (Spring 1984). *Wall Street Journal*, September 6, 1984, p. 1; James McClellan, "A Lawyer Looks at Rex Lee," *Benchmark*, 1 (March–April 1984), 5, 16–17.

9 *Washington Post*, May 1, 1985, p. A4; Caplan, *Tenth Justice*, 107.

10 *Ibid.*, 112–14; Aaron Louis Haberman, "Civil Rights on the Right: The Modern Christian Right and the Crusade for School Prayer, 1962–1996" (Ph.D. diss., University of South Carolina, 2006), 173–207, 223–24.

11 *Congressional Quarterly Almanac*, 33 (95th Cong., 1st Session: 1977), 15B–20B, 38B–41B; 35 (96th Cong., 1st Session: 1979), 34C; 36 (96th Cong., 2nd Session: 1980), 34C–35C; 37 (97th Cong., 1st Session: 1981), 3, 35C; *Washington Post*, December 1, 1980, p. A1.

12 *Ibid.*, A1, A8; *Ibid.*, January 17, 1982, p. A2; Peter Ross Range, "Thunder from the Right," *New York Times Magazine*, February 8, 1981, pp. 23, 64.

13 Range, "Thunder from the Right"; Mike Shanahan, "Popsicle Brigade Tries to Get in Step with the Senate," *Associated Press*, December 18, 1981, AM cycle. *Christian Science Monitor*, November 24, 1980, p. 23; *New York Times*, May 24, 1981, sec. 4, p. 19; *Washington Post*, January 17, 1982, p. A2.

14 *Ibid.*, December 1, 1980, p. A1; *Congressional Quarterly Almanac*, 37 (97th Cong., 1st Session: 1981), 3, 14, 35C, 407.

15 Range, "Thunder from the Right." *Congressional Quarterly Almanac*, 37 (96th Cong., 2nd Session: 1980), 34C–35C; 38 (97th Cong., 2nd Session: 1982), 37A; 39 (98th Cong., 1st Session: 1983), 39C; 41 (99th Cong., 1st Session: 1985), 39C. John Lofton, "Helms Is Driving Hill Liberals Batty," *Washington Times*, September 24, 1982.

16 Range, "Thunder from the Right"; *Congressional Quarterly Almanac*, 37 (95th Cong., 1st Session: 1977), 307; 39 (98th Cong., 1st Session: 1983), 600–606. See William A. Link, *Righteous Warrior: Jesse Helms and the Rise of Modern Conservatism* (New York: St. Martins, 2008); and Ernest B. Fergurson, *Hard Right: The Rise of Jesse Helms* (New York: Norton, 1986). On Helms's pre-Senate career, see Bryan Hardin Thrift, *Conservative Bias: How Jesse Helms Pioneered the Rise of Right-Wing Media and Realigned the Republican Party* (Gainesville: University Press of Florida, 2014).

17 Range, "Thunder from the Right"; "Jesse Helms's Hour," *Washington Post*, July 17, 1980, p. D1.

18 Range, "Thunder from the Right"; *Christian Science Monitor*, November 24, 1980, p. 23; *Washington Post*, December 1, 1980, pp. A1, A8–9; *Ibid.*, January 17, 1982, p. A2. James McClellan interview by Robert Daniel Rubin, October 14, 2004 (interview was conducted by telephone), 3. Brief amicus curiae for John P. East, United States senator, in support of appellees, *Ishmael Jaffree et al.* v. *Board of School Commissioners*, before the United States Court of Appeals for the Eleventh Circuit, March 21, 1983, 1983–87: Wallace File, SG 5012, Legal Case Files, ADAH, 12. East's commitment to arresting judicial activism can be gleaned from John P. East, "The Case for Withdrawal of Jurisdiction," in *A Blueprint for Judicial Reform*, ed. by Patrick B. McGuigan and Randall R. Rader (Washington, D.C.: Free Congress Research and Education Foundation, 1981), 29–36; John P. East, legislative analysis, "Judicial Reform Act of 1982," submitted by the Subcommittee on Separation of Powers, Senate Judiciary Committee, October 10, 1982, Wallace File, 1–4; and the statements of John P. East, United States Senate, Committee on the Judiciary, Subcommittee on Separation of Powers, hearings on "Federalism and the Federal Judiciary," March 16, March 25, April 28, May 4, May 25, and June 10, 1983 (9th Congress, 1st Session: 1983: Senate hearing 98–749), 1–4, 110, 114–20.

19 The impact of religious conservatism on the federal government at this time is explored in William Martin, *With God on Our Side: The Rise of the Religious Right in America* (New York: Broadway, 1996), 191–237; and Matthew C. Moen, *The Christian Right and Congress* (Tuscaloosa: University of Alabama Press, 1989), 89–98. On the role of religious conservatives in the 1980 election, see George Gallup Jr. and David Poling, *The Search for America's Faith* (Nashville: Abingdon: 1980); Norman Podhoretz, "The New American

Majority," *Commentary*, 71 (January 1981), 19–28; Seymour Martin Lipset and Earl Raab, "The Election and the Evangelicals," *Commentary*, 71 (March 1981), 25–31; Arthur H. Miller and Martin P. Wattenberg, "Politics from the Pulpit: Religiosity and the 1980 Elections," *Economic Outlook USA*, 9 (Summer 1982), 61–64; Stephen J. Whitfield, "'One Nation under God': The Rise of the Religious Right," *Virginia Quarterly Review*, 58 (Autumn 1982), 557–74; Jerome Himmelstein and James A. McRae Jr., "Social Conservatism, New Republicans, and the 1980 Election," *Public Opinion Quarterly*, 48 (Fall 1984), 592–605; Robert Zwier, "The New Christian Right and the 1980 Elections," in *New Christian Politics*, ed. by David G. Bromley and Anson Shupe (Macon: Mercer University Press, 1984), 173–94; Corwin Smidt, "Evangelicals within Contemporary American Politics: Differentiating between Fundamentalist and Non-Fundamentalist Evangelicals," *Western Political Quarterly*, 41 (September 1988), 601–20; and Nigel Ashford, "A New Conservative Majority?," in *Reagan's First Four Years: A New Beginning?*, ed. by John D. Lees and Michael Turner (New York: St. Martin's, 1988), 21–35. *New York Times*, May 24, 1981, sec. 4, p. 19; *Ibid.*, May 31, 1981, sec. 4, pp. 5–6; *Washington Post*, December 20, 1981, p. H1; *Ibid.*, February 16, 1982, p. A4; *New York Times*, September 25, 1982, sec. 1, p. 9. Steve Bruce, *The Rise and Fall of the New Christian Right: Conservative Protestant Politics in America, 1978–1988* (New York: Clarendon, 1988), 93–94.

20 *Congressional Quarterly Almanac*, 37 (97th Cong., 1st Session: 1981), 4–5, 10, 407; *Christian Science Monitor*, November 18, 1980, p. 1.

21 *New York Times*, November 12, 1981, p. A24; Steven P. Brown, *Trumping Religion: The New Christian Right, the Free Speech Clause, and the Courts* (Tuscaloosa: University of Alabama Press, 2002).

22 *Brown* v. *Board of Education*, 347 U.S. 483 (1954). Edward Keynes with Randall K. Miller, *The Court vs. Congress: Prayer, Busing, and Abortion* (Durham: Duke University Press, 1989), 1, 146, 169–71, 188–89, 221, 292–97.

23 Keynes with Miller, *Court vs. Congress*, 195–97. McClellan served on Helms's staff from 1974 through 1977. James McClellan interview by Robert Daniel Rubin, October 14, 2004 (interview conducted by telephone), 1–2, 19–20. *Congressional Quarterly Almanac*, 37 (94th Cong., 2nd Session: 1976), 16S, 198–200, 426–27.

24 Alexander M. Bickel, *The Least Dangerous Branch: The Supreme Court at the Bar of Politics* (1962; New Haven: Yale University Press, 1986), 14–29.

25 John Hart Ely, *Democracy and Distrust: A Theory of Judicial Review* (Cambridge, Mass.: Harvard University Press, 1980), 7–8; Jesse H. Choper, *Judicial Review and the National Political Process: A Functional Reconsideration of the Role of the Supreme Court* (Chicago: University of Chicago Press, 1980), 7, 27, 48, 60.

26 Stephen Macedo, *The New Right v. the Constitution* (Washington, D.C.: Cato Institute, 1987), 1. Raoul Berger, *Government by Judiciary: The Transformation of the Fourteenth Amendment* (Cambridge, Mass.: Harvard University Press, 1977), 312–18; Robert H. Bork, "Neutral Principles and Some First Amendment Problems," *Indiana Law Journal*, 47 (Fall 1971), 1–35. Robert H. Bork, *Tradition and Morality in Constitutional Law* (Washington, D.C.:

American Enterprise Institute, 1984), 9; Edwin Meese III, speech before the American Bar Association, July 9, 1985, in *The Great Debate: Interpreting Our Written Constitution*, ed. by Paul G. Cassell (Washington, D.C.: Federalist Society, 1986), 7.

27 Keynes with Miller, *Court vs. Congress*, 5, 149–51. McClellan, "Congressional Retraction of Federal Court Jurisdiction to Protect the Reserved Powers of the States," 1028; James McClellan, "The Judicialization of the American Republic," in *The Judges War: The Senate, Legal Culture, Political Ideology, and Judicial Confirmation*, ed. by Patrick B. McGuigan and Jeffrey P. O'Connell (Washington, D.C.: Free Congress Research and Education Foundation, 1987), 62. *Congressional Record*, 128 (97th Cong., 2nd Sess.), March 17, 1982, pp. 4463–64.

28 *Congressional Record*, 127 (97th Cong., 1st Sess.), June 18, 1981, p. 13120; *ibid.*, 128 (97th Cong., 2nd Sess.), November 29, 1982, p. 27667. Berger, "Congressional Contraction of Federal Jurisdiction," 801–2. McClellan, "Congressional Retraction of Federal Court Jurisdiction to Protect the Reserved Powers of the States," 1029.

29 *Congressional Record*, 128 (97th Cong., 2nd Sess.), March 17, 1982, pp. 4463–64, 4478; December 13, 1982, p. 30143.

30 Haberman, "Civil Rights on the Right," 77, 83–99, 115–16; Keynes with Miller, *Court vs. Congress*, 174.

31 Keynes with Miller, *Court vs. Congress*, 174, 195–200; Haberman, "Civil Rights on the Right," 129, 134–37; *Congressional Quarterly Almanac*, 37 (96th Cong., 2nd Session: 1980), 404. Falwell quoted in Haberman, "Civil Rights on the Right," 136.

32 Keynes with Miller, *Court vs. Congress*, 200–201; *Congressional Record*, 128 (97th Cong., 2nd Sess.), 1982, pp. 2184–86.

33 *Ibid.*, 2186.

34 *Congressional Quarterly Almanac*, 37 (97th Cong., 1st Session: 1981), 15; United States Senate, Committee on the Judiciary, Subcommittee on Separation of Powers, hearings on "Federalism and the Federal Judiciary," 707; *New York Times*, November 22, 1981, p. A3; Patrick B. McGuigan and Randall R. Rader, "Judicial Oligarchy: Have the People Ceased to be Their Own Rulers?," in *Blueprint for Judicial Reform*, ed. by McGuigan and Rader, 366.

35 *Congressional Record*, 128 (97th Cong., 2nd Sess.), February 4, 1982, pp. 917–19; March 16, 1982, pp. 4364–65; March 17, 1982, p. 4432. *New York Times*, November 12, 1981, p. A24; *U.S. News & World Report*, February 15, 1982, p. 33; *New York Times*, April 29, 1982, p. B12.

36 Bruce J. Dierenfield, "'A Nation under God': Ronald Reagan and the Crusade for School Prayer," in *Ronald Reagan's America*, vol. 1, ed. by Eric J. Schmertz, Natalie Datlof, and Alexej Ugrinsky (Westport, Conn.: Greenwood, 1997), 236. *Washington Post*, March 27, 1981, p. A1; *New York Times*, March 28, 1981, sec. 1, p. 9; *New York Times*, May 31, 1981, sec. 4, p. 6; *Washington Post*, July 21, 1981, p. A2; *New York Times*, September 6, 1981, sec. 1, p. 20; *Ibid.*, September 11, 1981, p. B11. William French Smith, "Urging Judicial Restraint," *American Bar Association Journal*, 68 (January 1982), 60; *Washington Post*, November 30, 1981, p. A1; *New York Times*,

January 26, 1982, p. B8; *Ibid.*, April 29, 1982, p. B12; *Congressional Quarterly Almanac*, 38 (97th Cong., 2nd Session: 1982), 404.

37 *Washington Post*, May 8, 1982, p. A2; *Christian Science Monitor*, May 10, 1982, p. 2. William French Smith to Strom Thurmond, May 6, 1982, United States House of Representatives, Committee on the Judiciary, Subcommittee on Courts, Civil Liberties, and the Administration of Justice, Hearings on Statutory Limitations on Federal Jurisdiction (June–July 1981), pp. 324–39, Su. Doc. Y4 .J89/1:97/104.

38 *New York Times*, May 7, 1982, p. B10; *Washington Post*, May 7, 1982, p. A1; *Congressional Quarterly Almanac*, 38 (97th Cong., 2nd Session: 1982), 405.

39 *New York Times*, May 7, 1982, p. B10; *Ibid.*, May 8, 1982, p. A2; *Montgomery Advertiser and Alabama Journal*, June 20, 1982, p. B3; *Christian Science Monitor*, June 23, 1982, p. 23; Haberman, "Civil Rights on the Right," 150–52.

40 *Ibid.*, 152–55; Robert S. Alley, *School Prayer: The Courts, the Congress, and the First Amendment* (Amherst, N.Y.: Prometheus, 1994), 198–99.

41 *Congressional Quarterly Almanac*, 38 (97th Cong., 2nd Session: 1982), 405; emphasis added.

42 *Congressional Record*, 128 (97th Cong., 2nd Sess.), June 30, 1982, pp. 15530–32. Meyer coauthored the petition for a writ of mandamus that James tried to submit to the Supreme Court in October 1982, as well as Wallace's *Jaffree* appellate brief to the Eleventh Circuit in February 1983. Defendant Fob James's petition for a writ of mandamus (never filed), *Jaffree* v. *James*, 1983–1987: Wallace File, SG 5012, Legal Case Files, ADAH; Brief for appellee George C. Wallace, governor of Alabama, *Ishmael Jaffree et al.* v. *Board of School Commissioners*, February 28, 1983, Wallace File. Brief amicus curiae, Center for Judicial Studies, *Jaffree* v. *Board.*

43 *Congressional Quarterly Almanac*, 38 (97th Cong., 2nd Session: 1982), 404–05; *New York Times*, May 24, 1981, sec. 4, p. 19. *Congressional Record*, 128 (97th Cong., 2nd Sess.), August 18, 1982, pp. 22356–57; September 21, 1982, pp. 24473, 24484.

44 *Ibid.*, 128 (97th Cong., 2nd Sess.), August 18, 1982, pp. 21470, 21843, 21855–56, 21862; September 17, 1982, pp. 24125, 24444; September 21, 1982, pp. 24481–82; September 23, 1982, p. 24770. Moynihan borrowed from Chief Justice John Marshall, who identified, as "the very essence of judicial duty," that "it is emphatically the province and duty of the judicial department to say what the law is." *Marbury* v. *Madison*, 5 U.S. 137 (1803), 177.

45 *Congressional Record*, 128 (97th Cong., 2nd Sess.), August 19, 1982, pp. 22365, 22375–76; September 21, 1982, p. 24171; October 1, 1982, p. 27046.

46 *Congressional Record*, 128 (97th Cong., 2nd Sess.), August 19, 1982, pp. 22352–53; August 21, 1982, pp. 24464–65; September 23, 1982, p. 24772.

47 *Congressional Record*, 128 (97th Cong., 2nd Sess.), September 20, 1982, p. 24171; September 21, 1982, p. 24473; September 22, 1982, pp. 24575–76; September 23, 1982, p. 24776.

48 *Congressional Quarterly Almanac*, 38 (97th Cong., 2nd Session: 1982), 405; *Congressional Record*, 128 (97th Cong., 2nd Sess.), September 23, 1982, pp. 24776–77.

49 *Congressional Record*, 129 (98th Cong., 1st Sess.), January 26, 1983, p. 869; February 16, 1983, p. 2372.

50 *Congressional Record*, 128 (97th Cong., 2nd Sess.), October 1, 1982, p. 27052; John P. East, legislative analysis, "Judicial Reform Act of 1982," 3–4; James McClellan, letter to the editor, *Washington Times*, December 21, 1982.

51 United States Senate, Committee on the Judiciary, Subcommittee on Separation of Powers, hearings on "Federalism and the Federal Judiciary," 113–17, 707.

52 *Ibid.*, 116–17.

53 *Congressional Record*, 128, September 23, 1982, pp. 24776–77; *Congressional Quarterly Almanac*, 38, 97th Cong., 2nd Session: 1982), pp. 404–05; 39 (98th Cong., 1st Session: 1983), pp. 301–02; Caplan, *Tenth Justice*, 99–103.

54 *New York Times*, October 30, 1981, p. A1; *Washington Post*, November 30, 1981, p. A1; *New York Times*, January 24, 1984, p. A14. McClellan, "Lawyer Looks at Rex Lee," 5.

55 Haberman, "Civil Rights on the Right," 164–65; *Congressional Quarterly Almanac*, 39 (98th Cong., 1st Session: 1983), pp. 301–02; Alley, *School Prayer*, 201.

56 Haberman, "Civil Rights on the Right," 157, 161.

57 *Congressional Record*, 130 (98th Cong., 2nd Sess.), March 5, 1984, p. 4330; March 6, 1984, p. 4585; March 8, 1984, p. 4891; March 12, 1984, pp. 5124, 5153; March 20, 1984, p. 5912.

58 *Ibid.*, March 5, 1984, p. 4344; March 6, 1984, p. 4589; March 7, 1984, p. 4748; March 15, 1984, pp. 5727–28.

59 *Ibid.*, March 5, 1984, p. 4344; March 6, 1984, pp. 4585, 4589; March 7, 1984, p. 4748; March 15, 1984, pp. 5727–28; March 20, 1984, p. 5912.

60 *Ibid.*, March 5, 1984, p. 4328; March 7, 1984, p. 4750; March 19, 1984, p. 5836; March 20, 1984, p. 5895.

61 *Ibid.*, 5919–20; *Congressional Quarterly Almanac*, 40 (98th Cong., 2nd Session: 1984), p. 247. Haberman, "Civil Rights on the Right," 147–59, 173–74. Stephen Monsma labels such evenhandedness "positive neutrality." Stephen V. Monsma, *Positive Neutrality: Letting Religious Freedom Ring* (Westport, Conn.: Greenwood, 1993), 226–35. See also Michael W. McConnell, "Equal Treatment and Religious Discrimination," in *Equal Treatment of Religion in a Pluralistic Society*, edited by Stephen V. Monsma and J. Christopher Soper (Grand Rapids, Mich.: Eerdmans, 1998), 30–54.

62 *Congressional Quarterly Almanac*, 40 (98th Cong., 2nd Session: 1984), p. 247. *Widmar* v. *Vincent* 454 U.S. 263 (1981), 263, 277.

63 Haberman, "Civil Rights on the Right," 158. Not long after *Widmar*, the Court limited its reach in *Brandon* v. *Board of Education of the Guilderland Central School District*, 454 U.S. 1123 (1981); and *Lubbock Civil Liberties Union* v. *Lubbock Independent School District*, 459 U.S. 1155 (1983).

Congressional Record, 128, September 17, 1982, pp. 24133–39; 129, October 20, 1982, p. 28656; United States Senate, Committee on the Judiciary, report on S. 1059, the Equal Access Act, February 22, 1984 (Washington, D.C.: U.S. Government Printing Office, 1984), 20. On Hatfield's evangelicalism and liberalism, see Mark O. Hatfield and Diane N. Solomon, *Against the Grain: Reflections of a Rebel Republican* (Ashland, Or.: White Cloud, 2001).

64 *Congressional Record*, 129, February 3, 1983, pp. 1645–46, quoting *Tinker* v. *Des Moines*, 393 U.S. 503 (1969).

65 *Congressional Record*, 129, March 15, 1983, p. 5357; October 20, 1983, p. 28656; April 15, 1983, p. 8722. United States Senate, Committee on the Judiciary, hearings on S. 815 and S. 1059, "Equal Access: A First Amendment Question," Ninety-eighth Congress, First Session, April 28, 1983 (Washington, D.C.: U.S. Government Printing Office, 1983). United States Senate, Committee on the Judiciary, report on S. 1059, the Equal Access Act, February 22, 1984 (Washington, D.C.: U.S. Government Printing Office, 1984), 8.

66 *Congressional Quarterly Almanac*, 40 (98th Cong., 2nd Session: 1984), pp. 488–491; *Congressional Record*, 130, March 20, 1984, p. 5922; April 12, 1984, p. 9321; June 6, 1984, pp. 15003–05; June 27, 1984, pp. 19218, 19232. Allen D. Hertzke, *Representing God in Washington: The Role of Religious Lobbies in the American Polity* (Knoxville: University of Tennessee Press, 1988), 168–71. Joan DelFattore, *The Fourth R: Conflicts over Religion in America's Public Schools* (New Haven: Yale University Press, 2004), 199–205.

67 *Congressional Record*, 130, June 27, 1984, pp. 19217, 19224, 19233–34.

68 *Congressional Quarterly Almanac*, 40 (98th Cong., 2nd Session: 1984), pp. 491, 496; Haberman, "Civil Rights on the Right," 174; *Congressional Record*, 130, June 27, 1984, pp. 19211–52.

5

Showdown

NO EXCLUSION

Constitutional counterrevolution faced as uphill a battle in the Supreme Court as in the Senate and the Justice Department. Embodied in the Court's constitutional law since World War II was an expansive reading of the religion clauses, one that aimed to ensure marginalized religious groups their rightful place within society. The Court's religion-clause rulings were part of a larger jurisprudence through which a panoply of liberties were protected against usurpation by government. Minorities of all kinds came to enjoy a greater dignity under law than they previously had known. This became possible, in large part, because of the incorporation doctrine, which prohibited state governments as much as the federal government from treading on minority rights. When Jesse Helms, James McClellan, and the counter-establishment waged their battle on behalf of majority rule and judicial restraint, they confronted a Court accustomed to seeing itself as protector of groups not easily able to advance their interests through the political process, especially at the state level.[1]

In its religion-clause decisions, the Court executed robust judicial review. The liberal judicial activism that would enrage Hand and McClellan was embraced especially by Justices William Douglas and William Brennan, who read the Bill of Rights expansively, as a framework for moral constitutional government, rather than merely a set of constraints on government. By the time of *Jaffree*, the most prominent articulator of this "living Constitution" had become Brennan, who sought consistently and unambiguously to protect the dignity of members of minority groups against ravages by disdainful popular majorities. Among Brennan's most notable opinions in this regard was his concurrence in *Abington* v. *Schempp*, the landmark case prohibiting Bible reading and recitation of the Lord's Prayer in public schools. In *Schempp*, Brennan singled out, as most important for First Amendment law, the ideals and values, running deeply throughout the Constitution, that gave it its greatest contemporary relevance. The devotional exercises examined in *Schempp* "offend[ed] the First Amendment," Brennan maintained, not because they violated any precise constitutional provision, but "because they sufficiently threaten [ed] in our day those substantive evils the fear of which called forth the Establishment Clause of the First Amendment." It was not enough for the Court to inquire only about "details of the Framers' deliberations." Rather, the justices' "interpretation of the First Amendment must necessarily be responsive to the much more highly charged nature of religious questions in contemporary society." So oriented, the Court prioritized contemporary social problems and its own responses to them.[2]

One social question that engrossed the justices was whether religious minorities felt fully included in American public life. Surrounded by a predominantly Christian society, religious dissenters were vulnerable to alienation. Most of the justices considered it their responsibility to help minimize that alienation. Establishment Clause rulings through 1980 sought to cordon off public institutions from the bitter partisan pressures created by religious differences, so that citizens of all religious persuasions – or none at all – felt fully welcomed. "When the power, prestige and financial support of government is placed behind a particular religious belief," warned Justice Hugo Black, "the indirect coercive pressure upon religious minorities to conform to the prevailing officially approved religion is plain." Justice Felix Frankfurter worried as well about the "inevitability" of society's attempt to marginalize religious dissenters, which, he believed, had always been "the very reason for Constitutional provisions primarily concerned with the protection of minority groups." Nor could majorities rightly hide behind the free exercise of religion to justify policies that excluded or otherwise dishonored religious minorities. The Establishment Clause provided a bulwark against majoritarian tyranny.[3]

The Court was troubled by more than coercive pressures brought upon religious minorities within state-run institutions. Even if a law or customary practice did not coerce citizens into conformity, it still ran afoul of the Constitution, the justices decreed, if it marked citizens as alien or lowly. A violation of the Establishment Clause, unlike a free-exercise violation, did not require a finding of coerciveness. Whereas the Free Exercise

Clause ensured citizens' right to choose freely, preserving religious voluntarism was not the primary concern of the Establishment Clause. Enforcement of the Establishment Clause, in the words of Justice Tom Clark, "does not depend upon any showing of direct governmental compulsion." The Establishment Clause "is violated by the enactment of laws which establish an official religion whether those laws operate directly to coerce nonobserving individuals or not." The Court set the bar low for an establishment infraction. Through 1980, it would require only a showing that an unpopular minority member had been excluded from public life. Proscribed was any law or policy that could diminish a citizen's status or sense of belonging as a result of her or his religious convictions.[4]

The Court's famous of "wall of separation" metaphor performed more than rhetorical work. In separating church from state with a wall, the post–World War II First Amendment required all branches and levels of government to remain neutral toward religion – neither to advance nor to hinder it. Beginning in 1947 with *Everson* v. *Board*, "neutrality" was conceived in a particular way fraught with great portent. The Court did not define neutrality as complete inclusivity among practices both religious and secular; rather, the Court identified neutrality with secularism itself. Religion was seen as a source of inherent bias. A policy or statute deriving from religious motives would inevitably lack the objectivity and rationality necessary to avoid discriminating against minorities. Government could maintain a neutral stance toward religion, and avoid alienating minorities, only by acting in a fully secular manner.[5]

In order to enforce its neutrality-as-secularism standard, the Court suggested that, in state-run schools, religious parochialism needed to be transcended and prejudice be supplanted by reason. Justice Wiley Rutledge asserted that public education was "organized on the premise" that it "be isolated from all religious teaching so that the school can inculcate all needed temporal knowledge and also maintain a strict and lofty neutrality as to religion." Empiricism and critical thinking alone could cultivate open-mindedness. Only "after the individual has been instructed in worldly wisdom," Rutledge wrote, will he "be better fitted to choose his religion." And only then, Frankfurter argued, would he learn religious tolerance. The strictly secular classroom "promot[ed] cohesion among a heterogeneous democratic people," Frankfurter held, "in an atmosphere free from pressures in a realm ... where conflicts are most easily and most bitterly engendered." This, Brennan added, permitted the schools to carry out their essential function: the "training of American citizens in an atmosphere free of parochial, divisive, or separatist influences of any sort – an atmosphere in which children may assimilate a heritage common to all American groups and religions."[6]

The Court reiterated those sentiments in its two remaining rulings, prior to *Jaffree*, that addressed religious content in the classroom. In 1968, the Court overturned an Arkansas statute prohibiting public educators from teaching the theory of human evolution. Justice Abe Fortas's majority opinion in *Epperson* v. *Arkansas* emphasized the reasonableness – the neutrality – of secular teaching standards. Quoting Brennan's assertion that the First Amendment "does not tolerate laws that cast a pall of orthodoxy over the classroom," Fortas insisted that state laws not require adherence to dogma, in order that they remain universalistic in their orientation and goals. Neutrality, for Fortas, mandated viewpoint inclusivity; inclusivity, in turn, mandated secularism. Because Arkansas lawmakers had acted out of religious motives, their anti-evolution law lacked the requisite objectivity. "Arkansas' law cannot be defended as an act of religious neutrality," Fortas maintained, given that the state had "sought to prevent its teachers from discussing the theory of evolution because it is contrary to the belief of some [legislators] that the Book of Genesis must be the exclusive source of doctrine as to the origin of man."[7]

Epperson's insistence on secular motives was reiterated in *Stone* v. *Graham*, a 1980 ruling declaring unconstitutional Kentucky's requirement that the Ten Commandments be posted inside every classroom. No secular designs had guided Kentucky legislators, the *Stone* majority concluded. Lawmakers had failed to act with the needed objectivity. The Court dismissed as self-serving the state's contention that it had presented the text in a secular manner, concluding that "the Ten Commandments are undeniably a sacred text in the Jewish and Christian faiths, and no legislative recitation of a supposed secular purpose can blind us to that fact." Born of religious designs, the law lacked the required neutrality.[8]

By the time of *Stone*, the Court had crafted a tripartite test for verifying the religious neutrality of any statute – a test that would, with few exceptions, henceforth determine the criteria through which the Establishment Clause would be applied to practices within the public-school classroom. The first prong of the test was articulated in *Engel* v. *Vitale*, the historic 1962 case prohibiting state-run schools from conducting aloud, organized religious exercises during regular instructional hours. *Engel* would provide Ronnie Williams with the most crucial precedent for his argument in *Jaffree*. Black's majority opinion in *Engel* read the Establishment Clause as requiring that public officials not intend to advance religion – that all legislation be informed by secular motives. A year later, *Schempp* added a second prong: that no law or policy result in the advancement of religion. "To withstand the strictures of the Establishment Clause," a statute needed to contain "a secular legislative purpose and a primary effect that neither advances nor inhibits religion." In *Walz* v. *Tax Commission* (1970), the two criteria were supplemented by a third, a requirement that no law or policy cause government and religion to become excessively entangled. The Court combined these into a single test for the first time in 1971's *Lemon* v. *Kurtzman*, which posited that the three prongs could "be gleaned from our cases" and comprised "cumulative criteria" for enforcing the Establishment Clause. Known thereafter as the *Lemon* test, these would be straightforwardly applied in nearly every establishment case through *Stone*.[9]

Lemon reinforced the non-exclusionary principle and crystallized the strict-separationist doctrine articulated in *Everson, Engel*, and *Schempp*. According to the *Lemon* test, even the most subtle and indirect harms suffered by dissenters constituted an establishment of religion. To violate the Establishment Clause, government need only act with religious purposes, cause favoritism toward religion, or generate undue intimacy between church and state. Through 1980, the Court looked disdainfully at majoritarian practices that promoted religion or marginalized religious minorities. As early as *Schempp*, the justices showed little patience with judges who would interpret the Establishment Clause narrowly – who would strike down nothing short of "governmental preference of one religion over another." Clark's majority opinion appeared to anticipate and rebuke Brevard Hand's *Jaffree* decision. Even though the "basic conclusions of the Court" had "been long established, recognized, and consistently reaffirmed," Clark complained, some critics "continue[d] to question their history, logic and efficacy." Such obstinacy lacked credibility. Any refusal to enforce strict separationism, "in the light of the consistent interpretation in cases of this Court, seem[ed] entirely untenable and of value only as academic exercises."[10]

NEUTRALITY

With the coming of the Reagan era, critics of the separationist doctrine – justices William Rehnquist and Byron White and Chief Justice Warren Burger – altered the Court's trajectory. Although the Court would not reconsider the role of religion in the public schools until *Wallace* v. *Jaffree* in 1985, it would, in the interim, issue several rulings that threw doubt on the continued reign of the *Lemon* test, the definition of neutrality as secularism, and the post–World War II enterprise of protecting religious minorities. Whereas neutrality had long implied a cordoning off of the state from religious influences – a thoroughgoing secularization – the Court increasingly came to understand the term, alternatively, as signifying an equivalence between religion and non-religion and demanding evenhanded treatment between the two. The conservative justices conceived of secularism not as a non-position toward religion, but as a decidedly hostile position. A couple of the Court's noteworthy rulings between *Stone* and *Jaffree* even went beyond this turn toward positive neutrality, or "nonpreferentialism," and evinced an overt deference toward the religious majority. By the time the Court heard arguments in *Jaffree*, it had set in place precedents that opened the possibility of vindicating Hand's majoritarian logic.[11]

The first decision to challenge the hegemony of separationism on the Court was *Widmar* v. *Vincent* (1981). Congress would base its 1984 Equal Access Act on *Widmar*'s determination that public universities had to accommodate religious student organizations as fully as they accommodated secular groups. Although the trial court ruled that the Establishment Clause required a state university to disallow religious meetings in its facilities, the Supreme Court disagreed. It did not consider the Establishment Clause controlling under those circumstances. The Court focused not on the university as a public authority shaping citizens' character, but on students as private citizens entitled to express themselves openly and remain free from censorship based on the content of their speech. De-emphasizing the *Lemon* test, the Court instead asserted a doctrine of accommodation – that the state must sometimes avoid invoking the Establishment Clause, in order to protect affirmatively the speech and exercise rights of religious citizens. *Widmar* disrupted postwar religion-clause jurisprudence by requiring that religious expression be restricted no more severely than nonreligious expression, even within government-run educational institutions. The Establishment Clause had effectively been disabled from certain applications.[12]

Widmar's transformative potential became apparent in a different sort of case decided two years later. In *Mueller* v. *Allen* (1983), the Court approved a Minnesota statute that provided aid to parochial schools. Rehnquist's majority opinion asserted that the Court would no longer be bound by the *Lemon* test and would utilize other methods of analysis as well. Whereas the *Lemon* test mandated that all laws be secular in purpose and effect, *Mueller* contended that such a mandate, if interpreted too strictly, discriminated against religion. What struck Rehnquist as most significant about the Minnesota statute was its neutrality, that it "permitt[ed] all parents – whether their children attend[ed] public school or private – to deduct their children's educational expenses." In asserting that the state should treat students attending private religious schools no worse than it treated public-school students, *Mueller*, like *Widmar*, defined neutrality as evenhandedness between religion and non-religion. Once again, the justices declared it unacceptable for a state to deny generally available benefits to residents on the basis of their religious orientation or needs.[13]

Less than a week after *Mueller* was decided, the Court ruled in another Establishment Clause case, one that redoubled *Mueller*'s assault on neutrality-as-secularism. In *Marsh* v. *Chambers*, Burger, writing for the majority, defended the Nebraska legislature's long-standing practice of commencing daily sessions with a prayer by a chaplain paid by taxpayer funds. Whereas *Mueller* had downplayed the controlling influence of the *Lemon* test, *Marsh* ignored the test altogether. *Marsh* relied on its own version of neutrality-as-evenhandedness, declaring Nebraska's practice neutral largely on the basis on the chaplain's trial deposition, which had described his prayers as nonsectarian, non-proselytizing, and consonant with America's civil religion. The Court's opinion also ignored post-*Engel* case law by focusing on the prayers' alleged non-coerciveness, thereby raising the bar for establishment violations. "The individual [legislator] claiming injury by the practice is an adult," Burger pointed out,"presumably not readily susceptible to 'religious indoctrination' or peer pressure." Nebraska's practice thus passed constitutional muster largely because it did not place coercive pressure on the lawmakers whom it affected. The lawmakers were easily able, if they wished, to ignore the prayer. That they might feel excluded from the majority of their peers within a government setting was immaterial.[14]

Marsh's radicalism lay in its appeal to the long-standing historical nature of legislative prayer. The nation's predominating traditions deserved accommodation, Burger asserted, because of their lofty tenure and their preeminence within "the fabric of our society." So widespread and established was the practice that it constituted a "tradition" exception to the *Lemon* test. "To invoke Divine guidance on a public body entrusted with making the laws" was, according to Burger, "simply a tolerable acknowledgement of beliefs widely held among the people of this country." Because the nation's civil religion was comprised of deeply entrenched, widely held faith – essentially, the faith of the Christian majority – it was this that warranted accommodation. Only the majority faith enjoyed the necessary historical pedigree to be granted "traditional" status. That government might disregard the dignity of dissenters and further marginalize them within the public sphere was not a relevant concern. [15]

Eight months after *Marsh,* the Court reinforced its sudden willingness to accommodate dominant religious traditions. *Lynch* v. *Donnelly* (1984) sanctioned a Pawtucket, Rhode Island, public Christmas display that included a nativity scene. A concurring opinion by Justice Sandra Day O'Connor reflected the accommodationist argument contained in the solicitor general's brief. Day's concurrence would hereafter provide a precedent for requiring evenhanded treatment between religion and non-religion. The majority opinion, by Burger, echoed the more explicitly majoritarian logic of *Marsh.* The chief justice interpreted the nativity scene as elemental to a holiday celebration whose long history and widespread performance gave it commonplace social status. With that came immunity from the Establishment Clause. With *Lynch*, the Court undermined the requirement of demonstrating a secular purpose by refusing "to be confined to any single test or criterion in this sensitive area." The majority opinion described the wall of separation concept as inadequate for characterizing church-state relations in the United States. Never, throughout American history, had government been insulated from religious influences, Burger claimed, "nor d[id] the Constitution require complete separation of church and state." The *Lynch* Court denied that it possessed the constitutional authority to prohibit public expression of the nation's most firmly established religious tradition.[16]

As William Van Alstyne recognized, recent Establishment Clause rulings had revised the separationist doctrine advanced from *Everson* through *Stone.* No longer imagining the United States as "one nation out of highly diverse but equally welcome states and people," the Court now entertained "an increasingly pressing enthusiasm in which government re-establishes itself under distinctly religious auspices." This trend alarmed Van Alstyne. *Lynch*, he warned, was "the clearest expression to date that acts affiliating government and religion may be deemed consistent with the first amendment, at least if accomplished gradually, that is, incrementally." Much like *Marsh*, with its constitutional grandfather clause, *Lynch* had established that "the absorption of a dominant religion within government itself may be deemed altogether unexceptionable – as though it were but a part of natural history." These decisions, in Van Alstyne's view, announced an "overt alignment of government with the particular theology of one, politically dominant, religious sect." They reversed Clark's finding, in *Schempp*, "that the Free Exercise Clause ... has never meant that a majority could use the machinery of the State to practice its beliefs."[17]

By the mid-1980s, there remained only three justices fully committed to church-state separation and the concept of neutrality-as-secularism: Brennan, Thurgood Marshall, and John Paul Stevens. These three watched with concern as the Court's conservative bloc challenged the Establishment Clause edifice built up since *Everson*. Brennan stood as the jurist most eloquent and unflinching in his defense of the rights and dignity of minorities. In his dissents, the Constitution remained a living document, not one frozen in the past and susceptible only to originalist treatment based on its precise text and historical adoption. Originalists did not, as they intimated, remain above politics, Brennan contended; rather, such judges were political activists committed to majority rule over civil rights. Their calls to constitutional transparency rang hollow, given that constitutional law inevitably embodied one or another set of social and political values. Foremost among Brennan's values was the worthiness of all of society's voices, even the most powerless and despised. The Constitution, as Brennan saw it, expressed an "aspiration to social justice, brotherhood, and human dignity," a "sublime oration on the dignity of man," a "sparkling vision of the supremacy of the human dignity of every individual." Such a Constitution could do no less than prohibit laws dishonoring religious minorities. This remained Brennan's vision, even as he became primarily a dissenter among the justices.[18]

Brennan spearheaded separationism's defense with stinging dissents. Our system of government dared not allow religious majorities to disenfranchise minorities, he proclaimed in *Marsh*. "No American should at any point feel alienated from his government because that government has declared or acted upon some 'official' or 'authorized' point of view on a matter of religion," no matter how entrenched in tradition the viewpoint may be. Stevens echoed this point in his own *Marsh* dissent. Because, "in a democratically elected legislature, the religious beliefs of the chaplain" would undoubtedly "reflect the faith of the majority of the lawmakers' constituents," Stevens argued, the prayers in the Nebraska legislature "constitute[d] the preference of one faith over another in violation of the Establishment Clause." Brennan's *Lynch* dissent condemned Pawtucket's unmistakable "step toward establishing the sectarian preferences of the majority at the expense of the minority." Members of minority groups deserved better, he believed. "To be so excluded on religious grounds by one's elected government" was "an insult and an injury that, until today, could not be countenanced by the Establishment Clause." At least so it seemed to Brennan, Stevens, and Marshall, who were left trying to ward off further erosion of the Court's thirty-five-year-old Establishment Clause jurisprudence.[19]

MAJORITARIAN ON THE BENCH

Since his confirmation by the Senate in 1972, Rehnquist, more consistently than any other justice, worked to reverse the Warren Court's legacy of ensuring equality among all citizens. During his and Brennan's nineteen years of serving together, the two would establish themselves as the Court's ideological poles, each providing intellectual leadership to his allies while recruiting uncommitted justices. Peter Irons points out that while the overriding aim of Brennan's opinions was to honor the dignity of powerless citizens, Rehnquist's opinions evinced a paramount concern with ensuring citizens' deference to government. For Rehnquist, self-reliance and obedience to authority were the means and ends of healthy citizenship. This, and his majoritarian political vision, made him an emblem of Reagan-era conservatism.[20]

Not surprisingly, the Reagan administration – including many in the Justice Department – found in Rehnquist a well-situated partner for constitutional counterrevolution. "This administration is much more in line with Rehnquist than with Brennan," remarked William Bradford Reynolds, who frequently based his legal briefs on Rehnquist's opinions. So close was the synchronization that some department lawyers complained about a "Rehnquist connection." One of Rehnquist's former clerks, for instance, had become a Reynolds aide, while another, future Supreme Court Chief Justice John Roberts, would serve as a special assistant to Attorney General William French Smith. Like Reagan and his closest advisors, Rehnquist sought to restore the independence of the states to antebellum levels so that they could resume responsibility for protecting civil rights. Unlike Reagan, Rehnquist did not face term limits or congressional oversight. He was the counter-establishment's best hope for instituting long-lasting constitutional change.[21]

Rehnquist's willingness to use his position to help remake government earned him a reputation as a judicial activist who decried judicial activism. Biographer Donald Boles notes that, to realize his political goals, Rehnquist "read right-wing conservative meanings into the Constitution" that enabled him "to institute a variety of new social and judicial policies" at odds with his alleged judicial minimalism. Owen Fiss and Charles Krauthammer similarly charge Rehnquist with pursuing a political agenda inappropriate for a judge – especially one with his judicial philosophy. Rehnquist routinely disregarded or distorted Supreme Court precedent, Fiss and Krauthammer contend, and, by inserting seemingly inconsequential asides into his opinions, he created inconspicuous precedents on which he would base later rulings. In this regard, his calls to judicial restraint rang hollow.[22]

But if Rehnquist was an activist in imposing his own moral and political vision on the law, he remained a strict constructionist on the role that he prescribed to the Court vis-à-vis the "political" branches. His juridical behavior may have constituted political activism, but, paradoxically, the content of his jurisprudence was largely to advocate for judicial restraint and majoritarian democracy. As Derek Davis points out, Rehnquist routinely promoted the central assumptions of strict constructionism: that correct constitutional interpretation can be gleaned objectively, through limiting one's reading to the text and its original history, and that moral judgments are hopelessly subjective and so are "better left to the legislator who, while no wiser than the judge, is at least more democratically accountable in a majoritarian-based republic." Rehnquist was a judicial activist seeking to curtail judicial activism.[23]

Rehnquist consistently advocated for political democracy based on majority will. The primary principle in U.S. government, he wrote in 1980, was "rule of the majority," which provided government's actions with "moral sanction." Judges, he insisted, must not usurp the legislative function. In a 1976 speech, he cautioned that, "however socially desirable the goals sought to be advanced" by an activist judge, "advancing them through a freewheeling, nonelected judiciary is quite unacceptable in a democratic society." Rehnquist especially tried to keep the Court from interfering with state legislatures, except when those legislatures violated the letter of the constitutional text or the history of its adoption. It was "unhealthy" for a democracy, he warned in *Richmond Newspapers* v. *Virginia* (1980), "to have so much authority concentrated in a small group of lawyers who have been appointed to the Supreme

Court and enjoy virtual life tenure." Dissenting in *Furman* v. *Georgia* (1972), a landmark case declaring the death penalty unconstitutional, Rehnquist chastised his colleagues for caring more about the government's restriction of "individual protections" than about the "right of the people to govern themselves." Over and over, he rebuked the Court for using judicial review to curtail popular sovereignty.[24]

The minority rights jurisprudence of the Warren Court, Rehnquist believed, was both careless and unconstitutional. Its robust judicial review violated the essence of our democratic system, rule by popular majorities rather than by a handful of elites abusing their judicial power. The living Constitution championed so fervently by the liberal justices was dismissed by Rehnquist as "a formula for an end run around popular government," a permission slip for judges to impose, on the majority, rules of conduct of which the majority itself would never have approved. The "living Constitution," he complained, was "genuinely corrosive of the fundamental values of our democratic society." Judicial review, when premised on the living Constitution, became a license for judges to substitute their own moral convictions for those of the popular majority.[25]

Rehnquist accused his liberal colleagues of falsely assuming that moral judgments were objective and thus a sound basis for judicial review. Moral judgments, he maintained, were inexorably subjective. No law exhibited a moral correctness ascertainable from some detached point of reference. According to Rehnquist, the justices' moral preferences possessed no extrapolitical wisdom, no deep, exclusive insight that might justify a living Constitution. A law gained legitimacy only through its democratic enactment and its comportment with the Constitution's precise text and original history. Like Robert Bork, Rehnquist believed that judges needed to restrict judicial review to morally neutral principles. In lieu of moral certainty, they needed to suspend their personal judgments and defer to the political majority – including the Constitution's authors, who, through ratifying the document, became America's "permanent majority." Partisans of the living Constitution, Rehnquist charged, "ignore[d] totally the nature of political value judgments in a democratic society." Nor did they sidestep the problem by claiming to act on behalf of some esoteric constitutional vision. The protection of human dignity, lauded by Brennan, properly bound judges only to the extent that the American people explicitly ratified it. "The laws that emerge after a typical political struggle in which various individual value judgments are debated" attain "moral goodness" solely "because they have been enacted into positive law." Lacking any legislative authority, judges could turn their insights into law only as other citizens could – by voting, supporting legislation, or advocating for constitutional amendments.[26]

For Rehnquist, judges' deferential imperative was most acute in regard to state legislatures. He urged his colleagues, in *Mueller*, to exhibit special "reluctance to attribute unconstitutional motives to the states," particularly when a constitutional motive could "be discerned from the face of [a] statute." Rehnquist's concern for state sovereignty derived from his strong support for majority rule. As Jeff Powell points out, Rehnquist supposed "that the chief threat to freedom comes from a powerful central government," while state governments remained "closer to the people," and more willing to honor their political authority. Determined to bolster majority rule wherever possible, he tried repeatedly to free the individual states from strictures placed on them over the past several decades by the Court. He deferred to "the understanding of those who drafted and ratified the Constitution that the States were sovereign in many respects," and that the "sovereignty attaching to every state government ... may not be impaired" by the federal government. He remained on guard as liberals continued to "smother [the] healthy pluralism which would ordinarily exist in a national government embracing fifty states."[27]

Rehnquist's advocacy for states' rights led him to what Derek Davis calls a "systematic rejection of the Court's doctrine of selective incorporation." While recognizing the states' general obligations under the Fourteenth Amendment to honor due process and equal protection, Rehnquist denied that those obligations encompassed all of the freedoms contained in the Bill of Rights. He conveyed his disgust with incorporation throughout his first decade on the Court. The states, he argued, could not reasonably be held to civil-rights standards designed specifically for the federal government. Rehnquist sardonically complained about "the mysterious process of transmogrification by which this [Fifth] Amendment was held to be 'incorporated' and made applicable to the States by the Fourteenth Amendment." He spouted disdain for what he considered his colleagues' recklessness and "express[ed] the hope that the Court will eventually return to [the] constitutional paths which, until recently, it ha[d] followed throughout its history." Incorporation, for Rehnquist, was nothing more than an aphorism obscuring a given decision's lack of constitutional grounding. For the justices to speak of the "selective incorporation" of the Bill of Rights, he charged, was to employ a "catchword" in order "to justify a given result."[28]

By resisting the Bill of Rights' application to the states, Rehnquist sought to insulate majority will against civil-rights complaints. In 1953, while clerking for Justice Robert Jackson, Rehnquist demonstrated his antipathy toward minority rights in a memorandum on *Brown* v. *Board of Education* (1954). "It was not part of the judicial function to thwart public opinion except in extreme cases," he wrote. If the citizens of Kansas thought racial segregation good, then the federal courts had no business telling them otherwise. "It is the majority who will determine what the constitutional rights of the minority are," he posited, in words that would serve as his operative ideology for half a century. Rehnquist did not oppose incorporation merely because he favored the states over the federal government; more essential was his solicitude toward the majority and its capacity to fashion policies embodying its moral and political preferences. To honor dissenters' rights more jealously than states' laws was to disgrace the democratic process. "From the point of view of the majority," he declared, "the minority, no matter how disaffected or disenchanted, owes an unqualified obligation to obey a duly enacted law." Rehnquist thought he could see plainly, even if others could not, that "neither idealism of purpose nor self-proclaimed moral superiority on the part of the minority qualifies in the slightest way its obligation to obey the law." He worried that the courts' coddling of dissenters had been passively accepted by an American public in whose mind the Constitution became reduced to the Bill of Rights. "The original Constitution was adopted not to ... guarantee *individual* freedom, but to create a limited national government which was empowered to *curtail. . . individual* freedom."[29]

Rehnquist brought this same majoritarian advocacy to cases involving the religion clauses. More fervently than any other justice, Rehnquist opposed the Court's separationist doctrine as a suppression of the Christian majority's right to craft good and decent public policy. Following *Everson*, the Court had, he believed, slavishly favored "those who believe in no religion over those who do believe." Writing frequently in dissent, Rehnquist aimed to discredit secularism-as-neutrality. Government, he argued, should not be prevented from accommodating its religious citizens more generously than it accommodated secularists, atheists, and other objectors. Rehnquist wanted to strip *Lemon* of its mandatory status. He looked to protect the right of states to pass laws and permit practices embodying the people's religious preferences.[30]

Rehnquist's opposition to church-state separation did not indicate a universally pro-religion stance. His position on the religion clauses was characterized by his solicitude not toward religion in general, but toward the religious proclivities of popular majorities. Although Rehnquist urged the Court not to overturn state laws based on majoritarian religious preferences, he also urged the Court to uphold the right of states not to exempt religious minorities from statutes burdening their free exercise of religion. That is, he favored the majority's prerogative to issue laws accommodating its own religious practices but disfavored the entitlement of minorities to have their religious interests accommodated. Dissenting in *Thomas* v. *Review Board*, he castigated the Court for finding unconstitutional an Indiana law denying worker's compensation benefits to a citizen quitting his job for religious reasons. By forcing Jehovah's Witnesses to work at objectionable tasks or on objectionable days, he reasoned, the state no more violated their religious liberty than it did to devout Christians by denying them the right to pray in schools. Rehnquist stood behind government and its laws rather than behind an individual dissenting on religious grounds. "Where, as here, a State has enacted a general statute, the purpose and effect of which is to advance the State's secular goals," he wrote in *Thomas*, "the Free Exercise Clause does not in my view require the State to conform that statute to the dictates of the religious conscience of any group." While conceding that "a State could choose to grant exemptions to religious persons from state unemployment regulations," Rehnquist steadfastly maintained that it "is not constitutionally compelled to do so." He held as paramount not the rights of religious citizens but the prerogative of lawmakers and the popular majorities that kept them in office.[31]

Rehnquist's religion-clause opinions illustrated his bias toward states' rights and constitutional originalism. His *Thomas* dissent tied his rejection of separationism to his renunciation of the expanding power of the federal government vis-à-vis the states. He emphasized that, "as originally enacted, the First Amendment applied only to the Federal Government, not the government of the States," and that "the Framers could hardly anticipate ... the 'selective incorporation' doctrine adopted by the Court." That doctrine, which Rehnquist skeptically placed inside quotation marks, remained for him at best a dubious way of treating the religion clauses. Rehnquist had expressed similar misgivings five months earlier while dissenting in *Stone* v. *Graham*, his first opinion regarding religion in the public schools. There, Rehnquist defended the Kentucky's legislature's right to mandate the posting of the Ten Commandments inside all public-school classrooms. For the federal courts to deny a state that authority was to go far beyond what the Framers would have allowed. It was to expropriate the state's right to design its own public institutions. This Rehnquist would not abide.[32]

SUPREME TEST

Rehnquist got his first opportunity to weigh in on the constitutionality of school prayer in 1985, when the justices finally heard arguments and ruled in the *Jaffree* case. As the solicitor general had urged in his brief, the Court decided in April 1984 to review neither the 1982 law containing the prayer composed by the governor's son nor the Mobile school board's sanctioning of teacher-led religious exercises in the classroom. The justices agreed to review only the 1981 Alabama statute permitting teachers each day to "announce that a period of silence not to exceed one minute in duration shall be observed for meditation or voluntary prayer." That July, the parties submitted their briefs. Representing George Wallace was John S. Baker of Louisiana State University. Bob Sherling, Tom Kotouc, and Tom Parker remained counsel for the intervenors. Ronnie Williams continued as Ishmael Jaffree's attorney. At last, the nation's highest tribunal would become involved in the case.[33]

The solicitor general's amicus brief, prepared by Rex Lee and Paul Bator, tried to nudge the Court further along its rightward trajectory by appealing to recent decisions that would restore pre-*Engel* standards to public-education policy. Lee and Bator built on *Marsh's* application of the coercion test for scrutinizing a state legislature's religious activities. Alabama's silent-prayer law passed constitutional muster, the solicitor general reasoned, because it did not coerce religious dissenters, but instead preserved an atmosphere of absolute voluntarism. Lee and Bator implored the Court to raise the bar for establishment violations high enough to enable teacher-led silent prayer to pass under unscathed. "By providing a brief opportunity for contemplative activity at the beginning of the school day," the brief posited, "all the [Alabama] government does is to create an opportunity that the students may use, if they wish, for prayer – or for meditation or other quiet contemplation if they prefer." The schools did not coerce. "Nothing is asked of a student who wishes not to pray or meditate but that he remain silent, respecting the rights of his fellow students whose views may be different."[34]

Emboldened by the civil-libertarian logic of *Widmar*, which it invoked repeatedly, the government's brief argued that Establishment Clause must not be construed to require what it called discrimination against religion. "The animating ideal of that approach" was "a pristinely secular society in which all public manifestations of religious faith and practice are deemed inappropriate" and "where religion, if it is to be practiced at all, is relegated to the purely private sphere of home and church." This, Bator and Lee claimed, impinged on acts of conscience. It turned devout persons into second-class citizens.[35]

The administration turned the silent-prayer law into a vehicle for ensuring fairness and inclusivity. Citing *Schempp*, it contended that silent classroom prayer "serve[d] the wholesome purpose of 'fostering harmony and tolerance among the pupils'" by enabling "young people to learn that each individual is free to worship and believe (or not believe) according to the dictates of his own conscience, and that the religious practices of others do not threaten or interfere with their own." Posing as the defender of an intimidated minority, Lee and Bator suggested that disallowing silent prayer would deprive students of their right to free exercise. "Religious people, especially children, find it somewhat embarrassing to be caught in the act of prayer." During a moment of silence, however, "all are free to pray or meditate as they choose, without having to appear 'different.'" If the Court continued to deny religious children any opportunity to pray, Lee and Bator maintained – indeed, if it continued to insinuate that praying was somehow wrong – it would then abolish the precise sort of "neutral forum for expressive activity" that lay "at the heart of First Amendment law."[36]

Three other briefs on behalf of the appellants struck an explicitly majoritarian stance. One was the brief for Governor Wallace. The governor's brief was prepared by Baker, an expert on the religion clauses and a member of the board of directors for McClellan's Center for Judicial Studies. Baker did not quite fulfill McClellan's hope that he present the justices with "all the same arguments and all the same evidence regarding States' Rights and jurisdiction" that the Center for Judicial Studies had been advancing. But Baker did encourage the Court to build on its own burgeoning "realization that strict separation and related theories do not accurately reflect the meaning of the Religion Clauses." The brief seemed especially calculated to curry favor with Justice Rehnquist. At several points it cited Rehnquist's opinion in *Mueller*, as when it asked the Court to trust the state's avowal of its own secular legislative purposes. The brief also appealed to Rehnquist's understanding of the Establishment Clause in terms of early American history. "The way to guarantee that the Constitution will last for the ages," Baker averred, "is not by wandering from the wisdom of the Founders, especially on issues of religion." Even Congress, "throughout its early history," had "promoted religion as an integral part of public education." Reading the Establishment Clause in light of such history was the only way to make case law comport with the organic nature of American government.[37]

In his most counterrevolutionary move, Baker, like McClellan, relied on the writings of early nineteenth-century justice Joseph Story. Story had declared that "the real object of the [First A]mendment was not to countenance, much less to advance mohametanism, or Judaism, or infidelity, by prostrating Christianity; but to exclude all rivalry among Christian sects." While admitting that such "statements about this country being a Christian nation ... might appear to us today to constitute intolerance," Baker lauded them as an appropriate blueprint for modern Establishment Clause jurisprudence. "The duty of supporting religion, and especially the Christian religion, is very different from the right to force the conscience of other men," Baker insisted. He urged the justices to find that government's active promotion of Christianity, rather than violating the First Amendment, satisfied its requirements by facilitating all citizens' ability to worship freely. In so doing he made obvious the ever-present connection between Christianity and conservative constitutional theory.[38]

That connection shone through brightly in the McClellian briefs of the intervenors. Although attorneys Bob Sherling, Tom Kotouc, and Tom Parker remained hopeful that their civil-libertarian trial arguments might at some point triumph, during this phase of the *Jaffree* case they pragmatically adopted Rehnquist's originalist position. The intervenors celebrated the *Jaffree* case for "provid[ing] the Court with a unique opportunity to affirm the clear language of the Constitution, the intent of the Founding Fathers, and history of the contemporaneous period regarding the constitutionality of a moment of silence for permissive prayer or meditation." Helping the Court render such an affirmation became the intervenors' quest. They echoed the governor's detailed history of the Constitution and early congressional legislation, seeking to demonstrate that the nascent federal government had never intended to purge religion from public schools – indeed, that it had understood public religion as filling salutary secular functions necessary for social order and good government. And it was early American constitutional history, they asserted, that should be controlling.[39]

Sherling, Kotouc, and Parker embraced all the conclusions reached by Hand. If the Court were to render a decision properly based on text, intent, and history, the intervenors asserted, then it would surely find, as Hand had, that the Establishment Clause was in no way intended to be "applied to the states by the fourteenth amendment." Unlike Baker or Lee and Bator, the intervenors explicitly rejected the incorporation doctrine. They found it "remarkable that a jurisdictional challenge has heretofore not been made to federal jurisdiction asserted over state religious matters left beyond the reach of federal intervention by the first amendment and unaffected by the fourteenth amendment." Relying on *Marsh* and *Lynch*, the intervenors painted their own arguments as consistent with the Court's recent findings. They cited Rehnquist's dissents in *Thomas* and *Stone*, along with the writings of McClellan, Robert Cord, and Raoul Berger, to support their assertions that "the establishment clause forbids only the creation of a national established church" and that "the fourteenth amendment did not apply the establishment clause to the states." Selecting carefully, the intervenors found fragments among Court opinions and scholarly writings that reflected credibility on their own McClellian assertions.[40]

One of the amicus briefs stood out for its audacity. McClellan's Center for Judicial Studies, which viewed the case as an opportunity to shift the Court's fundamental stance on judicial review, straightforwardly called on the federal judiciary to rectify its mistakes and reverse its position regarding religion in public schools. Writing for the center was Charles Rice of the Notre Dame Law School, a Christian-conservative expert on constitutional law and a leading proponent of Helms's and John East's court-stripping legislation. Rice's brief did not once mention the word "accommodation" or suggest that the Court should protect religious liberty against infringement by the states. Nor did the brief abide by the justices' decision in *Wallace* v. *Jaffree* to focus only on silent prayer. Rather, Rice asserted the constitutionality of all prayer in state-run schools. "Since the exercise of the reserved power to acknowledge and honor God is not forbidden to the States by any provision of the Constitution of the United States," he said, "officially sanctioned, voluntary public school prayer is not in violation of that constitution." The Court may have chosen not to reconsider the Eleventh Circuit's rulings on the 1982 spoken-prayer law and the practices of the Mobile schoolteachers, but McClellan's organization proceeded as if it had – as if the entire original case was now before the justices, with Judge Hand ready to be vindicated.[41]

The singular message running through Rice's brief was that the evidence presented and the decision rendered in the *Jaffree* trial broke such new ground and made such an important contribution to the nation's understanding of the Constitution that the Court now needed to pay them careful heed. Hand had done no less than "demonstrate that the Court's current interpretation of the Establishment Clause [had been] based upon a misunderstanding of the history and purpose of that clause." Moreover, Hand had proven the spuriousness of the incorporation doctrine. Brazenly, Rice informed the justices that their Establishment Clause "rulings should be reexamined and rejected on the ground that they are unconstitutional." After all, he maintained, "in a matter of such importance, it is appropriate to reverse an erroneous interpretation no matter for how long that error has been accepted by the Court." Rather than disregard Hand, the Court needed to answer his courageous, clearheaded call to reverse decades of judicial error.[42]

WHETHER TO ACCOMMODATE

Of course, neither the Senate nor the Justice Department had answered Hand's call. The Court's robust Establishment Clause jurisprudence appeared firmly embedded; especially sturdy was the incorporation doctrine. Advocates for protecting religion's place in the public schools attained their only legislative victory, the Equal Access Act, by trumpeting Court-protected First Amendment rights. By 1984, many conservatives in and around the federal government grew wary of the uncompromising spirit of Hand's school prayer opinion and Helms's court-stripping bills. Typical were the remaining amicus briefs supporting the *Jaffree* appellants, which evinced a conservative civil-libertarianism that neither disparaged activist judges nor denounced the incorporation doctrine, but defended Alabama's silent-prayer statute as a reasonable accommodation of free-exercise rights. The three briefs, written by veteran constitutional lawyers representing well-connected Washington organizations, asked simply that Christian conservatives be tolerated as fully as other members of society. These amici curiae included the Rutherford Institute and Freedom Council, represented by John W. Whitehead; the Moral Majority, represented by William Bentley Ball; and the Christian Legal Society and National Association of Evangelicals, represented by Samuel Ericsson, who had played a key role in the Equal Access Act. Like the solicitor general, they perceived a limited possibility for change open to them and pursued their clients' interests within those limits.[43]

All three attorneys explicitly described their efforts as attempts to secure freedom of speech and freedom of religious exercise. Whitehead claimed to be battling "content-based censorship of thoughts" carried out "solely because the meditation" by Alabama schoolchildren might happen to "be of religious significance." Ericsson cited *Widmar, Mueller*, and *Lynch* to demonstrate that the Court had already sanctioned "reasonable means of accommodating the spiritual needs of . . . students." The Founding Fathers' "universal sentiment toward religion," in Whitehead's view, suggested "accommodation, not merely toleration." For Ball, "statutory allowance" for silent prayer "accommodates ... a religious need of children, the fulfilling of which is presently denied them." None of these attorneys called on the federal judiciary to recuse itself from enforcing the First Amendment; to the contrary, they asked that their clients' First Amendment rights be fully protected by the courts.[44]

Ball and Whitehead reiterated the argument, made at trial by the *Jaffree* intervenors, that, for the sake of fairness, public schools needed to accommodate the Christian worldview as fully as they accommodated the secular-humanist orientation. Currently, Ball and Whitehead asserted, America's public schools were promoting only the "religion" of secular humanism. To balance the scales, government needed to accommodate Christians, whose beliefs and practices had been singled out and disfavored by the education system and the courts. "The wisdom of this Court has generally worked toward balance," Ball claimed, "as opposed to the perfectionist ideological extreme." He urged the justices to work toward balance by "upholding the statute for the benefit of religiously disadvantaged children" whose prayers were being silenced. Throughout the three briefs rang out echoes of *Widmar*'s and *Mueller*'s call for neutrality-as-evenhandedness, which, in Whitehead's estimation, simply "recognizes in neutral fashion the freedom of conscience of each teacher and student."[45]

For Ball and Whitehead, the advancement of the secular-humanist religion necessarily degraded what they took to be the worldview of Christianity. Ball contended that prohibiting silent prayer amounted to "teaching that man's relationship to God has not the stature or meaningfulness of everything else in the entire educational process and plainly [was] not essential to the formation of the whole person." This, in turn, promoted the sort of "nontheistic value judgments" that "constitute what is known as Secular Humanism" – which, Ball maintained, clearly "is a religion." Whitehead agreed. By failing to accommodate children who wished to pray to God, he wrote, government erects "a de facto establishment of what this Court has previously identified as a 'religion of secularism' which seeks fervently to eradicate all mention of religion from public life."[46]

These civil-libertarian arguments were refuted, in three other briefs, as slight-of-hand attempts to reestablish Christianity as the nation's official religion. Writing as amici curiae, the American Civil Liberties Union (ACLU), the American Jewish Congress (AJC), and Connecticut Senator Lowell Weicker countered that accommodation remained irrelevant to the case at hand. Only an ongoing suppression of religious liberties could rightly trigger accommodation, each maintained. Accommodation would not apply here, the AJC held, unless citizens' "pre-existing religious choices" had been proscribed or suppressed through passage of the 1981 statute. In fact, this was not the case. Alabama Christians had articulated no such interests prior to the law. To the contrary, the Alabama legislature was "seeking to generate a religious choice where none existed before." The statute constituted facilitation rather than accommodation; to categorize it as accommodation rendered fraudulent the neutrality standard required by the religion clauses. Its meaning thusly distorted, "accommodation then becomes," according to the ACLU, "just a pretext for permitting the governmental advancement of religion, and the promotion of particular religious practices such as prayer."[47]

The three briefs vigorously defended the Court's separationist doctrine and maintained that the religious designs of the Alabama legislature made the law a clear violation of the Establishment Clause. Striking down this law would protect an indispensable good: the protection of religious minorities' right to dissent. Weicker, the Connecticut senator who spearheaded the defeat of Helms's 1982 court-stripping bill and Reagan's 1984 prayer amendment, lamented that "dominant religious groups" had, throughout U.S. history, "utilized the power of government to persecute members of minority sects." Such "religious extremism," he charged, had been tempered only by Court's rulings in *Engel* and *Schempp*, which had "removed from the school child the stigma of being a member of a religious minority." The ACLU worried that "students in the public schools" remained "particularly vulnerable to majoritarian pressures for religious conformity." This, for the AJC, confirmed that the silent-prayer law presented an acute problem for American Jews. "As a small religious minority in an overwhelmingly Christian country, commitment to the separation principle serves to help maintain the Jewish community's status as political and civic equals in a religiously alien society." All three briefs insisted that the precariousness of religious minorities' inclusion in society rendered indispensable a robust reading of the Establishment Clause. Alabama's silent-prayer law needed to be struck down by the courts, lest religious minorities suffer unbearable exclusion within Alabama classrooms.[48]

The arguments of Weicker, the AJC, and the ACLU were seconded by Williams in December 1984, as he, Baker, and Bator stood before the justices and presented oral arguments. By adding the word "prayer" to its classroom mediation statute, Alabama, Williams opined, had unconstitutionally endorsed religion, to the detriment of the Jaffree children. Williams also held that, because Alabama schoolchildren had suffered no infringement on their right to free exercise, the 1981 law did not constitute a legitimate accommodation of religion. Opposing counsel, unsurprisingly, rejected this line of reasoning. Bator painted silent prayer as an inoffensive classroom activity uniquely able to accommodate the religious rights of all students. Baker concurred. "A statute providing a minute of silence for meditation or voluntary prayer," he told the justices, merely "constitutes a common sense accommodation of the religious diversity of our people which is consistent with the purposes of the religion clauses." He and Bator appealed to neutrality-as-evenhandedness rather than neutrality-as-secularism. The Constitution required laws only to avoid coercing students, they insisted; it did not require purging the classroom of all traces of religion.[49]

During oral arguments, the Court heard pleas for government's separation from religion, accommodation of religion, and freedom to operate with impunity. Together, these arguments presented the justices with a range of ideas about how to treat the school prayer issue. More generally, the justices were given an opportunity to weigh in about judicial review and its role in adjudicating cases involving the Establishment Clause. For Rehnquist and his allies on the bench, now was the moment to advance the cause of counterrevolution.

WALLACE V. *JAFFREE*

In June 1985, six months after hearing oral arguments, the Court handed down its ruling in *Wallace* v. *Jaffree*. Because Chief Justice Burger did not vote with the majority of the justices, the senior-most justice aligned with the majority, Brennan, got to assign the opinion. He selected Stevens, who, like himself, was apt to issue a broadly worded ruling with the potential to be applied sweepingly as precedent. Stevens did just that. Writing for a 6–3 majority, he confirmed that § 16-1–20.1, Alabama's 1981 law authorizing daily silent prayer, violated "the established principle that the government must pursue a course of complete neutrality toward religion." Not only did the Court's opinion derail the Reagan administration's effort to win an accommodation for certain kinds of prayer activities in the classroom; even more forcefully, it rebuked the attempt, by McClellan and the counter-establishment, to convince the Court to renounce its own jurisdiction over state laws regulating school prayer. What Weicker had done in the Senate, Stevens did in the Court: repudiate the early-Eighties moral majoritarianism that unabashedly clamored to reassign religious dissenters to society's margins.[50]

Stevens's majority opinion dismissed the claim, raised by the governor and the solicitor general, that Alabama's 1981 silent-prayer law passed constitutional muster because it enabled the state legitimately to accommodate religion. It was, Stevens said, "undisputed that at the time of the enactment of § 16-1–20.1 there was no governmental practice impeding students from silently praying." Therefore, "there was no need to 'accommodate' or to exempt individuals from any general governmental requirement." Stevens rejected Alabama's claims of secular designs. "Not motivated by any clearly secular purpose," the legislature had passed the 1981 law "for the sole purpose of expressing the State's endorsement of prayer activities." This violated the neutrality that the Establishment Clause requires. Quoting *Schempp*, Stevens repudiated the subtle majoritarianism lodged in the accommodationist argument. "While the Free Exercise Clause clearly prohibits the use of state action to deny the rights of free exercise to anyone, it has never meant that a majority could use the machinery of the State to practice its beliefs."[51]

Less categorical yet was Stevens's rejection of the jurisdictional challenge posed by Hand and McClellan. "The District Court's remarkable conclusion that the Federal Constitution imposes no obstacle to Alabama's establishment of a state religion" now compelled the Court "to recall how firmly embedded in our constitutional jurisprudence is the proposition that the several States have no greater power to restrain the individual freedoms protected by the First Amendment than does the Congress of the United States." He informed the counterrevolutionaries that the Due Process Clause of the Fourteenth Amendment had "imposed the same substantive limitations on the States' power to legislate that the First Amendment had always imposed on the Congress' power," and that the Supreme Court had "confirmed and endorsed this elementary proposition of law time and time again." For Stevens, the incorporation doctrine was part of the Court's inviolable commitment to a set of substantive social goods, which included both the rights of dissenters and the dignity of minorities. The Court would not allow an individual state to dictate moral or political orthodoxy to its citizens. "Just as the right to speak and the right to refrain from speaking are complementary components of a broader concept of individual freedom of mind, so also the individual's freedom to choose his own creed is the counterpart of his right to refrain from accepting the creed established by the majority."[52]

Establishment Clause violations did not require a showing of coercion by government, Stevens pointed out. Yet, in fact, "voluntary" religious exercises in the classroom such as silent prayer did, indirectly, coerce students. "When the power, prestige and financial support of government is placed behind a particular religious belief," he wrote, "the indirect coercive pressure upon religious minorities to conform to the prevailing officially approved religion is plain." Alabama had coerced and insulted its religious minorities – something unacceptable in our pluralistic polity and society. Stevens made clear where he thought such conditions might lead. "Those who begin coercive elimination of dissent," Stevens warned, "soon find themselves exterminating dissenters. Compulsory unification of opinion achieves only the unanimity of the graveyard."[53]

Without breaking any new ground, the *Jaffree* majority staked a bold claim about the meaning and function of the Establishment Clause. Stevens bolstered the *Lemon* test against continued assault. So, too, did the two justices who concurred. Lewis Powell, who voted with the majority and joined in its opinion, also wrote a concurring opinion. Stipulating that a silent-prayer statute did not, in itself, suffer constitutional infirmity, Powell nonetheless found that the religious motives of Alabama lawmakers had rendered this particular law unconstitutional. In so doing he confirmed the ongoing legitimacy of the *Lemon* test, "the only coherent test a majority of the Court has ever adopted." Moreover, *stare decisis* demanded Powell's commitment to the secularist standard for measuring neutrality. "*Lemon* has not been overruled or its test modified," he pointed out. It "has been applied consistently in Establishment Clause cases since it was adopted in 1971. In a word, it has been the law. Respect for *stare decisis* should require us to follow *Lemon*." Judicial restraint, not activism, compelled him to enforce the separationist doctrine.[54]

Powell's openness to silent-prayer statutes in general was shared by O'Connor, who likewise voted with the majority but wrote her own concurrence. O'Connor reiterated her supplement to *Lemon* – the endorsement test formulated in *Lynch* – indicating that government may neither approve nor disapprove of religion nor determine a citizen's political standing based on her adherence to religion. The endorsement test did not prohibit all conceivable silent-prayer laws, O'Connor contended. Hypothetically, a moment of silence could serve as an open forum, equally welcoming to students of all persuasions, accommodating any sort of meditation or none at all. But, like Powell, O'Connor did not believe that free exercise was at issue in the present case, claiming that "no law prevents a student who is so inclined from praying silently in public schools." To her mind, "the conclusion is unavoidable that the purpose of the statute is to endorse prayer in public schools." For O'Connor, *Lemon*, its shortcomings notwithstanding, retained its important place in First Amendment law.[55]

Not every justice belonged to the *Jaffree* majority. Three voted against the majority's ruling, and each issued his own dissent. Together, they belied any suggestion that the Court had neatly resumed its longtime trajectory on the religion clauses. In a brief dissent, Burger chastised the majority's adherence to *Lemon*, which, he charged, demonstrated "a naive preoccupation with an easy, bright-line approach for addressing constitutional issues." The Court was obligated, he insisted, "not to apply tidy formulas by rote," but "to determine whether the statute or practice at issue is a step toward establishing a state religion" – something that Alabama's statute certainly did not do. Like the solicitor general, the chief justice declared the statute a legitimate accommodation of religious liberty. Relying heavily on the absence of direct coercion, Burger contended that the Alabama law "accommodates the purely private, voluntary religious choices of the individual pupils who wish to pray while at the same time creating a time for nonreligious reflection for those who do not choose to pray." If it advanced any idea at all, it was "the view that the religious observances of others should be tolerated and, where possible, accommodated." Such accommodation hardly violated the Establishment Clause, Burger maintained; rather, it fostered the exact kind of "benevolent neutrality" that the First Amendment assured.[56]

White's dissent went further. Whereas Burger aligned himself with the *Widmar*-style civil-libertarianism advocated in the administration's brief, White gestured toward "a basic reconsideration of our precedents" regarding the Establishment Clause. Frustrated, he feared that the majority's opinion took the Court yet one step further in its perilous departure from the Framers' intentions. Properly applying the Constitution required the justices to turn to early American history for guidance, which would surely prompt them to "reassess our cases dealing with these Clauses, particularly those dealing with the Establishment Clause." White's only source of reassurance was the dissenting opinion written by his most conservative colleague. "I appreciate Justice Rehnquist's explication of the history of the Religion Clauses," White wrote, clinging to the hope that *Lemon* might still, at some point, be reversed.[57]

White's hope was sustained by Rehnquist's ambitious twenty-five-page dissent, which read more like a law review article than a judicial opinion. Encapsulating the arguments of McClellan and Cord, Rehnquist's dissent resembled nothing so much as McClellan's "Making and Unmaking of the Establishment Clause," which had served as the basis for McClellan's *Jaffree* testimony. Pent-up frustration came pouring out into Rehnquist's opinion – frustration toward his liberal colleagues, their predecessors, and the edifice of civil-libertarianism that they had helped construct at the center of American government. His tone throughout was stern and even caustic. Much in the manner of McClellan, he conveyed exasperation with a legal-political establishment that either did not understand or did not care about good government. Rehnquist used the *Jaffree* case as an opportunity to correct what he considered decades of faulty thinking and faulty adjudicating. Remarkably, the facts surrounding the case played almost no role in his opinion, which mentioned the case itself only once – in two sentences in the penultimate paragraph. His mind seemed focused not on Alabama classrooms or silent prayer, but on American jurisprudence since the 1940s. While the Court's majority utilized *Jaffree* to shore up the postwar Establishment Clause, Rehnquist took the opportunity to carry out counterrevolution.[58]

The centerpiece of Rehnquist's dissent was his originalist reading of the Establishment Clause. Rehnquist made clear his belief that a correct understanding of the clause could be founded only on an accurate history of the First Amendment's composition and ratification. "As drafters of our Bill of Rights, the Framers inscribed the principles that control today." Their words and intentions had been set for all time, he explained, and remained the lodestar of our system. "Any deviation from their intentions frustrates the permanence of that Charter and will only lead to the type of unprincipled decisionmaking that has plagued our Establishment Clause cases since Everson." Happily, his opinion provided substantive evidence to be utilized in some future, principled decisionmaking. His examination of the Establishment Clause revealed its "well-accepted meaning: it forbade establishment of a national religion, and forbade preference among religious sects or denominations." The clause meant nothing more. Any alternative reading amounted to fabrication. "As its history abundantly shows," he reported, "nothing in the Establishment Clause requires government to be strictly neutral between religion and irreligion." Nor, he added, "does that Clause prohibit Congress or the States from pursuing legitimate secular ends through nondiscriminatory sectarian means." Careful scrutiny of the record demonstrated the Clause's tight parameters.[59]

Rehnquist showed little respect for the incorporation of the First Amendment. In the time since his strongly worded dissents in *Buckley* and *Thomas*, he had conceded the First Amendment's application to the states. Perhaps Rehnquist had pragmatically chosen to excise his agenda's least attainable item. But, while admitting the de facto legality of the First Amendment's incorporation, his words cast doubt on its fundamental constitutionality. He reluctantly admitted that the states, like the federal government, were now "prohibited as well from establishing a religion or discriminating between sects," but only "given the 'incorporation' of the Establishment Clause." The word "given" and the quotation marks surrounding "incorporation" suggested his lingering disagreement with the doctrine.[60]

Rehnquist repeated the call, issued in Hand's *Jaffree* opinion and echoed in the amicus brief of the Center for Judicial Studies, to uproot diseased precedent and plant a new interpretation of the Establishment Clause. So distorted was existing case law that he could recommend nothing less than its complete makeover. His frustration and bitterness were apparent as he charged generations of Supreme Court justices with producing spurious, insubstantial work. This work was not worth preserving, he maintained, given that "no amount of repetition of historical errors in judicial opinions can make the errors true." Nor was there any good reason not to implement his recommended changes. Lecturing the other justices, he declared that, although "stare decisis may bind courts as to matters of law ... it cannot bind them as to matters of history." Bad history called out to be refuted. Rehnquist, for one, would not countenance sloppy jurisprudence. "If a constitutional theory has no basis in the history of the amendment it seeks to interpret, is difficult to apply, and yields unprincipled results, I see little use in it." *Jaffree* was yet one more instance of bad decision-making, and he would have no part of it.[61]

Left to dissent, Rehnquist could not catalyse the wholesale changes he sought. He proved no more able than McClellan, Helms, or East to return prayer to public-school classrooms. Nor could he circumscribe the federal courts' authority over the matter. For the time being, there would remain constitutional constraints on a religious majority's ability to use public education to instill its moral preferences into young citizens. In and around government, counterrevolutionaries found themselves stymied. The interests of religious majorities, it appeared, could best be defended as First Amendment rights, as in the *Widmar* case and the Equal Access Act. Rather than playing a reduced role, federal judges seemingly would retain the final word on the place of religion in the classroom. Hand may have declared himself and other federal judges powerless to impose the Establishment Clause on state and local government, but his superiors decreed otherwise. The Court admonished him to ensure that Alabama and its public education system establish no religion. When the justices remanded the *Jaffree* case back to him, to enjoin Alabama's prayer laws and prohibit devotional practices in Mobile schools, Hand was finally forced to do what he had resisted doing for so long. It fell on him to purge Alabama classrooms of any and all religious activity.

Notes

1 Lucas A. Powe, *The Warren Court and American Politics* (Cambridge, Mass.: Belknap, 2000); Morton J. Horwitz, *The Warren Court and the Pursuit of Justice* (New York: Hill and Wang, 1998). On the history of the incorporation doctrine, see Henry F. Abraham and Barbara A. Perry, *Freedom and the Court: Civil Right and Liberties in the United States* (Lawrence: University Press of Kansas, 2003), 47–83.

2 William J. Brennan, "The Constitution of the United States: Contemporary Ratification," *South Texas Law Review*, 27 (Fall 1986), 433–45. Peter Irons, *Brennan* v.*Rehnquist: The Battle for the Constitution* (New York: Knopf, 1994), xi–xii, 20–22, 33–39; Frank I. Michelman, *Brennan and Democracy* (Princeton: Princeton University Press, 1999), 3–62. *School District of Abington, Pa.* v.*Schempp*, 374 U.S. 203 (1963), 241 (Brennan, J., concurring).

3 Scott Titshaw, "Sharpening the Prongs of the Establishment Clause: Applying Stricter Scrutiny to Majority Religions," *Georgia Law Review*, 23 (Summer 1989), 1087; Brook Millard, "*Lee* v.*Weisman* and the Majoritarian Implications of Establishment Clause Jurisprudence," *Denver University Law Review*, 71 (1994), 761–62. *Engel* v.*Vitale*, 370 U.S. 421 (1962), 430–32; *McCollum* v. *Board of Education*, 333 U.S. 203 (1948), 216–17, 231 (Frankfurter, J., dissenting); *Abington* v. *Schempp*, 225–26.

4 Daniel O. Conkle, *Constitutional Law: The Religion Clauses* (New York: Foundation, 2003), 122; *Abington* v.*Schempp*, 233; *Engel* v.*Vitale*, 430.

5 *Everson* v.*Board of Education*, 330 U.S. 1 (1947), 18.

6 *Ibid.*, 23–24 (Rutledge, J., concurring); *McCollum* v.*Board*, 215–17 (Frankfurter, J., concurring); *Abington* v.*Schempp*, 241–42 (Brennan, J., concurring).

7 *Epperson* v. *Arkansas*, 393 U.S. 97 (1968), 105–09. Brennan quotation comes from *Keyishian* v.*Board of Regents*, 385 U.S. 589 (1967), 603.

8 *Stone* v.*Graham*, 449 U.S. 39 (1980), 41–42.

9 *Engel* v.*Vitale*, 425; *Abington* v.*Schempp*, 222; *Board of Education* v.*Allen*, 392 U.S. 236 (1968), 243; *Walz* v.*Tax Commission of the City of New York*, 397 U.S. 664 (1970), 674; *Lemon* v.*Kurtzman*, 403 U.S. 602 (1971), 612–13; *Stone* v.*Graham*, 41.

10 *Abington* v.*Schempp*, at 216. *Ibid.*, 217.

11 Titshaw, "Sharpening the Prongs of the Establishment Clause," 1113–16; Steven K. Green, "(Un)Equal Jurisprudential Pedigree: Rectifying the Imbalance between Neutrality and Separationism," *Boston College Law Review*, 43 (September 2002), 1112–16; William P. Marshall, "What Is the Matter with Equality?: An Assessment of the Equal Treatment of Religion and Nonreligion in First Amendment Jurisprudence," *Indiana Law Journal*, 75 (Winter 2000), 193–221; Russell M. Mortyn, "The Rehnquist Court and the New Establishment Clause," *Hastings Constitutional Law Quarterly*, 19 (Winter 1992), 573–89.

12 *Widmar* v.*Vincent* 454 U.S. 263 (1981). Titshaw, "Sharpening the Prongs of the Establishment Clause," 1088, 1113–14.

13 *Mueller* v.*Allen*, 463 U.S. 388 (1983), 394, 397–99.

14 *Marsh* v.*Chambers*, 463 U.S. 783 (1983), 792–93.

15 *Ibid.*, 792. Conkle, *Constitutional Law*, 126–30. Scott Titshaw characterizes the tradition exception as "a constitutional grandfather clause." Titshaw, "Sharpening the Prongs of the Establishment Clause," 1108.

16 In place of *Lemon*'s secular-purpose and no-advancement prongs, O'Connor specified that laws and practices must not, in their purpose or effect, "endorse" religion. *Lynch* v.*Donnelly*, 465 U.S. 668 (1984), 687–90 (O'Connor, J., concurring); *Ibid.*, 673–80.

17 William Van Alstyne, "Mr. Jefferson's Crumbling Wall: A Comment on *Lynch* v.*Donnelly*," *Duke Law Journal* (September 1984), 771, 781. *Abington* v.*Schempp*, 226.

18 Irons, *Brennan* v.*Rehnquist*, xi–xii, 20–22, 33–39; *Washington Post*, Oct. 28, 1985, p. A1; Joel M. Gora, "A Justice for All Seasons," *American Bar Association Journal*, 72 (October 28, 1985), p. 18; Brennan, Constitution of the United States," 433–39; Michelman, *Brennan and Democracy*.

19 *Marsh* v.*Chambers*, at 805–06 (Brennan, J., dissenting). *Ibid.*, 822–23 (Stevens, J., dissenting). *Lynch* v.*Donnelly*, at 725 (Brennan, J., dissenting). *Ibid.*, 709 (Brennan, J., dissenting). Marshall expressed similar convictions in *Mueller* v.*Allen*, at 404–15 (Marshall, J., dissenting).

20 Owen Fiss and Charles Krauthammer, "The Rehnquist Court," *New Republic*, March 10, 1982, p. 21; Irons, *Brennan* v.*Rehnquist*, ix–xii.

21 *Congressional Quarterly Almanac*, 42 (99th Cong., 2nd Session: 1986), 69; *Washington Post*, February 17, 1982, p. A6.; Fiss and Krauthammer, "Rehnquist Court," 21.

22 Donald E. Boles, *Mr. Justice Rehnquist, Judicial Activist: The Early Years* (Ames: Iowa State University Press, 1987), 34, 55; Fiss and Krauthammer, "Rehnquist Court," 15–16.

23 Jeff Powell, "The Compleat Jeffersonian: Justice Rehnquist and Federalism," *Yale Law Review*, 91 (June 1982), 1317–70; Davis, *Original Intent*, 15–16; Robert E. Riggs and Thomas D. Proffitt, "The Judicial Philosophy of Justice Rehnquist," *Akron Law Review*, 16 (Spring 1983), 579–83.

24 William H. Rehnquist, "Government by Cliché," *Missouri Law Review*, 45 (Summer 1980), 384; Riggs and Proffitt, "Judicial Philosophy of Justice Rehnquist," 573–78; Sheri J. Engelken, "Majoritarian Democracy in a Federalist System: The Late Chief Justice Rehnquist and the First Amendment," *Harvard Journal of Law & Public Policy*, 30 (Spring 2007), 720–22; Davis, *Original Intent*, 18–19; Irons, *Brennan* v.*Rehnquist*, 61–63; William H. Rehnquist, "The Notion of a Living Constitution," *Texas Law Review*, 54 (May 1976), 699. *Richmond Newspapers* v.*Virginia*, 448 U.S. 555 (1980), 605–6 (Rehnquist, J., dissenting); *Furman* v.*Georgia*, 408 U.S. 238 (1972), 470 (Rehnquist, J., dissenting). Rehnquist articulated his majoritarian conception of democracy in string of dissenting opinions. See *Furman* v.*Georgia; Roe* v. *Wade*, 410 U.S. 113 (1973); *Sugarman* v.*Dougall*, 413 U.S. 634 (1973); *Trimble* v.*Gordon*, 430 U.S. 762 (1977); *Richmond Newspapers* v.*Virginia;* and *Bob Jones University* v.*United States*, 461 U.S. 574 (1983).

25 Rehnquist, "Notion of a Living Constitution," 696–98, 706; *Trimble* v. *Gordon*, 777–79.

26 Rehnquist, "Notion of a Living Constitution," 704–06; Robert H. Bork, "Neutral Principles and Some First Amendment Problems," *Indiana Law Journal*, 47 (Fall 1971), 1–35; *Furman* v.*Georgia*, 466–68; Rehnquist, "Government by Cliché," 389–92.

27 *Mueller* v.*Allen*, at 394–95; Powell, "Compleat Jeffersonian," 1365; *Fry* v. *United States*, 421 U.S. 542 (1975), 557 (Rehnquist, J., dissenting); *National League of Cities* v.*Usery*, 426 U.S. 833 (1976), 845 (Rehnquist, J., dissenting). *Nevada* v.*Hall*, 440 U.S. 410 (1979), 432–43 (Rehnquist, J., dissenting); *Richmond Newspapers* v.*Virginia*, 606.

28 Davis, *Original Intent*, 21–22, 91. *Buckley* v.*Valeo*, 424 U.S. 1 (1976), 291 (Rehnquist, J., dissenting); *Carter* v.*Kentucky*, 450 U.S. 288 (1981), 309–10 (Rehnquist, J., dissenting); *Snead* v.*Stringer*, 454 U.S. 988 (1981), 988–90.

29 Engelken, "Majoritarian Democracy in a Federalist System," 720–22; Irons, *Brennan* v.*Rehnquist*, xi–xii, 50–51, Rehnquist, "Government by Cliché," 386–87, emphasis in original. Rehnquist quoted in Irons, *Brennan* v. *Rehnquist*, 51–52; and in Boles, *Mr Justice Rehnquist, Judicial Activist*, 58–59.

30 *Meek* v.*Pittenger*, 421 U.S. 349 (1975), 396 (Rehnquist, J., dissenting); *Committee for Public Education* v.*Nyquist*, 413 U.S. 756 (1973), 812–13 (Rehnquist, J., dissenting); *Mueller* v.*Allen*, 394.

31 *Thomas* v.*Review Board*, 450 U.S. 707 (1982), 722–27 (Rehnquist, J., dissenting); *Hobbie* v.*Unemployment Appeals Commission of Florida*, 480 U.S. 136 (1987), 146 (Rehnquist, J., dissenting).

32 Davis, *Original Intent*, 27, 88–91; *Thomas* v.*Review Board*, 721 (Rehnquist, J., dissenting); *Stone* v.*Graham*, 45 (Rehnquist, J., dissenting).

33 *Wallace* v.*Jaffree*, 466 U.S. 924 (1984); *Ibid.*, 466 U.S. 926 (1984); *Code of Alabama*, 1975, vol. 13, pp. 14–15.

34 *Marsh* v.*Chambers*, 792. Brief for the United States as amicus curiae supporting petitioners, July 1984, at *Wallace et al.* v.*Jaffree et al.*, before the Supreme Court of the United States, on appeal from the United States Court of Appeal for the Eleventh Circuit, 8, 11, 14–15.

35 Brief for the United States as *amicus curiae* supporting petitioners, *Wallace* v. *Jaffree*, 7–9, 26.

36 *Ibid.*, 19–22.

37 James McClellan, "When Prayer Fell in Alabama: Reflections on the Jaffree Case," *Southern Partisan*, 4 (Spring 1984); Brief of petitioner George C. Wallace, Alabama governor, July 3, 1984, at *Wallace* v.*Jaffree*, 12–13, 16–29, 42.

38 Brief of petitioner Wallace, at *Wallace* v.*Jaffree*, at 35–36, 40. Story quoted in James McClellan, *Joseph Story and the American Constitution: A Study in Political and Legal Thought* (Norman: University of Oklahoma Press, 1971), 128. See also R. Kent Newmyer, *Supreme Court Justice Joseph Story: Statesman of the Old Republic* (Chapel Hill: University of North Carolina Press, 1985).

39 Brief of petitioners Douglas T. Smith et al., July 3, 1984, at *Wallace* v.*Jaffree*, 5, 8, 15–39, 42. The intervenors submitted their first brief on July 3, 1984–the same day as the governor submitted his. *Ibid.* They submitted a subsequent, "reply" brief on November19. Reply brief of petitioners Douglas T. Smith et al., November19, 1984, at *Wallace* v.*Jaffree*. The two documents made essentially the same argument.

40 Brief of petitioners Smith et al., July 3, 1984, at *Wallace* v.*Jaffree*, 1–8, 16, 28–29, 43–45.

41 Brief for the Center for Judicial Studies as amicus curiae supporting petitioners, July 3, 1984, at *Wallace* v.*Jaffree*, esp. 30. Rice consistently opposed incorporation and church-state separation. *Congressional Quarterly Almanac*, 42 (99th Cong., 2nd Session: 1986); Charles E. Rice, "Judicial Supremacy and the Balance of Powers," in *A Blueprint for Judicial Reform*, ed. by Patrick B. McGuigan and Randall R. Rader (Washington, D.C.: Free Congress Research and Education Foundation, 1981); *Congressional Record*, 128 (97th Cong., 2nd Sess.), July 16, 1982, p. 16630; United States Senate, Committee on the Judiciary, Subcommittee on Separation of Powers, hearings on "Federalism and the Federal Judiciary," March 16, March 25, April 28, May 4, May 25, and June 10, 1983 (9th Congress, 1st Session: 1983: Senate hearing 98–749), 113–17; Charles E. Rice, "Withdrawing Jurisdiction from Federal Courts," *Harvard Journal of Law and Public Policy*, 7 (Winter 1984), 13–15.

42 Brief for the Center for Judicial Studies, 2–4, 23, 26.

43 Brief for the Moral Majority as amicus curiae supporting petitioners, July 3, 1984, at *Wallace* v.*Jaffree*; Brief for the Christian Legal Society and National Association of Evangelicals as amici curiae supporting petitioners, July 3, 1984, at *Wallace* v.*Jaffree*; Brief for the Freedom Council and the Rutherford Institute as amici curiae supporting petitioners, July 5, 1984, at *Wallace* v. *Jaffree*.

44 *Ibid.*, 4, 20; Brief for the Christian Legal Society and National Association of Evangelicals, 4, 6–7; Brief for the Moral Majority, 2.

45 *Ibid.*, 16–17; Brief for the Freedom Council and the Rutherford Institute, 2, 21–23.

46 Brief for the Moral Majority, 5, 15; Brief for the Freedom Council and the Rutherford Institute, citing *Abington* v.*Schempp*, 225.
47 Brief for the American Jewish Congress as amicus curiae supporting respondents, September 4, 1984, at *Wallace* v.*Jaffree*, 30–31; Brief for the American Civil Liberties Union, the Alabama Civil Liberties Union, and the National Coalition for Public Education and Religious Liberty as amici curiae supporting respondents, September 4, 1984, at *Wallace* v.*Jaffree*, 22–23, 29–30.
48 Brief for Lowell P. Weicker Jr. as amicus curiae supporting respondents, Sept. 4, 1984, at *Wallace* v.*Jaffree*, 4–5, 12, 15–17; Brief for the American Civil Liberties Union, the Alabama Civil Liberties Union, and the National Coalition for Public Education and Religious Liberty, 19.
49 Transcript of oral arguments, December 4, 1984, at *Wallace* v.*Jaffree*, www.oyez.org/cases/1980–1989/1984/1984_83_812/argument.
50 *Congressional Quarterly Almanac*, 42, p. 70; *Wallace* v.*Jaffree*, 472 U.S. 38 (1985), 39.
51 *Wallace* v.*Jaffree*, 56, 58n45, 60.
52 *Wallace* v.*Jaffree*, 48–49, 52–55.
53 *Wallace* v.*Jaffree*, 55n39, 60–61n51. Stevens compares the silent-prayer law to a law requiring citizens to salute the American flag. *West Virginia Board of Education* v.*Barnette*, 319 U.S. 624 (1943), at 640–41.
54 *Wallace* v.*Jaffree*, 62–63 (Powell, J., concurring).
55 *Wallace* v.*Jaffree*, 67, 69, 72–73, 77, 83–84 (O'Connor, J., concurring). *Lynch* v.*Donnelly*, 465 U.S. 668 (1984), 687–90 (O'Connor, J., concurring).
56 *Wallace* v.*Jaffree*, 89–90 (Burger, J., dissenting). Burger himself was the author of the majority opinion in *Lemon* v.*Kurtzman*.
57 *Wallace* v.*Jaffree*, 91 (White, J., dissenting).
58 *Ibid.*, 91–114 (Rehnquist, J., dissenting); James McClellan, "The Making and Unmaking of the Establishment Clause," in *Blueprint for Judicial Reform*, 295–325.
59 *Wallace* v.*Jaffree*, 106, 113 (Rehnquist, J., dissenting).
60 *Ibid.*, 113 (Rehnquist, J., dissenting); *Buckley* v.*Valeo*, 291 (Rehnquist, J., dissenting); *Thomas* v.*Review Board*, 721 (Rehnquist, J., dissenting). Davis, *Original Intent*, 93–94.
61 *Jaffree* v.*Board of School Commissioners of Mobile County*, 554 F.Supp. 1104 (1983), 1126–28; Brief for the Center for Judicial Studies, 2–4; *Wallace* v. *Jaffree*, 99, 107, 112 (Rehnquist, J., dissenting).

6

The Trouble with Secularism

OPPORTUNITY

The *Jaffree* case fell back into Brevard Hand's lap. He, staunch opponent of government by judiciary, was tasked with implementing the orders of the Eleventh Circuit Court of Appeals and the Supreme Court to purge all traces of religion's advancement within Alabama public schools. Meanwhile, in the two and a half years since Hand had wailed his cry in the wilderness against judicial tyranny and the incorporation doctrine, champions for expanding religion's public role had scored notable victories. In *Widmar* v. *Vincent*, the Court had decreed that, under certain circumstances, the First Amendment required evenhanded treatment of religion and non-religion. This new formulation had been reinforced by Sandra Day O'Connor's concurrence in *Lynch* v. *Donnelly*, which nudged the Court away from its all-but-automatic reliance on the secular standard for adjudicating Establishment Clause claims. The Equal Access Act of 1984 had extended religious-viewpoint neutrality to extracurricular activities in the nation's public high schools. During the Supreme Court phase of *Jaffree*, prominent evangelical litigators had submitted amicus briefs utilizing the idiom of civil rights in advocating for viewpoint pluralism. The Court remanded *Jaffree* back to Hand at a moment when segments of the New Right were recognizing the practical value of adopting elements of the 1960s rights revolution rather than continuing to resist its legacy.[1]

This posed a challenge for the judge, who had spent his career battling liberal judicial activism. He had been ordered to constrain the legislature of his state and the public schools in his town – institutions whose right to home rule he strongly supported. The wide majority of Alabamians wished for their public schools to conduct devotional exercises, and it fell now to Hand to scuttle their plans, to tell them that the federal judiciary – that he – would silence any worship that might fill their classrooms. His superiors had determined that the Establishment Clause forbade organized prayer in the classroom, but it was he who would strike down his neighbors' public policies if those policies lacked secular purpose and secular consequence. Locally, he alone would exercise the federal judicial oversight that he had always so fervently opposed.

Hand recognized, better than most, how firmly ensconced the rights revolution had become. In the nation's courts, and throughout much of its political culture, the right of minority groups to express themselves was now sacrosanct. Critics such as George Wallace and Jesse Helms may have dented the reputation of the federal judiciary, but they hadn't diminished public expectations that the courts would serve as final guardians of individuals' constitutional liberties. That much was obvious to the judge charged with ensuring that Alabamians established no religion in their public schools. But, like some others who shared his political inclinations, Hand was learning that conservative goals could sometimes be accomplished through liberal means. He needed look no further than the *Jaffree* trial, where Christian Right intervenors leveled arguments that in key respects mirrored the arguments of Ishmael Jaffree. Posing as a religious minority, the intervenors purported that they, and not the plaintiffs, were the aggrieved party. Although their argument played no role in Hand's ultimate ruling, it remained on the record, an instructive example of religious conservatives turning the tables on atheists and dissenters. Moreover, with his own single-handed attempt to reverse religion clause doctrine, Hand himself had waged an audacious act of judicial activism, reminding anyone who might be paying attention that conservatives would defend their constitutional vision by any legal means necessary.

Conservative activists such as the intervenors had gained a crucial insight. The early 1980s was a time when identity politics – fighting for the interests of a subculture or social group – had become a widespread and effective means for instigating political change. As discussed in Chapter 2, a number of successful Christian conservative legal firms had arisen over the past decade. Taking cues from progressive groups such as the National Association for the Advancement of Colored People and the American Jewish Congress, these conservative "cause-lawyering" firms specifically identified themselves as Christians and their work as Christian advocacy. All three of the intervenors' attorneys exemplified this tendency. Two of them, Tom Kotouc and Tom Parker, remained affiliated with the Rutherford Institute, whose founder and director, John W. Whitehead, called on Christians to "go on the offensive like Jesus Christ" – not only to defend their rights but also to sue for them. Christian Right leaders such as Whitehead, his mentor Rousas John Rushdoony, and theologian Francis A. Schaeffer had advanced the notion that traditional, "biblical" Christians, on the basis of their moral convictions, stood outside and apart from the broad swath of American culture and society. Increasingly, religious conservatives of all stripes were deciding that people such as them constituted a minority, not ethnically or racially, but by virtue of their worldview. If other minority groups could succeed politically on the basis of identity, then so could they. And if other minority groups could use the federal courts in their quest, then so could religious conservatives.[2]

Hand was no religious activist. His love was the law. He did feel distressed by what he thought to be a nation "slouching towards Gomorrah," and, to help arrest that declension, he was inclined to uphold classroom practices that cultivated Christian morality. From his involvement in the 1964 presidential campaign of Barry Goldwater through his rulings limiting court-ordered desegregation and affirmative action, Hand had bristled indignantly at liberalism run amok – in both America's culture and its courts. He remained a political creature, willing and able to enforce a view of the Constitution that promoted his political vision. Faced with implementing a Court order to enjoin local schools from engaging in what he considered legitimate activities, Hand remained as resourceful as his situation was challenging.[3]

REALIGNMENT

The Supreme Court's ruling in *Wallace* v. *Jaffree* marked a turning point in the nearly four-year-long saga begun when Chioke Jaffree revealed that he and his classmates recited daily prayers in their kindergarten classroom. Upon hearing the Court's ruling, the entire Jaffree family felt enormous relief. They also felt no small measure of vindication. Ishmael Jaffree declared that the Court had taken a "giant step" in assuring the nation that public-school teachers "cannot get involved in promoting religion," and that "the minute they start promoting religion it's unconstitutional." With a trace of glee Jaffree predicted that the Court's ruling would "stir up to no end the religious right." Yet he was also relieved to be finished with the matter, given how difficult it had made life for his family and him.[4]

Not everyone in Alabama celebrated the Court's decision. State senator Donald Holmes, sponsor of the 1981 silent-prayer law, feared that the nation was "drift[ing] away" from its moral foundations. U.S. senator Jeremiah Denton lamented the "continuation of a distorted rationale that equates the opportunity to pray with the establishment of a 'state religion.'" Governor Wallace saw fit to "speak for the vast majority of Alabamians in stating ... that the Supreme Court is in error in its ruling." The "God fearing and God loving" people of Alabama "believe that these are matters that have been reserved to the states and that the federal government has no legitimate cause to prohibit any state action with regard to a statute of this type." Wallace reminded the justices that "this nation ... was conceived and ... has [as] its entire basis the belief in a supreme being." And once again, that basis had been undermined by a small band of unelected elites who had struck down the people's laws.[5]

Along with its moral-majoritarian strain, the rhetoric of Denton, and even Wallace, emphasized liberty and diversity. The governor insisted that school prayer advocates "believe[d] in treating all children (and all persons) equally" and "in letting all children (and all persons) use their own conscience to dictate how they will deal with matters of a religious nature." At this late juncture in his career, he had made peace with the enforcement of civil rights, and he remained crafty enough to make use of its language. So, too, did Denton, who encouraged "Americans everywhere" to "seek full implementation of [the Equal Access] law" – which, he noted, ensured that any students who wished could, for any reason, "gather peacefully in fellowship during their free time in the school day."[6]

As much as Denton and Wallace, Hand remained committed to conservative governance, and creative in its attainment. He had recognized, in the intervenors' earliest arguments, a civil-libertarian legal strategy with the potential for achieving conservative results. At the injunction hearing of August 2, 1982, he had responded raptly when Bob Sherling questioned whether the public schools had effectively promoted a non-Judeo-Christian religion, or "what has been described by the courts as the religion of humanism." Hand's ruling found "that miscellaneous doctrines such as evolution, socialism, communism, secularism, humanism, and other concepts are advanced in the public schools." "Make no mistake," he warned, "these are to the[ir] believers religions; they are ardently adhered to and ... advanced in the teachings and literature that is presented to the fertile minds of the students." It was "time to recognize that the constitutional definition of religion encompasses more than Christianity and prohibits as well the establishment of a secular religion."[7]

At the end of his trial opinion, issued five months later, Hand reminded readers that he would not forget the intervenors' claims. If his ruling were struck down, he promised, then he would "look again at the record in this case and reach conclusions which [he was not yet] forced to reach." And what might those conclusions be? Hand was clear. "If this Court is compelled to purge 'God is great, God is good, we thank Him for our daily food' from the classroom, then this Court must also purge from the classroom those things that serve to teach that salvation is through one's self rather than through a deity." When teachers taught that people can determine their fundamental values through their own efforts, then, as the intervenors had suggested, those teachers established a religion of secular humanism. What was more, multiple witnesses had "pointed out in the testimony that the curriculum in the public schools of Mobile County [wa]s rife with efforts at teaching or encouraging secular humanism – all without opposition from any other ethic – to such an extent that it becomes a brainwashing effort." This religious imbalance could be traced back to the secularist leanings of the Court, whose "case law deals generally with removing the teachings of the Christian ethic from the scholastic effort but totally ignores the teaching of the secular humanism ethic." Accordingly, he promised, he would once again hold the justices responsible for their errors "should this [current] judgment be reversed."[8]

When the Supreme Court upheld the Eleventh Circuit's reversal of his ruling and remanded the case back to him, Hand saw an opportunity to challenge Establishment Clause jurisprudence in a novel way. He was stirred by the constitutional and political potential in the intervenors' argument. To him, the *Jaffree* case demonstrated the Court's resolve to monitor the classroom and halt any religious instruction. This, he believed, had put the justices in an untenable position. If they were truly to reckon with all that constituted religion, then they would be forced either to apply their doctrine arbitrarily or to scour every textbook and lesson plan for traces of religion in all its myriad forms. If the Court were to abide by its own occasional suggestions that secular humanism were indeed a religion, then "all the courts [would] have time to do" would be "dry clean the curriculum on complaint by anybody as to" the religious content therein.[9]

Hand saw, in the intervenors' argument, a vehicle for making clear that federal court control over state schools was untenable and unwise. If the justices insisted on retaining final authority over the nation's classrooms, then perhaps he could demonstrate the unmanageability of their task. Perhaps he could show that religion, of one variety or another, necessarily structured all teaching – that education could be purged of religion no more than it could be purged of language. In mending the hanging threads in the intervenors' case, Hand set out to prove that genuinely removing faith from the classroom would prove as distasteful to liberals as to conservatives. In his mind, those threads remained loose. The intervenors' complaint that the Alabama public schools had violated their First Amendment rights lay unaddressed. Hand was ready to resolve the outstanding issues and deliver a badly needed lesson to his judicial superiors.[10]

On August 15, 1985, Hand directed the various parties to submit memoranda indicating their positions on reopening the case and on the intervenors' argument. He summarized their argument. "If Christianity is not a permissible subject of the curriculum of the public schools, then neither is any other religion, and under the evidence introduced it is incumbent upon this Court to strike down those portions of the curriculum demonstrated to contain other religious teachings." On his own initiative, Hand realigned the parties, designating the erstwhile intervenors as plaintiffs. He informed Jaffree, the original plaintiff, that he was free to withdraw if he considered his claim "fully justified" by the Supreme Court's ruling. The remaining defendants were free to challenge or accede to the complaint of the new plaintiffs, should the plaintiffs choose to lodge such a complaint. Hand had put in place the pieces for a new phase of the case. It remained now with the parties litigant to set events into motion.[11]

In a September 9 letter to the judge, Mobile school board attorney Robert Campbell indicated that, while he sympathized with the plaintiffs' likely position, he strongly wanted the case not to be continued. Defending it, he feared, would "place the defendant in a position of incurring additional attorney's fees," something that the board could hardly afford. On September 11, Hand received a letter from Charles Coody, counsel for the state board of education and superintendent of schools, who conveyed his clients' reluctance to go forward or take a position on a plaintiff's complaint. Hand granted a motion filed that same day by Ronnie Williams, who asked that Jaffree be permitted to withdraw from the case. Five days later came word from the original intervenors.

Sherling filed a brief reaffirming that "the curriculum used in the Mobile County School System unconstitutionally advances the religion of Humanism." The new plaintiffs planned to "seek declaratory judgment from this Court . . . and proper injunctive relief." In early October, Hand informed the parties that the case would indeed go forward as *Smith* v. *Board of School Commissioners*, with Sherling's clients to assume the burden of demonstrating that Mobile County and the state of Alabama had, through their public-school curricula, established the religion of secular humanism.[12]

RENEWING OLD COMPLAINTS

The *Smith* plaintiffs met Hand's challenge with an extensive memorandum of law. Including its several appendices, the memorandum totaled nearly seven hundred pages in length. In it, the plaintiffs put forward an ambitious legal argument aimed ultimately at remaking Supreme Court case law through the use of Supreme Court case law. Sherling, Kotouc, and Parker appealed to civil-libertarian themes in asserting that the Mobile public schools had deprived Christian students and teachers of their freedom of speech and freedom to exercise religion. The textbooks used in Mobile schools, through their anti-Christian bias, had prevented children from receiving information regarding their own religion; teachers, limited to using only those textbooks, had been prohibited from sharing about their faith and explaining its relevance to topics under study. The plaintiffs held the local school board and the state board of education responsible for denying their clients' First Amendment freedoms.[13]

The plaintiffs' primary argument, like that driving Jaffree's complaint, looked most emphatically to the Establishment Clause. The plaintiffs reminded the judge that their nine witnesses had "testified on the contents and the effects of the curriculum used in the Mobile County schools." It remained for the court to confirm that the schools were, in fact, "advancing the religion of Humanism and inhibiting Christianity," and that in so doing the schools had violated the Establishment Clause by generating a primary effect that was not neutral. It was up to Hand to rule for or against their claim that the Mobile schools and the state board of education had promoted one religion, humanism, while denigrating and silencing another, Christianity.[14]

According to the plaintiffs, the Supreme Court had laid the groundwork for a broad definition of "religion." In the present case, they averred, it would make most sense for Hand to utilize the broadest definition ever given by the justices. The plaintiffs admitted that, through the middle of the twentieth century, a narrow definition – religion as God-centered belief, or theism – had remained the Court's standard. The Court's conception widened with *Torcaso* v. *Watkins* (1961), in which Hugo Black held that a state could not "aid those religions based on a belief in the existence of God as against those religions founded on different beliefs." A nontheistic religion deserved the same consideration as a theistic one. And "among [the] religions in this country which do not teach what would generally be considered a belief in the existence of God," according to Black, were "Buddhism, Taoism, Ethical Culture, Secular Humanism and others." With *Torcaso*, the plaintiffs maintained, the Court had defined religion expansively enough to account for the religious and ideological diversity of contemporary American society.[15]

The *Torcaso* case was central to the plaintiffs' memorandum and to their entire case going forward. Black, they held, had asserted a functional equivalence between a God-centered morality and a morality not based on God. A worldview that functioned as a religion was, for Black, a religion. The plaintiffs acknowledged that the Court's subsequent rulings defining religion functionally and broadly addressed only the Exercise Clause and not the Establishment Clause. Those cases, *United States* v. *Seeger* (1965) and *Welch* v. *United States* (1970), exempted conscientious objectors from military service on the basis of their strongly held non-theistic convictions. The nontheists benefited from the Court's functional definition of religion. While the plaintiffs applauded this, they lamented that a gap had opened between how the Court conceived of religion for purposes of the respective religion clauses. Such a "bifurcated definition," they asserted, "would create a 'systemic bias' in favor of newer, less familiar religions." If the functional definition were applied to the Establishment Clause, then humanists would be prevented from commandeering the curriculum with their religion and the rights of Christians such as themselves would be protected.[16]

The plaintiffs tied the definition of religion to another issue, one that had garnered the justices' attention more recently. In a few rulings, the Court had called for government to treat religion and non-religion with "benevolent neutrality." Those decisions held that, whenever government makes benefits generally available, religious organizations and individuals should have no less access to those benefits than was enjoyed by their secular counterpart. The "benevolent neutrality" prescribed in these cases suggested an equivalence between God-centered religion and its secular competitors, the plaintiffs argued. If neutral treatment required the state to act evenhandedly between groups with theistic and nontheistic orientations, then benevolent neutrality implied a functional equivalence between these competing orientations.[17]

What was this secular humanist religion? The memorandum suggested that many Americans – including some who considered themselves Christians or Jews – were shaped by the humanistic worldview, which viewed moral and epistemological issues through a liberal, modernist, human-centered lens. Humanism was poisonous, they insisted; it corrupted faith in God and converted many Christians into humanists without their knowledge. Yet the plaintiffs did not, in describing the tenets of the secular-humanist religion, draw on ideas espoused by these supposed converts from Christianity. Instead, the plaintiffs relied on a doctrine articulated by a small cadre of self-defined humanists. The plaintiffs thus linked an untold number of unsuspecting converts to a religion that they probably would not claim as their own or even be able to describe.[18]

From rarified publications such as *Free Inquiry* and the *Humanist*, and from the philosophical treatises *Humanist Manifesto* and *Humanist Manifesto II*, the plaintiffs distilled humanism's five core principles. The first, they claimed, "captures the heart of Humanism: a preoccupation with man as the supreme value in the universe and as the sole solver of the problems of the universe." The humanist made decisions by turning to human intelligence rather than to Godly scripture. This implied the second principle, that "God is either nonexistent or irrelevant to modern man," a tenet that placed humanism "in direct conflict with traditional Christianity," given that "traditional Christianity holds God, not man, to be the supreme value in the universe." Detachment from the law of God led to the third principle. For the humanist, "no absolute morals or values exist"; right and wrong were simply matters of personal preference. The fourth principle concerned the nature of humankind. For the humanist, "man is purely a material or biological creature," not a moral being with a soul, and so did not turn to God for salvation. According to the fifth principle, the humanist believed that "man, through the use of his scientific reason, will save himself." In discerning an "absence of absolute morals," the humanist trusted his own intelligence to uncover truth and ensure his ultimate destiny. These five principles, gleaned from the writings of predominantly secular philosophers, revealed to the plaintiffs a discrete humanistic orientation shared, if unknowingly, by countless Americans, including most educators.[19]

The plaintiffs' memorandum pointed to "uncontroverted evidence by educational experts, theologians, teachers, parents, and students," that, in fact, secular humanism was "being advanced in the curriculum of the Mobile County school system." For evidence of this, the plaintiffs relied on the accounts of three employees of the county school system – two teachers and one guidance counselor – who, at the *Jaffree* trial, had testified that the schools had forced them to disseminate the humanist religion among their students. This, according to the plaintiffs, proved that the Mobile schools had violated the *Lemon* test's second prong, which stipulated that no public policy may have, as its primary effect, the advancement of religion. As the Supreme Court had confirmed in recent decisions, including *Jaffree*, the primary-effect prong of its test for establishment required states to act with "complete neutrality" toward religion, displaying no favor or disfavor toward religious belief or toward its absence. The primary-effect prong and the complete neutrality it demanded had been violated by Mobile County.[20]

Accordingly, the plaintiffs petitioned Hand "to enjoin the inculcation of the beliefs of the religion of Humanism that is being perpetrated by the curriculum used in the Mobile County school system." They asked Hand to remedy as well a closely related process, the inhibition of Christianity. Not only had Mobile schools shown hostility toward Christianity; by attempting to indoctrinate students into the rival religion of humanism, the schools had coerced Christian students into adopting a negative attitude toward their own religion and threatened ultimately to alienate them from their own faith. The memorandum asked that the federal courts apply their well-developed Establishment Clause doctrine in this case, to protect schoolchildren against the heavy-handed religious advocacy of the Mobile County public schools.[21]

CULTURE WAR

The plaintiffs did not construct their critique of liberalism out of whole cloth. Their October 1985 memorandum relied on an analysis of post–World War II American culture and society that, by 1985, had spread widely among conservative evangelicals. All of their claims about secular humanism and its religious function derived from a polemical critique of modernity advanced initially by a few key thinkers and then applied by a number of Christian Right authors. Familiar with these works, the plaintiffs cited them repeatedly. Parker and Kotouc enjoyed particular familiarity with this critique through their work with the Alabama chapter of the Rutherford Institute, which utilized the critique extensively in its First Amendment litigation. As they prepared their case in *Smith* v. *Board*, the plaintiffs had at their disposal a cottage industry of Christian social criticism on which to draw.[22]

Increasingly over the 1960s, Christian conservatives had grown alarmed at the liberalization of personal fashion, sexual mores, religious beliefs, and attitudes toward authority in the home, church, and school. By the 1970s, moral and cultural issues had begun informing American politics, resulting in the advent of what James Davison Hunter labeled "culture wars." A vocal religious right emerged, explicitly connecting politics to moral worldview. This movement witnessed the assertion, by Christian conservative thinkers, of a prophetic political stance – a warning of decadence and moral decline. America's historical declension was traced to the ascendancy of a worldview antithetical to what these thinkers conceived of as "Christianity." They alternately labeled this ascendant worldview "humanism" and "secular humanism." Assigning a name to the broad swath of attitudes and beliefs confronting and alarming them allowed these thinkers to make sense of the world and fix responsibility for its hazards. By identifying secular humanism as the cause of their own supposed social marginalization, Christian conservatives discovered a useable "other." Secular humanism constituted for them all that had gone wrong with society and government since at least the Sixties – all that stood in the way of the restoring the Christian society, government, and law of America's past.[23]

For these conservative critics, secular humanism wreaked perhaps its most severe damage in the public schools. Nowhere, they believed, did liberal "change agents" more fully disseminate their morally bankrupt, anti-Christian orientation than in the classroom, where humanist teachers brainwashed vulnerable children. These teachers, it was alleged, functioned as agents of a state hostile to biblical Christianity and undertook to purge all traces of Christianity from children's hearts and minds. Many evangelicals had, by the time of *Smith*, come to view the public schools as ground zero in a battle to sustain the nation's Christian civilization. Over the past decade, at least twenty-eight states had hosted, either in the courts or among community activists, challenges to the propagation of secular humanism in the classroom. These efforts targeted not simply the content of the curricula but also the humanistic ideology supposedly underlying the curricula. Christian conservatives' focus on the schools provided them an entry point into a larger struggle to define and refashion America. The stakes in this struggle were enormous, as nothing less than the American people's continued faith in the common school ideal lay in danger. At issue was the ideological neutrality of the public schools and their treatment of Christian conservatives.[24]

Christian Right authors spun a history of American politics, religion, and education that ran parallel to standard accounts. Theirs was a history based on the decline of conservative evangelical Protestantism and the ascendance of secular humanism. The individual who largely commenced this alternative account of history was Rushdoony, whose testimony at the *Jaffree* trial provided intellectual ballast to the case of the then-intervenors. In the early 1960s, the Orthodox Presbyterian minister began a prolific surge of writing and generated many of the ideas utilized later by the *Smith* plaintiffs and others in the battle against humanism. Several authors have estimated Rushdoony's influence on the 1980s Christian Right to be unsurpassed. As much as anyone else, he was the movement's godfather.[25]

Rushdoony's early publications averred the profoundly un-Christian nature of the public education system of the United States. From these works later critics would absorb an animus against the schools and a resolve to transform or eliminate them. In his 1961 book *Intellectual Schizophrenia*, Rushdoony purported that schoolchildren were not learning to think for themselves, were not acquiring the capacity to act freely. By stripping children of their connection to biblical morality, the schools – arms of the secular government – were rendering them passive and malleable. The state was colonizing the individual, refashioning their instincts so as to duplicate its own and cause her to do its bidding. According to Rushdoony's 1963 *The Messianic Character of American Education*, the public schools assumed that "the child is the ... property of the state," that "the state 'priesthood' of educators [was] best able to rear the child and prepare him for life," and that the state alone possessed "the impartiality and transcendence of a god." In so doing public education broke the child down, equipped her with Godless values, and provided her "entrance into the true catholicity of the civil religion of the modern state."[26]

Within a few years, Rushdoony began to articulate his legal philosophy, which would influence the *Smith* plaintiffs as much as did his critique of public education. Religion and the state could never be separated, Rushdoony posited, given that "a state cannot exist without laws," and that "all laws are expressions of one or another religious faith." Inevitably, a state would promulgate its foundational religion, its underlying "faith in what constitutes true and ultimate order." For Rushdoony, religious neutrality could never possibly be attained. And because the laws of the state necessarily advanced a particular moral worldview, "every legal system is inescapably an establishment of religion." No government could exist shorn of its religious establishment. The essential nature of the state precluded it.[27]

For Rushdoony, the "important question" remained "this: since every state or civil government is an establishment of religion, what will the religion of the state be?" As things now stood, humanism was the religion established by the U.S. government. "Humanism," which "seeks to destroy Christian doctrines of law in favor of humanistic doctrine, is increasingly the religion of our laws and of our courts." Rushdoony observed that "non-theistic religions" may deny that they are religions simply because they make humankind, not God, "the working god of their system." But "the denial of God," he insisted, did "not eliminate the fact there is an operative god in every religious system or faith," and that "the religious motivation, impetus, and fervor behind our present law structure, our state establishment of religion, is humanism." Given the direness of this threat, American Christians needed to fight to restore the religion that the Founders had intended to establish – not directly through the state, but "from the ground level," through the people's freely chosen submission to God. The Christian people now needed to return to the original Constitution, which was meant to keep the state out of their way – a Constitution whose purpose "was not to express Christian faith but to allow such faith freedom from the state in order to dominate society, law, and education."[28]

At its most superficial level, Rushdoony's political and legal vision might seem consonant with the majoritarian constitutionalism of James McClellan and William Rehnquist. His influence on the intervenors-turned-plaintiffs might appear not unlike McClellan's impact on the Mobile school board. Such an apparent similarity only distorts Rushdoony's radical divergence from the majoritarian path. Although Rushdoony would agree that popularly elected legislators ought to be able to act with nonsecular purposes, Rushdoony would arrive at his position from entirely different premises. For McClellan, Rehnquist, and Robert Bork, the operative issue was democratic rule. Laws attained moral authority, Rehnquist held, only from their passage, not because of "any independent virtue they may have in any particular citizen's own scale of values." For Rushdoony, the enactment of laws, in and of itself, entailed no moral claim. Only if the people acted on the basis of the expressed imperatives of Christian law – as he understood it – did civil law possess legitimacy. Rushdoony claimed that majoritarian democracy, extended through the modern state, ultimately destroyed the sovereignty of Christianity and the true freedom to which it alone gave rise. "Standards perish before majority rule," he warned. "The group morale outweighs morality; the insistence on rights nullifies the doctrine of responsibility." Severed from any transcendent morality, such a society tolerates "no value apart from the democratic majority, or any appeal against it." This had become the case in our own "humanistic society," where "untruth becomes the majority opinion and will" and "the rule of numbers ... means that the will of man prevails, not an objective standard." For Christians to base law on state sovereignty or majority rule was improper. Rather, they needed to declare their inalienable rights as Christians and compel the state to accommodate them.[29]

Beginning in the late 1960s, another conservative evangelical attained vast influence by propounding social and political ideas similar to Rushdoony's. Presbyterian theologian and missionary Schaeffer developed a widespread following, in the United States and Europe, largely from his ability to explain theology and its social implications in concrete terms that made intuitive sense to the many Christians who read his books and heard him speak. Schaeffer, more than anyone else, convinced evangelical thinkers that societies were comprised of holistic worldviews, "the overall way[s] people think and view the world and life as a whole." In his seminal 1981 book *A Christian Manifesto*, Schaeffer contended that contemporary American society had witnessed a shift in the balance of power, "*from* a world view that was at least vaguely Christian" and "*toward* something completely different." Society and its many institutions – especially its public schools – had increasingly fallen under the influence of the humanist worldview, which Schaeffer defined as a belief in "Man beginning from himself, with no knowledge except what he himself can discover and no standards outside of himself." The humanist, Schaeffer claimed, assumed that "man is the measure of all things." Schaeffer urged Christians to take notice of the comprehensiveness and the mutual incompatibility of these worldviews. He maintained that Christianity could regain its foothold in society only if its followers grasped the totality of its truth and then lived according to that truth, to transform not only themselves but government and law.[30]

Like Rushdoony, Schaeffer rejected majoritarian political appeals. He alleged that most who comprised Richard Nixon's "silent majority" and became diligent Republican Party voters did so for selfish, unprincipled reasons. It was, instead, only a "*minority* of the Silent Majority ... who were standing on some kind of principle ... with at least a memory of Christianity." The masses sought primarily to satisfy themselves, not to live according to God's law. The humanistic worldview, Schaeffer lamented, had become their religion. More perverse yet, the majority of Americans now identified religious liberty precisely with humanism and its boundless moral relativism. The freedom of choice prized by most citizens implied "that all types of situations are spread out before us, and that it really is up to each individual to grab one or the other on the way past, according to the whim of personal preference." Schaeffer reached the same non-majoritarian conclusion as Rushdoony did – that genuine liberty depended not on republican government but on the shared belief "that Christianity is the Truth of total reality." Any foundation less absolute deprived people of the capacity to act freely, not addicted to caprice and convenience. For Schaeffer, as for Rushdoony, true religious liberty made space for Christianity to dominate society and law. And true religious liberty demanded personal restraint and unwavering commitment. Schaeffer championed a version of freedom rooted in an absolute adherence to conservative Christian principles.[31]

Schaeffer found that the humanist worldview had manifested great shifts in the nation's lawmaking since World War II. It seemed to him that "the state deliberately is committed to destroying its ethical commitment to God." Christian resistance to the state's lawmaking enterprise was thus called for. "*We must not be satisfied with mere words*," Schaeffer declared. In the present day, resistance should come "most often ... by legal action." Schaeffer urged Christians, as Christians, to go to court and defend public policy based on the Christian worldview. "Lawsuits should be initiated to stop [government] funds from flowing to" social institutions trying to wipe out Christianity, "even when it is extremely costly in money, time, and energy." For humanism's terrible permeation of society he blamed "the Christian lawyers," who "should have seen the change taking place and stood on the wall and blown the trumpets loud and clear." Because they had "not blow[n] the trumpets clearly," America had gone "very, very far down the road toward a totally humanistic culture."[32]

The writings of Rushdoony and Schaeffer radiated among Christian Right activists who, during the 1970s and 1980s, looked to constrain the influence of secular humanism on society, government, and, especially, public schools. Several helped lay the groundwork for the *Smith* plaintiffs. One, constitutional scholar Whitehead, founded the powerful Rutherford Institute with Rushdoony's patronage. In an important 1978 article that would guide activists such as Kotouc and Parker,

Whitehead tried to show that the Court, in *Torcaso*, had adopted a conception of "belief-as-religion." The justices' own logic, he argued, dictated that "Secular Humanism, being no less a religion than theism, is equally susceptible to the establishment clause" as to the Free Exercise Clause, and that, in the classroom, "its expression, in any form, is clearly unconstitutional." Whitehead went beyond asserting that the teaching of secular humanism violated the Establishment Clause. Even the omission of theistic values from the curriculum, he claimed, constituted an establishment of humanism. "If all moral teaching is eradicated in public education," Whitehead posited, then "the problem of religious secularism is still present because the state would be effectively establishing a preference for those who believe in no morals over those who do." In such a situation, "the ideology of the religion of Secular Humanism would be the only ideology in public education offering answers to moral questions." Citing Rushdoony and Schaeffer extensively, Whitehead maintained that neither liberty nor order was safe when law floated freely, unanchored in Christian morality. The establishment of secular humanism had led to a state of "judicial relativism" in which the justices rubber-stamped the arbitrary results of the state's lawmaking enterprise. Far from charging the federal courts with disregarding the majoritarian political process, Whitehead accused them of slavishly submitting to that process.[33]

A number of other prominent Christian conservatives joined the effort. Claiming that secular humanism was a religion, they painted themselves as members of a besieged religious minority: true Christians. Among them was the well-known activist Phyllis Schlafly, who reminded her readers that "parents have the right to assure that their children's beliefs and moral values are not undermined by the schools." Shortly before Ronald Reagan assumed office as president, she expressed satisfaction in that, although liberals had "made secular humanism our de facto state religion in government and education," they now "realize[d] that those who believe in the eternal verities and the Ten Commandments of the Judeo-Christian culture are starting to exercise their inalienable political rights." The war against secular humanism was waged with equal vigor by Mel and Norma Gabler, a Texas couple who founded a highly effective grassroots organization dedicated to removing secular humanism from the textbooks used in American public schools. Perhaps the best-known popularizer of Rushdoony's and Schaeffer's ideas was Tim LaHaye, who found the widest audiences for the claim that Christianity faced mortal danger from an antithetical religion, secular humanism. They and others provided a groundswell of antihumanist literature that would help prepare the *Smith* plaintiffs to litigate their case.[34]

SECULAR HUMANISM AND THE COURTS

On multiple occasions in the years leading up to *Smith*, the federal courts considered whether secular humanism constituted a religion for purposes of the Establishment Clause. Litigants arguing that it did drew on relevant Supreme Court precedent. One ruling commonly cited was *Zorach* v. *Clauson* (1952), which interpreted the Establishment Clause as directing government not to disfavor religion and, in fact, to accommodate it whenever possible. To prohibit such accommodation would be mistakenly "to find in the Constitution a requirement that the government show a callous indifference to religious groups," which, in turn, would be to favor "those who believe in no religion over those who do believe." Neutrality, in that case, would be breached. Antihumanists also invoked *Torcaso*'s provision that government show no partiality toward either theistic religion or nontheistic religion. A third foundation for conservatives' arguments came from Potter Stewart's solo dissent in *Abington* v. *Schempp* (1963), which proclaimed that, because of the schools' profound influence on students, any student who needed to engage in devotional activities during the day had to be accommodated. "Permission of such exercises for those who want them is necessary if the schools are truly to be neutral in the matter of religion," Stewart held, "and a refusal to permit religious exercises thus is seen, not as the realization of state neutrality, but rather as the establishment of a religion of secularism."[35]

Following *Schempp*, the federal courts would mandate that public schools neither show hostility toward religion nor promote an antitheistic religion. At no point, however, did a court find that any school system had actually demonstrated such hostility or promoted an antitheistic religion in contravention of the Establishment Clause. In *Reed* v. *Van Hoven* (1965), a district judge admitted "that, in light of the [Court's] decided cases, the public schools, as between theistic and humanistic religions, must carefully avoid any program of indoctrination in ultimate values." Yet the judge denied that he was "espous[ing] a particular philosophy of secularism" in disallowing classroom prayer during the school day. The trial judge in *Cornwell* v. *Board of Education* (1970) made no serious attempt to comprehend the plaintiffs' claim "that the teaching of sex [education] in the Baltimore County Schools will in fact establish religious concepts." Likewise, the district judge in *ACLU* v. *Wallace* (1972) concluded that, while the Alabama legislature had to avoid establishing a religion of secularism, that did not require the state to permit Bible reading in the schools.[36]

These rulings asserted that, by requiring school boards and legislators to demonstrate secular intent, case law fomented religious neutrality and not an antireligious ethos. So argued the Ninth Circuit in *Jackson* v. *California* (1972), in which the parents of private-school students contended that the state had established the religion of secular humanism by refusing to extend them tuition credits. The plaintiffs in *Wright* v. *Houston* (1974) similarly alleged "that, by restricting the study of human origins to an uncritical examination of the theory of evolution," without exploring alternative theories, the schools were "lending official support to a 'religion of secularism'" and thereby "'establishing' a particular religion in contravention of the first amendment." Here again, the trial judge rejected the allegation, insisting that "the offending material," by not referencing God, remained only "peripheral to the matter of religion."[37]

Crowley v. *Smithsonian* (1978) spoke to an important claim made by the *Smith* plaintiffs. Here, a district judge held that a publicly funded exhibit on natural selection did not, in excluding information on Biblical creation, establish a secular religion. Omitting religious accounts of human origins did not violate neutrality of religion but, rather, preserved it. A court of appeals upheld the ruling in 1980, pointedly rejecting the appellants' argument that because natural selection could not be observed and so could not be proven, it constituted a religious belief, an article of faith. The *Smith* plaintiffs would later echo this argument. The court, in Crowley, thought otherwise. Even if scholars' acceptance of evolutionary theory did rest ultimately on "faith" in science, the court determined, any such faith was far removed from the religion proscribed by the Establishment Clause. Maintaining faith that one's powers of observation and critical thinking were reliable tools for knowledge was not at all the same as basing one's knowledge of the world on scripture or dogma.[38]

Another federal case addressed issues central to *Smith*. In *Rhode Island Federation of Teachers* v. *Norberg* (1979), a district judge struck down, on Establishment Clause grounds, a state law allowing tax deductions to parents of private schoolers. The judge rejected arguments made by an intervening group of ten parents charging that the statute was needed to redress the public schools' establishment of secular humanism. Like the

Smith plaintiffs, the *Norberg* intervenors purported to resolve the "religious" imbalance inclusively, by getting the schools to accommodate a wider array of worldviews. Upholding the judge's ruling against the statute and the intervenors, the First Circuit determined that, if any imbalance did exist, then only an *exclusive* remedy would honor the wall of separation required by the Establishment Clause. "No establishment" denoted a ban on religious establishment, not an establishment of multiple, counterbalancing religions. "If secular humanism is, in fact, a religion, and if it is taught in Rhode Island's public schools," the court reasoned, then the only remedy available would be a "prohibition of the teaching of secular humanism, not the adoption of state tax deductions which ... would facilitate [the] attending [of] schools that teach other religions" such as Christianity. The appellate court almost certainly considered its propposition merely rhetorical: If the Constitution yielded no solution less preposterous than a prohibition against secularism itself, then the intervenors' quest obviously could not be accommodated.[39]

TEXTBOOK OFFENSIVE

Throughout these years, activists across the United States protested the issue that would become most central to *Smith*. Christian conservatives applied the secular-humanism-as-religion argument to school books, which they depicted as promoting secular-humanism and disparaging Christianity. Some of these accusations ended up as federal court cases, others made it to state courts, and still others never made it to trial. Among the latter was a protest waged in 1974 in Kanawha County, West Virginia. Alice Moore, a school-board member and wife of a fundamentalist preacher, led a campaign against a series of language-arts textbooks supposedly promoting secular humanism. The books, Moore charged, were "disrespectful of authority and religion, destructive of social and cultural values, obscene, pornographic, unpatriotic, or in violation of individual and familial rights of privacy." Moore drew the attention of the nation's best-known textbook critics, Mel and Norma Gabler, whose writings provided the basis for Moore's campaign. The Gablers journeyed to Kanawha County to help instruct local citizens, turning the conflict into a lightning rod in the battle against humanism in the textbooks.[40]

From 1977 to 1979, a group of schoolteachers tried to prevent the Warsaw, Indiana school board from purging the classrooms of textbooks such as Sidney Simon's *Values Clarification* and novels such as Sylvia Plath's *The Bell Jar*. According to Stephen Arons, the school board was defending traditional authority – the "authority of men over women, of fundamentalism over secular humanism, of the school board over the teachers, of the family over the school board, and of parents over children." Believing "that their value system was seriously threatened," they were willing to censor ideas, obstruct the legal system, and ruin teachers' careers. Although neither the Kanawha County nor Warsaw conflict went to trial, both evinced the start of a right-wing movement protesting the use of books that purportedly established a secularist religion antithetical to true Christianity.[41]

During that same time, a group of Californians sued their state's board of education, portraying as unconstitutional its prohibition against the adoption of biology curricula referencing creationism. The litigants pursued a dual strategy. On the one hand, their brief argued that creationism was supported by scientific evidence and so constituted a science as much as did evolution. But, while asserting that the science of creationism deserved equal representation in the curriculum, the brief also asserted that evolution was a religion and so deserved no accommodation that was denied to other religions. Much as the *Crowley* plaintiffs did that same year, these litigants argued that "the theory of evolution cannot be proven beyond doubt and necessarily involves an element of faith." The "requisite government neutrality toward religion," they argued, could "be satisfied by requiring equal time for the two theories, whether they be scientific or religious." Although the court never heard testimony or issued a ruling, the case left a record of yet one more accusation that public-school textbooks were contravening the Establishment Clause by advancing the religion of secular humanism.[42]

During the 1980s, several cases about textbooks and curricula were heard in state and federal courts. The judges in all of them equated secular curricula with religious neutrality. The Commonwealth Court of Pennsylvania, in *Fink* v. *Board of Education* (1982), denied that prohibiting Bible reading and prayer in the classroom "show[ed] a hostility for religion or establish[ed] a religion of secular humanism." According to the court, the petitioner mistook governmental neutrality for hostility. A year later, in *Crockett* v. *Sorenson*, a Virginia district court admitted, citing *Zorach*, that familiarity with religion is so necessary for understanding society that to deprive students of such familiarity is to attenuate their education. Nonetheless, the court relied on the *Lemon* test in striking down a Bible-reading program in Bristol, Virginia public schools. "Although a stated purpose of the program [wa]s the objective teaching of the Bible, the evidence [demonstrated] that the program was originally designed to inculcate religious beliefs in the students."[43]

Most notable were three federal cases, in the years immediately leading up to *Smith*, that addressed especially important elements of the case. While Jaffree was learning about the devotional exercises conducted in Mobile classrooms, a group of parents, teachers, and religious leaders was suing the Arkansas Board of Education for enforcing a statute that, the group claimed, violated the Establishment Clause. That law, the "Balanced Treatment for Creation-Science and Evolution-Science Act," signed in March 1981, mandated that "public schools within this State shall give balanced treatment to creation-science and to evolution-science" in the curriculum. The district court in *McLean* v. *Arkansas* struck down the law as "simply and purely an effort to introduce the Biblical version of creation into the public school curricula." Lawmakers had based the statute on a model, distributed to Christian conservatives nationwide, asserting that creationism and evolution were both religions. As in the 1978 creationism conflict in California and the 1979–1980 *Norberg* case, Christian conservatives demanded that the schools disestablish secular religion. The *McLean* court ruled, as the First Circuit had in *Norberg*, that the Establishment Clause required that no religion be taught, not that competing religions be jointly accommodated. If evolution actually were a religion, the judge maintained, then "the remedy [would be] to stop the teaching of evolution" rather than to "establish another religion in opposition to it."[44]

In *Grove* v. *Mead* (1985), another district judge applied *Lemon* in dismissing a complaint that public schools in Mead, Washington, were establishing the religion of secular humanism. The plaintiff's daughter had been required to read a novel that the plaintiff considered abhorrent to her Christian values. Serving as her attorney was Michael Farris, a prominent Christian Right litigator who was then chief counsel for Concerned Women for America. Farris claimed to be fighting for the rights of not only his client but the many Christians who "wonder[ed] whether religious neutrality is a guise for throwing Christianity out of schools while allowing antagonistic philosophies to fill the vacuum." The judge, less skeptical of religious neutrality than Farris, concluded that "use of the book" simply "served a secular educational function." The Ninth Circuit upheld the ruling. Because the book had been "included in a group of religiously neutral books in a review of English literature," the three-judge panel found, "its use [did] not constitute establishment of religion or anti-religion." Even if secular humanism were a religion, the curriculum as a whole had not advanced it – or any other religion.[45]

In a concurring opinion, one of the judges went further, castigating the plaintiffs for "divid[ing] the universe of value-laden thought into only two categories – the religious and the anti-religious," and for simply assigning all products of secular, nonreligious thinking to the antireligious category. Such a coarse parsing would render pointless any attempt at religious impartiality and would "erect an insurmountable barrier to meaningful application of the establishment clause to controversies like this one." This made the court's job much harder. "The difficulty," the judge noted, was "that plaintiffs might well concede that the [law's] primary purpose and effect was secular; indeed, that is precisely their point." Secularism itself was under attack. Attorney Farris was attempting to turn case law on its head by denying that the schools could provide neutrality by ensuring a secular classroom. For Farris, as for other religious conservatives, the constitutional rights of Christians could be protected only if the schools taught Christianity alongside the anti-Christian religion now enjoying exclusive reign.[46]

Farris again championed his brand of religious pluralism as lead counsel in a federal case that grabbed national headlines. *Mozert* v. *Hawkins* was brought by a group of parents and concerned residents in Hawkins County, Tennessee, contending that their Christian sensibilities had been offended by a series of books used in county public schools. Although the group initially attempted to have the entire series removed from the schools, the suit it filed in December 1983 asked only that their children be permitted to read alternative textbooks. Farris portrayed his clients as members of a disrespected minority seeking to defend their religious liberty. "There's a widespread feeling amongst Christians" such as his clients, Farris told the press, "that the religion of secular humanism has permeated public education." One of the plaintiffs expounded on this theme. Insisting that she was interested only in academic freedom and the presentation of "viable multiple alternatives," she accused the school system of censoring Christianity by excluding it from the curriculum. "Secular humanism is a religion, according to the U.S. Supreme Court," she informed the Hawkins County school board. "Since we believe in separation of church and state we cannot allow this series of books to teach religion contrary to the laws of our land."[47]

In June 1985, while Hand was reviewing the parties' briefs and preparing to set a date for the *Smith* trial to begin, *Mozert* came to trial. The specter of the Tennessee case, so similar to *Smith*, loomed over the proceedings in Alabama. Journalists drew frequent comparisons between *Mozert* and *Smith*. So, too, did political and constitutional theorists. The underlying issue in both cases was whether evangelicals could accomplish more by using the courts than by eschewing them – whether they could better preserve the place of religion in public schools if they demanded their own constitutional rights than if they disregarded the rights of others.[48]

HARDBALL

The path ahead remained uncertain for Sherling, Kotouc, and Parker. Perhaps they could count on Hand's solicitude. Perhaps their chances for ultimate success lay more squarely with some out-of-court arrangement. No federal court had ever ruled that an exclusively secular curriculum amounted to an unconstitutional establishment of religion. Even if Hand found that it did, his judicial superiors could hardly be expected to affirm his ruling. The Supreme Court, having just disallowed a moment of silence in the classroom, seemed highly unlikely to buy into the plaintiffs' argument. The plaintiffs recognized the difficulty of their task. Over the next several months, they worked to settle the case out of court. Threatening the Mobile school board, the governor, and the state board of education with another costly trial, they tried to strong-arm the three parties defendant to accede to their demands. The plaintiffs presented each opposing counsel with the opportunity to sign a "consent decree" stipulating that secular humanism was a religion, that the systematic omission or denigration of theistic religion indicated the dissemination of secular humanism, and that secular humanism's dissemination in the classroom violated the Establishment Clause. Any of the defendants, by signing the decree, would agree not to authorize the use of textbooks that disseminated the religion of secular humanism.

The plaintiffs scored their first victory on November 7, 1985, when the governor signed a consent decree. Carefully incorporated into the decree were all elements of the plaintiffs' October 10 memorandum of law, other than an admission that secular humanism was actually being taught in Alabama schools. Wallace confirmed the plaintiffs' assertions that humanism was a religion, that its promotion violated the First Amendment, and that the suppression of Christianity in the classroom did likewise. Rather than denouncing the Court, as he had famously done throughout in his career, Wallace now acceded to the binding authority of "the test established by the U.S. Supreme Court in *Lemon*

v. *Kurtzman*." The governor also agreed to the creation of state guidelines protecting students against indoctrination by the humanist religion – guidelines to be administered by Hand. In exchange for the governor's signature, the plaintiffs promised not to request legal fees and expenses from his office. Both sides agreed, for the moment, not to publicize the accord. For nearly three months, the agreement remained confidential.[49]

In mid-January 1986, the plaintiffs were given a boost. Sherling announced that the National Legal Foundation (NLF), the legal arm of Pat Robertson's Virginia-based Christian Broadcasting Network, would provide funding and legal assistance to the plaintiffs. Founded in 1982, the NLF represented the televangelist's first foray into law. Later in the decade, the organization would win a high-profile victory in *Mergens* (1990), the Supreme Court's confirmation of the 1984 Equal Access Act. Although the organization would disband by the early 1990s, superseded by Robertson's American Center for Law and Justice, the Christian–civil-libertarian strategy that the NLF helped pioneer would continue exerting influence among Christian Right litigators. The *Smith* plaintiffs benefited from the assistance of the NLF, whose general counsel, Robert Skolrood, would advise Sherling, Kotouc, and Parker. The NLF covered approximately 70 percent of the plaintiffs' legal expenses. Not that its contributions came without cost – the participation of a high-powered, nationally known advocacy group with a sharp ideological bent would, over time, contribute to the perception among some Mobilians that the parties supporting the suit were using the local schools and taxpayers to advance their own political agenda.[50]

The plaintiffs' eagerness to purge the schools of non-Christian textbooks alarmed some local liberals. Among those was Michael Seider, minister of the Unitarian Universalist Church of Mobile, who worried that a triumph by the plaintiffs would annihilate schoolchildren's freedom to learn. Seider was joined in his concern by Ishmael Jaffree, who was rethinking his decision to bow out of the case. Fearing that none of the defendants would resist the plaintiffs' threats, the two men set out to find parents of Mobile schoolchildren who might be willing to intervene in the case against the plaintiffs. Seven of Seider's congregants, along with five other parents, agreed to organize themselves as prospective intervenors. These individuals were better situated than Jaffree to contest the plaintiffs' claim that modernism and liberalism constituted an anti-Christian religion, as none of them, unlike Jaffree, renounced religion or openly questioned God's existence. Two, Corinne and Malcolm Howell, called themselves "historical Baptists who believe in separation of church and state." They denied that their humanism conflicted with their Christianity. To the contrary, Malcolm Howell contended, "humanism elevates people to the highest that they can become." He suggested that "Jesus Christ was a humanist.... If he were in Mobile walking the streets today, he would call out the very best in each one of us. That, as I understand it, is humanism."[51]

Seider acted quickly. He got Mobile attorney Richard Dorman to handle the case locally and to prepare the motion to intervene. The prestigious Washington, DC, law firm Hogan and Hartson offered its services pro bono. The liberal advocacy group People for the American Way (PFAW) agreed to help pay costs, as did the American Civil Liberties Union (ACLU). With the proposed entry of the intervenors and their supporters, along with the plaintiffs' assistance from Robertson's NLF and continued affiliation with the Rutherford Institute, the conflict began publicly to assume a pitched, ideological character. So it seemed to William Bradford, Hogan and Hartson's top attorney involved in the case, who saw the conflict as "a clash of cultures." Primed to preserve academic freedom in every American classroom, Seider's group presented Hand with its motion to intervene on January 15, 1986. Written by Dorman, the motion warned that the remedy sought by the plaintiffs would "require a costly and lengthy restructuring of the school system curriculum" and might even bankrupt the schools.[52]

Immediately, the would-be intervenors tried to persuade the parties defendant to support their intervention. Two lawyers from Hogan and Hartson traveled to Mobile and met with Mobile school board attorney Campbell, who remained wary of another extended, expensive trial. One week later, Campbell told the school commissioners of his meeting. The firm was convinced, he reported, that the case "could be one of landmark importance" and that the plaintiffs, if successful, would spur censorship throughout the nation's public schools. Campbell did not advise the board on whether or not to sign off on the intervention. He did indicate to reporters that the board would zealously guard its own interests. If the plaintiffs were "going to attack our curriculum," then his clients might be forced to collaborate with Hogan and Hartson.[53]

There was more. Campbell explained to the commissioners that their decision was bound up with a bigger choice, about whether to resist the plaintiffs or accede to their demands. Within the past couple of days, he told the board, he had learned that Wallace had reached an accord with the plaintiffs – nearly three months earlier. Parker and Sherling had now shown him the consent decree signed by the governor and were requesting that Campbell sign an identical agreement. The plaintiffs were asking the Mobile board, as they would soon ask the Alabama Board of Education, to foreswear approving for classroom use any textbooks that advanced the religion of secular humanism. If it consented, the board would promise to adopt only textbooks authorized by a recent Department of Education study by Paul Vitz, a conservative critic of public education. The commissioners needed to decide on one or the other path. They could either defend themselves against accusations of promoting an anti-Christian religion, or they could sign the decree and thereby avoid preparing for a court battle and paying legal fees. Of course, many of their textbooks might be removed from classroom use. And defending themselves came with an additional cost: the prospective intervenors, it seemed, would be receiving assistance from PFAW and the ACLU, organizations with obvious ideological agendas. (Campbell did not note the plaintiffs' ideological agenda.) If the board declined to sign the consent decree, then it would fight alongside these liberal interest groups. The commissioners were instructed to align themselves with either one side or the other.[54]

By the board's next meeting, on February 12, Campbell's position had decidedly firmed. Having conferred again with plaintiffs' counsel, he concluded that the plaintiffs would triumph at trial. Hand seemed poised to rule favorably on their argument that secular humanism met the First Amendment standard for a religion. The plaintiffs had forwarded Campbell materials demonstrating the religious status of secular humanism, which he had then shared with all the board members. These materials had persuaded him; he asked if the materials had persuaded them as well. Campbell also told them of the footnote Hand had appended to his *Jaffree* decision. The judge had warned that, if the appellate courts rejected his jurisdictional argument, then he would revisit the erstwhile intervenors' claims about humanist indoctrination – claims on which Hand looked sympathetically. Campbell let the board know that he and the plaintiffs' attorneys had agreed further to discuss the consent decree and, he hoped, reach an accord. He then announced that the plaintiffs' attorneys were there in attendance that evening. They wished to speak, in order to clarify certain matters.[55]

Addressing the board, the plaintiffs' lawyers painted themselves and their suit as reasonable, deserving of the board's cooperation. They also warned that the cost of defying them would be unbearably steep. Speaking first was Sherling, who insisted that the plaintiffs' actual goal was not to restrict the curriculum but to expand it, to ensure that God-centered religions were accommodated alongside human-centered faiths. Parker expounded. His clients, he said, simply wished for religious accounts of history and society to be accorded their rightful place alongside secular explanations. As to prescribing any particular religion, his clients were staunchly opposed. Parker emphasized how unwieldy it would be for Hand to purge textbooks of secular humanism, and how frustrated the board might feel if the federal courts assumed control over textbook selection. All this could be avoided, Parker assured the board members, if they signed a consent decree.[56]

FIGHT OR FLIGHT

The plaintiffs' ultimatum generated mixed reactions. The board's two African American members, Robert Gilliard and Norman Cox, reiterated the skepticism they had registered during *Jaffree*. This time around, Gilliard was especially mistrustful. The board, he insisted, had done nothing wrong and was not obligated to submit to a private group's attempt to harm the county schools. Mobile's desegregation battles still fresh in his mind, Gilliard remained on guard against what he perceived to be continuing efforts by conservatives to destroy public education. The current controversy appeared to him "some kind of political move to generate solidarity among groups which promote ghosts." On the other side of the issue stood white board member Steve Belk, who wished for Christianity to be taught alongside its humanist counterpart. With Sherling and Parker in attendance, Belk confirmed his support for signing the decree. His exasperation at the decline of "the traditional family unit in America, the ideology of moral absolutes, patriotism, [and] free enterprise" signaled his close sympathy with the plaintiffs' cause. Board president Judy McCain agreed that the board ought to sign, having concluded, from the documents provided by the plaintiffs, "that humanists do seem to view their doctrines as a very definite religion." Gilliard continued to deny that humanism was a precise or meaningful concept or that Mobile public schools were brainwashing students. Fellow African American school commissioner Cox similarly saw no evidence that secular humanism was being advanced in the schools. After voting to oppose the intervention by Seider's group, the commissioners agreed to table a decision on the decree until the next meeting. They did, however, grant Campbell the authority to "negotiate" with the plaintiffs.[57]

The Alabama Board of Education also chose not to support the intervenors' motion. Although the state board initially indicated that it had no objection, it shifted position in mid-February, "instruct[ing] its attorney to oppose the intervention of this group using all legitimate grounds of opposition." The board's motives were based in politics as well as law. The intervenors, like the plaintiffs, wanted to mold Alabama schools according to their political agenda – or so it seemed to the state board, which bristled at the involvement of the ACLU and PFAW. Board counsel Coody complained that, while "it's one thing for a group of citizens to assert their rights," it was entirely "another thing for an organization to control citizens' assertion of their rights and their views." In fact, the board had no evidence that the two civil-rights organizations were shaping how the intervenors understood the issues. Not surprisingly, Hogan and Hartson attorney George Mernick quickly countered that it was "an absolutely false allegation to say the ACLU is controlling these individuals." What was true was that the board was resisting what it saw as an attempt to infringe on its authority over the selection of curricular materials for Alabama public schools.[58]

Clinging tightly to its control over the selection process, the state board remained unready to compromise on the other matter still before it, whether or not to sign the plaintiffs' consent decree. Sherling and Parker attended the board meeting on February 13 and brought with them the consent decree that they had presented to the Mobile board the previous day. Alabama Superintendent of Schools Wayne Teague expressed wariness with the plaintiffs' proposal. Teague especially didn't want to give a federal judge authority to determine what gets taught in Alabama schools, and Teague feared that, by signing the consent decree, the board would cede to Hand the "power to set up a curriculum for the state." Along with Vice President John Tyson, Teague encouraged the board to continue deliberation and resist the mounting pressure to sign – which was coming not only from the plaintiffs but from the many Christian Right activists statewide bombarding the board members with daily letters and phone calls. With Hand insisting they hasten their process, the asked their attorneys, Coody and James Ippolito, to begin negotiations with the plaintiffs' attorneys and to report their findings at the board's February 27 meeting, when the board would make its decision.[59]

It remained uncertain whether any of the defendants would resist the plaintiffs. Nor, it appeared, did any of the parties wish to align themselves with the prospective intervenors. The direness of the situation was grasped by Jaffree, who, on February 14, sent the Mobile board a letter urging it to support the intervenors and resist the plaintiffs. Jaffree insisted that the plaintiffs' demands would not hold up on appeal. Campbell knew full well, the letter charged, that not a single federal court had "held that text books [that] include language or sentence fragments which affect the sensibilities of some religious fundamentalists ... violate the Establishment Clause." Jaffree charged the board with kowtowing to religious fanatics. He refused to tolerate such capitulation. He had withdrawn from the case only because he had assumed that the board would protect the curriculum, and because he was willing to let the intervenors represent his interest as a parent. If the board remained unwilling to defend itself, and if the court barred the intervenors from any involvement, then he would reenter the case.[60]

The board's attorney was less than happy to receive new directives from his old adversary. Campbell forwarded the letter to Hand, who seemed to recognize that the likelihood of a trial was growing dimmer with the defendants' failure to rise up and defend the textbooks. On February 20, he granted the twelve parents' request to intervene in the *Smith* case. Developments, he acknowledged, had "demonstrate[d] that these defendants may have ... an interest adverse to the petitioning intervenors-defendants or, at the very least, [had] clearly indicate[d] a reluctance on the part of these defendants to vigorously defend against the plaintiffs' claims."[61]

At its February 26 meeting, the Mobile board set about to decide whether to abide by the demands of the plaintiffs. Campbell maintained that he was not personally invested in the decision, that he only wished to save the board from financial liabilities and endless litigation. He recommended signing the decree, but only if the board members trusted that signing did not threaten the interests of students. The opposition rallied on exactly that objection. Gilliard and Cox remained adamant that their only commitment lay in protecting the quality of public education in Mobile County – even if doing so required the board to spend money. To fail to defend the teachers, they charged, was to allow the schools to be compromised by parochial interests. Gilliard reported that he had researched similar court cases, and that, without fail, the courts had refused to honor claims such as those now presented by the plaintiffs. Recalling Mobile's desegregation controversy, he painted the present case as another instance of conservatives denying the best-quality education to public schoolchildren. To educate fully, textbooks needed to "expose children to as much of the thinking process as possible," not to censor controversial ideas. Cox declared that the plaintiffs' "threat to rip the pages from the textbooks" was "only one step removed from book-burning." He and Gilliard urged the board to "fight this case all the way."[62]

The three remaining commissioners wanted to sign the decree. Doing so made practical sense, opined McCain. To her, this was not the Mobile school board's fight to wage. The board's sole concern was to minimize its own liability and to protect its limited financial resources. Belk responded to Gillard's and Cox's charges by echoing the plaintiffs' position that the only censorship here was being practiced by the secular humanists. If anyone had the right to complain about bias in the textbooks, Belk contended, it was Christians. Full religious inclusion – and not censorship – was all that he wanted. That was also the goal of the fifth commissioner, Howard Mathis, who championed the evenhanded treatment of all religions. Mathis reminded his colleagues that the Court had identified secular humanism as a religion and that the justices had forbade the schools from promoting any religion at all. How then, he asked, could the board sanction the promotion of this one religion alone? Perhaps a bold trial decision would convince the Court to reverse itself.[63]

Belk called for a vote. Voting "aye" were Belk, McCain, and Mathis; voting "no" were Gilliard and Cox. By a 3–2 vote, the motion carried, as cries of "All glory be to God!" and "Praise the Lord" filled the audience. Campbell immediately signed the "Stipulation for Consent Decree," which hewed closely to the document signed by the governor. While the decree did not stipulate that the books used in Mobile schools promoted secular humanism, it did mandate "the establishment of court-approved standards, criteria, or guidelines, designed to protect the constitutional rights stipulated herein." The board agreed to full "retention of jurisdiction by the court to monitor compliance with its order," thereby placing final authority for curricular decisions with Hand. The decree included a constitutional argument based largely on *Lemon*'s effect prong. The Court's own rulings were used to demonstrate that the teaching of humanism ran afoul of the Establishment Clause – both directly, by promoting a particular religion, and indirectly, by "inhibit[ing] other religions." The decree also incorporated Vitz's finding "that the existence, history, contributions, and roles of Protestantism, Catholicism, and Judaism have been excluded from textbooks" used in American schools. After weeks of debate, the board signed on to the plaintiffs' case that secular humanism was a religion whose teaching was prohibited by the First Amendment.[64]

The Alabama Board of Education was not willing to offer any such concession. The state board wasn't ready to act in any direction, wary of staking an ideological position or incurring legal costs. Resistance to signing the decree was led by Tyson and Teague, who held that the state had in no way promoted religion, even if its textbooks were seriously flawed by virtue of their failure to describe religion's historical role. At its March 13 meeting, the board was up against Hand's deadline for signing a decree. Supporters of the decree, lacking the needed votes, did not ask for a vote that evening. By not acting, the board effectively declined to placate the plaintiffs. Tyson and Teague remained determined not to take sides and to defend themselves against anyone who would infringe on their authority to manage their own affairs. The board also passed a resolution that underlined its moderate position. Admitting that "historically important facts about the contributions of Protestantism, Catholicism, and Judaism to the development of the United States do not appear in many textbooks," the resolution directed the state textbook committee to notify the board whenever it discovered that textbooks were lacking such content. It likewise directed Teague to contact publishers and request that they incorporate such "factually-based content" into their textbooks. The board of education was ready to fight but not to appear unreasonable.[65]

On August 29, Hand scheduled the *Smith* trial to begin on October 6, 1986. He accepted the accords reached between the plaintiffs and the two parties defendant, the governor and the Mobile school board. Hand also declared the plaintiffs to be a class, a status that he enhanced soon afterward by splitting the plaintiffs into two classes: Alabama schoolteachers who believed in God, and parents who believed likewise. The plaintiffs had charged that the schools were violating the rights of teachers as much as the rights of any other Alabamians. Hand agreed. If the state infringes on the First Amendment rights of even a single "theistic teacher," he ruled, "it infringes [on] the right of all theists who are teachers, because there is one textbook list for all teachers in the state." Teachers, as much as their pupils, would have been subjected to the state's established religion. In Hand's courtroom, Christian schoolteachers would enjoy every bit as much constitutional protection as did humanistic teachers, students, and parents.[66]

WHOSE *LEMON* IS IT?

The *Smith* plaintiffs, defendants, and intervenors readied to square off. Theirs was a fight about government, law, culture, morality, and epistemology. What had begun four years earlier as a struggle to decide the scope of judicial review over state laws and local customs had grown into a contest to determine the appropriateness of secular standards in public education. Throughout it all remained Hand. While his motives were multifaceted, one thing remained clear – his disdain for a Supreme Court that seemed to him impervious to the will of the people. The arguments presented by the parties at trial would provide him with materials to be used in his widely anticipated ruling. Soon would commence the events that would allow him to speak, in a trial that was sure to garner widespread attention.

Prior to trial, the intervenors submitted a brief advancing their position fully. In places, the brief refuted the plaintiffs' claim to the status of injured religious minority; more often, the intervenors proceeded as if the plaintiffs' argument were such sheer nonsense that it need not be contested. The intervenors expounded the conventional, commonsense meaning of Establishment Clause jurisprudence – that the Court intended to proscribe the establishment not of any comprehensive worldview but of conventional, God-centered religion. *Engel* and *Schempp* remained controlling and continued to require a secular classroom. The intervenors failed to grapple seriously with the plaintiffs' charge that "secularism-as-neutrality" comprised an oxymoron. Although the plaintiffs had argued persuasively that the secular standard obstructed their own equal treatment by the state, the intervenors largely looked past that argument and simply reasserted standard case law.[67]

Secularism – and only secularism – could, according to the intervenors, provide the religious neutrality required by the Establishment Clause. They flatly rejected the plaintiffs' contention that secularism was an antireligious religion. "The plaintiffs' sweeping and unsupported definition of religion as anything someone thinks is important" caused "the term 'religion' [to lose] all independent significance." To the intervenors, the plaintiffs' suggestion that "neutrality is impossible, [that] everything is either for or against theistic religion," effectively "renders the religion clauses of the first amendment meaningless and unworkable." If nontheistic norms for religious neutrality could not universally be trusted as impartial, then government-run institutions would have no chance at welcoming and including all citizens. The intervenors cited the concurring opinion in *Grove*, which declared that, "if the establishment clause is to have any meaning, distinctions must be drawn to recognize not simply 'religious' and 'anti-religious,' but 'non-religious' governmental activity as well. In the parlance of *Lemon v. Kurtzman*, 'secular' must mean 'non-religious.'"[68]

The intervenors painted secularism as an ethos of objectivity that remained apart and detached from all religious worldviews, an ethos that permitted and fostered autonomous thinking. Secularism gave students the freedom to choose to adhere to any religion or to none at all. In maintaining secular standards, Alabama educators were clearly "committed to the transmission of values essential to a free and democratic society," the values of personal autonomy and independent judgment. The state had acted properly in adopting "an approach to teaching that encourages students to think independently rather than an approach that is dogmatic and indoctrinating." The Hogan and Hartson attorneys paid no heed to the plaintiffs' insistence that, by instilling an autonomous way of evaluating one's own place in the world, the schools were violating the plaintiffs' Christian values. While the intervenors did take careful note of the plaintiffs' "claim that the use of these textbooks infringes upon their children's religious development by exposing them to viewpoints contrary to those of their own religion," the intervenors did not find this claim compelling. To them, it seemed obvious that "such exposure to alternative viewpoints" served only "to strengthen, not undermine, religious conviction." That the plaintiffs' convictions might be harmed by "exposure to alternative viewpoints" seemed unbelievable to them, hardly worthy of retort.[69]

According to the intervenors, it was the remedy proposed by the plaintiffs, and not the actions of the state, that ran afoul of the *Lemon* test. They characterized the plaintiffs' case as a "demand that the State Board of Education remove from the public schools all textbooks that are inconsistent with the plaintiffs' religious views and replace them with books that are consistent with those views." Were the state to accede to that demand, they asserted, it would violate all three of *Lemon*'s prongs. But, in fact, the plaintiffs claimed not to be asking that the state adopt books consistent with their views. They claimed to be asking the state evenhandedly to remove all books showing traces of any religion. The plaintiffs spun around the intervenors' accusation and aimed it back at the intervenors. It was the resolution sought by the intervenors, they maintained, that would impose its religious designs on the Christian minority.[70]

The *Smith* plaintiffs posed an unusual challenge. To meet it, the intervenors needed to do more than utilize *Engel, Schempp*, and their progeny to defend the rights of religious minorities. The intervenors had to recognize that Sherling, Kotouc, and Parker had not disregarded Establishment Clause case law, but had done quite the opposite. The intervenors needed to acknowledge that their opponents had embraced the rules of the game and used those rules to attack the very parties who typically benefited from them. The plaintiffs had employed the *Lemon* test, along with Justice O'Connor's endorsement test, to challenge "the unconstitutional advancement of the religion of Humanism." Mobile schools, they alleged, had expressed disapproval toward children who believed in God, conveying to those children "that they are outsiders, not full members of the political community." The Court's requirement that schools not exclude politically powerless groups had been put to new uses. The plaintiffs had grabbed hold of the standard method for identifying religious establishment; the intervenors were now tasked with seizing it back.[71]

Not only was the secularist educational establishment marginalizing Christians, the plaintiffs contended. The schools had installed secular humanism as a dogma that they inculcated into young, impressionable minds. The free exchange of ideas had been forestalled. The plaintiffs quoted *West Virginia* v. *Barnett*, in which the Court upheld the free-speech right of Jehovah's Witnesses not to salute the American flag. In Alabama, secular humanism had become state orthodoxy, and "no official, high or petty, can prescribe what shall be orthodox in politics, nationalism, religion or other matters of opinion." Christian schoolchildren were enduring great pressure to abandon their worldview for the prevailing orthodoxy. This, as *Engel* had made plain, was intolerable. "When the power, prestige and financial support of government is placed behind a particular religious belief, the indirect coercive pressure upon religious minorities to conform to the prevailing officially approved religion is plain."[72]

The plaintiffs' stance in *Smith* signaled the New Right's daring civil-libertarian turn away from court-stripping. Full membership in the civil rights revolution of the 1960s and 1970s had become one of its goals. Christian conservatives now called on the federal courts to protect *their* rights as a minority. Soon, the case would come before Hand, who would carry the story forward. So, too, would the appellate courts that were sure to review the case. The twentieth-century history of the Establishment Clause was about to gain a dramatic new chapter.

Notes

1 *Widmar* v. *Vincent* 454 U.S. 263 (1981); *Lynch* v. *Donnelly*, 465 U.S. 668 (1984), 687–94 (O'Connor, J., concurring); *Congressional Record*, 130, June 27, 1984, pp. 19211–52. Brief for the Moral Majority as amicus curiae

supporting petitioners, July 3, 1984, at *Wallace et al.* v. *Jaffree et al.*, before the Supreme Court of the United States, on appeal from the United States Court of Appeal for the Eleventh Circuit; Brief for the Christian Legal Society and National Association of Evangelicals as amici curiae supporting petitioners, July 3, 1984, at *Wallace* v. *Jaffree*; Brief for the Freedom Council and the Rutherford Institute as amici curiae supporting petitioners, July 5, 1984, at *Wallace* v. *Jaffree*.

2 Francis Wilkinson, "Judge Hand's Holy War," *American Lawyer*, 9 (May 1987), 112; "Lawyer: Christians Must Mount the Offensive," *Birmingham News*, April 4, 1986.

3 The term was popularized by Robert H. Bork, *Slouching towards Gomorrah: Modern Liberalism and American Decline* (New York: HarperCollins, 1996). W. Brevard Hand interview by Robert Daniel Rubin, December 5, 2000, Mobile, Ala., 2–3; *Montgomery Advertiser and Alabama Journal*, November 26, 1987, p. A2; *Los Angeles Times*, March 29, 1987, sec. 5, p. 3.

4 Burt Rieff, "Conflicting Rights and Religious Liberty: The School-Prayer Controversy in Alabama, 1962–1985," *Alabama Review*, 54 (July 2001), 200; *Montgomery Advertiser*, June 5, 1985, pp. A1–A2; Ron Williams interview by Robert Daniel Rubin, March 19, 2002, Mobile, Ala., 12–13.

5 "Wallace, Denton Blast School Prayer Ruling," *Huntsville Times*, June 5, 1985; *Mobile Beacon*, June 22, 1985, p. 2; Statement by Governor Wallace on Supreme Court ruling, 1983–1987: Wallace File, SG 5012, Legal Case Files, ADAH, June 4, 1985, pp. 1–2.

6 Statement by Wallace on Supreme Court ruling, 2; *Mobile Beacon*, June 22, 1985, p. 2.

7 Transcript, *Ishmael Jaffree et al.* v. *Gov. Fob James et al.*, August 5, 1982, Civil case no. 82–0792–H, box no. 7, accession no. 021–93–0423, location no. C0681974 SAN (Federal Records Center, East Point, Ga.), 212–13, 223–29, 263–64; *Jaffree by and through Jaffree* v. *James*, 544 F.Supp. 727 (1982), 732.

8 *Jaffree* v. *Board of School Commissioners of Mobile County*, 554 F.Supp. 1104 (1983), 1129.

9 W. Brevard Hand interview by Robert Daniel Rubin, April 12, 2000, Mobile, Ala., 14–15; W. Brevard Hand interview by Robert Daniel Rubin, October 10, 2002, Mobile, Ala., 3–5. The Court suggested that secular humanism constituted a religion in *Torcaso* v. *Watkins*, 367 U.S. 488 (1961), 495 n11; *School District of Abington, Pa.* v. *Schempp*, 374 U.S. 203 (1963), 313, 225; *United States* v. *Seeger*, 380 U.S. 163 (1965), 165–66; and *Welsh* v. *United States*, 398 U.S. 333 (1970), 342–43.

10 Hand interview, April 12, 2000, pp. 14–15; Hand interview, October 10, 2002, pp. 12–13; *Smith* v. *Board of School Commissioners of Mobile County*, 827 F.2d 684 (1987), 687–88.

11 *Ibid.*, 688; *Mobile Register*, June 24, 1987, pp. 1, 6; *Douglas T. Smith et al.* v. *Board of School Commissioners of Mobile County et al.*, 655 F.Supp 939 (1987), 943–44; Charles S. Coody to W. Brevard Hand, September 11, 1985, Wallace File, 1; Plaintiff's memorandum of law, October 10, 1985, at *Douglas T. Smith et al.* v. *Board of School Commissioners of Mobile*

County et al., consolidated with *Douglas T. Smith et al.* v. *George Wallace*, Wallace File, 1–2.

12 "Judge to Decide If Prayer Case to Go On," *Birmingham News*, October 13, 1985; Minutes of the regular meeting of the Board of School Commissioners of Mobile County, Alabama, January 22, 1986, Central Administrative Office of the Mobile County Public School System, Barton Academy (504 Government Street, Mobile, Ala.), 49; Charles S. Coody to W. Brevard Hand, September 11, 1985, Wallace File, 1–2. *Smith* v. *Board*, 944; Memorandum on position of plaintiffs Smith, September 15, 1985, at *Jaffree* v. *Board*, records of *Smith* v. *Board*, 1–2. Wilkinson, "Judge Hand's Holy War," 113. The case assumed its name from the individual listed first in the original motion to intervene, Douglas Smith.

13 Plaintiff's memorandum of law, October 10, 1985, at *Smith* v. *Board*, records of *Smith* v. *Board*, 2–3.

14 *Ibid.*, i–ii, 2–3.

15 *Ibid.*, 16–23, quoting *Torcaso* v. *Watkins*, 367 U.S. 488 (1961), 495. The plaintiffs cited two lower-court rulings labeling secular humanism a religion. *Washington Ethical Society* v. *District of Columbia*, 249 F.2d 127 (1957); *Fellowship of Humanity* v. *County of Alameda*, 315 F.2d 394 (1957).

16 *United States* v. *Seeger*, 380 U.S. 163 (1965); *Welsh* v. *United States*, 398 U.S. 333 (1970). Plaintiff's memorandum of law, 20–28.

17 *Walz* v. *Tax Commission of the City of New York*, 397 U.S. 664 (1970); *Widmar* v. *Vincent* 454 U.S. 263 (1981); *Mueller* v. *Allen*, 463 U.S. 388 (1983). Plaintiff's memorandum of law, 23–25.

18 *Ibid.*, 35–37.

19 *Ibid.*, 29–32, 46–49.

20 *Ibid.*, 58–77. Transcript, *Jaffree* v. *Board*, 641–55, 663–79, 699–721. *Lemon* v. *Kurtzman*, 403 U.S. 602 (1971), 612–13; *Wallace* v. *Jaffree*, 472 U.S. 38 (1985), 60.

21 Plaintiff's memorandum of law, 78–102.

22 R. Jonathan Moore, *Suing for America's Soul: John Whitehead, the Rutherford Institute, and Conservative Christians in the Courts* (Grand Rapids, Mich.: Eerdmans, 2007). Kotouc shared with me the large collection of books that he used in preparing for the case. Throughout these books ran the evangelical critique of secular humanism.

23 Hunter sees this "orthodox" worldview as framing political conservatism as a whole. James Davison Hunter, *Culture Wars: The Struggle to Define America* (New York: BasicBooks, 1991). Andrew Hartman, *A War for the Soul of America: A History of the Culture Wars* (Chicago: University of Chicago Press, 2015), 200–21; Jonathan Zimmerman, *Whose America? Culture Wars in the Public Schools* (Cambridge, Mass.: Harvard University Press, 2002); Michael Lienesch, *Redeeming America: Piety and Politics in the New Christian Right* (Chapel Hill: University of North Carolina Press, 1993), 157–66; Steve Bruce, *The Rise and Fall of the New Christian Right: Conservative Protestant Politics in America, 1978–1988* (New York: Clarendon, 1988), 76–80.

24 Rosemary C. Salomone, *Visions of Schooling: Conscience Community, and Common Education* (New Haven: Yale University Press, 2000), 1;

Eugene F. Provenzo, *Religious Fundamentalism and American Education: The Battle for the Public Schools* (Albany: State University of New York Press, 1990), xiv–xv, 1, 8; Amy Guttmann, *Democratic Education* (Princeton: Princeton University Press, 1999), xi, 3. Alarm at liberal "change agents" is expressed in Barbara M. Morris, *Change Agents in the Schools: Destroy Your Children, Betray Your Country* (Upland, Calif.: Barbara M. Morris, 1979).

25 Testimony of Rousas John Rushdoony, November 15, 1982, at *Jaffree* v. *Board*, pp. 290–370. On Rushdoony's profound influence on Christian Right thinkers, see Hartman, *War for the Soul of America*, 78, 81–82, 213–14; Fritz Detweiler, *Standing on the Premises of God: The Christian Right's Fight to Redefine America's Public Schools* (New York: New York University Press, 1999), 15–16; Richard John Neuhaus, "Why Wait for the Kingdom? The Theonomist Temptation," *First Things*, no. 3 (May 1990), 13–21; Salomone, *Visions of Schooling*, 106; Provenzo, *Religious Fundamentalism and American Education*, 4–8; Anson Shupe, "The Reconstructionist Movement and the New Christian Right," *Christian Century*, October 4, 1989, 881; Rob Boston, "Thy Kingdom Come," *Church & State*, 41 (September 1988), 174–76; and Rodney Clapp, "Democracy as Heresy," *Christianity Today*, February 20, 1987.

26 Rousas John Rushdoony, *Intellectual Schizophrenia: Culture, Crisis, and Education* (Philadelphia: Presbyterian and Reformed Publishing, 1961), 5–10; Rousas John Rushdoony, *The Messianic Character of American Education: Studies in the History of the Philosophy of Education* (Vallecito, Calif.: Ross House, 1963), 323.

27 Rousas John Rushdoony, *Law and Liberty (1966–1967)* (Vallecito, Calif.: Ross House, 1984); Rousas John Rushdoony, "Religion and the State," Chalcedon Report No. 152 (April 1978), *The Roots of Reconstruction* (Vallecito, Calif.: Ross House, 1991), 986; Rousas John Rushdoony, "The State as an Establishment of Religion," in *Freedom and Education: Pierce* v. *Society of Sisters Reconsidered*, ed. by Donald P. Kommers and Michael J. Wahoske (Notre Dame, Ind.: Center for Civil Rights, 1978), 42.

28 Rushdoony, "Religion and the State," 986; Rushdoony, "State as an Establishment of Religion," 40–42; Rousas John Rushdoony, foreword to John W. Whitehead, *The Separation Illusion: A Lawyer Examines the First Amendment* (Milford, Mich.: Mott, 1977), 9; Rousas John Rushdoony, "America Wake Up!," *Fundamentalist Journal*, 2 (July–August 1983), 22–24.

29 William H. Rehnquist, "The Notion of a Living Constitution," *Texas Law Review*, 54 (May 1976), 693–706; Robert H. Bork, "Neutral Principles and Some First Amendment Problems," *Indiana Law Journal*, 47 (Fall 1971), 1–35; Robert H. Bork, *Tradition and Morality in Constitutional Law* (Washington, D.C.: American Enterprise Institute, 1984). Rousas John Rushdoony, "The Meaning of Theocracy," Chalcedon Position Paper No. 15 (August 1979), *The Roots of Reconstruction* (Vallecito, Calif.: Ross House, 1991), 63–68; Rushdoony, *Messianic Character of American Education*, 31, 302; Rousas John Rushdoony, *Christianity and the State* (Vallecito, Calif.: Ross House, 1986), 97.

30 D. G. Hart, *That Old Time Religion in Modern America: Evangelical Protestantism in the Twentieth Century* (Chicago: Dee, 2002), 134–41; William Martin, *With God on Our Side: The Rise of the Religious Right in America* (New York: Broadway, 1996), 159–60, 194–97. Barry Hankins tells that Schaeffer was quite taken with Rushdoony during the 1960s. Barry Hankins, *Francis Schaeffer and the Shaping of Evangelical America* (Grand Rapids, Mich.: Eerdmans, 2008), 193–94. Schaeffer gained widespread attention from his first three publications. Francis A. Schaeffer, *The God Who Is There: Speaking Historic Christianity into Twentieth Century* (Chicago: Intervarsity, 1968); Francis A. Schaeffer, *Escape from Reason: A Penetrating Analysis of Trends in Modern Thought* (Chicago: Intervarsity, 1968); and Francis A. Schaeffer, *He Is There and He Is Not Silent* (Wheaton, Ill.: Tyndale, 1972). Francis A. Schaeffer, *A Christian Manifesto* (Wheaton, Ill.: Crossway, 1981), 17–20, 24, 111–13.

31 *Ibid.*, 46–47, 77–82.

32 *Ibid.*, 47–49, 103, 118, 132–33, emphasis in original.

33 John W. Whitehead and John Conlan, "The Establishment of the Religion of Secular Humanism and Its First Amendment Implications," *Texas Tech Law Review*, 10 (Winter 1978), 10–20, 61–65. Schaeffer was "deeply appreciative" of Whitehead's work. Schaeffer, *Christian Manifesto*, 10. The body of work decrying humanism's influence is immense. It includes David Ehrenfeld, *The Arrogance of Humanism* (New York: Oxford University Press, 1978); Homer Duncan, *Secular Humanism: The Most Dangerous Religion in America* (Lubbock: Christian Focus on Government, 1979); Charles F. Stanley, *Stand Up, America!* (Atlanta: In Touch Ministries, 1980); Tim LaHaye, *The Battle for the Mind* (Old Tappan, N.J.: Revell, 1980); James Hitchcock, *What Is Secular Humanism? How Humanism Became Secular and How It Is Changing Our World* (Ann Arbor, Mich.: Servant, 1982); Norman Geisler, *Is Man the Measure: An Evaluation of Contemporary Humanism* (Grand Rapids, Mich.: Baker, 1982); Josh McDowell and Don Stewart, *Understanding Secular Religions* (San Bernadino, Calif.: Here's Life, 1982); John W. Whitehead, *The New Tyranny: The Ominous Threat of State Authority over the Church* (Ft. Lauderdale, Fla.: Coral Ridge Ministries, 1982); and Donald Wildmon, *The Home Invaders* (Wheaton, Ill.: Victor, 1985).

Denouncing humanism's alleged control over curricula and textbooks are Onalee McGraw, *Secular Humanism and the Schools: The Issue Whose Time Has Come* (Washington, D.C.: Heritage Foundation, 1976); Connaught Marshner, *Blackboard Tyranny* (New Rochelle, N.Y.: Arlington House, 1978); Morris, *Change Agents in the Schools*; Rockne M. McCarthy, James W. Skillen, and William A. Harper, *Disestablishment a Second Time: Genuine Pluralism for American Schools* (Grand Rapids, Mich.: Eerdmans, 1982); Tim LaHaye, *The Battle for the Public Schools* (Old Tappan, N.J.: Revell, 1983); Paul C. Vitz, *Censorship: Evidence of Bias in Our Children's Textbooks* (Ann Arbor, Mich.: Servant, 1986); and Daniel D. McGarry, *Public Schools Teach Religion without God and Should Not Have a Monopoly: Secularism in American Public Education and the Unconstitutionality of Its Exclusive Governmental Support* (St. Louis: White Educational Foundation, 1986).

34 Schlafly quoted in Provenzo, *Religious Fundamentalism and American Education*, 17; and Donald Critchlow, *Phyllis Schlafly and Grassroots Conservatism: A Woman's Crusade* (Princeton: Princeton University Press, 2005), 268. Aaron Louis Haberman, "Civil Rights on the Right: The Modern Christian Right and the Crusade for School Prayer, 1962–1996" (Ph.D. diss., University of South Carolina, 2006), 126–27. Mel Gabler and Norma Gabler, "Mind Control through Textbooks," *Phi Delta Kappan*, 64 (October 1982), 96; Mel Gabler and Norma Gabler, *Humanism in Textbooks: Secular Religion in the Classroom* (Longview, Tex: Educational Research Analysts, 1983); William Martin, "The Guardians Who Slumbereth Not," *Texas Monthly*, November 1982, pp. 144–50, 266–71; *Washington Post*, Friday, August 6, 1982, pp. D1, D4; Provenzo, *Religious Fundamentalism and American Education*, 32–40. LaHaye, *Battle for the Mind*; LaHaye, *Battle for the Public Schools*.

35 *Zorach* v. *Clauson*, 343 U.S. 306 (1952), 313–14; *Torcaso* v. *Watkins*, 495; *Abington* v. *Schempp* (Stewart, J., dissenting), 313.

36 *Reed* v. *Van Hoven*, 237 F.Supp. 48 (1965), 53–54; *Cornwell* v. *State Board of Education*, 314 F.Supp. 340 (1969), 342; *Alabama Civil Liberties Union* v. *Wallace*, 331 F.Supp. 966 (1971), 968–69.

37 *Jackson* v. *State of California*, 460 F.2d 282 (1972), 283; *Wright* v. *Houston Independent School District*, 366 F.Supp. 1208 (1972), 1209, 1211.

38 *Crowley* v. *Smithsonian Institution*, 462 F. Supp. 725 (1978), 726–28; *Ibid.*, 636 F.2d. 738 (1980) 741–42.

39 *Rhode Island Federation of Teachers, AFL-CIO*, v. *Norberg*, 479 F.Supp. 1364 (1979); *Ibid.*, 630 F.2d 855 (1980); Appeal of J. Fred Lipkind et al., *Rhode Island Federation of Teachers, AFL-CIO*, v. *Norberg*, 630 F.2d 850 (1980), 854–55.

40 James Moffett, *Storm in the Mountains: A Case Study of Censorship, Conflict, and Consciousness* (Carbondale: Southern Illinois University Press, 1988); John Egerton, "The Battle for the Books," *Progressive*, 39 (no. 6, 1976), 13; Martin, *With God on Our Side*, 117–43. The Gablers' views are presented sympathetically in James C. Hefley, *Are Your Textbooks Harming Your Children?* (Milford, Mich.: Mott, 1979), pp. 157–67.

41 Stephen Arons, *Compelling Belief: The Culture of American Schooling* (Amherst: University of Massachusetts Press, 1986), 3–13.

42 *Ibid.*, 31–33.

43 *Fink* v. *Board of Education of Warren County School District*, 65 Pa. Cmwlth. 320 (1982), 330–31; *Crockett* v. *Sorenson*, 568 F.Supp. 1422 (1983), 1426–30.

44 Ark.Stat.Ann. § 80–1663, *et seq.* (1981 Supp.), March 19, 1981; *McLean* v. *Arkansas Board of Education*, 529 F.Supp. 1255 (1982), 1274.

45 Concerned Women for America, petition for a writ of certiorari to the United States Court of Appeals for the Ninth Circuit, *Grove* v. *Mead School District No. 354*, 753 F. 2d 1528 (1985), June 21, 1985, 12–13; *Grove* v. *Mead School District*, 753 F2d 1528 (1985), 1534, 1528.

46 *Ibid.*, 1536.

47 *Mozert* v. *Hawkins County Public Schools*, 647 F.Supp. 1194 (1986); *Ibid.*, 827 F.2d 1058 (1987). Stephen Bates, *Battleground: One Mother's Crusade, the Religious Right, and the Struggle for Our Schools* (New York: Holt, 1993), 33–37. *New York Times*, February 28, 1986, p. A19.

48 Bates, *Battleground*, 165, 233.

49 George Wallace, stipulation for consent decree, November 7, 1985, at *Smith* v. *Board*, records of *Smith* v. *Board*, 1–2, 4; Thomas F. Parker IV to William A. Jackson, November 7, 1985, Wallace File; *Montgomery Advertiser*, January. 27, 1986, pp. A1–A2; *New York Times*, February 28, 1986, p. A19; Wilkinson, "Judge Hand's Holy War," 113.

50 *Alabama Journal*, January 8, 1986, p. 12; *Birmingham News*, January 19, 1986, p. 12A; *Montgomery Advertiser*, June 19, 1986, pp. D1–D2; *Birmingham News*, October 26, 1986, p. 2A; Steven P. Brown, *Trumping Religion: The New Christian Right, the Free Speech Clause, and the Courts* (Tuscaloosa: University of Alabama Press, 2002), 36–39; Wilkinson, "Judge Hand's Holy War," 112. *Board of Education of Westside Community Schools* v. *Mergens*, 496 U.S. 226 (1990).

51 *Birmingham News*, October 26, 1986, p. 2A; Minutes of the regular meeting of the Board of School Commissioners of Mobile County, February 12, 1986, 63; *Mobile Register*, August 30, 1997, pp. 1D, 3D.

52 *Birmingham News*, January 19, 1986, p. 12A; *New York Times*, February 28, 1986, p. A19; *Birmingham Post-Herald*, September 29, 1986, p. C3; *Birmingham News*, October 26, 1986, p. 2A; Wilkinson, "Judge Hand's Holy War," 112; Minutes of the regular meeting of the Board of School Commissioners of Mobile County, January 22, 1986, p. 49.

53 *Ibid.*; *Birmingham News*, January 19, 1986, p. 12A.

54 Minutes of the regular meeting of the Board of School Commissioners of Mobile County, Alabama, January 22, 1986, pp. 49–51; Minutes of the regular meeting of the Board of School Commissioners of Mobile County, Alabama, February 12, 1986, pp. 68–73. *Montgomery Advertiser*, January 27, 1986, pp. A1–A2; *New York Times*, February 28, 1986, p. A19. Vitz, *Censorship;* Paul C. Vitz, *Psychology as Religion: The Cult of Self-Worship* (Grand Rapids, Mich.: Eerdmans, 1977).

55 Minutes of the regular meeting of the Board of School Commissioners of Mobile County, February 12, 1986, pp. 68–73.

56 *Ibid.*, 73–75.

57 Minutes of the regular meeting of the Board of School Commissioners of Mobile County, January 22, 1986, pp. 51–52; Minutes of the regular meeting of the Board of School Commissioners of Mobile County, February 12, 1986, pp. 68–71, 76.

58 Defendants' response to defendant-intervenors' motion to intervene, January 17, 1986, at *Smith* v. *Board*, records of *Smith* v. *Board;* Defendants' amended response to defendant-intervenors' motion to intervene, February 19, 1986, at *Smith* v. *Board*, records of *Smith* v. *Board;* Minutes of the official session of the Alabama State Board of Education, Montgomery, Alabama, February 13, 1986, Gordon Persons Building (50 N. Ripley St., Montgomery, Ala.), 53;

Montgomery Advertiser, January 27, 1986, pp. A1–A2; *Montgomery Advertiser*, June 19, 1986, pp. D1–D2.

59 Minutes of the official session of the Alabama State Board of Education, February 13, 1986; *Montgomery Advertiser*, June 19, 1986, pp. D1–D2; Defendants' motion for extension of time, February 14, 1986, at *Smith* v. *Board*, records of *Smith* v. *Board;* "Prayer-in-School Advocates Try to Include Religion in Textbooks," *Birmingham News*, February 14, 1986; *New York Times*, February 28, 1986, p. A19.

60 Ishmael Jaffree to Board of School Commissioners of Mobile County, February 14, 1986, Wallace File. Howell defendants' memorandum in opposition to governor's motion to vacate and reconsider, March 7, 1986, at *Smith* v. *Board*, records of *Smith* v. *Board*, 1–2; Defendants' Board of School Commissioners of Mobile County response to defendant-intervenors' motion to intervene, February 21, 1986, at *Smith* v. *Board*, records of *Smith* v. *Board*; Minutes of the regular meeting of the Board of School Commissioners of Mobile County, February 26, 1986, p. 99.

61 Defendants' Board of School Commissioners of Mobile County response to defendant-intervenors' motion to intervene; Minutes of the regular meeting of the Board of School Commissioners of Mobile County, February 26, 1986, p. 99; Howell defendants' memorandum in opposition to governor's motion to vacate and reconsider, 2.

62 Minutes of the regular meeting of the Board of School Commissioners of Mobile County, February 26, 1986, pp. 99–103.

63 *Ibid.*, 101–03.

64 *Ibid.*, 103; *Mobile Register*, August 30, 1997, p. 3D; Wilkinson, "Judge Hand's Holy War," 113. Board of School Commissioners of Mobile County, stipulation for consent decree, February 26, 1986, *Smith* v. *Board*, 1–3.

65 *Montgomery Advertiser*, January 27, 1986, pp. A1–A2; *New York Times*, February 28, 1986, p. A19; "Tyson: Court Not Place to Set Policy," *Mobile Press*, March 7, 1986; *Mobile Register*, March 14, 1986, p. B5; "Deadline Passes in Textbook Case," *Mobile Press*, March 14, 1986; "Tyson Says Textbook Publishers Should Appear at Humanism Trial," *Mobile Press Register*, March 15, 1986; "The Humanism Suit," *Birmingham News*, March 17, 1986; Wilkinson, "Judge Hand's Holy War," 113; Minutes of the official session of the Alabama State Board of Education, March 13, 1986, p. 13.

66 *Birmingham News*, August 30, 1986, p. A2; *Birmingham Post-Herald*, September 24, 1986, p. C5.

67 Defendant-intervenors' pretrial brief, October 6, 1986, *Smith* v. *Board*.

68 *Ibid.*, 3–5.

69 *Ibid.*, 6–7.

70 *Ibid.*, 13–15.

71 Plaintiff's memorandum of law, 3, 87.

72 *Ibid.*, 98–99.

7

Religion by Any Other Name

SMITH V. BOARD OF SCHOOL COMMISSIONERS

At 9:00 a.m., on October 6, 1986, the trial got under way. From its onset, *Douglas T. Smith* v. *Board of School Commissioners of Mobile County* possessed a momentous, surreal air. Law clerks wheeled out cart after cart of elementary- and secondary-school textbooks for inspection by expert scholars, while true believers sat in the courtroom pews, leafing through well-worn copies of *Humanist Manifesto I* and *Humanist Manifesto II*, quoting passages as if confirming the devil's own handiwork. A reporter described, as "a scene out of the Dark Ages," a plaintiffs' lawyer accusing one defense witness of "yoking" herself "together with unbelievers." For the plaintiffs in particular, the events in Brevard Hand's courtroom took on a character of ultimacy. While examining a witness on the trial's second day, Bob Sherling was stopped mid-sentence by the crash of outside thunder; Sherling paused and then obediently withdrew the question. Theologians, philosophers, and historians testifying for the plaintiffs scoured home economics books for traces of secular humanism while pondering the consequences of schoolchildren's indoctrination with the teachings of an insidious, alien religion.[1]

All the while, the plaintiffs' lawyers kept their eyes on the prize – convincing Hand that if the First Amendment prohibited Alabama from establishing a religion, then it prohibited Alabama from establishing any religion at all, including the religion of secular humanism. In his opening remarks, Tom Parker reminded Hand that "the Supreme Court has read the first amendment to mean strict neutrality," that "no religion can be advanced in the public school classroom through its tenets of faith, its beliefs, its doctrines, dogma." Although this requirement had "been used heretofore to exclude [only] Judeo-Christian beliefs," the plaintiffs were now "asking that the Supreme Court position be equally applied" so "that there be no privileged religion that is beyond the touch of the constitution." The federal courts could not, in good conscience, stop midway through the disestablishment process, Parker reasoned. To dispense fair treatment, they had to extend the justices' proscription evenhandedly.[2]

Behind the plaintiffs' constitutional argument lay a more palpable objective. Parker, Sherling, and Tom Kotouc were asking Hand to protect Christianity's role in public education. To do this, the court needed to conceive of religion in functional terms. Hand needed to find that secular humanism was a religion, and not merely because secular humanists themselves had originally done so, or because the Court had done so in *Torcaso* v. *Watkins*. The reality was that if Hand applied a narrow, substantive definition to religion, then he would reinforce religious conservatives' lack of influence over the schools. Parker cautioned Hand not to be misled by secular humanism's relative newness in the religious landscape. By recognizing as religions only God-centered, conventionally organized sects, the courts were effectively awarding "protected status to newer religions which might not have the form of traditional religions," and were thereby "discriminat[ing] against the traditional religions." Christianity's slow but steady eradication from the public sphere was proceeding unarrested because neither the courts nor the surrounding culture saw secular humanism for the religion that it was.[3]

The plaintiffs' dire mission contrasted with the Alabama Board of Education's wish to preserve what it described as its straightforward, non-ideological policies. The defendants claimed only to be protecting the ability of state and local school boards to choose their own textbooks, free from interference by federal judges. Charles Coody, attorney for the Alabama board, insisted that his clients' process of textbook selection remained transparent and responsive to public feedback. Predominantly, the process was a grassroots one. "Simply because a book is on the state approved list does not mean that it will be used or ever get into the classroom," Coody reminded the court. Ultimately, it was "local people" who "decide what textbook goes in their classrooms, not the State." Moreover, "a number of counties" in Alabama retained "the legal right to choose textbooks that are not even on the State adopted list." Notwithstanding the plaintiffs' insinuation that some "monolithic unseen bureaucracy in Montgomery or in the State is controlling education," the truth was that, throughout Alabama, "education is controlled fundamentally at the local level." This, Coody suggested, was for the best. His concern was not for critical thinking or personal liberty, but for the common sensibility of locally, democratically managed public schools. Leave our schools alone, he beseeched the judge; let our teachers do their job.[4]

The defendants seemed not to grasp – and certainly did not acknowledge – the disorienting irony in the plaintiffs' case. From *Engel* through *Jaffree*, complainants had challenged school prayer not merely on grounds of direct coercion but also on grounds of indirect harm. The source of constitutional infirmity, they contended, was the marginalization suffered by children belonging to religious minority groups. These complainants had charged that majority rule, communally and statewide, had diminished the dignity and status of minorities. The *Smith* plaintiffs were leveling this same accusation at the Alabama Board of Education, which found itself waging a defense not unlike that by the New York Board of Regents in *Engel*. The defendants could only respond that exposure to troublesome material did not equal religious indoctrination because the schools had not forced the plaintiffs' children to adopt or renounce any religious values at all. No coercion had taken place; no infraction had occurred.[5]

In fact, the Supreme Court had repeatedly ruled that the Establishment Clause protected religious minorities and dissenters against the kind of systematic religious instruction, and resulting emotional distress, of which the *Smith* plaintiffs now complained. The justices had declared that, by permitting out-loud religious exercises during regular hours, schools did far more than "merely expose" students to alien or even offensive ideas. By allowing religious activities, schools marginalized and demeaned minority students. If the *Smith* plaintiffs could show that secular humanism was a religion, and that it had played a normative role in the classroom, then Hand might logically be led to find that the plaintiffs had suffered the sort of exclusion that the Establishment Clause forbade. The Court's doctrine was the basis for the plaintiffs' argument, which went largely unrefuted.

The intervenors came somewhat closer to addressing the plaintiffs' clever argument. Reiterating the case from his pretrial brief, William Bradford denied that secular humanism was a religion, that Mobile schools were promoting it, and that the Establishment Clause had been violated. Bradford correctly saw that the plaintiffs were staging *Jaffree* in reverse, with conservative Christians cast as dissidents scorned and repressed by the secularist majority. He responded by asserting the substantive definition of religion. "Secular humanism is not a religion," he told the court. "It does not have the spiritual, or supernatural, or transcendent [qualities] that the law requires of a religion," and, in reality, was "nothing more than a convenient label" that had been "attach[ed] to opinions and facts that d[id]n't comport with the religious worldview of these plaintiffs." As a non-religion, secular humanism could not be established by the state.[6]

If the plaintiffs' children felt marginalized in Mobile public schools, Bradford charged, then that was not the result of teachers or textbook authors belonging to one or another discrete religious group. The religious affiliation of educators was not the problem. The plaintiffs' children were victims of "a clash of cultures." Whereas most schoolteachers, school administrators, and textbook publishers advocated objectivity and critical thinking, the plaintiffs clung to their "biblical literalis[m]." Doggedly immersed in a premodern epistemology, the plaintiffs – and not the schools and the textbooks – rejected the neutrality required by the Supreme Court. Bradford brought the case back to the key underlying question of what constituted neutrality, and he defined neutrality as objectivity – the very objectivity that characterized his clients' worldview. This, he understood, was the intervenors' and their codefendants' burden. They needed to persuade Hand that the plaintiffs had misconstrued secular education – that it signified not an establishment of religion, but a neutral arena in which all citizens could participate as equals.[7]

ARMY OF EXPERTS

The plaintiffs called their witnesses first. Quickly it became apparent that the plaintiffs were not playing the role of the Mobile school board at the *Jaffree* trial. Nowhere to be found were witnesses asserting that the Bill of Rights did not apply to the individual states or that the advancement of religion in the classroom did not violate the Establishment Clause. None of their expert witnesses was a constitutional scholar; none focused on the Framers' original intentions or the Supreme Court's supposed misinterpretations. As fully as Ishmael Jaffree, the *Smith* plaintiffs embraced Establishment Clause doctrine from *Everson* through the present. They spent no time defending that doctrine. Rather, it remained in the background, assumed rather than stated.

The plaintiffs' witnesses called for robust, comprehensive enforcement of the First Amendment's ban against an establishment of any religion. One after another academic scholar took the stand, reporting that the social studies, U.S. history, and home economics textbooks on display in the courtroom – all approved for use in Alabama schools – were promoting secular humanism. The textbooks did this, the experts said, partly by omission. By failing to provide descriptive accounts of Christianity's and Judaism's role in America's past and present, the books taught that traditional religions were not valuable. The textbooks promoted secular humanism also, it was alleged, by inculcating anti-theistic values into readers. Emphasizing the paramount importance of human beings, the books implied God's relative unimportance. This, the plaintiffs experts would argue, created discomfort and confusion for students who had been taught at home that God's will, and not human intelligence, demanded their primary compliance. The seemingly endless parade of scholars called by the plaintiffs drove home the argument that, even in Alabama, the humanist majority had mistreated the Christians in its midst.

The plaintiffs' onslaught began with Timothy Smith, a historian of nineteenth-century U.S. religion at Johns Hopkins University and an ordained minister in the Church of the Nazarene. Smith had reviewed the fourteen U.S. history textbooks whose religious neutrality the plaintiffs were challenging. To his dismay, he discovered that none of the books devoted much attention to the religious dimension of social and political events; indeed, accounts of religion had been almost altogether left out. "The omissions so shocked me," he told Sherling, "the elimination or the absence of so much material [on] religion as an explanation for events," that he nearly could not believe what he saw. From the impact of the Puritans to the role of prophetic Christianity in the antiwar and civil rights movements, religion's historical role was effectively excised from the history textbooks used in Alabama public schools. In no meaningful sense, Smith suggested, did these textbooks account for religion's influence throughout American history.[8]

Smith's testimony enabled the plaintiffs to paint themselves as defenders of pluralism, in the tradition of the Warren Court. The textbooks' omission of religious factors in history, he averred, constituted discrimination against the many religious citizens who had contributed to American history. Such discrimination bore on any student who might conclude that his or her forbears had not contributed to America's past. This was unacceptable, Smith told the court, as all children needed and deserved to see themselves as full members of American society. Unable to find their people in the history books, Christian children became alienated from the wider community. Smith found, in these books, an implication that religion was "an outdated, outmoded [matter] which the age of modern science could safely lay aside." These books had missed a precious opportunity to foster tolerance toward religious diversity. Including religion would demonstrate to non-Christian students "the deep involvement of other peoples" in American history and make them "more tolerant citizens than before simply because they saw the religious contributions of other groups beside their own."[9]

Further to convince the court that Alabama was engaged in religious establishment, the plaintiffs called to the stand University of Virginia sociologist James Davison Hunter, author of the well-known book *Culture Wars*. Hunter laid out an elaborate analysis of secular humanism and its social function. He reported having reviewed twenty-two social studies textbooks used in Alabama elementary schools. Those books, he alleged, failed to acknowledge religion's prominent influence throughout all dimensions of American culture and society. This confirmed what Hunter already believed, that secular humanism had become the "dominant ideology of public school textbooks." Nothing less than a "secularization of public education" had taken place, he believed, the result of censorship in the classroom – a "censorship by omission or neglect of almost any reference to theistic religion in the description of American life and culture." Through such censorship, the textbooks expounded a clear message about religion. "It's a fallacy," he argued, to suppose that, "by omitting a subject, in this case religion," teachers "teach nothing about it. On the contrary, [they] teach that it is to be omitted and that it is therefore a matter of secondary importance."[10]

But did the schools, by denigrating traditional religion, actually establish an alternative religion? To answer this, Hunter explored the different ways in which sociologists defined religion. He spoke of the substantive approach, which defined religion in terms of what it was. Here, sociologists marked as "the sacred" anything their subjects held up as sacred in their lives, as "wholly other" than everything else. Hunter distinguished this from a functional approach defining religion "by what it does, by its function – its role or its consequences for individual and social existence." It was the functional approach that Hunter emphasized in his testimony. Religion, he said, provided the individual "a sense of order," a set of moral "coordinates" with which one could "know wrong from right," and gain "an explanation for the ... problem of suffering." For society, religion performed a "priestly function" that legitimated the existing order, along with a "prophetic function" that questioned the status quo or even called for its destruction. In his opinion, any comprehensive worldview that filled these several roles essentially constituted a religion.[11]

The religion permeating the textbooks that Hunter scoured was, he found, none other than secular humanism. This could be seen in how the books encouraged students to rely on their own moral judgment rather than defer to what Scripture commanded or what their parents told them. Through curricular materials such as these, secular humanists were propagating their worldview while denigrating the worldview taught to Christian children by their parents. From various manifestos written by self-declared humanists, as well as from the foundational documents of several humanist organizations, Hunter discovered a coherent worldview resting on five basic principles – five principles that he also saw reflected in the social studies books used in Alabama schools. According to his analysis, secular humanists believed "that the universe is self-existing and not created"; that the human race had evolved naturally; that knowledge should be acquired and truth should be tested rationally, through the use "of inquiry, logic, and evidence"; that morality and ethics should be discerned subjectively and situationally, not through absolute biblical standards; and that life's goal was not service to God, but "the full realization and actualization of human potentiality." Together, these five principles functioned as a religion within the subculture that embraced them. And their dissemination through textbooks indicated the advancement of a distinct religion in the public schools.[12]

ORTHODOXY

Hunter did more than argue that the social studies textbooks used in Alabama schools promoted the religion of secular humanism. Hunter helped make the plaintiffs' case that the humanistic worldview was so rigid – so assured of its universal validity – that its advancement necessarily closed off the possibility for any student to see the world from a biblical perspective without being ridiculed or silenced. The classrooms, Hunter said, were filled by "the orthodoxy of humanism." Secular humanism held so tightly to modernist ideals such as autonomy of the individual and tolerance for nearly all moral viewpoints that it could not countenance any disagreement with those ideals. The one thing it refused to tolerate was intolerance itself. The secular humanist documents examined by Hunter dismissed traditional religion as "obscurantist, unreasonable, outmoded, escapist, irrational, and unacceptable" and, on that basis, foreclosed religion's inclusion in the curriculum. For all of its supposed openness to difference, secular humanism signaled that there were "definable limits to toleration, that the world should be open to [only] a particular kind of diversity."[13]

Through Hunter's testimony, the plaintiffs looked to align themselves with the forces of multiculturalism and its precondition of exposure to different ways of seeing the world. Hunter posited that, by inculcating secular humanism, with its unyielding dogmatism and intolerance, educators obstructed the operation of America's pluralistic society. Hunter aimed to be clear. It was not his point that "public school textbooks should discuss matters from the perspective of a particular set of transcendent standards." Quite the opposite. The textbooks harmed society because they instilled in young citizens only one particular worldview – "a subjectivistic and implicitly relativistic approach to values, needs, emotions, and the nature of the individual." This worldview was disseminated "uncritically, without detachment, or without respect to cultural traditions that would strongly dissent." Based on their intolerance toward worldviews different from their own, secular humanists' "commitment to the traditions of democratic pluralism ... would seem dubious."[14]

Hunter also gave voice to the plaintiffs' contention that the dissemination of secular humanism should be understood sociologically as well as ideologically. In the United States, according to Hunter, proponents of secular humanism wielded greater social power than did Christians. Humanists' antireligious bias was amplified through their prominence in society's knowledge class, the sector that produced information and shaped public opinion and taste. The culture and values of this "new class" diverged sharply from traditional norms. Because of the strong influence of the new class over the content of public education, secular humanism found a large and susceptible audience.[15]

Hunter ran down a litany of psychological and social traits that new-class humanists supposedly exhibited: a tendency toward narcissism, a "therapeutic" mentality, an expressive individualism, a socio-political political liberalism, and a theological antinomianism or even "outright secularity." Given the prominence of these tendencies "within the highly educated sector of the upper-middle classes," it should come as no surprise, Hunter reasoned, that we find "an affinity ... between the ideological content of public education and the interests of certain cultural elites." Here, Hunter got at an essential element in the plaintiffs' complaint and in the wider political efforts of the Christian Right: the secularization of the schools was but a single front in America's culture wars, where secular humanists promote their worldview in order to establish social and political dominance. In the schools as elsewhere, one or another group's value system would always achieve preeminence. "No knowledge is value neutral; no knowledge is free of presuppositions," Hunter told the court. "All knowledge is rooted in the social structure in particular ways and reflects, even if indirectly, the particular interests of different sectors of the population. And this would hold true, as well, for the 'knowledge' passed on to children in the public schools." Hunter's testimony signaled the plaintiffs' determination, as they saw it, to level the religious playing field. If Christians were to be silenced within American culture and society, then the enemies of Christianity needed to be silenced as well.[16]

And so it continued with the plaintiffs' experts. Those who followed all described a secular humanist worldview largely shaping contemporary American culture and society. As Hunter had done, those witnesses provided a litany of characteristics allegedly comprising secular humanism. Its central-most characteristic was its hostility toward conventional religion. One witness, religious historian James Hitchcock, depicted humanism as "an explicitly anti-theistic philosophy" resting on "the exclusion of meaningful belief in God." Having scanned many of the humanist documents that Hunter also had examined, Hitchcock likewise discovered a worldview bent on eliminating all rival perspectives.[17]

Central to this antitheistic worldview, the plaintiffs' experts found, were moral relativism and subjectivism. Secular humanism, it was reported, denied that human beings could distinguish right from wrong through absolute, transcendent standards. Ethicist Richard Baer, who had given testimony at the *Jaffree* trial, now testified that secular humanists lacked the sort of firm, "authoritative moral codes" that could be verified "through revelation." Instead, they preached "that value judgments are matters of preference and taste and personal opinion" and so "cannot be known to be right or wrong, true or false." Baer's finding was confirmed by psychologist William Coulson, a former protégé and collaborator of renowned humanistic psychologist Carl Rogers. From the humanists' "foundational documents" Coulson learned that secular humanists espoused moral autonomy – that human beings could rely only on their own reason and observation to distinguish right from wrong. Hitchcock confirmed this finding. Humanists, he said, believed that human beings "are completely autonomous" and remain "perfectly free ... to discover or define meaning and value for themselves."[18]

The plaintiffs' experts assigned to secular humanism traits even more troubling than moral subjectivism and moral autonomy. They found, for instance, that the antitheistic religion lacked a tragic sensibility. Because secular humanism denied the human capacity for sinfulness, they charged, it could only gaze with sunny naïveté on even the most disturbing human impulses. This accusation was leveled by theologian Gordon Spykman, who considered secular humanism infatuated with "the apparent goodness of man and his potential" always "to do even better," to perfect himself. Hitchcock lamented that "humanism does not really recognize man as in need of salvation," nor see for humanity any moral imperative other than overcoming "whatever limits happen to be imposed upon human nature, either externally or internally."[19]

This supposed moral naïveté spoke to another trait, moral anthropocentrism. Here, the witnesses drew on Francis Schaeffer's often-cited observation that humanism worships "Man" with "no standards outside of himself," as "the measure of all things." Not only did human judgment stand alone, apart from divine rebuke; the goal of human self-realization meant nothing more than self-glorification. Coulson and Baer echoed Hitchcock's contention that secular humanism's "core notion" was "the central importance of man in the scheme of reality" and the unceasing need to maximize "man's dignity, man's self-fulfillment, man's power." For the plaintiffs' experts, this indicted secular humanism as a religion built on self-indulgence. Baer found that, for the secular humanist, "all motivation is pleasure-determined." So, too, discovered educational philosopher Kenneth Strike, who defined secular humanism as essentially hedonistic, its greatest good the pursuit of self-satisfaction. These experts found that, in secular humanism, the fulfillment of God's commands had been replaced by the fulfillment of human appetites.[20]

All of these witnesses designated this naïve, hedonist worldview a religion. Spykman characterized it by its function, which was to shape its adherents' "ultimate commitment" and determine their "life orientation." Others seconded Spykman's declaration that "humanism constitutes a religion as an alternative to, say, the Protestant, Catholic, and Jewish traditions." According to Hitchcock, it demanded "total and complete dedication from [its] adherents," purported "to teach the ultimate truth about existence," and imposed "a well-developed code of conduct or discipline." Baer argued that whenever an author expounded a humanistic morality and epistemology without explaining or justifying his position, he asked readers to make a leap of faith no different from what would be made by a true believer in God. And to "presuppose, without any argument or rational defense, a view of values" that was "consistent with secular humanist thinking" was effectively to "undermine ... much traditional Christian and Jewish thinking." To ask Christian or Jewish schoolchildren uncritically to accept secular humanism's premises was to erode those children's attachment to their parents' religion. Nor was this indoctrination any less insidious when executed by authors or teachers who considered themselves Christians. Indeed, Hitchcock alleged – echoing Rushdoony – the mainline sects were filled with individuals who called themselves Christians but thought and acted as humanists. When writers and teachers disseminated the humanist worldview, they proselytized a religion that severed students' attachments to the faith tradition bestowed on them by their families.[21]

Core tenets of the secular humanist religion allegedly permeated the textbooks used in Alabama schools. Echoing Hunter and Smith, psychology professor Paul Vitz, author of the textbook survey adopted in the plaintiffs' consent decree, found that theistic "religion was, for all practical purposes, ignored" in the books adopted by the state. These books made "almost no reference to [theistic religion's] importance in our present life, and very little reference to its significance in our history." This signaled that theistic religion was "either old fashioned or, let's say, exotic, or in some way characteristic of other peoples but not us." The "negation of God" found in Alabama textbooks, Spykman charged, was "just as real a response to His existence as the [overt] denial of His existence is."[22]

The home economics books especially, with their explicit advancement of humanist morality and epistemology, purportedly harmed Christian children by inculcating in them values that conflicted sharply with their families' belief systems. By teaching that "values are subjective," Coulson complained, the books suggested to children that they had "the right to make their own choices" without regard to their family's wishes. Indeed, according to Strike, the books encouraged children to reject "external influences, such as parents' advice [and] community values," as "inauthentic or inappropriate kinds of sources of values." Such children were at risk of becoming alienated from their own families and church communities. Their reprogramming by the state potentially caused them unbearable anguish.[23]

Although the plaintiffs' witnesses avoided explicitly constitutional arguments, they did challenge the Court's longtime assumption that a secular environment equally accommodated all students. Baer and Strike, in particular, emphasized the unfairness of the existing situation whereby secular humanists were permitted to advance their religion in the classroom while other religious groups were prohibited from doing likewise.

Secularism could not provide for neutrality, they suggested; to the contrary, the secular classroom environment created profoundly non-neutral conditions – conditions that, within "the framework of a democratic pluralistic society," generated "an intolerable condition." The detractors of Christianity were thereby awarded a "preferred status." Strike agreed. By excluding theistic viewpoints, the schools had "violate[d] the rule that ideas which are competitive with one another ought to function under the same rules" as one another.[24]

Through their witnesses, the plaintiffs put forward the crux of their complaint: that in not recognizing secular humanism as a religion, Alabama schools had failed to accommodate the religious diversity of their student body. Baer applauded the Supreme Court's occasional acknowledgment that "the first amendment had to be extended to include the atheist or the agnostic," and he called on the courts to extend that logic more fully. "As we've become a more diverse people philosophically and theologically," Baer maintained, "we have recognized that ordinary human fairness demanded that we extend the concept of religion to cover people who are not religious in that traditional [theistic] sense." Strike looked to publishers to foster religious diversity. By "develop[ing] a textbook [that] legitimated a variety of moral points of view," he told the court, educators could provide a more inclusive curriculum "without violating either the moral or religious sensibilities of individual students." As things now stood, the secularist majority of educators imposed a singular religion on all students. This, the plaintiffs claimed, harmed Christian families. The plaintiffs complained, much as Ishmael Jaffree had, that systematic religious indoctrination had deprived the religious minority of its right to pass its religious convictions on to its children.[25]

PLAYING DEFENSE

The two parties defendant – the Alabama Board of Education and the intervening public-school parents – needed to persuade Judge Hand either that the textbooks used in Alabama schools did not promote antitheistic principles or, if they did, that such principles did not comprise a religion for purposes of the Establishment Clause. The army of scholars testifying for the plaintiffs had spoken with a cohesive voice, delivering with consistency the plaintiffs' core argument. In response, each of the defendants' expert witnesses challenged one or another element in the plaintiffs' case. Yet the combined testimony of the intervenors' and board's witnesses lacked their opponents' singular thrust, remaining instead piecemeal, disparate. Fewer of the defense witnesses were academics; compared with the plaintiffs' experts, fewer demonstrated a comprehensive, long-term engagement with the theoretical issues on stage. The plaintiffs desired this trial and craved to present its issues in a way that the defendants did not. The arguments before Hand were arguments that the plaintiffs wanted the American public – and their leaders – to consider. Lacking similar motivation or sense of purpose, the defendants managed only to blunt the impact of their opponents' testimony.

The intervenors called two expert witnesses. Both wielded the potential to refute elements of the plaintiffs' case, having been tagged by them as notable promoters of secular humanism. The first was philosopher Paul Kurtz, former editor of the *Humanist* and current editor of *Free Inquiry* – the two flagship journals of the American secular humanist movement. Kurtz had drafted the movement's two most important documents of recent years, *Humanist Manifesto II* and *A Secular Humanist Declaration*. Having spent a career sketching the contours of secular humanism, Kurtz was ideally positioned to repair his movement's reputation after the beating it had received from the plaintiffs' experts.

Kurtz denied the plaintiffs' charges that secular humanism espoused hedonism and selfishness. He underlined the philosophy's ethical dimension. Rather than encouraging reliance on scriptural dictates, he pointed out, secular humanism "emphasizes rationality and reflective intelligence as the best method of solving human problems." To help bring about moral ends, "it seeks to develop moral awareness and to cultivate moral sensitivity in individuals." Kurtz denied that secular humanism advocated moral relativism or subjectivism; to the contrary, it stressed the capacity of human intelligence to discover "moral standards and moral values." Self-fulfillment was one of secular humanism's goals, but it was "only part of the creatively fulfilled or actualized life," which included compassion and commitment toward fellow human beings. In fact, self-fulfillment was a means of strengthening the individual and enabling her to care for society. Kurtz assured the court that, as a typical secular humanist, "I stand as a critic of subjective pleasure-seeking independent of social responsibility or the needs of others."[26]

Kurtz testified that the principles of secular humanism in no way comprised a religion. The philosophy's "nontheism," he insisted, should not be confused with atheism, as the movement took no position on God's existence or other supernatural matters. Nor did secular humanism possess the trappings of a religion. It had no spiritual or transcendent element, he pointed out; it touted no creed; its adherents engaged in no cultic practices and built no churches; they did not aim to foster piety in themselves or others; they did not proselytize; they embraced no doctrine or dogma; they preferred doubt to zealousness. Secular humanism's core principles remained "open to revisions or supplementation in the light of new experience and problems." Its foundational documents needed to be understood, not "as final or eternal truths," but as reflections of the zeitgeist "of modern science" – namely, that "intellectual inquiry [remain] open to modification."[27]

Kurtz rejected the plaintiffs' attempt to categorize as a religion any idea or movement that performed some of the functions of a religion. Defined functionally, he argued, religion "refers to almost everything." Libertarianism, vegetarianism, and Democratic Party politics could then be reduced to "religions." Proponents of a functional definition engaged in "a kind of Humpty Dumptyism" in which "everything is religious and nothing is not." Such frivolous reductionism obscured what secular humanism actually was: a school of thought that encouraged critical thinking about religion and all other matters of importance. Secular humanism provided an intellectual context for thinking about religion; it was not itself a religion.[28]

Also testifying to the textbooks' nonreligiosity was Verdene Ryder, a home economics teacher and the author of three home economics textbooks. Among those was *Contemporary Living*, perhaps the standard work in the field and one of the books accused by the plaintiffs of advancing secular humanism. Ryder maintained that she had no idea what secular humanism was. She reported being a lifelong member of the American Lutheran Church, attending church regularly, and helping organize church activities. Her book did not attack Christianity; "if anything," Ryder held, "it complements Christianity in building strength of families." According to its author, the book in no way contradicted the thoughts and wishes of the Christian students, parents, and teachers she knew. Throughout its years in publication, all it had earned was praise. Indeed, it was largely a product of the extensive feedback she had received at local panels, workshops, and speaking engagements, as well as from her students.[29]

Ryder advanced the subtle but important argument that books such as hers neither indoctrinated children into a secular-humanist religion nor failed to provide children with any moral instruction. Her testimony revealed the illogic in the plaintiffs' accusation that the textbooks, all at once, forced a religion-bound morality on children and deprived them of any morality at all. Neither extreme was the case. Ryder demonstrated, by reading passages, that the book did not brainwash readers; rather, it urged them to "accept some ideas and reject others in order to express [their] own beliefs." Her book recognized that students entered "the classroom with values that have been instilled in them in their home," and it respected their "ability to think and to reason," to act on their values intelligently and creatively. The critical-thinking skills fostered by her book did not erode students' respect for authority or deafen them to the needs of other people. She insisted that *Contemporary Living* did not tell its "readers that any choice students make" was "just as good as any other choice, that choice is a matter of whim or caprice." Nor did it "espouse self-gratification." To the contrary, it "emphasize[d] the individual's responsibility for making their own decisions." The book stimulated students to make not only independent decisions, Ryder told the court, but also "responsible decisions." It taught students that they had to consider others' needs as well as their own – to "accept responsibility not only for themselves but for the people that live around them, their families, their peers, their communities, and the world at large."[30]

Ryder demonstrated that, for high-school students, there was a necessary connection between critical thinking and moral development. If older children did not learn to think for themselves, she contended, then they did not fully mature into responsible moral actors. Here, Ryder helped the intervenors make their farthest-reaching claim: that pluralistic, modernistic pedagogy was not merely compatible with moral instruction but *necessary* to it. Only if high schoolers "develop[ed] effective valuing processes," she believed, could they then become "able to handle [their] own problems as they arise."[31]

At the same time, Ryder did not acknowledge the plaintiffs' fundamental assumption that Christian schoolchildren, when taught to execute judgment autonomously, became steeped in a religion foreign to their own. She felt certain that her book was simply conveying universal, commonsense instruction when it told readers "that they ha[d] the ability to make choices in life" and "to evaluate the consequences of those alternatives." For the plaintiffs, this did not constitute common sense. It was not universally valid. Ryder may have been correct that by enabling students "to work through the process of decision making," schools helped produce responsible, ethical citizens, not adherents of a secularist religion. But to its detractors, critical thinking was a faith-based pedagogy that violated their own deeply held faith.[32]

One of the witnesses for the state board of education made assumptions similar to Ryder's. Floyd Enfinger was neither a writer nor a college professor, but the pastor of a Methodist congregation. Enfinger refuted the plaintiffs' charges that the home economics textbooks in question conflicted with or disparaged Christianity. As he described it, the plaintiffs' witnesses had mischaracterized Christianity. They were mistaken in claiming that Christians were prohibited from making independent choices regarding ultimate values. To the contrary, he told the court, Christian values "would be meaningless if we did not have [the] freedom to choose those values and appropriate them" for ourselves. Enfinger also denied that the books' omission of information about religion constituted "a denial of God and the spiritual nature of man." Jesus, he believed, "did not come using the name of God or a specific formula couched in religious language to reach people." Christians were not required to talk about God or even "to believe in God," but to act morally, to respond "to human needs first" and not to the ritual requirements of any religion. Much as Ryder had, Enfinger suggested that the home economics books actually helped students act as good Christians.[33]

The defendants intended Enfinger's expert testimony to refute many of the plaintiffs' claims. He was a pastor, a Christian professional. But Enfinger's testimony did not refute the plaintiffs' characterizations of Christianity so much as forge a parallel conception. His assumptions about Christianity's requirements of its adherents were radically different from the plaintiffs'. When he averred that it was "the primary responsibility ... of the Christian faith" to enable young people to distinguish right from wrong "for themselves," he indicated a worldview not unlike the one that the plaintiffs ascribed to secular humanism, one where meaningful commitment derives from awareness that the commitment is chosen from among an array of choices. Christian thought and action, for Enfinger, properly emerged from a first-order autonomy, in which exposure to a range of ethical choices enables an actor to discern the one that is correct for her. Submitting to the strictures and requirements of being a Christian, he believed, ought to be a second-order obligation chosen from a position of first-order autonomy.[34]

For the parents represented by Kotouc, Parker, and Sherling, exposure to an array of equivalent moral viewpoints and encouragement of personal moral choice-making was anathema to the absolute morality instilled by the Christian family and community. Encouragement toward autonomy signaled harm. The harm was no less if a child freely chose the Christian faith commitment of her parents. A person who chose from such a position to live as a Christian was, as Hitchcock suggested in his testimony, a person who called himself a Christian despite really being a secular humanist. Of course, the plaintiffs ignored the troubling problem that their resistance to exposure to diverse viewpoints conflicted with the religious pluralism that they were championing. No matter. The contradiction did not impede the plaintiffs, who, notwithstanding their call for competing religions to be accommodated in the classroom, objected to the teaching of autonomous thinking. For the plaintiffs, Enfinger's Christianity was not real Christianity. For them, it failed to reckon with the alien and destructive nature of a morality based on critical thinking and personal choice.[35]

Another of the Board of Education's experts, educational psychologist Glennelle Halpin, confirmed Kurtz's testimony that secular humanism denied neither human beings' spiritual nature nor God's existence. Secular humanism, she insisted, merely emphasized an ethics based on reason. While conceding that secular humanist tenets permeated the home economics textbooks, she celebrated these as a source for building personal character. Humanistic psychology in particular, she maintained, provided public educators with effective tools for teaching children interpersonal skills and social values and instilling in them a sense of justice and compassion. Halpin distinguished between the humanist and hedonist, who were often confused with one another. The attitude of the hedonist, she explained, was "if it feels good, then do it." The hedonist cared only about himself. Nothing, Halpin insisted, could be further from the attitude of the humanist, which was "one of valuing, of caring, of being concerned, not only about the individual, but about humanity in general." The humanist, as much as any other educator, taught children to "love thy neighbor as thyself," that "it's okay to care for yourself," but not at "the exclusion of caring for other people."[36]

Only one of the board's experts, educational philosopher Charles Rudder, directly addressed humanism's status as a religion. More plainly than Kurtz, Rudder elucidated how little sense it made to define religion functionally. He began by assuming the reality and the uniqueness of the sacred, that "there is a real supernatural part of the world which is what it is, no matter what we think about it." From there he posited a sacred realm that remained distinct from all that was ordinary, different from all else that human beings knew about themselves and their world. Rudder rejected the propposition that the sacred amounted to whatever people considered sacred. The functional definition of religion on which this propposition rested was unsatisfactory in his eyes because it failed to honor God's independent, a priori reality. It confused religion with the ordinary spheres of life. "Religion – genuine religion – issues from an encounter with God, a personal, direct encounter with God," Rudder told the court. To note the great difference between God and everything else in the universe was "the proper distinction to make in identifying the difference between the secular and the religious."[37]

Having distinguished between secular and sacred, Rudder deduced that the two realms did not conflict with one another. What we knew about the secular, he insisted, had no bearing on our understanding of God's realm. Rudder considered it absurd that anyone would perceive secular knowledge as capable of threatening knowledge of God's reality. If God did not remain a realm apart, then human beings would fail to know God as God. "There has to be some contrast with what's ordinary before we recognize that extramundane, that non-ordinary dimension of experience" that "gives rise to the religious experience." Moreover, Rudder said, it behooved us to operate in the secular without saying anything at all about matters religious, to increase our chances of reaching broad agreement on worldly matters without touching on our varying understandings of the supernatural. A genuinely pluralistic education remained "within the ... confines of ordinary experience" but did not attempt to "extract from that a denial of the supernatural." Thus distinguished, the secular and sacred could "co-exist without any necessary conflict between them."[38]

With these claims, Rudder, along with the other defense experts, advocated for a method of bridging parents' and students' ideological differences that varied sharply from what the plaintiffs proposed. Secularism, for the defense, accommodated divergent religious affiliations. Secularism was the solution to a vexing problem; secularism was not the problem itself. The defense's understanding of secularism as the necessary ethos on which a neutral classroom rested did not, for the plaintiffs, begin to fathom the Christianity that structured their entire lives. The Christian values and habits that the plaintiffs wanted to instill in their children was violated by a secular ethos that guided students to make their own, contingent, flexible moral choices based on critical thinking. Because the public schools belonged to all taxpaying citizens, they argued, they were entitled to ensure that the curriculum not indoctrinate their children with secular values and habits. Judge-made law had determined that Christianity may not structure the curriculum. The only solution, then, was to make sure that secularism be likewise prohibited.

HAND'S OBJECTIVE

A seemingly clear-cut choice faced Judge Hand. As impartial arbiter, he needed to decide among the rival accounts placed before him by the plaintiffs and the defendants. Was secular humanism a religion or a neutral stance toward matters of ultimacy? Did the textbooks used in Alabama public schools undermine students' belief in God and commitment to moral decency, or did the books provide students the critical distance necessary for reaching ethical, intelligent understandings about the world? Perhaps Hand had not already answered those questions beforehand. Perhaps the judge needed to stand back and gain perspective before answering them. Or perhaps his choice had been made long before the trial's end. Perhaps what he needed was cover of some sort to provide his ruling the appearance of impartiality.

At the trial's very outset, Hand reported to the parties that he was considering bringing in his own expert witness, someone not working with either side, to help him determine as clearly as possible the actual content and meaning of secular humanism. He expressed concern that "the parties [might] not provide to this court an adequate discussion" of secular humanism's definition, that they might not answer the question, "Is it a religion and is it being taught?" At the end of the first day, in chambers, he provided a different reason for wanting a court's witness: his own need, not for more information, but for greater objectivity. Hand now worried that "the testimony that will be presented to this Court on the issue of secular humanism" was "going to be the testimony that most likely supports the position of the counsel that advances the witness." By "bringing in an expert ... on behalf of the Court," Hand informed the parties, he wished "to come to a neutral understanding." Hand gave the lawyers for all parties a list of potential experts who, he said, might help him gain an "independent view of the question." "If you have already counseled with any of them," he instructed the lawyers, then "I would like to know it." He told them that he would not "want to call [anyone] that you have discussed the matter with" and learn that the expert "would be unduly prejudiced in your side of the case." Each of the parties assured the judge that it hadn't approached any of the potential witnesses and that it had no objections to any of them being called as a court's expert on secular humanism.[39]

To find the person for the job, Hand contacted none other than James McClellan, his good friend and the source for most of his *Jaffree* opinion. This seemed like a reasonable course of action to Hand. "McClellan," he would later recall, "knew a good bit about a lot of people who had spoken out on conservative matters and on religious matters, particularly those that were dealing with secular humanism." Hand's friend urged him to contact "somebody who probably had about as much grasp of the problem that the court was facing as anybody," the philosopher and historian Russell Kirk – who, other than perhaps William F. Buckley, was the preeminent American conservative intellectual in the decades following World War II. "I wasn't looking for someone to reinforce my views," Hand insisted. "I was looking for someone who could give me an objective explanation of . . . secular humanism and the separation of church and state," a matter on which "I didn't have a view." It was disinterested information that he needed. Kirk as well as anyone, he believed, would provide such a service. Hand admitted that he already "knew something about him," having "read some of Russell Kirk's works." Although Hand discerned from them Kirk's philosophical and political opinions, he claimed not to detect a bias among those opinions. Dubious about most witnesses' objectivity, Hand felt no such reservations about Kirk, whom he considered not "doctrinaire" but "intellectually honest." From what he knew about Kirk, the philosopher-historian would sketch a broad and accurate context in which to evaluate secular humanism. With the trial already under way, Hand contacted Kirk, who agreed to come to Mobile and testify at the *Smith* trial.[40]

Among all the scholars who might have served as the court's objective lens on secularism, religion, and their interface, Kirk was a curious selection. McClellan's recommendation of him would seem to testify, if not to Kirk's bias, then at least to his right-wing orientation. More suggestive yet was a recent article by John East, Jesse Helms's Senate protégé and partner in championing legislation to eliminate federal court jurisdiction over state laws concerning school prayer and abortion. *Modern Age*, a journal founded by Kirk, had published a laudatory piece by East, in early 1984, dubbing Kirk's book *The Conservative Mind* "the definitive work among the intellectual contributions to the American conservative movement." Had Hand read the article, he would have learned of Kirk's essentially Christian conception of conservatism, as depicted by a sympathetic observer. "Being rooted in biblical love," Kirk's personal philosophy "looks beyond the self to the transcendent, enduring and permanent" and aims to bring about "the attunement of the individual to the moral order ordained by the Creator."[41]

Even if Hand had been unaware of East's essay, he would likely have known of a volume, published early in 1986, that Kirk had edited and introduced. The volume, titled *The Assault on Religion*, grew out of a 1984 National Conference on Religious Liberty, sponsored by McClellan's Center for Judicial Studies – on whose advisory board Kirk served. One of the panels at that conference considered Hand's *Jaffree* decision; another looked at Helms's and East's court-stripping bills. The book was dedicated "to Judge W. Brevard Hand: Defender of the Constitution and Religious Liberty." If Hand believed that Kirk stood neutrally on these matters, then his was an act of willful ignorance.[42]

Kirk may, as he testified at *Smith*, never have stated in writing precisely whether he considered secular humanism a religion. In fact, he had published countless books and essays that all but confirmed the testimony of the plaintiffs' experts. How Hand would not have known this, given his admitted familiarity with Kirk's work, seems incomprehensible. Kirk's 1953 magnum opus, *The Conservative Mind*, was rivaled only by Buckley's *God and Man at Yale* in its influence on a generation of conservative thinkers. Therein Kirk established the themes that would animate his entire corpus of scholarship, including that society must derive its norms from God's intentions and that social and political order must be grounded in tradition rather than abstract formulations. Subsequent works reiterated those themes. Again and again Kirk disparaged liberal morality, scientific epistemology, and modernist culture. Christianity alone, he insisted, could properly regulate government and society. Hand would have gleaned Kirk's position toward biblical morality and its properly political role if he had read *Roots of American Order* (1974), which celebrated America's "religious consecration of the civil social order" and strenuously rejected the "arid secularism" that, in recent decades, had crept into public life. Hand might also have done well to read a 1982 essay in which Kirk declared that "the foundation of our civil social order ... is the Christian religion," or his observation a year earlier that, while, "in theory, America knows no establishment of religion; in actuality, one is tempted to suggest, we experience an establishment of Holy Public Educationism and Holy Secular Bureaucracy." Kirk, it would appear, was no more enamored of secularism-as-neutrality than were the *Smith* plaintiffs.[43]

Most telling were two essays published just prior to the trial. One, Kirk's introduction to the volume dedicated to Hand, lambasted liberals' "assault on religion." Designs such as those laid out in the *Humanist Manifesto* had increasingly shaped the U.S. government, Kirk complained, resulting in the modern state's "flight from God" and concomitant suppression of public expressions of religious devotion. This tyranny extended to the public schools. There, "anti-religious fanatics" and "'separation' zealots aimed to expunge any vestige of religious observance," so "that universal ignorance of the life of spirit should prevail."

What remained was "schooling deprived of religious insights," the most "wretched education" imaginable.[44]

Kirk expanded on the above allegations in a paper given in April 1986 and published that August – more than a month before the *Smith* trial commenced. A symposium on "Content, Character, and Choice in Schooling," sponsored by Paul Weyrich's Free Congress Foundation, featured, along with Kirk's paper, presentations by *Smith* plaintiffs' witnesses Baer and Vitz. Kirk's talk on "Traditions of Thought and the Core Curriculum" previewed his *Smith* trial testimony. Over recent decades, he asserted, American public education had ceased to fulfill its traditional functions of fostering students' virtue and obligation to community and nation. These traditional functions had been replaced by the positivism, pragmatism, and instrumentalism of the humanists, who taught students not to treasure the "contract of eternal society" but to worship each new urge and insight and adjust to society's basest, most destructive tendencies. Worse yet, for Kirk, was the schools' emphasis on "values ... as a substitute for the religious assumptions about human existence that formerly were taken for granted in schools. A 'value,' as educationists employ that unfortunate word, is a personal preference, gratifying perhaps to the person who holds it, but of no binding moral effect upon others." No longer, Kirk lamented, did teachers teach "the dogma that human beings have a proclivity toward the sinful." No longer did students learn of the "transcendent order governing the universe" or "that man is made for eternity."[45]

On October 15, 1986 – day seven of a twelve-day trial – Kirk took the stand in *Smith* v. *Board.* His brief testimony reiterated much of what the plaintiffs' witnesses had claimed. Like them, he conceived of religion in functional terms. To prepare for trial, Kirk reported, he had researched religion's definition. His investigation had revealed that "a religion is a body of belief and practice which has some view of the cosmos" and of "the place of humankind in the cosmos, which posits a moral system, which has a body of doctrine or dogmata, which proselytizes with zeal, and which strongly criticizes or denounces rival credence." Belief "in a transcendent order or in a divine power," he learned, was not a necessary element. Kirk then consulted a number of works that he considered credible, including his own, to inform his analysis of secular humanism. "Secular humanism is a creed or world view which holds that [human beings] have no reason to believe in a creator," he told the court. Secular humanism posits "that the world is self-existing, that there is no transcendent power at work in the world," and "that we should not turn to traditional religion for wisdom." Instead, it taught that human beings needed to "develop a new ethics and a new method of moral order founded upon the teachings of modern natural and physical sciences." Kirk concluded, accordingly, that "secular humanism" fell "within the limits of this definition of religion."[46]

Kirk pointed, as had the plaintiffs' witnesses, to a problem extending beyond the textbooks used in Alabama schools. Brought in as an expert on secular humanism, Kirk had not been asked to examine the specific books in question. He did aver, on the basis of his experience as a textbook editor, that the textbooks used in American public schools reflected only "views which might be labeled those of secular humanism." Kirk went further, confirming one of the plaintiffs' boldest, if most implicit, claims: that the religious bias in those textbooks reflected a long-established intellectual strain, sprung from the Renaissance and Enlightenment, that disdained Christianity and wished to see it obliterated. This anti-Christian impulse, Kirk told, rejected the belief, long held by most prominent historians, that civilization depends on religion. The newer view, which virtually controlled the American education industry, originated with the first popular history of the world, François Voltaire's *Universal History*, which contained only a single reference to Christianity. Kirk considered Voltaire's immense intellectual influence the primary cause of religion's neglect and mistreatment by present-day educators. Indeed, Kirk maintained, we "may say that the attitude now called secular humanism begins pretty much in the French Enlightenment and most conspicuously of all with François Voltaire." That attitude had been passed on through American philosopher John Dewey, who aimed to build a society guided "not by old beliefs but by new ethics derived from modern scientific doctrine," a society regulated by "a religion quite different than any religion in the past, a religion that would have cast off transcendent properties or attributes."[47]

If Hand were looking to justify an audacious ruling with an air of "neutrality," then he had found his cover. Kirk's testimony allowed Hand, if he wished, to adopt the findings of a renowned, supposedly disinterested witness. If this was the judge's intention all along, then the court's expert did not disappoint. Kirk punctuated the thrust of the plaintiffs' case by giving it the one quality it could not give itself: the appearance of objectivity. Hand had recruited Kirk, persuaded him to testify, and stamped his testimony as nonpartisan. Whether or not Hand intended *Smith* to proceed exactly as it did, he searched for and found the best imaginable final ingredient for cementing the plaintiffs' case.

CIVIL-LIBERTARIAN

On March 4, 1987, Judge Hand handed down his ruling in *Smith* v. *Board of School Commissioners*. Hand found in favor of the plaintiffs. More specifically, he entered judgments for the two plaintiff classes: all parents and all teachers of Alabama public school students who "adhere by belief and practice to a theistic religion." Hand entered judgments against the defendants – the Mobile school board, the state board of education, and the state superintendent of schools. Those defendants, he declared, were "hereby permanently restrained and enjoined from using any of" the five home economics textbooks, nine U.S. history textbooks, and twenty-two social studies textbooks examined during the trial. Each of the banned books, in Hand's estimation, had advanced the religion of secular humanism, in violation of the Establishment Clause of the First Amendment to the U.S. Constitution. "With these books," he wrote, "the State of Alabama has overstepped its mark." It was now being forced to "withdraw" those books, in order "to perform its proper nonreligious function."[48]

Hand sought to justify his realignment of the *Jaffree* parties and resurrection of the trial. He recalled the caveat in his *Jaffree* ruling that, "in the event the appellate courts disagreed with this conclusion" that he had no jurisdiction over state and local religious practices, he "reserved the right to again look at the record and consider the positions raised by" the original intervenors. The appellate courts did indeed disagree with his conclusion that he lacked jurisdiction. The Supreme Court's order that he enforce the First Amendment to the U.S. Constitution prompted him to resolve those issues that he had earlier deemed outstanding. "Having reserved jurisdiction for further rulings not inconsistent with opinions already reached" in any of the *Jaffree* rulings, Hand acted on that jurisdiction by "reconsolidat[ing] the cases and realign[ing] the defendant-intervenors, Smith and others, as parties plaintiff in light of the relief they had requested." Because the original intervenors had been afforded no chance to win the relief they sought, adjudication of their claims remained appropriate and necessary, Hand opined. He was acting practically in allowing them to reissue their complaint through the existing case rather than bifurcating the case and forcing them to begin the entire process over. If the original intervenors were to file a new complaint, he pointed out, then "jurisdiction would appropriately have lodged to the same extent that it lodged originally in the case filed by Jaffree." His decision, he held, was logical, prudent, and fair.[49]

In formulating his *Smith* opinion, Hand began with determining, within the parameters set by the Court, the definition of religion. Doing so was complicated by the ambiguity of the Court's church-state rulings, which, he noted, "never stated an absolute definition of religion under the first amendment." In case law touching on public education, the boundaries of religion remained especially murky. Amid the uncertainty of the Court's rulings, he detected one overriding pattern: a broadening of the definition to include nontheistic values and orientation. Whereas the Court had, throughout most of its history, thought about religion in traditional terms, based on worship of God, by the 1970s it had adopted "an individualistic and subjective view of religion." For examples of the latter, Hand turned to the conscientious objector cases, *Seeger* and *Welsh*, in which the Court explicitly stated that religion included more than just theistic belief. Although both of those rulings focused primarily on a statute, the U.S. Selective Service Act, each ruling contained a concurring opinion that extended the Court's finding to the Constitution, thereby providing precedent for defining religion broadly. Hand seized upon this precedent and made it the basis for his *Smith* ruling.[50]

Hand maintained that other relevant cases, including *Torcaso, Sherbert* v. *Verner*, and *Wisconsin* v. *Yoder*, provided only vague guidelines for defining religion, So, too, he argued, did the string of Establishment Clause rulings associated with the three-pronged test for establishment – that a law or practice must have a secular purpose, have a neutral primary effect that neither advanced nor inhibited religion, and avoid excessively entangling government with religion. Notwithstanding the absence of a bright line with which to ascertain constitutional violations, these several opinions yielded four general principles, Hand wrote. The first was that "the Constitution protects every religious belief without regard to its theological foundation." The religion clauses did not, and could not, discriminate between religions; they could not designate some religions as conceptually legitimate and others as illegitimate. Second, the American people's present-day understandings of what they considered "religious" needed to guide the courts. If some citizens' conscience or moral sense was rooted in nontheistic sources, then those sources counted as religions. Third, according to Hand, "the government cannot hinder or prohibit the growth of new beliefs by its definition of religion"; that is, no statute or public policy may draw bounds of acceptability and stamp illegitimacy onto religions falling outside those bounds. Finally, the government reserved the right to limit religious freedom for the sake of carrying out its essential functions. The Court's expansive definition of religion could be circumscribed whenever government had compelling reason to do so.[51]

Having defined religion broadly, Hand wrapped his ruling in the rhetoric of civil-libertarianism, much in the manner that the plaintiffs had presented their arguments. "Religion must therefore be defined, for first amendment purposes," he declared, "in a way that protects the people's right to define their religious beliefs." Utilizing the Court's recent proscription against discrimination based on the religious content of speech or belief, Hand liberally expanded the field, recognizing a wider array of legitimate religions than the Court generally had. Because "any content-based decision must inevitably result in showing favoritism to some religions and disapproval of others," thereby thwarting "the purpose of the first amendment," he would instead "look to factors common to all religious movements to decide how to distinguish those ideologies worthy of the protection of the religion clauses."[52]

Looking to resolve the Court's ambiguity, Hand determined that "any definition of religion must not be limited ... to traditional religions, but must encompass systems of belief that are equivalent to them for the believer." The functional definition of religion put forward by several of the plaintiffs' witnesses – and, of course, by Kirk, the court's expert – became the judge's definition. "Religion need not posit belief in a deity, or belief in supernatural existence," he wrote. "Whenever [a] belief system deals with fundamental questions of [the] nature of reality and man's relationship to reality, it deals with essentially religious questions." To ascertain whether or not a philosophy was religious in nature, Hand would gauge the "sincerity of [an] adherent's claims, though not [the] validity of [his] ideas." A set of ideas would constitute a religion for Hand if it possessed the "social characteristics of [a] movement" and conformed to a "theory of human relationship." A religion operated wherever a movement or worldview functioned as a religion.[53]

Secular humanism satisfied Hand's conception of a religion because, he found, it performed four functions typical of a religion. By denying God's existence, secular humanism "makes a statement about supernatural existence a central pillar of its logic"; by describing morality as a human product, it "defines the nature of man"; by emphasizing human self-actualization, it "sets forth a goal or purpose for individual and collective human existence"; and, by relying on empirical and rational knowledge, it "defines the nature of the universe and thereby delimits its purpose." Hand saw, in secular humanism's various documents, publications, and manifestos, further "evidence that this belief system is similar to" that embraced by "groups traditionally afforded protection by the first amendment religion clauses." Neglecting to consider carefully the arguments made by defense witnesses such as Rudder and Ryder, he adopted – wholly and uncritically – the plaintiffs' position. Hand characterized secular humanism as "a belief system" that "erects a moral code" determined by "humans and the[ir] social relationship." Antitheistic, it was a religion nonetheless. From testimony provided exclusively by its opponents, Hand identified and analyzed a religion that few of its supposed adherents would claim as their own.[54]

In finding that secular humanism was a religion, Hand turned to an argument advanced in the plaintiffs' October 1985 memorandum of law, and in the trial testimony of Baer, their witness. Secular humanism's status as a religion, Hand reasoned, derived from, as much as anything else, its automatic assumption that its methods for accessing truth were valid. Notwithstanding their pretense to objectivity, secular humanists made as big a leap of faith as did the person who believed that Scripture revealed perfect truth. Hand rejected the argument of defense witness Kurtz that secular humanism represented a scientific attitude and method rather than a religion. Humanism was a religion, Hand wrote, because it posited without proof that truth can be ascertained only by rational-empirical means, and that moral behavior requires personal, reason-based judgment. The validity of these automatic assumptions themselves could not be demonstrated scientifically. According to Hand, "a statement that there is no transcendent or supernatural reality is a *religious* statement" because it assumed that only what is observable is real. In fact, he said, it made no sense at all for humanists to point to the nondemonstrability of the existence of the supernatural, he asserted, "because inquiry into the fundamental nature of man and reality itself may not be confined solely within the sphere of physical, tangible, observable science." Lack of scientific evidence did not conclusively indicate nonexistence, and to assume otherwise was to evince religious faith in the scientific method. How could humanists reasonably emphasize the nondemonstrability of the supernatural when their own fundamental assumptions were no more demonstrable? Moral subjectivism and skepticism were no more self-evidently valid than were the moral premises of Christian fundamentalism, Hand affirmed. Each required faith in a method of ascertaining truth. Each, as much as the other, was a religion.[55]

ESTABLISH NO RELIGION

Hand next addressed whether the textbooks approved for use in Alabama classrooms promoted secular humanism. To assess the history and social studies textbooks, Hand turned to reports provided to the court by Hunter, Smith, and Vitz – plaintiffs' witnesses all. Each of these reports had concluded that the books under examination demonstrated an indisputable pattern of downplaying or, more often, ignoring religion's role in American culture, society, politics, and law. The findings in those reports became the findings of the judge. So, too, did the conclusions reached at trial by Baer, Strike, Coulson, and Spykman regarding the home economics textbooks. Hand offered no excuse, no pretense, in straightforwardly adopting the plaintiffs' analysis of the books.[56]

As the plaintiffs' experts had found, so did Hand find that the books were permeated by a systematic, if implicit, message that students ought simply to accept and employ relativism and subjectivism as the only valid bases for moral judgment. Like the plaintiffs' experts, Hand determined that the home economics textbooks presented individual moral autonomy as a universally valid stance, when its validity, in fact, rested on faith. He observed that "the books require the student to accept that the validity of a moral choice is only to be decided by the student." This unquestioning advancement of such a "highly relativistic and individualistic approach," according to Hand, "constitutes the promotion of a fundamental faith claim opposed to other religious faiths.... Such a relativistic claim can only be made on the basis of a faith assumption." In his estimation, the textbooks typified secular humanist publications in multiple ways. The books took for granted "that man has no supernatural attributes or component, that there are only temporary and physical consequences for man's actions, and that these results, alone, determine the morality of an action." Not only did the books promote secular humanism, Hand maintained; they contradicted theism's core premise "that certain actions are in and of themselves immoral, *whatever the consequences.*"[57]

Did the ubiquity of secular humanism in the books constitute an establishment of religion? Hand had ducked that question in his *Jaffree* decision, contending that he lacked the jurisdiction to apply the Establishment Clause to an individual state. The Eleventh Circuit Court of Appeals and Supreme Court disagreed and ordered him to prohibit the state of Alabama from promoting religion. Now, having set in motion a trial where a different sort of religious promotion was alleged, Hand again confronted the same question. It remained to him to ascertain whether

Alabama public schools had established a religion, in contravention of the First Amendment as interpreted by the nation's highest tribunal. Was "this religious belief system of Humanism," he inquired, "involved in a constitutional controversy before this Court"?[58]

Hand would answer the question on his terms. He acknowledged the high constitutional hurdle to be cleared – he needed to demonstrate more than the "mere coincidence of ideas with religious tenets" within the textbooks. Inevitably, books would contain passages consistent with one religion or another. "Rather," he wrote, an establishment violation required him to show the "systematic, whether explicit or implicit, promotion of a belief system as a whole." The hurdle, he found, had been cleared. "The State of Alabama," he wrote, "has on its state textbook list certain volumes," currently "used by school systems in this state, which engage in such promotion." The home economics books especially proselytized the secular humanistic religion, in violation of the Establishment Clause, and forced his intervention. By "teaching that moral choices are purely personal and can only be based on some autonomous, as yet undiscovered and unfulfilled, inner self," Alabama had advanced "a sweeping fundamental belief that must not be promoted by the public schools." Having established a religion where none was permitted, Alabama had violated the U.S. Constitution.[59]

Whereas the home economics textbooks directly proselytized secular humanism, the history and social studies books had, according to Hand, advanced the religion in less direct though equally onerous terms. By failing to convey religion's prominent role in American life past and present, the state's history and social studies textbooks infringed on students' constitutional "right not to be prevented from learning material" simply "for religious reasons," outside of a compelling governmental interest. Hand utilized the creative argument, made by plaintiffs' expert Smith, that a child who didn't see his own subculture and way of living reflected positively in the textbooks would conclude that his subculture and way of life were not valuable. Such a child would feel marginalized, as the member of any neglected or disliked minority group would. By excluding any description of religion's historical role, the books effectively denied the existence of religious belief. And "some religious beliefs are so fundamental" to their adherents, Hand insisted, that "the act of denying them will completely undermine that religion." Hand went further, asserting that any "denial of *that* belief will result in the affirmance of a contrary belief and result in the establishment of an opposing religion." For the judge, the textbooks did more than injure theists. By failing adequately to account for theistic religion, the books actually established the humanistic religion, to the consternation of the non-humanist minority.[60]

Hand emphasized, beyond all else, the civil libertarian character of his ruling. He denied that the plaintiffs had used the schools to impose their own worldview on the residents of Alabama. The *Smith* case, he maintained, did not "represent an attempt of narrow-minded or fanatical proreligionists to force a public school system to teach only those opinions and facts they find digestible," nor was the case "an attempt by anyone to censor materials deemed undesirable, improper or immoral." The *Smith* plaintiffs had sought "objective education, not partisan indoctrination." It was not they who wished to proselytize. The plaintiffs wanted religious neutrality in the classroom. They desired only that their children might be spared the suffering that came with prejudice and marginalization. At bottom, "what this case *is* about," Hand wrote, was the "improper promotion of certain religious beliefs, thus violating the constitutional prohibitions against the establishment of religion, applicable to the states through the Fourteenth Amendment." Enforcing the Establishment Clause against an individual state was his charge. He did not seek out that charge, but he had incurred it nonetheless. And he would execute his responsibility according to his reading of the case law.[61]

Hand relished the opportunity to apply the Court's mandate toward an end that the liberal justices would surely find improper. As if to throw *Jaffree* back at the Court, he would enforce the Establishment Clause against the state of Alabama in order to constrain the very non-Christians who had historically benefited through the Bill of Rights' application to the states. "It is this Court's solemn duty and obligation under the first and fourteenth amendments as interpreted by the Supreme Court in *Jaffree* to protect the rights of these plaintiffs," Hand reminded his readers. He would see to it that all Alabama schoolchildren enjoyed an education "unimpaired by an officially sponsored version of history that ignores the facts" about religion. The Court had forced him to require Alabama to conform to notions of religious neutrality generated by liberals. Well, he would impose religious neutrality on the state, but the liberals might not like what they saw. If the state was permitted to establish no religion, then he would see to it that it established no religion at all.[62]

Notes

1 Francis Wilkinson, "Judge Hand's Holy War," *American Lawyer*, 9 (May 1987), 113; *Mobile Press Register*, Sunday, October 19, 1986, p. A11; Ken Englade, "The *Gospel* v. *Secular Humanism*," *Southern Magazine*, May 1987, p. 39; Joseph L. Conn, "Inquisition in Alabama: Federal Court Lends a Hand to Religious Right's 'Secular Humanism' Crusade," *Church & State*, 40 (April 1987), 79.

2 Transcript, *Douglas T. Smith et al.* v. *Board of School Commissioners of Mobile County et al.*, Civil case no. 82–0554–H, box no. 2, accession no. 021–93–0423, location no. C0681974 SAN (Federal Records Center), October 6, 1986, p. 29.

3 *Ibid.*, 37–39. *Torcaso* v. *Watkins*, 367 U.S. 488 (1961).

4 Transcript, *Smith* v. *Board*, 40–44.

5 Defendants' proposed findings of fact and conclusions of law, *Smith* v. *Board*, December 5, 1986, pp. 38–40.

6 Transcript, *Smith* v. *Board*, 44–45.

7 *Ibid.*, 44–50.

8 *Ibid.*, 52–57. Smith's major work was Timothy L. Smith, *Revivalism and Social Reform: American Protestantism on the Eve of the Civil War* (New York: Harper & Row, 1965).

9 Transcript, *Smith* v. *Board*, 98–108, 119–20.

10 James Davison Hunter, *Culture Wars: The Struggle to Define America* (New York: BasicBooks, 1991). Transcript, *Smith* v. *Board*, 246, 299–301. At the time of the *Smith* trial, Hunter had published several works that informed his testimony. These included James Davison Hunter, "The New Class and the Young Evangelicals," *Review of Religious Research*, 22 (December 1980), 155–69; James Davison Hunter, "The Liberal Reaction to the New Christian Right," in *New Christian Right*, ed. by Robert C. Liebman and Robert Wuthnow (New York: Aldine, 1983), 150–63; and James Davison Hunter, *American Evangelicalism: Conservative Religion and the Quandary of Modernity* (New Brunswick: Rutgers University Press, 1983), 103–11.

11 Transcript, *Smith* v. *Board*, 246, 249–50, 299–301.

12 *Ibid.*, 262–67, 279–88.

13 *Ibid.*, 269–71.

14 *Ibid.*, 269–71, 301–02.

15 *Ibid.*, 307. The idea of a "new class" is examined in Andrew Hartman, *A War for the Soul of America: A History of the Culture Wars* (Chicago: University of Chicago Press, 2015), 50–52; Daniel T. Rodgers, *Age of Fracture* (Cambridge, Mass.: Belknap, 2011), 82–93; and Christopher Lasch, *The True and Only Heaven: Progress and Its Critics* (New York: Norton, 1991), 509–22. See also the penetrating essays in B. Bruce Briggs, ed., The New Class? (New York: McGraw Hill, 1979).

16 Transcript, *Smith* v. *Board.*, 307, 310–14. Jonathan Zimmerman, *Whose America? Culture Wars in the Public Schools* (Cambridge, Mass.: Harvard University Press, 2002). On the alleged narcissism of cultural elites, see Daniel

Bell, *The Cultural Contradictions of Capitalism* (New York: BasicBooks, 1976); and Christopher Lasch, *The Culture of Narcissism: American Life in an Age of Diminishing Expectations* (New York: Norton, 1978). On their therapeutic mentality, see Philip Rieff, *The Triumph of the Therapeutic: Uses of Faith after Freud* (New York: Harper & Row, 1966). On their expressive individualism, see Robert N. Bellah et al., *Habits of the Heart: Individualism and Commitment in American Life* (New York: Harper & Row, 1985). On their theological antinomianism, see Bell, *Cultural Contradictions of Capitalism.*

17 Transcript, *Smith* v. *Board*, 740–41, 745, 761–63. Hitchcock's published works were among those that the plaintiffs consulted in preparing their case. James Hitchcock, *What Is Secular Humanism? How Humanism Became Secular and How It Is Changing Our World* (Ann Arbor, Mich.: Servant, 1982), 61–79, 99–151; James Hitchcock, "Disentangling the Secular Humanism Debate," in *Whose Values? The Battle for Morality in Pluralistic America*, ed. by Carl Horn (Ann Arbor, Mich.: Servant, 1985), 21–36. Long prior to *Smith*, Coulson had repudiated his former humanistic orientation. Transcript, *Smith* v. *Board*, 875–90, 500, 509–10. See also William R. Coulson, *Groups, Gimmicks, and Instant Gurus: An Examination of Encounter Groups and Their Distortions* (New York: Harper and Row, 1972).

18 Transcript, *Smith* v. *Board*, 814, 825. At the time of the trial, Baer had published several pieces related to the topic of his testimony, including Richard A. Baer Jr., "Values Clarification as Indoctrination," *Educational Forum*, 41 (January 1977), 155–65; Richard A. Baer Jr., "Teaching Values in the Schools," *American Education*, 18 (November 1982), 11–17; Richard A. Baer Jr., "Fighting the Wrong Battle in Public School Censorship Disputes," *Social Education*, 50 (March 1986), 164–65; and Richard A. Baer Jr., "Character Education and Public Schools: The Question of Context," in *Content, Character, and Choice in Schooling: Public Policy and Research Implications*, ed. by Onalee McGraw (Washington, D.C.: National Council on Educational Research, 1986), 73–83.

19 Transcript, *Smith* v. *Board*, 765, 1158. Spykman contributed to an important Christian Right critique of secularism-as-neutrality. Rockne McCarthy et al., *Society, State, and Schools: A Case for Structural and Confessional Pluralism* (Grand Rapids, Mich.: Eerdmans, 1981).

20 Francis A. Schaeffer, *A Christian Manifesto* (Wheaton, Ill.: Crossway, 1981), 24. Transcript, *Smith* v. *Board*, 498, 745, 814, 823, 957–59. At the time of *Smith*, Strike had written several relevant works, including Kenneth A. Strike, "Freedom, Autonomy, and Teaching," *Educational Theory*, 22 (Summer 1972), 262–77; Kenneth A. Strike, *Educational Policy and the Just Society* (Urbana: University of Illinois Press, 1982); and Kenneth A. Strike, *Liberty and Learning* (New York: St. Martin's, 1982).

21 Transcript, *Smith* v. *Board*, 747–48, 767–68, 822–25, 1160. Rousas John Rushdoony, "The State as an Establishment of Religion," in *Freedom and Education: Pierce v. Society of Sisters Reconsidered*, ed. by Donald P. Kommers and Michael J. Wahoske (Notre Dame, Ind.: Center for Civil Rights, 1978), 40–41.

22 Transcript, *Smith* v. *Board*, 1048–54, 1068, 1073, 1163. Vitz published his findings in Paul C. Vitz, *Censorship: Evidence of Bias in Our Children's Textbooks* (Ann Arbor, Mich.: Servant, 1986). See also Paul C. Vitz, "Ideological Biases in Today's Theories of Moral Education," in *Whose Values? The Battle for Morality in Pluralistic America*, ed. by Carl Horn (Ann Arbor, Mich.: Servant, 1985), 113–38.

23 Transcript, *Smith* v. *Board*, 518, 523, 949–50, 957–59.

24 *Ibid.*, 811, 986.

25 *Ibid.*, 809–10, 818–19, 967–68, 987. For an extended version of this argument, see Stephen Arons, *Compelling Belief: The Culture of American Schooling* (Amherst: University of Massachusetts Press, 1986).

26 Transcript, *Smith* v. *Board*, 1680–1719. "Humanist Manifesto II," in *Humanist Manifestos I and II*, ed. by Paul Kurtz (Amherst, N.Y.: Prometheus, 1973), 13–31; Paul Kurtz, *A Secular Humanist Declaration* (Amherst, N.Y.: Prometheus, 1980). For a representative sampling of essays written over Kurtz's career, see Paul Kurtz, *In Defense of Secular Humanism* (Amherst, N.Y.: Prometheus, 1983).

27 Transcript, *Smith* v. *Board*, 1688–90, 1706, 1710, 1721–23.

28 *Ibid.*, 1721–23.

29 *Ibid.*, 2306–2439. Verdene Ryder, *Contemporary Living* (South Holland, Ill.: Goodheart-Willcox, 1985).

30 Transcript, *Smith* v. *Board*, 2306–2439.

31 *Ibid.*, 2324.

32 *Ibid.*, 2319–25.

33 *Ibid.*, 2450, 2456–59.

34 Emily R. Gill, *Becoming Free: Autonomy and Diversity in the Liberal Polity* (Lawrence: University of Kansas Press, 2001), 20–22, 28, 140–42. Ideas similar to Enfinger's inform Amy Guttmann, *Democratic Education* (Princeton: Princeton University Press, 1999).

35 Nomi Maya Stolzenberg, "'He Drew a Circle That Shut Me Out': Assimilation, Indoctrination, and the Paradox of a Liberal Education," *Harvard Law Review*, 106 (1993), 581–667.

36 Transcript, *Smith* v. *Board*, 1953–54, 1959–61.

37 *Ibid.*, 2120–21.

38 *Ibid.*, 2121–23.

39 *Ibid.*, 22, 196–97, 200–201; W. Brevard Hand interview by Robert Daniel Rubin, April 12, 2000, Mobile, Ala., 20.

40 Hand interview, April 12, 2000, p. 20; W. Brevard Hand interview by Robert Daniel Rubin, October 10, 2002, Mobile, Ala., 1–3. Godfrey Hodgson, *The World Turned Right Side Up: A History of the Conservative Ascendancy in America* (Boston: Houghton Mifflin, 1996), 40–43; George H. Nash, *The Conservative Intellectual Movement in America since 1945* (Wilmington: ISI, 1996), 61–73. Transcript, *Smith* v. *Board*, 1151.

41 John P. East, "Russell Kirk as a Political Theorist," *Modern Age*, 28 (Winter 1984), 33, 44.

42 Russell Kirk, ed., *The Assault on Religion: Commentaries on the Decline of Religious Liberty* (Lanham, Md.: University Press of America, 1986), v.

43 Russell Kirk, *The Conservative Mind: From Burke to Eliot* (1953; Washington, D.C.: Regnery, 1995); William F. Buckley, *God and Man at Yale: The Superstitions of Academic Freedom* (Chicago: Regnery, 1951); Russell Kirk, *The Roots of American Order* (La Salle, Ill.: Open Court, 1974), 439. See also Russell Kirk, *Enemies of the Permanent Things: Observations of Abnormality in Literature and Politics* (New Rochelle, N.Y.: Arlington House, 1969). Russell Kirk, "The Living Edmund Burke," *Modern Age*, 26 (Summer–Fall 1982), 324; Russell Kirk, "Shelton College and State Licensing of Religious Schools: An Educator's View of the Interface between the Establishment and Free Exercise Clauses," *Law and Contemporary Problems*, 44 (Winter 1981), 184.

44 Russell Kirk, "Introduction," in *Assault on Religion*, 4–6.

45 Russell Kirk, "Traditions of Thought and the Core Curriculum," in *Content, Character, and Choice in Schooling: Public Policy and Research Implications*, ed. by Onalee McGraw (Washington, D.C.: National Council on Educational Research, 1986), 13–27.

46 Transcript, *Smith* v. *Board*, October 15, 1986, pp. 1348, 1358–59, 1371–72.

47 *Ibid.*, 1359–75. A similar take on modern intellectual history is advanced throughout Francis A. Schaeffer, *How Should We Then Live: The Rise and Decline of Western Thought and Culture* (Wheaton, Ill: Crossway, 1976).

48 *Smith* v. *Board of School Commissioners of Mobile County*, 655 F.Supp 939 (1987), 988.

49 *Ibid.*, 943–44, 974.

50 *Ibid.*, 975, 977. *United States* v. *Seeger*, 380 U.S. 163 (1965); *Welsh* v. *United States*, 398 U.S. 333 (1970).

51 *Smith* v. *Board of School Commissioners*, 975–77. *Torcaso* v. *Watkins; Sherbert* v. *Verner*, 374 U.S. 398 (1963); *Wisconsin* v. *Yoder*, 406 U.S. 205 (1972); *Lemon* v. *Kurtzman*, 403 U.S. 602 (1971).

52 *Smith* v. *Board*, 978–79. *Widmar* v. *Vincent* 454 U.S. 263 (1981); *Lynch* v. *Donnelly*, 465 U.S. 668 (1984).

53 *Smith* v. *Board*, 978.

54 *Ibid.*, 980–81.

55 *Ibid.*, 982, emphasis in original; Plaintiff's memorandum of law, October 10, 1985, at *Smith* v. *Board*, 49; Transcript, *Smith* v. *Board*, 822–25.

56 *Smith* v. *Board*, 983.

57 *Ibid.*, 986–87, emphasis in original.

58 *Ibid.*, 983.

59 *Ibid.*, 983, 988.

60 *Ibid.*, 984, 987, citing *Epperson* v. *Arkansas*, 393 U.S. 97 (1968).

61 *Smith* v. *Board*, 974–75, emphasis in original.

62 *Ibid.*, 985.

Conclusion

The Constitution and the People

CRYING IN THE WILDERNESS

Hand surprised no one with his *Smith* ruling. He did set the media ablaze, firing what Warren Nord labeled "the loudest salvo in the war of religion versus secular humanism." Liberals were predictably dismayed and disgusted; many conservatives praised the decision but doubted its chances of holding up on appeal. Hand rested assured that he had acted with consistency and integrity and had rendered the best possible decision, given what he considered the Court's absurd religion clause doctrine. Still, he viewed as less than ideal his ordered removal of textbooks from Alabama classrooms. He had never believed that it was his place to tell the state and local school boards how to manage their business, and he hoped that his order would show the public just how unwieldy and unfair it was to give a federal judge ultimate authority over the curricula of the public schools.[1]

Few people recognized the method in Hand's madness. Alabamians, by and large, failed to see the ruling as a defense of ordinary citizens' right to run their own schools. To the contrary, most felt burdened by his mandate that the schools collect up all of the offending textbooks and remove them from classroom use. Newspapers throughout the state, which typically assumed a conservative editorial stance, portrayed the plaintiffs as religious fanatics looking to mold school policy. For his part, Hand was depicted as a censor and a book burner. Schoolteachers resented him for usurping their authority and disregarding their judgment. Neither he nor the Christian conservatives whose interests he had defended enjoyed the support that had come their way four years earlier when his *Jaffree* verdict was announced.[2]

Local criticism of *Smith* raised three basic objections. One, expressed repeatedly by Alabama Board of Education Vice President John Tyson, was that the removal of the textbooks, without provision of adequate alternatives, would bring disorder to the classrooms. Tyson feared that Hand's lack of clear directives for replacing the books had placed teachers and administrators in a confusing, untenable position. The second objection, seen often in the newspapers' editorial pages, was that "far too much of the public's money ha[d] been spent on this question." Third, schoolteachers, journalists, and public officials complained that the federal courts had, yet again, substituted their own authority for the rightful authority of teachers, local administrators, and state legislators. The plaintiffs were castigated, not unlike the way Ishmael Jaffree had been, for "censor[ing] textbooks and insert[ing their] own sectarian beliefs through a federal judge's orders." In their recourse to the methods of civil-libertarianism – using the courts to defend minority rights against local majoritarian rule – the plaintiffs and the judge found themselves viewed in the way that liberals often were in Alabama: as enemies of the democratic process.[3]

Many Alabamians lacked an understanding of the issues involved in the case and so felt little enthusiasm for the draconian remedy prescribed by Hand. Plaintiff Douglas Smith lamented that, while the attorneys had "explain[ed] things in legal terms," the "average person on the street's not thinking that way" or "us[ing] that vocabulary," so that, despite the plaintiffs' victory in the courtroom, "what [we] didn't do was win a victory in the public mind." Smith's analysis was confirmed by Joseph Newman, who determined that local support for the *Jaffree* verdict dwarfed support for *Smith* because of the highly complex issues at the heart of the latter. Whereas ordinary Alabamians understood and felt the importance of restoring prayer to the classroom, they were not similarly stirred by the call to purge the schools of secular humanism. People had an especially hard time grasping that the absence of religion in the classroom constituted the presence of an alternative religion. "Fundamentalists have rarely presented their appeal in such an abstract, theoretical way," Newman pointed out. "The Smith litigation cast Judge Hand and the most fundamental of Mobile's fundamentalists in the unaccustomed role of outsiders."[4]

Hand's sophistry found an even less receptive audience among the appellate judges assigned to review the *Smith* decision. On June 23, 1987, a three-judge panel from the Eleventh Circuit heard oral argument from the lawyers for the respective parties. All three judges asked critical questions of Tom Parker; one judge in particular expressed sharp skepticism over Hand's role in initiating the *Smith* case. The skeptical judge was none other than Frank M. Johnson Jr., Alabama's most famous defender of minority civil rights. An undeterred liberal judicial activist, Johnson believed that courts could and should interpret the law to protect those citizens whose rights and liberties were most precarious. Although he and Hand enjoyed an amicable relationship, the two could not have adhered to more diametrically opposed judicial philosophies. Hand's creative inversion of the Establishment Clause was reviewed by a judge who had spent a career enforcing the Bill of Rights as a moral obligation toward those marginalized by the political process. The entire *Smith* case rankled Johnson, who announced, "I'm trying to find out who instigated this lawsuit. Was it the district judge or the parties?" Under direct questioning by Johnson, Parker admitted that neither his clients nor any of the other principles to the conflict had requested that the *Jaffree* case be continued or the parties realigned. Before the three judges, Hand was outed as the initiating force behind the case.[5]

The judges handed down their unanimous opinion two months later, on August 26. Writing for the court was Johnson, who not only reversed Hand's judgment but ridiculed it as well. Johnson scoffed that Hand's conclusions "reflect a misconception of the relationship between church and state mandated by the establishment clause." Hand's elaborate discursion on the religious status of secular humanism did not even draw a response from Johnson. The court of appeals considered only whether Alabama, through its choice of textbooks, had violated its obligation to act with religious neutrality. The court answered flatly in the negative. "Even assuming that secular humanism is a religion for purposes of the establishment clause," Johnson wrote, the plaintiffs had "failed to prove a violation of the establishment clause through the use in the Alabama public schools of the textbooks at issue in this case." Where Hand had detected disapproval toward religion, Johnson saw secular neutrality. Nor, for Johnson, did secular treatment in and of itself constitute an antireligious position. Under the Establishment Clause, the state was not obligated to avoid offending anyone's religious sensibilities, but simply to act with secular purposes. Johnson also denied that the state had an affirmative obligation to ensure that its history books addressed religious topics or any other topics. No "objective observer could conclude from the mere omission of certain historical facts regarding religion that the State of Alabama was conveying a message of approval of the religion of secular humanism."[6]

That a giant of liberal judicial activism such as Johnson would overturn Hand's ruling was to be expected. Hand had acted audaciously in declaring secular humanism a concrete ideology that could be described with precision. That he found it to constitute a religion was unconventional; that he found its advancement by government to violate the Establishment Clause was nothing short of radical. Still, no matter how startling Hand's theory might have been, it did reflect the beliefs of many religious conservatives. As such, it deserved, at the least, thoroughgoing refutation. Regardless of whether Johnson reached the correct conclusion under law, he failed to contend with the serious, if unusual, challenge presented by the trial court. The Eleventh Circuit indicated either that it had not grappled with Hand's theory or that it found the theory so mistaken as not to warrant the least bit of thoughtful consideration.[7]

Although Johnson claimed to have conceded, for the sake of argument, that secular humanism was a religion, he implied throughout his opinion that secular humanism was not a religion. Even if the home economics books did reflect some sort of humanistic orientation, he suggested, "the message conveyed" therein was "not one of endorsement of secular humanism or any religion," but, rather, "one of a governmental attempt to instill in Alabama public school children such values as independent thought, tolerance of diverse views, self-respect, maturity, self-reliance and logical decision-making." Correct though he may have been, he did not demonstrate the correctness of his assertion. He evaded any consideration of what secular humanism actually was, much less whether, for present purposes, it constituted a religion. Johnson berated Hand: "What is required of the states under the establishment clause is not 'comprehensive identification of state with religion,' but *separation* from religion." But, to Hand, it was he himself who was striking down an existing "comprehensive identification of state with religion" – the religion of secular humanism. By disallowing the advancement of any all-encompassing worldview, it was he, he believed, who was trying to ensure the state's complete "separation from religion." The Eleventh Circuit did not dignify this with as much as a counterargument. The judges stamped Hand's opinion as fanatical and nonsensical – as if its supporting arguments had never even been made.[8]

Hand was not troubled by the judges' ruling, which he considered inevitable. All along, "they gave the impression that they were determined to find that [the] books didn't do" what he had found that the books did do – promote a secular religion – because confirming his finding would have "shut the school system down." Hand knew that, by using

Supreme Court opinions such as *Torcaso, Seeger,* and *Welsh* to upend the Court's own Establishment Clause doctrine, he had put the Eleventh Circuit in a difficult position. He suspected, not unreasonably, that the circuit court recognized this as well. Had the judges not glossed over his theory of religious establishment, he believed, they would have risked "bog[ging] the courts down *ad infinitum* in censoring everything that went on in the schools." Summarily cutting him down had been "a practical decision by the court of appeals to end that right there, because of what those judges perceived to be the real problem that they were going to bring upon themselves." All of this was fine with Hand, who hoped that the Supreme Court, on appeal, would be forced to reckon with every one of its opinions suggesting that secular humanism was a religion.[9]

After the Eleventh Circuit's decision, the plaintiffs and their supporters shared Hand's hopeful optimism. But, in late November, after Justice Sandra Day O'Connor refused to stay the circuit court's ruling, the plaintiffs reversed course and decided not to appeal. They explained their decision publicly by reasoning that because they had already achieved their goals, continuing on was not necessary. Actually, the plaintiffs had come to believe that the Court would refuse even to hear the case. This, they feared, would dissuade future litigation along the lines of *Smith.* Continued funding, it seems, had also become a problem for the plaintiffs. To Hand's disappointment, his act of breathtaking audacity died an ignominious death, denied the national spotlight that he and his supporters had wanted for their theory that secular humanism was a religion whose promotion by the state violated the First Amendment.[10]

Smith failed to attract the support that would have infused the plaintiffs with confidence. Instead, their cause attracted resistance and resentment, even among people who wanted religion to have a place in public life. Despite drawing on the popular conviction that government was obligated to treat religious citizens as well as it treated nonreligious citizens, the theory informing the plaintiffs' argument lacked the appeal of the free-speech theory driving opinions such as *Widmar* v. *Vincent.* Whereas *Widmar* and its progeny appeared to expand the range of voices permitted to be heard in public education, *Smith* and cases like it appeared to narrow the range. Opponents of "equal access" could be portrayed as censors, while, in *Smith,* it was the plaintiffs and their sympathetic judge who were accused of censoring the curriculum. The latter looked as if they, and not their opponents, were strong-arming the system.[11]

At this moment in history, religious instruction in the public schools would remain prohibited by the Court's continued application of the "neutrality-as-secularism" formula. Although William Rehnquist and the conservative justices would increasingly apply the doctrine of "non-preferentialism," or evenhandedness between religious and secular expression, that doctrine did not supplant the secularist reading of the Establishment Clause as authoritative over the place of religion in the classroom. Even at a historical moment when the rights of Christians were gaining recognition, it strained the Court to interpret the Establishment Clause as requiring public-school curricula to accommodate God-centered worldviews. In the short term, at least, neither *Jaffree* nor *Smith* directly changed how the Court treated religion in the classroom.

MAJORITARIAN JUSTICES

Hand had nonetheless articulated an ascending view on federal judicial review and republican majoritarianism. His rulings advanced a right-wing vision of what was good for polity and society. They typified the rulings and writings of a generation of conservatives who tried to limit or dissolve the influence of the "living Constitution" promulgated by the Warren Court. When Antonin Scalia and Clarence Thomas joined together with Rehnquist to give the Court a conservative bloc, they breathed life into the ideals behind *Jaffree* and *Smith*. Hand's originalist views on the Establishment Clause and the incorporation doctrine would live on, albeit largely in dissenting opinions. His republican majoritarianism and religious "civil-libertarianism" would help bring clarity and coherence to the constitutional dimension within the post-1960s American conservative worldview. As Daniel Rodgers writes, "Hand's and McClellan's quixotic venture into Constitutional 'intention' brought a tangle of threads to the surface: the vulnerability of the Warren Court's ventures into new realms of rights declaration; the multiple, rival American histories in circulation"; and "the counter-mobilization of expertise which the conservative foundations were now able to bring to bear against the legal and educational establishments."[12]

In the years following *Smith*, the constitutional counterrevolution appeared not to have taken hold as Hand and McClellan had hoped. The Court's conservative bloc could only dissent in key Establishment Clause cases such as *Edwards* v. *Aguillard* (which disallowed a law requiring the teaching of evolutionary theory always to be accompanied by the teaching of "creation science"); *Lee* v. *Weisman* (which barred the reciting of prayers at public-school graduation ceremonies); and *Santa Fe* v. *Doe* (which prohibited the delivery of invocations at public-school sporting events). Writing for the Court in *Santa Fe* was John Paul Stevens, author of the *Jaffree* opinion and, by that point, chief spokesperson on the Court for liberal ideals. Stevens assured Americans that, despite two decades of right-wing pressure, the federal courts would continue to defend religious minorities against out-loud, "public expression of the views of the majority of the student body delivered with the approval of the school administration." The Court's position in *Jaffree* maintained its traction. Perhaps a different strategy for advancing Christian constitutional interests was in order.[13]

As discussed in Chapter 6, a different strategy was available. Indeed, the Christian Right had successfully been implementing an alternative constitutionalism for a number of years. Beginning with *Widmar* and the 1984 Equal Access Act, state-run educational facilities became obligated, under certain circumstances, to accommodate groups whose members spoke from a religious viewpoint. In its equal-access rulings, the Court held that the Establishment Clause did not necessarily prohibit private citizens from advancing religious beliefs within the walls of a public school facility. At issue in these cases were the free-speech rights of private individuals, the Court ruled, not Establishment Clause proscriptions that might be incurred by public schools. To prohibit religious groups from meeting in an open forum where groups of all kinds were generally permitted to meet was to discriminate against them on the basis of the viewpoint from which their members spoke. This jurisprudential thread was reinforced by O'Connor's endorsement test. As Noah Feldman points out, the endorsement test's insistence that government "treat religion and nonreligion equally in order to make certain that all citizens feel like equal participants in civic life" quickly "opened the door to a creative and original legal strategy" for religious conservatives, who "started describing *themselves* as minorities, discriminated against by powerful government institutions that were refusing to treat them equally when it came to government support."[14]

Bolstered by the Court's equal-access rulings and endorsement test, conservatives made a stunning strategic pivot. In the two decades after *Smith*, a number of Christian Right litigants would, like the plaintiffs in *Smith*, argue on behalf of their own First Amendment rights. Rather than continuing the effort to suppress the power of the federal courts or limit the reach of the First Amendment, these evangelicals sought to harness the power of the courts in order to utilize the First Amendment's guarantee of individual rights. Pioneering litigators such as Michael McConnell and Jay Sekulow broke from the well-tread majoritarian path by arguing that the courts were obligated to protect the civil liberties of religious conservatives as fully as those of all other groups. These litigators recognized a loophole in liberal theory whereby an emphasis on ideological diversity creates an opportunity for non-liberals to attain a share of influence within public institutions such as schools.[15]

Hand looked to slip through that loophole and provide self-identified Christians with a say in what takes place in the classroom. The *Smith* plaintiffs also recognized their opportunity. However fiercely they may have denounced liberals' "moral relativism," they nonetheless based their legal argument on the need for state-run schools to honor students' full range of worldviews. By agreeing with their position, Hand created a crucial precedent. A federal judge established that the law might – if not now, then at some point – ensure the influence of Christianity within the classroom. Hand shone a beacon for conservative litigators and judges determined to end the courts' penalization of religious citizens on account of their theistic worldview.

The civil-libertarian turn represented a compromise by the Christian Right. Christian conservative leaders knew the history of the federal courts as defenders of minority rights. They recognized the trajectory of constitutional law toward accommodating society's ever-increasing diversity. With this in mind, law professor Stephen Carter famously called on government to accommodate "epistemic diversity" along with "diversity of other kinds," so that citizens with a God-centered worldview might cease to be marginalized and disrespected by what Carter saw as the dominant secular culture. Failing to undo *Engel, Schempp,* and *Epperson*, some Christian Right lawyers and activists became willing to play by the civil-libertarian rules – to accept an invitation simply to participate in the game. They became willing to enter the courts as political players attempting to win their share of the prize.[16]

Its benefits aside, the civil-libertarian turn incurred long-term potential to disadvantage Christians. Byron White, the lone dissenter in *Widmar* and a conservative, worried about the impact on religion from the Court's reliance on the Free Speech Clause to protect religious expression. His brethren, he said, were "plainly wrong" in asserting that "religious worship *qua* speech is not different from any other variety of protected speech as a matter of constitutional principle," for if they were correct, then "the Religion Clauses would be emptied of any independent meaning in circumstances in which religious practice took the form of speech." If religious expression deserved the same protection as every other public utterance, then religious expression would cease to signify sacredness. The power of religion, White recognized, lay in its ultimate difference from all else, its unassimilability into the mundane. Government's evenhanded treatment of all viewpoints, and the utterances that they informed, threatened to rob religion of its essential difference. The same constitutional provision that now protected religious student groups might also protect atheists and gay-rights organizations. Perhaps, over time, churches would lose their tax exemptions and other privileges that came with being essentially different from all other institutions. Whatever its advantages, reliance on the equal-treatment principle carried hazards for religiously devout citizens.[17]

Christian Right leaders embraced the civil-libertarian turn not because they failed to recognize its hazards but because it offered them a "foot in the door" to the public sphere. The opportunity to challenge neutrality-as-secularism moved Hand, in *Smith*, to embrace the equal-treatment principle. Hand had no desire to de-sacralize religious ideas; he did not wish public schools ultimately to present Christian values exactly as they presented socialism, feminism, or atheism. The equal-treatment principle provided Hand with a strategy for making judges realize how untenable it would be to apply the First Amendment to the states if those judges were forced to apply it in a fair, evenhanded manner. For Christian Right leaders, as for Hand, the goal remained to achieve familiarity incrementally and to win acceptance for religious conservatives' voices in government and public institutions. Playing the "pluralism card" is not the same as genuinely welcoming nontheistic worldviews in public discourse, as the *Smith* plaintiffs claimed at moments to be doing. Asking the courts to guarantee equal treatment made sense to these leaders as a means to a contrary end. The Christian Right intended to win the culture wars. "By definition, they are missionaries," in the words of Eugene Provenzo, "whose purpose in life is to convert those who have not yet discovered Absolute Truth. As a result, it is impossible for them not to challenge the pluralistic model implicit in the public school system in the United States." If they accepted the pluralistic model, it was for strategic purposes only.[18]

In fact, the Court's civil-libertarian turn augured not a new respect for religious pluralism, but an enhancement of the power of local majorities to turn their religious preferences into public policy. In effect, nonpreferentialism granted religious majorities, in their private capacities, permission to use public institutions to advance their worldview. The conservative justices made Hand's *Jaffree* and *Smith* opinions more relevant later than at the time of their issuing. The Court's majority rulings in *Rosenberger* and *Good News* and dissent in *Santa Fe* completely spun around the earlier rationale for judicial review. Whereas *Engel, Schempp*, and *Epperson* protected religious minorities against marginalization by state legislatures and the religious majorities whose interests they served, the later rulings protected majorities of students, teachers, and legislators from being restrained by the judiciary and the interests of religious minorities. The Court became less concerned with tyranny of the majority and more concerned with its own tyrannical capacity. Writing for the Court in *Rosenberger*, Anthony Kennedy refused to tolerate "governmental censorship" intended "to ensure that all student writings and publications meet some baseline standard of secular orthodoxy." The *Rosenberger* Court would not play the role of censor. Nor would Hand, who had declared, years earlier, that "the Constitution speaks not to the manner in which individuals are treated by others, but rather to the manner in which individuals are treated by government."[19]

The majoritarianism underlying the civil-libertarian turn shows through starkly in the opinions of Thomas. His majority opinion in *Good News* flatly denied "that any risk that small children would perceive endorsement" of religion necessitated that the Court prohibit an evangelical organization from meeting on school premises. To the contrary, prohibiting the group from meeting would publicly demonstrate governmental disapproval of religion, allowing "any bystander" to "suffer as much from viewpoint discrimination as elementary school children could suffer from perceived endorsement." With the new century, the justices embraced a position that the *Schempp* Court never could have imagined. If the majority of a community favors the performance of a religious activity in public space, then the Court will not interfere simply to pacify a handful of malcontents. Christians have rights, too. As Hand had declared in *Jaffree*, "A member of a religious minority will have to develop a thicker skin if a state establishment offends him." And "tender years are no exception."[20]

Bald-faced majoritarianism stripped of all pretense of civil libertarianism, is evinced in three characteristically sharp opinions by Scalia. In *Employment Division* v. *Smith*, the Court reversed nearly thirty years of Free Exercise Clause jurisprudence. *Employment Division* determined that a state could restrict citizens' religiously motivated behavior if that restriction applied in all cases, regardless of the motivation for a party's behavior. Writing for the Court, Scalia suggested that the justices would no longer protect minority religions against the hostility they sometimes encountered within legislatures. Scalia was comfortable letting the majoritarian process sort out tolerable from intolerable religious conduct. He acknowledged that this process might harm religious minorities. "It may fairly be said that leaving accommodation to the political process will place at a relative disadvantage those religious practices that are not widely engaged in." For Scalia, as for Hand, this was an "unavoidable consequence of democratic government." Scalia's opinion, as David Sehat contends, made "apparent, if it had not been obvious all along, that conservatives were not interested in equally maximizing religious liberty for all – just those of Judeo-Christian heritage."[21]

In *Romer* v. *Evans*, the justices upheld lower court rulings striking down an amendment to the Colorado Constitution, approved by popular referendum, that would prohibit any law or ruling treating gays and lesbians as minorities against whom discrimination was disallowed. In dissent, Scalia echoed Robert Bork in insisting that majorities were entitled to make laws based on their moral preferences. Scalia characterized the amendment as "a modest attempt by seemingly tolerant Coloradans to preserve traditional sexual mores against the efforts of a politically powerful minority to revise those mores." He insisted that the Court had "no business imposing upon all Americans the resolution favored by the elite class from which the members of this [federal judicial] institution are selected, pronouncing that 'animosity' toward homosexuality is evil." The prejudices of the Court, it appeared, and not the prejudices of the majority of Coloradans, was at issue. Scalia reiterated his majoritarian proclivities dissenting in *Lawrence* v. *Texas*, which struck down a Texas statute forbidding two persons of the same sex to engage in intimate sexual conduct. Again, the popular majority's traditional values, for Scalia, deserved priority over the unpopular minority's fundamental rights. He accused the Court of signing on to the "homosexual agenda ... directed at eliminating the moral opprobrium that has traditionally attached to homosexual conduct." In passing this law, Texas had acted "well within the range of traditional democratic action." It was "the premise of our system that [such] judgments are to be made by the people, and not imposed by a governing caste that knows best."[22]

Hand's legacy endures powerfully in several opinions where Thomas renounced the Establishment Clause's application to the individual states. Thomas wrote for the majority in *Zelman* v. *Simmons-Harris*, in which the Court upheld an Ohio program allowing public school vouchers, even though many of the students using the vouchers were attending religiously affiliated schools. "While the Federal Government may 'make no law respecting an establishment of religion,'" Thomas opined, "the States may pass laws that include or touch on religious matters so long as these laws do not impede free exercise rights or any other individual religious liberty interest." Apparently, the Establishment Clause did not constrain state governments. For Thomas, "there would be a tragic irony in converting the Fourteenth Amendment's guarantee of individual liberty into a prohibition on the exercise of educational choice." Thomas reversed *Schempp*'s declaration that "the Free Exercise Clause ... has never meant that a majority could use the machinery of the State to practice its beliefs." For Thomas, the Ohio program embodied private citizens' free exercise; to use the Establishment Clause to infringe on that freedom was nonsensical as well as indefensible.[23]

Thomas further developed this idea in *Elk Grove* v. *Newdow*, where the Court upheld California's policy mandating teacher-led recitation of the Pledge of Allegiance, including its reference to "one nation under God." Concurring, Thomas labeled the Establishment Clause a "federalism provision." Just as McClellan had argued in his *Jaffree* testimony, Thomas maintained that the clause "does not restrict state governments but, rather, protects state establishments from federal interference." Thomas expanded on this theme concurring in *Greece* v. *Galloway*, which upheld the recitation of a Christian prayer at the opening of a town meeting. Here, Thomas tried to show the illogic of incorporating the Establishment Clause by comparing it to an incorporation of the Tenth Amendment, which would nonsensically bind the states from infringing on the very right guaranteed to them by that amendment. Like the Tenth Amendment, the Establishment Clause could not possibly restrict the states, Thomas insisted, because its entire purpose was to guard states' rights against infringement by the federal government. The Establishment Clause was, by its very nature, a federalism provision prohibiting Congress from transgressing against the right of states to establish a religion. Hand, it seemed, was "crying in the wilderness" no longer. His *Jaffree* ruling had found a sympathetic Supreme Court justice.[24]

THE GREAT DEBATE

Hand's impact went beyond Court rulings. As seen in Chapters 3 and 4, his *Jaffree* ruling inspired conservatives in the Justice Department and the Senate. The most publicly visible set of events with which he was associated was launched by Rehnquist's dissent in *Jaffree*, which had been informed and inspired by Hand's ruling in that case. Like the other battles, this one was as much political as legal. Hand was essentially a political creature who used the law to advance an ideological understanding of the Constitution. Along with many other political actors of his era, he subscribed to the belief that federal judges, of whom he was one, had improperly inserted their own views into constitutional law. In so doing they had become lawmakers. He charged that the laws they made far too often supplanted the laws made through state legislatures – the proper lawmaking channel in a democratic republic. In his view, federal judges generally embraced a kind of morality held mostly by cultural elites, one divorced from traditional religious precepts. Judge-made laws readily obstructed the attempts of popular majorities to encode their religious values into law. By vitiating self-government, federal judges had become enemies of the people.[25]

Rehnquist's dissent in *Jaffree* gave rise to an unusual series of public jabs and ripostes by key government officials concerned about how the Constitution was being interpreted and enforced. In the immediate aftermath of *Jaffree*, President Reagan's new attorney general, Edwin Meese, gave a series of addresses in which he saluted Rehnquist's dissent while rejecting the spirit and substance of the Supreme Court's jurisprudence over the past half-century. Meese's ideas were entirely in keeping with Hand's; the content of his speeches mirrored writings by the *Benchmark* editorial staff, especially McClellan and former assistant deputy attorney general Bruce Fein, now a legal analyst at the American Enterprise Institute. Meese sounded the call to constitutional counterrevolution still ringing in conservative circles. The justices of the Supreme Court needed to curtail their habit of inserting their own values into their interpretation of the Constitution, Meese asserted. They needed not to read between the lines of the text but, rather, to limit themselves to the text itself and the intentions of the men who wrote and ratified it. Any method of interpretation other than a "Jurisprudence of original intention ... suffer[ed] the defect of pouring new meaning into old words, thus creating new powers and new rights totally at odds with the logic of our Constitution and its commitment to the rule of law." The improvidence of activist justices, Meese said, was destroying the credibility of the Court.[26]

Liberal judicial activism had damaged American government, Meese charged. It had weakened the role of the states within the nation's federal system of government, creating a potentially hazardous situation. Only by "allowing the States sovereignty sufficient to govern," he contended, do "we better secure our ultimate goal of political liberty through decentralized government." Not only was federalism endangered; democracy itself lay threatened by liberal judicial activism. According to Meese, the nation's "deeply rooted commitment to the idea of democracy" could bear fruit only when the Constitution was interpreted narrowly. By reading their own views into the Constitution, the liberal justices were usurping the people's right to make their own laws. The constitutional text represented "the fundamental will of the people." To tamper with its integrity was to frustrate democracy.[27]

Meese staked a claim beyond even what Rehnquist asserted in *Jaffree*. Like Hand, the attorney general openly repudiated the doctrine of incorporation. He based his position entirely on the writings of McClellan. "The Bill of Rights, as debated, created and ratified," he declared, "was designed to apply *only* to the national government." Thus, the first ten amendments did not properly attach to the individual states. Like McClellan, Meese emphasized the novelty of the incorporation doctrine. He insisted that, despite its repeated invocations over recent decades, "nothing can be done to shore up the intellectually shaky foundation upon which the doctrine rests." The damage it had caused, especially to the states, was incalculable. "Nowhere else," he said, had "the principle of federalism been dealt so politically violent and constitutionally suspect a blow as by the theory of incorporation.[28]

For evidence of that damage, Meese claimed, one needed look no further than the Court's disastrous church-state rulings. Yet there was one ray of hope. "One finds much merit in Justice Rehnquist's recent dissent in *Jaffree*," the attorney general announced. Like Rehnquist, Meese believed that the Court's religion clause jurisprudence rested on "a mistaken understanding of constitutional theory." Meese adopted Robert Cord's interpretation of the Establishment Clause – the very interpretation adopted by Hand in *Jaffree*. "The Establishment Clause of the First Amendment," he insisted, "was designed to prohibit Congress from establishing a national church." It was meant to do nothing more. "To have argued, as is popular today, that the Amendment demands a strict neutrality between religion and irreligion would have struck the founding generation as bizarre." For Meese, the Establishment Clause was never meant to secularize government. Its "purpose was to prohibit religious tyranny, not to undermine religion generally."[29]

Shortly after Meese's address, the *Wall Street Journal* ran a front page article supporting his take on incorporation and the Establishment Clause. The article was written by Charles Rice – law professor at Notre

Dame, contributor at *Benchmark*, and attorney representing McClellan's Center for Judicial Studies during the Supreme Court phase of *Jaffree*. Rice's article precisely encapsulated McClellan's trial arguments. Rice attributed to "this incorporation doctrine" the "greatest change in the legal institutions of this country since the Constitutional Convention of 1787." The doctrine, he alleged, was "a total fraud." It signaled "a judicial seizure of power." In his estimation, no one deserved more praise than Hand, who had "squarely challenged the incorporation doctrine." Partly because of Hand's efforts, Rice predicted, the doctrine would likely be overturned. Accordingly, he forecasted, "some law school [would] someday establish the Brevard Hand Chair of Constitutional Principle."[30]

Meese gave two further addresses during the upcoming weeks. In them, he reiterated his accusations that liberal judicial activism was corroding democracy. Meese derisively labeled federal judges "political power brokers." By "transforming courtrooms into mini-legislatures," he charged, judges had "attempt[ed] to make an end run around popular government." Through their tyranny, those judges had enforced "an aggressively secular liberalism." This came at a great cost to the people. "The result has been nothing less than an abandonment of many of the traditional political and social values the great majority of Americans embrace." Out of touch with ordinary citizens, federal judges had usurped their authority and insulted their sensibilities.[31]

No administration official since Franklin Roosevelt had denounced the Supreme Court in such a manner. Indeed, there was nothing ordinary about the counter-establishment and its attempt to change the way government conceived of and used the Constitution. Like Hand and McClellan, Meese looked to start a public conversation about the Constitution. He succeeded. Meese's criticism provoked Justice William Brennan, leader of the Court's liberal wing, into an impassioned response directed implicitly but clearly at the attorney general. Addressing students at Georgetown University on October 14, Brennan portrayed a Constitution whose essence lay in its loftiest ideals. Because those ideals survived and evolved over time, the Constitution was, at its core, a living document. Not to understand that, Brennan scolded Meese, was to misconstrue the Constitution and the system of government it informs. Brennan rose to the occasion, staking out a position utterly at odds with the counterrevolution's. Where Meese saw a clear-cut set of fixed constitutional limitations on government, Brennan saw nothing less than a "sparkling vision of the supremacy of the human dignity of every individual."[32]

Brennan described Meese's supposed "depoliticization of the judiciary" as, in reality, "a choice no less political than any other." Meese had used his power as a government official, Brennan charged, to promote his own vision of the proper place of the respective branches and levels of government. In looking to tie the hands of the federal judiciary, Meese "expresse[d] antipathy to claims of the minority rights against the majority." Brennan insisted that, without federal judicial oversight, the political branches would go unchecked and be liable to tread over the interests of parties lacking political power. "The view that all matters of substantive policy should be resolved through the majoritarian process ... will not do," he maintained. "Unabashed enshrinement of majority will would permit the imposition of a social caste system ... so long as a majority of the authorized legislative body, fairly elected, approved." Brennan considered it "the very purpose of a Constitution – and particularly of the Bill of Rights – to declare certain values transcendent, beyond the reach of temporary political majorities." No responsible government official could "read the text without admitting that it embodie[d] substantive value choices" that it placed "beyond the powers of any legislature."[33]

Conservative legal scholars publicly rebuked Brennan. On October 23, the *Wall Street Journal* published a piece by Walter Berns, a well-known constitutionalist at the American Enterprise Institute. Berns condemned the justice as reckless and driven by resentment at the New Right. "This sort of public posturing," he wrote, was "almost unseemly and is certainly injudicious." Those sentiments were echoed five days later by Raoul Berger, a friend of Hand, confidant of McClellan, and well-known opponent of the incorporation doctrine. In *Jaffree*, Hand had mentioned his great appreciation for and reliance on Berger's work. Berger now presented those same views in a *Washington Post* editorial. Meese, he said, was correct in claiming that contemporary jurists could "gauge accurately the intent of the Framers." Berger charged with arrogance in pretending that the justices had the authority to create new rights out of whole cloth, rights not at all contained within the Constitution's text. To Berns and Berger, Brennan deserved to be called out.[34]

Another justice weighed in. John Paul Stevens, author of the Court's *Jaffree* opinion, took Meese to task for what Stevens considered his naïveté. Stevens pointed out that the attorney general's position glossed over critical constitutional events that occurred after the adoption of the Bill of Rights. Meese's "position overlook[ed] the profound importance of the Civil War and the post-war amendments on the structure of our government, and particularly upon the relationship between the Federal Government and the separate States." History, Stevens believed, had settled the matter. It was dispositive "that no Justice who has sat on the Supreme Court during the past sixty years has questioned the proposition that the prohibitions against state action that are incorporated in the Fourteenth Amendment include the prohibitions against federal action that are found in the First Amendment." Court precedent was binding unless and until the Court itself overruled it. Just as his *Jaffree* opinion had chastised Hand, so did Stevens now chastise Meese for unabashedly insulting the justices.[35]

The next turn in the debate came with a tongue-in-cheek speech delivered three days later by Justice Rehnquist. Speaking at the University of Wyoming Law School, Rehnquist suggested that his fellow conservatives need not force the issue – that their influence over government and law was on the increase. He reminded Meese that "the political branches of the federal government" did, in fact, "have something to say as to who shall judge the constitutionality of [the justices'] actions." After all, "any vacancy in the federal judiciary, including of course the Supreme Court, is filled by presidential nomination subject to Senate confirmation." The justices did not act in a vacuum. Ours remained a government with a separation of powers. As Laurence Tribe of Harvard Law School noted, Rehnquist was subtly advising the attorney general, "Bide your time and you'll have the real Reagan revolution."[36]

Meese's critique of liberal judicial activism riled many liberals in the government, press, and academia largely because of its open attack on the Court and the process of judicial review. But it stung also because of what it implied about secularism and pluralism and the counterrevolution's intentions toward them. Behind Meese's critique of judicial activism lay a broader moral and cultural critique of the values that liberal judges purportedly tried to impose on all Americans. Not only did Meese consider neutrality-as-secularism a sham; he insinuated that political majorities were fully entitled, through their state representatives, to establish any religion they chose. The unspoken assumption here was that "ordinary" citizens – those unlike the justices and the cultural elites for whom they spoke – knew what was best for society and government.[37]

A couple of years after Meese made his public mark, Judge Robert Bork, the era's best-known legal intellectual, joined the discussion, bringing great sophistication to the ideas behind Meese's antijudicial broadsides. Bork made headlines when the Senate thwarted his attempt to gain confirmation to the Supreme Court. His conservative constitutional views so troubled Senate liberals that they waged the most fearsome battle ever carried out against a Court nominee. In his testimony before the Senate Judiciary Committee, and in his many published essays, Bork made no secret of his disdain for the living Constitution, as well as for modern, liberal culture. No public figure more effectively and eloquently articulated the interconnection between the moral and political dimensions running through Meese's and Hand's "jurisprudence of original intention."[38]

In the wake of his tumultuous Senate confirmation hearings, Bork published a best-selling book that tied together his thoughts on the Constitution, federal judges, and morality. *The Tempting of America* excoriated liberals not only for circumventing the Constitution and the will of the popular majority, but for holding values that could attain the force of law only if federal judges circumvented the Constitution and the will of the popular majority. "Judges are by definition members of the intellectual class," Bork posited. Because "the morality and politics of the intellectual or knowledge class" reflected the preferences of a cultural elite, they could "be made into constitutional law" only, and ironically, if judges disregarded the Constitution. Although "an elite moral or political view may never be able to win an election or command the votes of a majority of a legislature," it was likely to "influence judges and gain the force of law in that way." This corrupted America's political system, given that the authority of federal judges was extrapolitical, beyond the reach of popular majorities. A federal judge was "free to reflect the 'better' opinion because he need not stand for reelection and because he can deflect the majority's anger by claiming merely to have been enforcing the Constitution."[39]

Tempting of America deftly tied political majoritarianism to conservative morality. It returned to an argument that Bork made twenty years earlier, that a judge must apply the Constitution without imposing his own values and beliefs, or those he believed to undergird society or to lie between the lines of the document. Bork called this restraint on judges "the American orthodoxy." It prescribed a limited role for judicial review. The American orthodoxy, as Bork explained it, consisted of a long-established political axiom that judges should not make law. Violations against the orthodoxy constituted the political heresy, committed over recent decades, that judges may render decisions based on their own personal values. The heresy, Bork insisted, eroded the Constitution – regardless of the particular kinds of values injected into the process by judges. "The heresy described is not peculiar to any political outlook," Bork maintained. The heresy had nothing intrinsically to do with federal judges' liberal inclinations. "When it has suited their purpose, conservatives as well as liberals have surrendered to its temptation." The orthodoxy concerned the separation of powers between branches of government; it did not concern morality or culture.[40]

And yet it did. We learn that it was liberals in particular who "hate the American orthodoxy," and that they did so "because they have moral and political agendas of their own that cannot be found in the Constitution and that no legislature, or at least none whose members wish to be reelected, will enact." By necessity, liberals appealed to activist judges, who generally shared their liberal cultural orientation, in order to "win their victories for them by altering the Constitution." Conservatives might hypothetically, at some point, hijack the democratic process, but liberals did so in fact – because they needed to do so, because they could not realize their agenda in any other way. Bork sought to slay "left-liberal constitutional revisionism," which, he told us, was "rooted in a powerful American subculture whose opinions differed markedly from those of most Americans." These culturally elite revisionists spoke for a class of citizens who stood "in opposition to business-class or bourgeois values, indeed to the values of a majority of Americans." These elites comprised "an adversary culture" seeking to impose its fundamentally un-American views on the rest of the nation. The orthodoxy that these elites violated, it turned out, was cultural and moral as well as constitutional. It was the orthodoxy of basic decency, established custom, self-reliance, and personal accountability.[41]

Democracy, for Bork, was threatened by liberalism in two ways. It was threatened by the political fact that liberals used federal judges, who themselves usually were liberals, to usurp the people's right to make their own laws. Democracy, for Bork, was also threatened by the culture – the decadence, dependency, and egalitarianism – that liberals forced on real Americans through the federal judiciary. Liberals stifled the people's ability to protect themselves legislatively against moral harm. While the people sought to pass laws based in traditional, Bible-based morality, liberals, through their judges, declared such laws unconstitutional on the basis of their nonsecular purposes. So fully had liberals cordoned off public policy and public institutions from conventional morality that they had created an "establishment of secularism as our official creed." Because "any healthy society needs a view of itself as a political and moral community," the ban on religiously motivated lawmaking deprived society of its moral moorings. The decent, traditional society became frustrated in its attempt to reproduce itself.[42]

Meese and Bork championed the conservative counterrevolution called for by Hand and McClellan. Their manifestos against liberalism paved the way for the most important legal movement of the period. From a few renegade law-school students arose what became the Federalist Society, a conservative cadre of lawyers whose influence would pervade legal scholarship, legal advocacy, and the American judiciary. The Federalist Society saw itself as the vanguard of conservative counterrevolution. Many of the movement's founders clerked for or otherwise assisted Bork and Meese. The Reagan Justice Department sparked these young lawyers and provided them a platform for battling liberal judicial activism and promoting constitutional originalism. According to Reagan's second solicitor general, Charles Fried, the public addresses that they composed for Meese advanced "extreme positions such as ... suggesting that the president need not obey Supreme Court decisions with which he disagrees." Members of the Federalist Society reached out to and influenced conservative politicians, inserting their legal ideas in conservative politics. Hand's legacy was not to cry in the wilderness, but to ring out through the ideas and actions of a young generation of conservative politicians and lawyers.[43]

THE IMPERIAL JUDICIARY

The call to counterrevolution impacted the world of journalism. The line of thinking that would inform Hand and McClellan first crystalized with a 1975 article by sociologist Nathan Glazer. "Towards an Imperial Judiciary?" declared that "American courts" were "now far more powerful than ever before, while "public opinion [had grown] weaker." Glazer accused federal courts, "through interpretation of the Constitution and the laws," of "reach[ing] into the lives of the people, against the will of the people." With impunity, judges "overrul[ed] legislatures, executives, and administrators, for the purpose indeed of replacing democratic procedures with [their own] authoritarian decisions." For years after the article's publication, conservative writers excoriated the Court in terms similar to Glazer's. Running throughout these criticisms was the accusation that the "imperial judiciary" had usurped the people's right and responsibility to make their own laws through their elected representatives.[44]

The imperial judiciary thesis would be wailed in an alarming symposium in the November 1996 issue of *First Things*. Journal editor John Richard Neuhaus was a longtime critic of liberal culture and its supposed hegemony over government. His 1984 book *The Naked Public Square* focused ire over the alleged social and political marginalization of Christians. The *First Things* symposium diagnosed the problem further and considered how Christians, and conservatives more generally, ought to react. The essays were collected, along with introductions and printed responses, in a collection titled *The End of Democracy? The Judicial Usurpation of Politics*. There, Neuhaus proclaimed that the nation was "witnessing the displacement of a constitutional order in which the people, through the institutions of representative democracy, are thought to have the capacity and the right to govern themselves." He and other contributors were distressed by "something much more profound than conventional concerns about judicial activism." They were alarmed that law had "declared its independence from morality." This "judicial usurpation of politics" – a transformation of democracy into an oligarchy of secularist federal judges – was intolerable. The symposium's contributors, referring back to "the most elementary principles of Western Civilization," announced that "laws which violated the moral law are null and void and must in conscience be disobeyed." Whether and how to disobey such laws were the questions before them.[45]

The contributors spared no hysteria. One was Russell Hittinger, a professor of religion at the University of Tulsa. Hittinger celebrated the people's wish to pass laws that would provide the public sphere with traditional moral guidelines able to discipline and strengthen the individual. Much like the *Smith* plaintiffs, Hittinger deplored society's creation of the morally autonomous individual – not to be confused with the politically free citizen, who, liberated from slavish self-seeking, may take part in the creation of laws likely to encourage conservative moral conduct. Hittinger condemned the Court both for acting anti-democratically and for prohibiting religious motivations within the lawmaking enterprise. The conventional order of things had been turned upside down. "The new constitutional regime ... has made what used to be its most loyal citizens – religious believers" into "enemies of the common good." This had given rise to a legitimacy crisis. "Insofar as private citizens give tacit consent to the new regime, and thus allow it to speak in their name," they now faced "an unavoidable moral crisis." The judicial oligarchy had alienated its most responsible, thoughtful subjects. Its authority over them lay in doubt.[46]

Not only had the Court bypassed the people, claimed Hadley Arkes, political scientist at Amherst College. Worse, the Court had stamped into law the notion, engrained in the political culture, that citizens informed by Christianity were simpletons and bigots whose influence needed to be contained. As Arkes saw it, "judges form a virtual concert to advance the interests of gay rights and other parts of the liberal agenda," while "those who would resist these initiatives, even with the most modest measures, are branded as the aggressors and the zealots." Although, according to Arkes, ordinary citizens considered gay marriage abominable, public debate on the matter had been foreclosed. "The 'Christian Right' is tagged," by the Court and its minions, "with the responsibility for unsettling our national politics by injecting the issues of abortion and school prayer." The federal courts were celebrated for protecting extraconstitutional rights that removed those issues from the people's rightful purview. What was to be done?[47]

That question was answered in near-apocalyptic terms by the one of the era's most prominent evangelicals. Charles Colson, convicted years earlier as part of Richard Nixon's Watergate scandal, had found a second career as a public critic of all things not Christian conservative. The *First Things* symposium brought out his most panicky qualities. In his contribution, Colson painted American democracy as a defiled, perhaps illegitimate political order. "We have nearly reached the completion," he reported, of a "systematic usurpation of ultimate political power by the American judiciary – a usurpation that compels evangelical Christians and, indeed, all believers to ask sobering questions about the moral legitimacy of the current political order and our allegiance to it." Colson suspected that "events in America may have reached the point where the only political action believers can take is some kind of direct, extrapolitical confrontation of the judicially controlled regime." Yet "would even active disobedience be effective against our current judicial state?" If not, Colson prescribed still more drastic steps. "When peaceable means and limited civil disobedience fail," he warned, "revolution can be justified from a Christian viewpoint."[48]

In no sense at all did Americans "still live in a functioning democracy," confirmed fellow evangelical James Dobson. Founder of the highly influential Focus on the Family, Dobson wrote an essay responding to the symposium. Like the symposium contributors, Dobson concluded that, "on the most essential matters of human life and conscience, the courts have systematically invalidated the will of the people." Moreover, the courts had left "no doubt they intend to continue ruling by judicial fiat for the foreseeable future." This posed a terrible dilemma for Christians, who believed that political authority, to be legitimate, must not transgress the will of God. "The Supreme Court ha[d] placed on notice all citizens animated by religious beliefs"; it had "thrown down the gauntlet" to Christians who would resist its totalitarian regime. While Dobson did not explicitly advocate resistance to the law, he did urge Christians to take whatever steps might restore them to their rightful place in American democracy.[49]

The most comprehensive critique came from none other than Bork. As in *The Tempting of America*, the circuit-court judge carefully tied together conservatism's political and cultural strains. In his contribution to the symposium, Bork charged the Supreme Court justices – America's oligarchs – with substituting the values of the elite cultural minority in place of the values of the rest of the people. The justices, he opined, "firmly believe they have access to wisdom denied the rest of us." Flouting the people's will, they made "homosexual conduct a constitutional right, adopted the radical feminist view that men and women are essentially identical," and "continued to view the First Amendment as a protection of self-gratification rather than the free articulation of ideas." Bork suggested that judicial review itself might be illegitimate. When the Court declared a statute unconstitutional, he complained, "it *overrides* current popular desires." It imposed the "counter-majoritarian preferences" it shared among "a wider cultural elite that includes journalists, academics, [and] entertainers." Bork confirmed the connection he had made in *Tempting*. Federal judges eviscerated democracy both by usurping the people's legislative authority and by imposing on them an un-American morality.[50]

Bork now took his earlier argument one step further. He labeled the justices as the people's "robed masters." "They order our lives," he charged, "and we have no recourse, no means of resisting, no means of altering their ukases." Were they, in fact, a "band of outlaws"? Yes, they were. Defining an outlaw as "a person who coerces others without warrant in law," Bork found that such coercion was "precisely what a majority of the present Supreme Court does." Accordingly, the people needed to consider radical solutions. "Only a change in our institutional arrangements can halt the transformation of our society and culture by judges," he counseled. "Decisions of courts might be made subject to modification or reversal by majority vote of the Senate and the House of Representatives." Or, "alternatively, courts might be deprived of the power of constitutional review." Still, the easiest solution might be if "an elected official ... simply refuses to comply with a Supreme Court decision." Whatever course the people decided on, they were entitled, and probably compelled, to take extraordinary measures to regain control over their lives and their government. Bork could only hope that the people had the courage to resist the judicial oligarchy.[51]

Although Bork and the others incurred some opposition from conservative thinkers, they spoke for a wide swath of the American right. Over the subsequent twenty years, conservatives of all stripes would routinely vent populist animus against federal judges. The far right edge of the Republican Party, dubbing itself the "Tea Party," pointed to the federal government's disregard for the constitutional text as justification for a new American revolution. Christian conservatives and fiscal conservatives alike accused federal judges of treachery. 2008 vice-presidential candidate Sarah Palin excoriated them as un-American. Many other Republican politicians, finding that antijudicialism made for good politics, incorporated it as a cornerstone of their public rhetoric. Evangelical organizations routinely urged resistance to the tyranny of the Court. Throughout conservative culture could be seen republican-majoritarian condemnations of the people's "robed masters."[52]

At the time that *Jaffree* and *Smith* took place, the conservative counterrevolutionaries who seized on those cases appeared out of touch with settled constitutional law and politics. Hand, McClellan, and the *Jaffree* intervenors seemed quixotic, extremist. Time may proving otherwise. Whether or not conservatives actually comprise majorities within their states, they continue to take recourse in the language of majoritarianism – not a plebiscitary majoritarianism, but one in which elected representatives, especially on the state level, give voice to the supposed popular will. Notwithstanding the civil-libertarian turn, the American right continues mostly to present itself in majoritarian terms. The conservative imagination has become a populist one – as made clear by the rise to power of Donald Trump. In the conservative imagination, self-identified ordinary citizens try their hardest to reassert their influence over law and society. Regardless of whether they overtly embrace religious values, they look to restore to prominence a traditional morality emphasizing self-discipline and self-reliance. Hand did his part to help along the counterrevolution, fearing He feared that his fellow citizens would passively allow secularism and liberal judicial activism to take over and destroy his nation. Resistance, it turns out, has been carried out with greater vigor than Hand imagined, even if its ultimate success remains yet unknown.

Notes

1 Warren A. Nord, *Religion and American Education: Rethinking a National Dilemma* (Chapel Hill: University of North Carolina Press, 1995), 169. Francis Wilkinson, "Judge Hand's Holy War," *American Lawyer*, 9 (May 1987), 112, 114; *Mobile Press Register*, March 14, 1987, p. 1, 8; "Arguments Set Tuesday in Mobile Textbook Case," *Mobile Register*, June 22, 1987; "Textbook Case Sent Spasms through Local School Systems," *Mobile Press Register*, December 27, 1987. W. Brevard Hand interview by Robert Daniel Rubin, April 12, 2000, Mobile, Ala., pp. 14–15 (in Robert Daniel Rubin's possession); W. Brevard Hand interview by Robert Daniel Rubin, December 5, 2000, Mobile, Ala., transcript, 16–17 (in Robert Daniel Rubin's possession).

2 Joseph W. Newman, "Organized Prayer and Secular Humanism in Mobile, Alabama's, Public Schools," in *Curriculum as Social Psychoanalysis: The Significance of Place*, ed. Joe L. Kincheloe and William F. Pinar (Albany: SUNY Press, 1991), 70–72; Wilkinson, "Judge Hand's Holy War," 114; Joseph L. Conn, "Inquisition in Alabama: Federal Court Lends a Hand to Religious Right's 'Secular Humanism' Crusade," *Church & State*, 40 (April 1987), 10–11. *Alabama Journal*, January 8, 1986, p. 12; "The Humanism Suit," *Birmingham News*, March 17, 1986; *Mobile Press Register*, October 25, 1986; "State Board Acts Correctly to Appeal," *Mobile Press Register*, March 14, 1987; "Teague Recommends Storing Textbooks," *Mobile Press Register*, March 21, 1987. Bob Sherling interview by Robert Daniel Rubin, November 14, 2000, Mobile, Ala., pp. 19–20 (in Robert Daniel Rubin's possession); John Webster and Sue Webster interview by Robert Daniel Rubin, October 22, 2002, Mobile, Ala., pp. 11–12, 21–22 (in Robert Daniel Rubin's possession); Douglas Smith interview by Robert Daniel Rubin, March 21, 2002, Mobile, Ala., transcript, pp. 7–9, 13 (in Robert Daniel Rubin's possession).

3 "State Board Acts Correctly to Appeal"; *Mobile Press Register*, March 21, 1987, p. 9B; "Teague Recommends Storing Textbooks"; Wilkinson, "Judge Hand's Holy War," 114. *Alabama Journal*, January 8, 1986, p. 12; "Humanism Suit"; "State Board Acts Correctly to Appeal"; *Mobile Press Register*, March 21, 1987, p. 9B; Wilkinson, "Judge Hand's Holy War," 114. *Mobile Press Register*, October 25, 1986; "Humanism Suit"; *Birmingham News*, October 26, 1986, p. 2A; "State Board Acts Correctly to Appeal"; "Appeal Has Appeal to Plaintiffs in Humanist Trial," *Mobile Press Register*, March 28, 1987; *Mobile Register*, April 17, 1987, p. 10; "Textbook Case Sent Spasms through Local School Systems," *Mobile Press Register*, December 27, 1987; Sherling interview, 19–20.

4 Smith interview, 13; Newman, "Organized Prayer and Secular Humanism," 71–72.

5 *Mobile Register*, June 24, 1987, p. 1. Frank M. Johnson, *Defending Constitutional Rights*, ed. Tony A. Freyer (Athens: University of Georgia Press, 2001); Jack Bass, *Taming the Storm: The Life and Times of Frank M. Johnson, Jr., and the South's Fight over Civil Rights* (New York: Doubleday, 1993); Jack Bass, *Unlikely Heroes* (Tuscaloosa: University of Alabama Press, 1990), 16. Hand interview, December 5, 2000, p. 6. *Mobile Register*, June 24, 1987, p. 1.

6 *Smith* v. *Board of School Commissioners of Mobile County*, 827 F.2d 684 (1987), 689–95.
7 *Ibid.*, 692.
8 *Ibid.*, 692, 695, emphasis in original.
9 Hand interview, April 12, 2000, p. 12. *Torcaso* v. *Watkins*, 367 U.S. 488 (1961); *United States* v. *Seeger*, 380 U.S. 163 (1965); *Welsh* v. *United States*, 398 U.S. 333 (1970).
10 Hand interview, April 12, 2000, p. 12. *Mobile Press Register*, August 27, 1987, p. 8; "Textbook Ruling Said No Surprise," *Mobile Press Register*, August 27, 1987; *Washington Post*, August 27, 1987, p. A1; *New York Times*, August 27, 1987, p. A1; *Christian Science Monitor*, August 28, 1987, p. 3; *Mobile Register*, August 28, 1987, p. A15; "Textbook Rulings Appeal Promised," *Mobile Press*, August 28, 1987. *Mobile Register*, October 15, 1987, pp. 1, 8; Textbook Case Emergency Appeal Nixed," *Mobile Press*, October 22, 1987. "Plans to Appeal Textbook Ruling Are Abandoned," *Mobile Register*, November 26, 1987; "Fundamentalists Say Book Issue Still Alive," *Mobile Press Register*, December 2, 1987; Kirsten Goldberg, "Alabama Group Closes Its 'Secular Humanism' Suit," *Education Week*, December 9, 1987, p. 8; Newman, "Organized Prayer and Secular Humanism in Mobile, Alabama's, Public Schools," 72.
11 *Widmar* v. *Vincent*, 454 U.S. 263 (1981); *Board of Education of Westside Community Schools* v. *Mergens*, 496 U.S. 226 (1990); *Lamb's Chapel* v. *Center Moriches Union Free School District*, 508 U.S. 384 (1993); *Rosenberger* v. *Rector and Visitors of University of Virginia*, 515 U.S. 819 (1995); *Good News Club* v. *Milford Central School*, 533 U.S. 98 (2001). Rosemary C. Salomone, *Visions of Schooling: Conscience Community, and Common Education* (New Haven: Yale University Press, 2000), 117–20. Several federal cases, in the years following Smith, featured plaintiffs arguing unsuccessfully that public schools had established a religion of secular humanism. These included *Roberts* v. *Madigan*, 702 F.Supp. 1510 (1989); *Doe* v. *Human*, 725 F.Supp. 1503 (1989); *Seidman* v. *Paradise Valley Unified School District No. 69*, 327 F.2d 1098 (2004); and *Harper* v. *Poway Unified School District*, 445 F.3d 1166 (2006).
12 Justin Driver, "The Consensus Constitution," *Texas Law Review*, 89 (2011), 787, 801. Daniel T. Rodgers, *Age of Fracture* (Cambridge, Mass.: Belknap, 2001), 236–37.
13 *Edwards* v. *Aguillard*, 482 U.S. 578 (1987); *Lee* v. *Weisman*, 505 U.S. 577 (1992); *Santa Fe Independent School District* v. *Doe*, 530 U.S. 290 (2000), esp. 308.
14 The Court's equal-access rulings include *Widmar* v. *Vincent; Board* v. *Mergens; Lamb's Chapel* v. *Center Moriches Union; Rosenberger* v. *Rector;* and *Good News Club* v. *Milford.* O'Connor first articulated the endorsement test in three concurring opinions: *Lynch* v. *Donnelly*, 465 U.S. 668 (1984), 687–94; *Wallace* v. *Jaffree*, 472 U.S. 38 (1985), 67–84; and *County of Allegheny* v. *American Civil Liberties Union*, 492 U.S. 573 (1989), 623–37. The test informed Justice Blackmun's majority opinion in *Allegheny* and O'Connor's majority opinion in *Mergens* – the case in which a plurality of

justices affirmed Congress's Equal Access Act of 1984. *Allegheny* v. *ACLU*, at 578–621; *Board* v. *Mergens*. Noah Feldman, *Divided by God: America's Church-State Problem—and What We Should Do about It* (New York: Farrar, Straus, and Giroux. 2005), 205–06, emphasis in original.

15 Steven P. Brown, *Trumping Religion: The New Christian Right, the Free Speech Clause, and the Courts* (Tuscaloosa: University of Alabama Press, 2002), 5–7, 59, 76–77; Feldman, *Divided by God*, 207–10. The conundrum of liberalism accommodating illiberalism is explored in Rob Reich, *Bridging Liberalism and Multiculturalism in American Education* (Chicago: University of Chicago Press, 2002); and Stephen Macedo, "Liberal Civic Education and Religious Fundamentalism: *The Case of God* v. *John Rawls?*," *Ethics*, 105 (April 1995), 468–96.

16 Stephen L. Carter, *The Culture of Disbelief: How American Law and Politics Trivialize Religious Devotion* (New York: Anchor, 1994), 15, 229–30.

17 *Widmar* v. *Vincent*, 282. On the hazards to religion brought on by adoption of the equal-treatment principle, see Winnifred Fallers Sullivan, "The Difference Religion Makes: Reflections on *Rosenberger*," *Christian Century*, March 13, 1996, pp. 292–95; Gregg Ivers, "American Jews and the Equal Treatment Principle," in *Equal Treatment of Religion in a Pluralistic Society*, ed. by Stephen V. Monsma and J. Christopher Soper (Grand Rapids, Mich.: Eerdmans, 1998), 177; Brown, *Trumping Religion*, 10, 60, 139–45; and Aaron Louis Haberman, "Civil Rights on the Right: The Modern Christian Right and the Crusade for School Prayer, 1962–1996" (Ph.D. diss., University of South Carolina, 2006), 185–86, 207.

18 Hand interview, April 12, 2000, pp. 12–15; Hand interview, December 5, 2000, pp. 16–17. John S. Detweiler, "The Religious Right's Battle Plan in the 'Civil War' of Values," *Public Relations Review*, 18 (Fall 1992), 247–55; Justin Watson, *The Christian Coalition: Dreams of Restoration, Demands for Recognition* (New York: St. Martin's, 1997); Chip Berlet and Matthew N. Lyons, *Right-Wing Populism in America: Too Close for Comfort* (New York: Guilford, 2000), 255–64; Michelle Goldberg, *Kingdom Coming: The Rise of Christian Nationalism* (New York: Norton, 2006); Dan Gilgoff, *The Jesus Machine: How James Dobson, Focus on the Family, and Evangelical America are Winning the Culture War* (New York: St. Martin's, 2008). Provenzo, *Religious Fundamentalism and American Education*, 91.

19 *Rosenberger* v. *Rector*, 844–45. *Clark* v. *Marengo*, 469 F.Supp. 1150 (1979), 1173 n31.

20 *Good News Club* v. *Milford*, 118, 120. See also Thomas's concurrence in *Rosenberger* v. *Rector*, 862 (Thomas, J., concurring); and Rehnquist's dissent in *Santa Fe* v. *Doe*, 318–26 (Rehnquist, J., dissenting). *Jaffree* v. *Board*, 554 F. Supp. 1104 (1983), 1118 n24. See Ivers, "American Jews and the Equal Treatment Principle," 167–77; and Matthew A. Peterson, "The Supreme Court's Coercion Test: Insufficient Constitutional Protection for America's Religious Minorities," *Cornell Journal of Law and Public Policy*, 11 (Fall 2001), 261–63.

21 *Employment Division, Department of Human Resources of Oregon* v. *Alfred L. Smith*, 494 U.S. 872 (1990), 890. Stephen M. Feldman, "Conservative Eras

in Supreme Court Decision-Making: *Employment Division* v. *Smith*, Judicial Restraint, and Neoconservatism," *Cardozo Law Review*, 32 (May 2011), 1798–99; David Sehat, *The Myth of American Religious Freedom* (New York: Oxford University Press, 2011), 277–78.

22 *Romer* v. *Evans*, 517 U.S. 620 (1996), 636 (Scalia, J., dissenting); Robert H. Bork, *Tradition and Morality in Constitutional Law* (Washington, D.C.: American Enterprise Institute, 1984). *Lawrence* v. *Texas*, 539 U.S. 558 (2003), 602–4 (Scalia, J., dissenting).

23 *Zelman* v. *Simmons-Harris*, 536 U.S. 687 (2000), 679–80 (Thomas, J. concurring); *Abington* v. *Schempp*, 374 U.S. 203 (1963), 226.

24 *Elk Grove* v. *Newdow*, 542 U.S. 1 (2004), 45, 49 (Thomas, J., concurring); *Van Orden* v. *Perry*, 545 U.S. 677 (2005), 692–93 (Thomas, J. concurring); *Greece* v. *Galloway*, 134 U.S. 1811 (2014), 1835–36 (Thomas, J., concurring). *Ishmael Jaffree* v. *Board of School Commissioners of Mobile County*, 554 F.Supp 1104 (1983), 1128.

25 The idea that judges are often driven by ideology is put forward in Driver, "Consensus Constitution"; and John C. Jeffries Jr. and James E. Ryan, "A Political History of the Establishment Clause," *Michigan Law Review*, 100 (November 2001), 279–300.

26 Edwin Meese III, speech before the American Bar Association, July 9, 1985, Washington, D.C., in Edwin Meese III, *Major Policy Statements of the Attorney General: Edwin Meese III, 1985–1988* (Washington, D.C.: United States Government Publications Office, 1989), 7–8. The signature importance of Meese's speeches to the concept of constitutional originalism is asserted in numerous law-review articles. Among them is Jonathan K. Van Patten, "The Partisan Battle over the Constitution: Meese's Jurisprudence of Original Intention and Brennan's Theory of Contemporary Ratification," *Marquette Law Review*, 70 (Spring 1987), 389–422; and Howard Ball, "The Convergence of Constitutional Law and Politics in the Reagan Administration: The Exhumation of the 'Jurisprudence of Original Intention' Doctrine," *Cumberland Law Review*, 17 (no. 3, 1986–1987), 877–90.

27 Meese, speech before the American Bar Association, July 9, 1985, pp. 4, 7.

28 *Ibid.*, 5–6, emphasis in original.

29 *Ibid.*, p. 6.

30 *Wall Street Journal*, July 31, 1985, p. 1.

31 *Christian Science Monitor*, July 18, 1985, p. 2; *New York Times*, July 18, 1985, p. A7; Lincoln Caplan, *The Tenth Justice: The Solicitor General and the Rule of Law* (New York: Knopf, 1987), 119.

32 William J. Brennan Jr., paper delivered at the Text and Teaching Symposium, Georgetown University, October 12, 1985, Washington, D.C., in *The Great Debate: Interpreting Our Written Constitution*, ed. Paul G. Cassell (Washington, D.C.: Federalist Society, 1986), 11, 18–19.

33 Brennan, Text and Teaching Symposium paper, 15–16.

34 *Wall Street Journal*, October 23, 1985, p. 1; *Washington Post*, October 28, 1985, p. A15; *Jaffree* v. *Board*, 554 F.Supp. 1104 (1983), 1113 n5.

35 John Paul Stevens, speech before the Federal Bar Association, October 23, 1985, Chicago, Ill., in *Great Debate*, ed. Cassell, 28.

36 UPI Archives, Oct. 25, 1985, www.upi.com/Archives/1985/10/25/Supreme-Court-Justice-William-Rehnquist-said-Friday-the-US/2658499060800/; *Christian Science Monitor*, October 29, 1985, p. 3.

37 Among the liberals publically criticizing Meese were senator and future vice president Joseph R. Biden and historian Arthur Schlesinger Jr. *New York Times*, November 7, 1985, p. A20; *Wall Street Journal*, January 17, 1986, p. 1.

38 Robert H. Bork, "The Case against Political Judging," *National Review*, December 8, 1989, pp. 23–28; Robert H. Bork, *Tradition and Morality in Constitutional Law* (Washington, D.C.: American Enterprise Institute, 1984); Robert H. Bork, "The Struggle over the Role of the Court," *National Review*, September 17, 1982, pp. 1137–39. See Laura Kalman, *Yale Law School and the Sixties: Revolt and Reverberations* (Chapel Hill: University of North Carolina Press, 2005).

39 Robert H. Bork, *The Tempting of America: The Political Seduction of the Law* (New York: Free Press, 1990), 8, 15–16; Robert H. Bork, "Neutral Principles and Some First Amendment Problems," *Indiana Law Journal*, 47 (Fall 1971), 1–35.

40 Bork, *Tempting of America*, 4–8, 78, 145.

41 Bork, *Tempting of America*, 7, 242–43.

42 Bork, *Tempting of America*, 247–49.

43 Amanda Hollis-Brusky, *Ideas with Consequences: The Federalist Society and the Conservative Counterrevolution* (New York: Oxford University Press, 2015), 7, 147–48, 159–64; Michael Avery and Danielle McLaughlin, *The Federalist Society: How Conservatives Took the Law Back from Liberals* (Nashville: Vanderbilt University Press, 2013), 7–8.

44 Nathan Glazer, "Towards an Imperial Judiciary?" *Public Interest*, 41 (Fall 1975), 106, 120. See also Lino A. Graglia, "Judicial Imperialism: The Supreme Court's Abuse of Power," *National Review*, July 21, 1978, pp. 892–96. This line of critique is explored most fully in Mark Kozlowski, *The Myth of the Imperial Judiciary: Why the Right Is Wrong about the Courts* (New York: New York University Press, 2003), 1–50. See also Philip Kennicott, "Judge Not: In the Court of Public Opinion, the Bench Is in the Hot Seat," *Washington Post*, May 17, 2005, p. C1.

45 "First Things First," *National Review*, November 11, 1996, pp. 16–17; Richard John Neuhaus, *The Naked Public Square: Religion and Democracy in America* (Grand Rapids, Mich.: Eerdmans, 1984); Mitchell S. Muncy, ed., *The End of Democracy? The Judicial Usurpation of Politics* (Dallas: Spence, 1997), viii, 6.

46 http://cslr.law.emory.edu/fileadmin/media/PDFs/CV_-_updated_2008/Hittinger_CV.pdf. Russell Hittinger, "A Crisis of Legitimacy, in *End of Democracy?*, ed. by Muncy, 18–29, esp. 26–27.

47 Hadley Arkes, "A Culture Corrupted," in *End of Democracy?*, ed. by Muncy, 31, 38.

48 Charles W. Colson, "Kingdoms in Conflict," in *End of Democracy?*, ed. by Muncy, 41, 44, 50.

49 James C. Dobson, essay in *End of Democracy?*, ed. by Muncy, 81.

50 Robert H. Bork, "Our Judicial Oligarchy, in *End of Democracy?*, ed. by Muncy, 10–13 (emphasis in original).

51 *Ibid.*, 16–17.

52 Theda Skocpol and Vanessa Williamson, *The Tea Party and the Remaking of Republican Conservatism* (New York: Oxford University Press, 2012), 48–51; Jeffrey Rosen, "Radical Constitutionalism," November 26, 2010, www.nytimes.com/2010/11/28/magazine/28FOB-idealab-t.html?_r=2&pagewanted=1; *New York Times*, December 27, 2010, p. A18. Sarah Palin, *America by Heart: Reflections on Family, Faith, and Flag* (New York: HarperCollins, 2010). Jenny Kutner, "Tom DeLay Urges Americans to Defy the 'Ten' Supreme Court Justices if They Rule in Favor of Same-Sex Marriage," Salon.com, June 16, 2015, www.salon.com/2015/06/16/tom_delay_urges_americans_to_defy_the_ten_supreme_court_justices_if_they_rule_in_favor_of_same_sex_marriage/; Ted Cruz, "Constitutional Remedies to a Lawless Supreme Court," *National Review Online*, June 26, 2015, www.nationalreview.com/article/420409/ted-cruz-supreme-court-constitutional-amendment; Mike Huckabee, "Gay Marriage Could Criminalize Christianity," June 20, 2015 www.mikehuckabee.com/articles?ID=D7E61E4D-754A-4D4E-B6C0-BFCA92831BC1. Tony Perkins and Ken Blackwell, "The American Founders Never Intended 'Government by the Judiciary,' So Why Do We Tolerate It?," Family Research Council, July 22, 2015, www.frc.org/op-eds/the-american-founders-never-intended-government-by-the-judiciary-so-why-do-we-tolerate-it; Tim Wildmon, "AFA Action Alert: Three Things Churches Must Do to Protect Themselves," American Family Association, June 30, 2015, www.afa.net/who-is-afa/press-releases/2015/06-june/afa-action-alert-three-things-churches-must-do-to-protect-themselves/.

Index